Rainbow Days

■ ■ ■ ■ ■ ■ ■ ■

3

Story and Art by
Minami Mizuno

CONTENTS

CHARACTERS

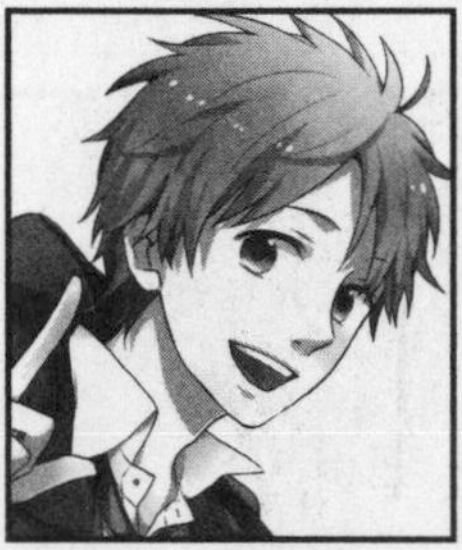

NATSUKI HASHIBA
A dreamer with a pure and romantic heart. Nickname: Natchan.

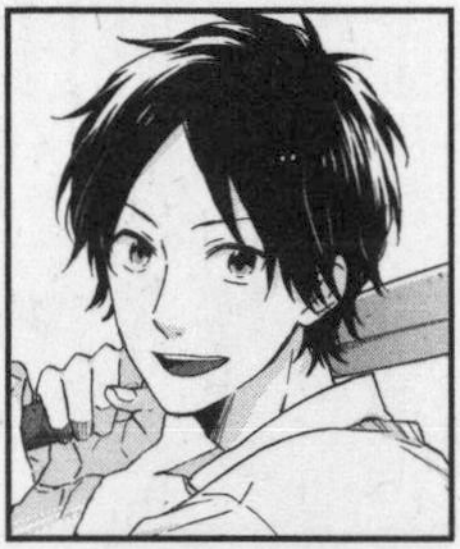

KEIICHI KATAKURA
Always smiling, but actually a sadist. Never without his whip. Nickname: Kei-chan.

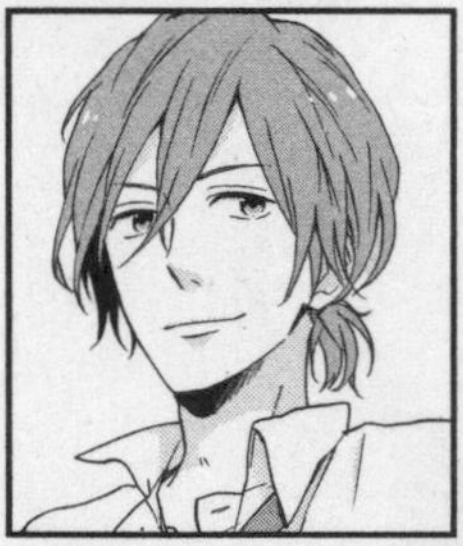

TOMOYA MATSUNAGA
A narcissist playboy who loves girls. Tends to involve himself in other people's problems. Nickname: Mattsun.

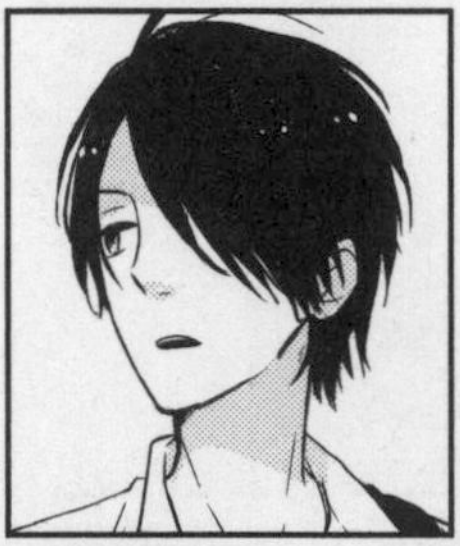

TSUYOSHI NAOE
An otaku. Cannot read the room, but gets great grades. Nickname: Tsuyopon.

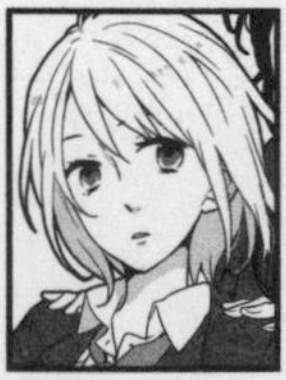

ANNA KOBAYAKAWA
The oblivious object of Natsuki's affections. Doesn't talk much. Does things at her own pace.

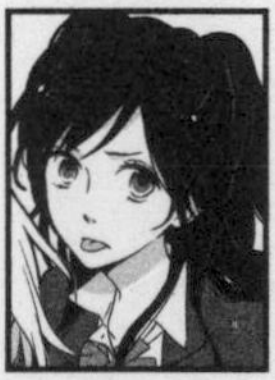

MARI TSUTSUI
A beautiful girl besotted with Anna. She and Mattsun loathe each other.

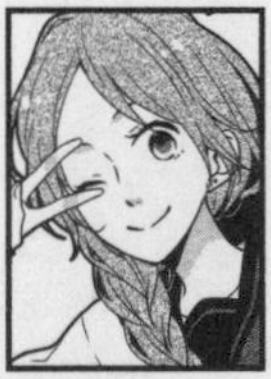

YUKIKO ASAI
Tsuyoshi's girlfriend. A cosplayer. Nickname: Yukirin.

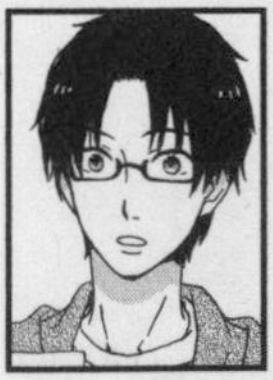

MR. KATAKURA
Kei-chan's big brother. Teaches math at their school.

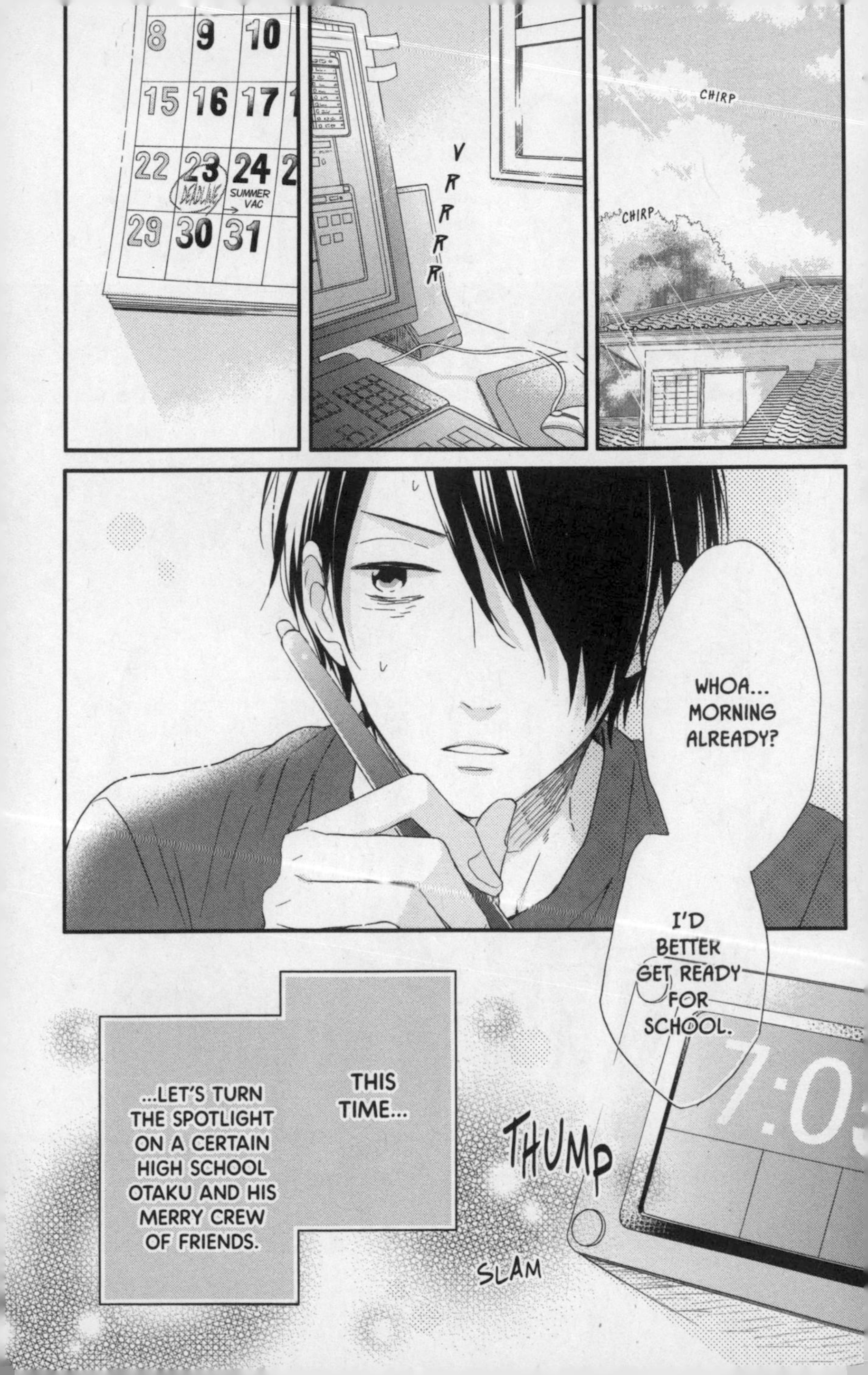
CHIRP
CHIRP
VRRRRR
SUMMER VAC
WHOA... MORNING ALREADY?
I'D BETTER GET READY FOR SCHOOL.
THUMP
SLAM
THIS TIME...
...LET'S TURN THE SPOTLIGHT ON A CERTAIN HIGH SCHOOL OTAKU AND HIS MERRY CREW OF FRIENDS.

Rainbow Weather

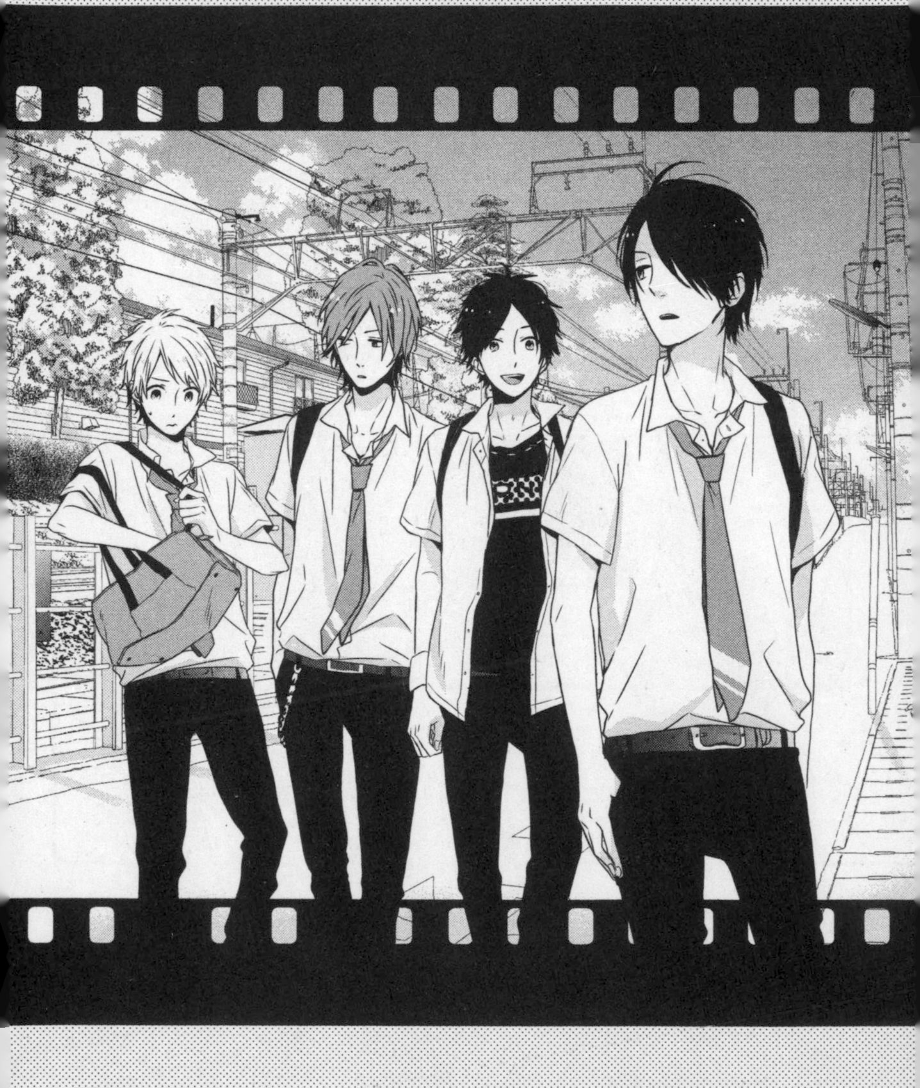

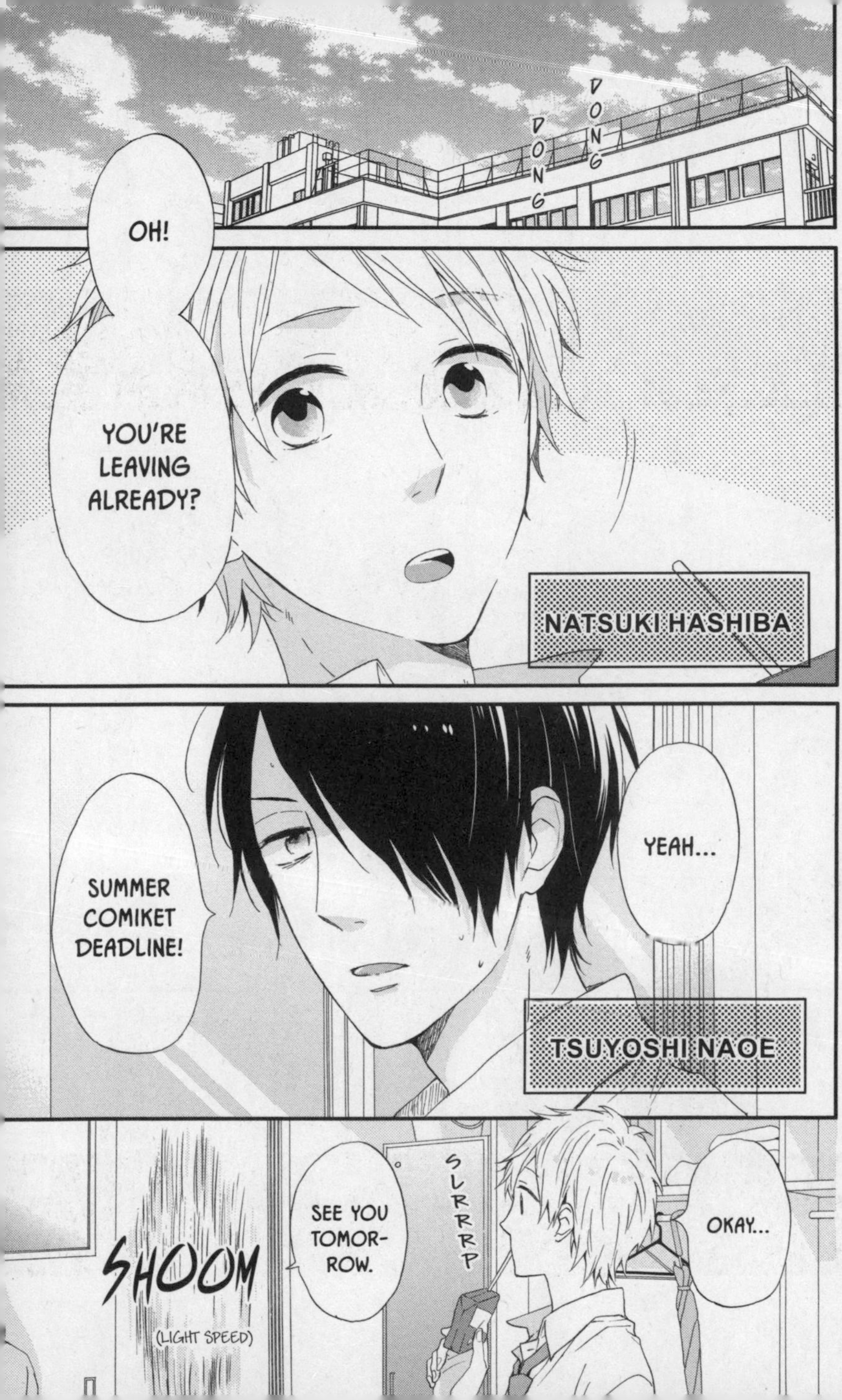
DONG
DONG
OH!
YOU'RE LEAVING ALREADY?
NATSUKI HASHIBA
YEAH...
SUMMER COMIKET DEADLINE!
TSUYOSHI NAOE
OKAY...
SLRRRP
SEE YOU TOMOR-ROW.
SHOOM
(LIGHT SPEED)

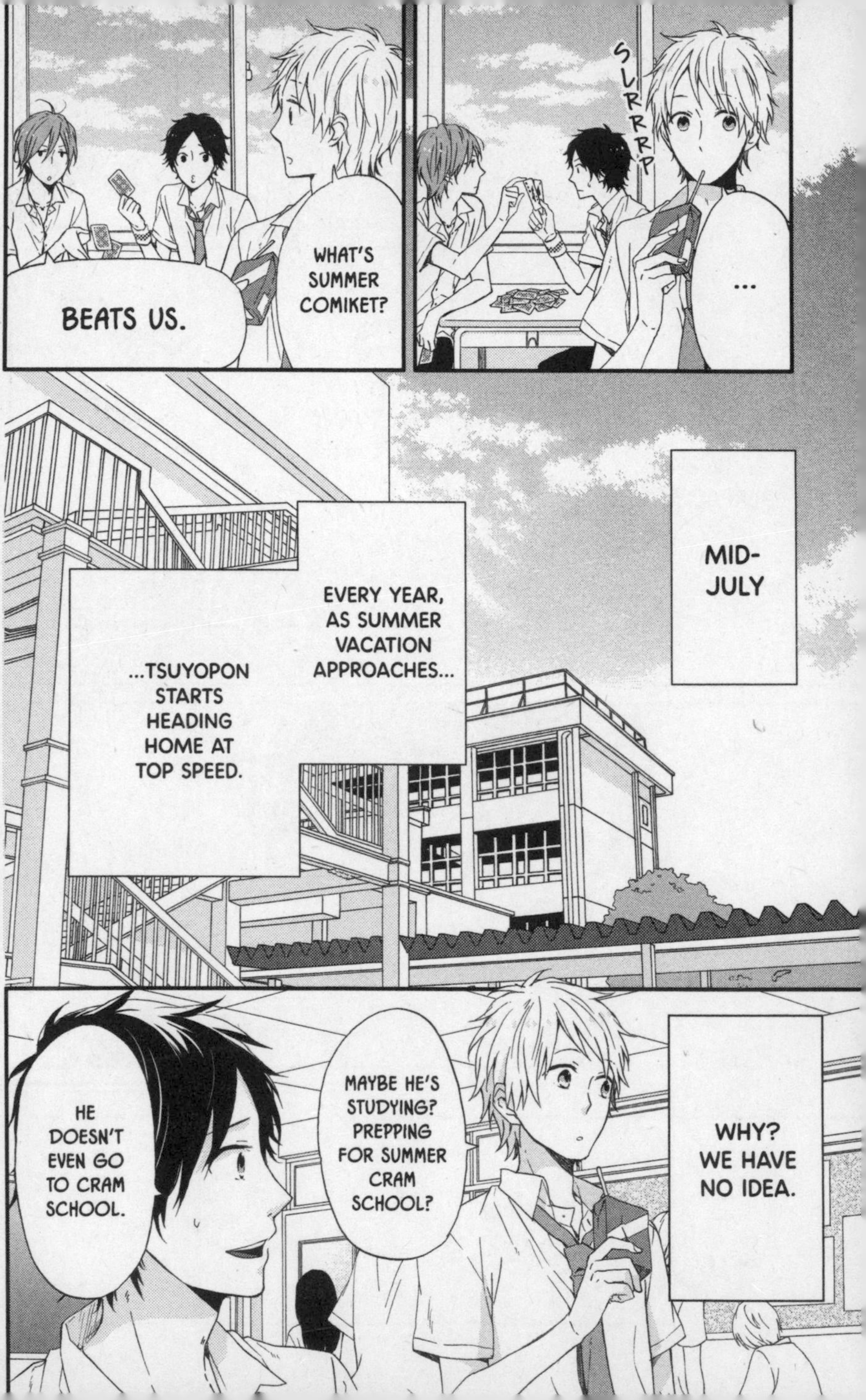
SLRRRP
...
WHAT'S SUMMER COMIKET?
BEATS US.
MID-JULY
EVERY YEAR, AS SUMMER VACATION APPROACHES...
...TSUYOPON STARTS HEADING HOME AT TOP SPEED.
WHY? WE HAVE NO IDEA.
MAYBE HE'S STUDYING? PREPPING FOR SUMMER CRAM SCHOOL?
HE DOESN'T EVEN GO TO CRAM SCHOOL.

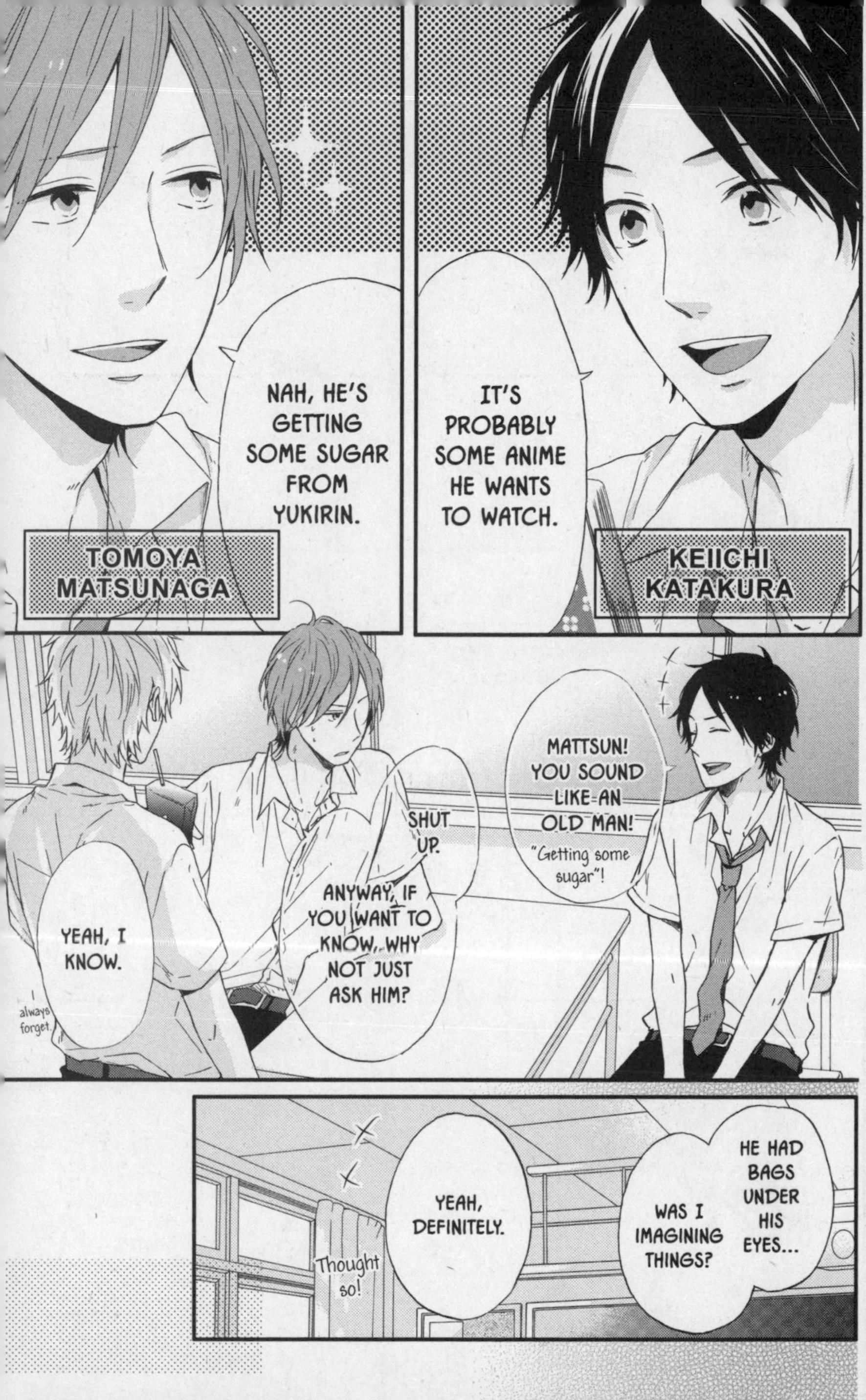
IT'S PROBABLY SOME ANIME HE WANTS TO WATCH.
KEIICHI KATAKURA
NAH, HE'S GETTING SOME SUGAR FROM YUKIRIN.
TOMOYA MATSUNAGA
MATTSUN! YOU SOUND LIKE AN OLD MAN!
"Getting some sugar"!
SHUT UP.
ANYWAY, IF YOU WANT TO KNOW, WHY NOT JUST ASK HIM?
YEAH, I KNOW.
I always forget.
HE HAD BAGS UNDER HIS EYES...
WAS I IMAGINING THINGS?
YEAH, DEFINITELY.
Thought so!

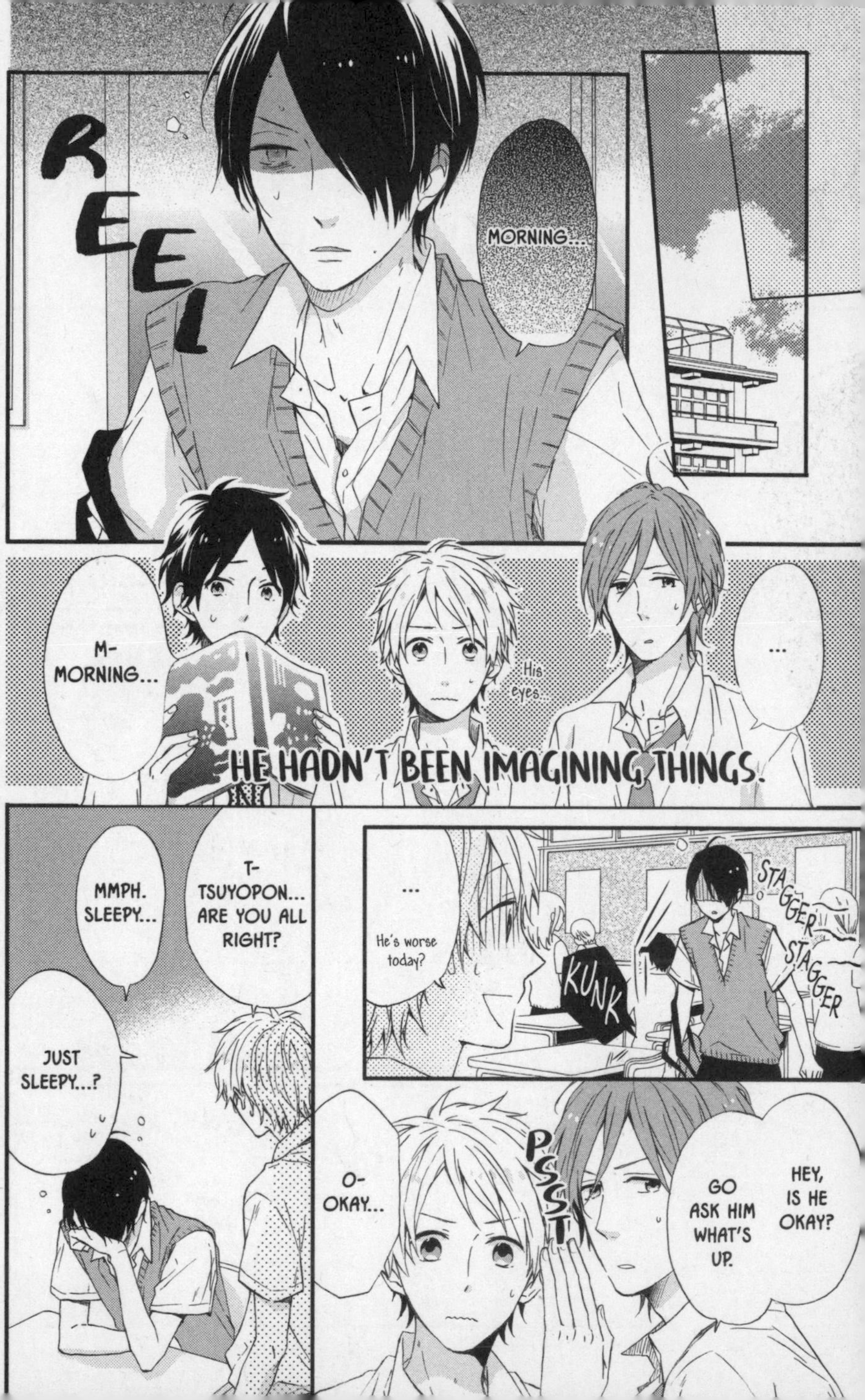
MORNING...
REEL
...
His eyes...
M- MORNING...
HE HADN'T BEEN IMAGINING THINGS.
STAGGER STAGGER
KUNK
...
He's worse today?
HEY, IS HE OKAY?
GO ASK HIM WHAT'S UP.
PSST
O- OKAY...
T- TSUYOPON... ARE YOU ALL RIGHT?
MMPH. SLEEPY...
JUST SLEEPY...?

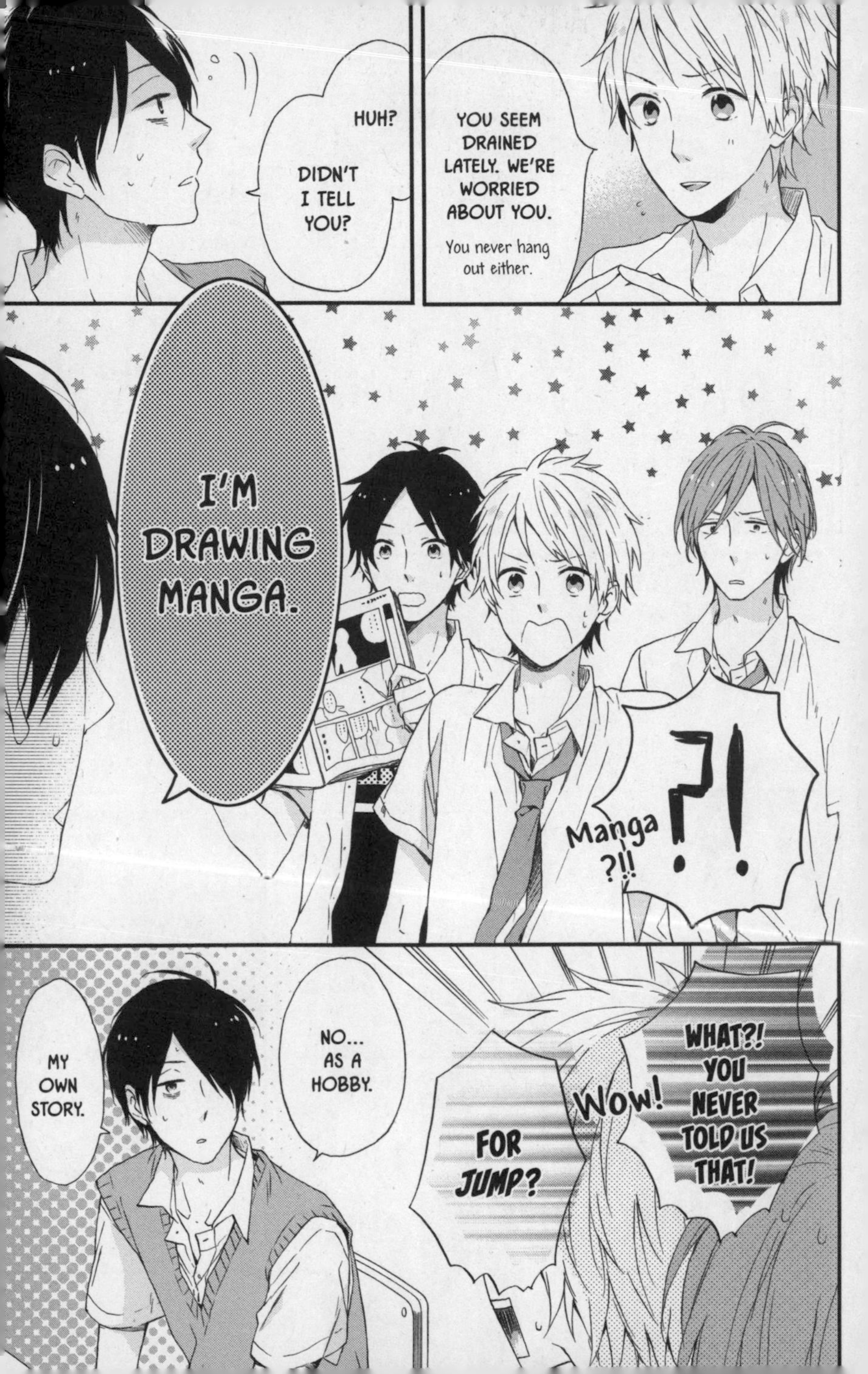
YOU SEEM DRAINED LATELY. WE'RE WORRIED ABOUT YOU.
You never hang out either.
HUH?
DIDN'T I TELL YOU?
I'M DRAWING MANGA.
?!
Manga ?!!
WHAT?! YOU NEVER TOLD US THAT!
Wow!
FOR *JUMP*?
NO... AS A HOBBY.
MY OWN STORY.

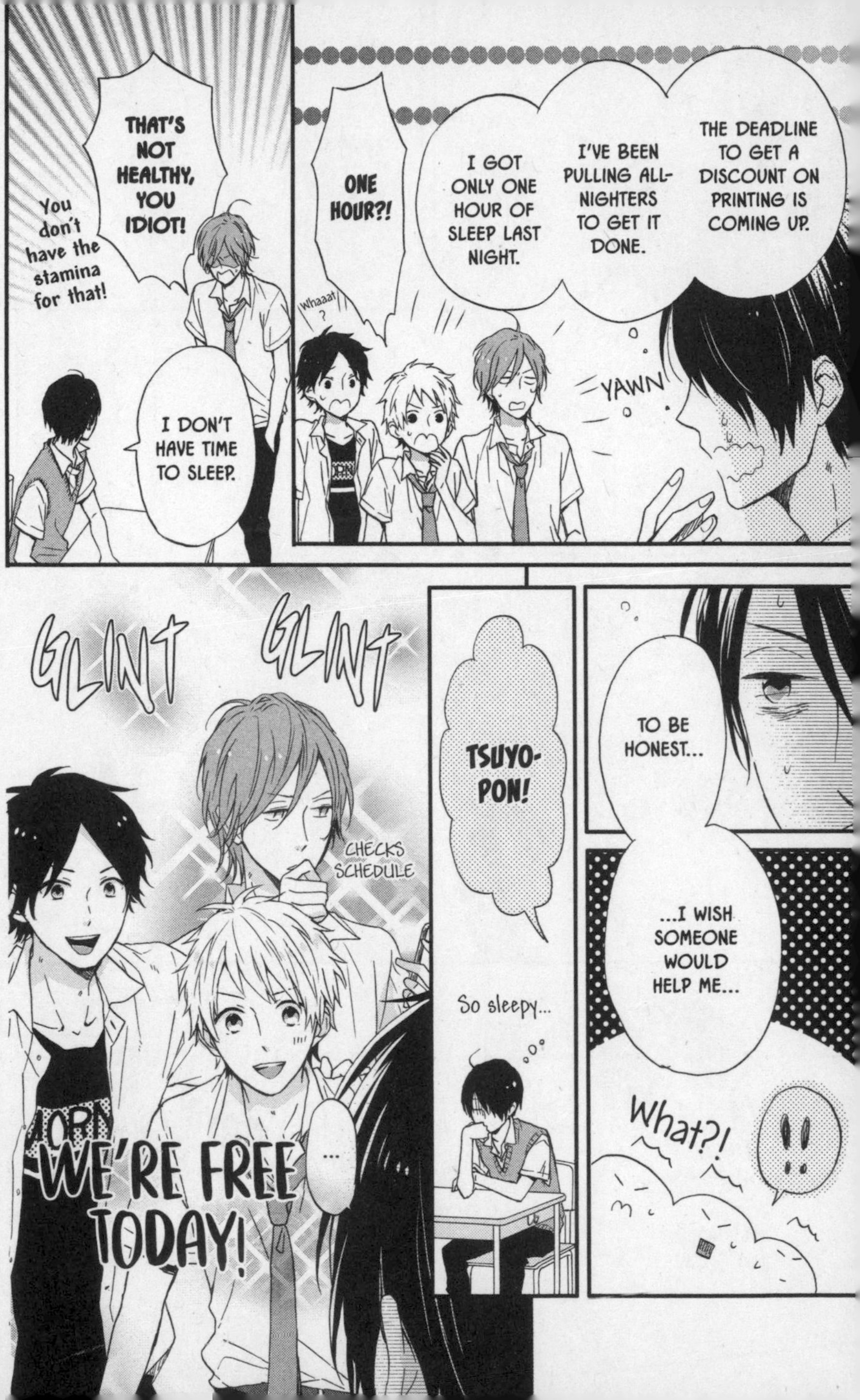
THE DEADLINE TO GET A DISCOUNT ON PRINTING IS COMING UP.
I'VE BEEN PULLING ALL-NIGHTERS TO GET IT DONE.
I GOT ONLY ONE HOUR OF SLEEP LAST NIGHT.
YAWN
ONE HOUR?!
Whaaat?
THAT'S NOT HEALTHY, YOU IDIOT!
You don't have the stamina for that!
I DON'T HAVE TIME TO SLEEP.
TO BE HONEST...
...I WISH SOMEONE WOULD HELP ME...
What?!
!!
TSUYO-PON!
So sleepy...
GLINT
GLINT
CHECKS SCHEDULE
WE'RE FREE TODAY!
...

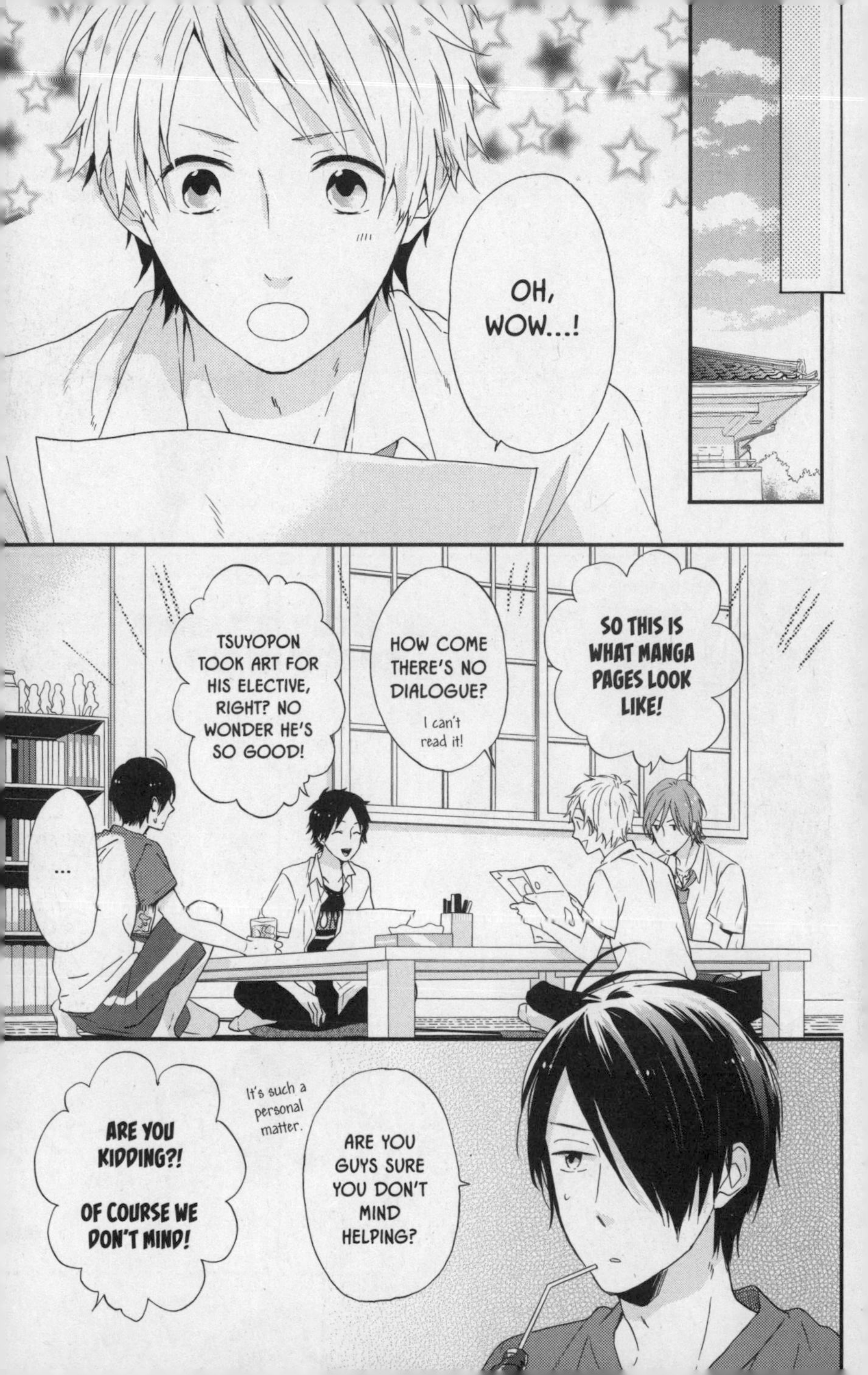
OH, WOW...!
SO THIS IS WHAT MANGA PAGES LOOK LIKE!
HOW COME THERE'S NO DIALOGUE?
I can't read it!
TSUYOPON TOOK ART FOR HIS ELECTIVE, RIGHT? NO WONDER HE'S SO GOOD!
...
ARE YOU GUYS SURE YOU DON'T MIND HELPING?
It's such a personal matter.
ARE YOU KIDDING?! OF COURSE WE DON'T MIND!

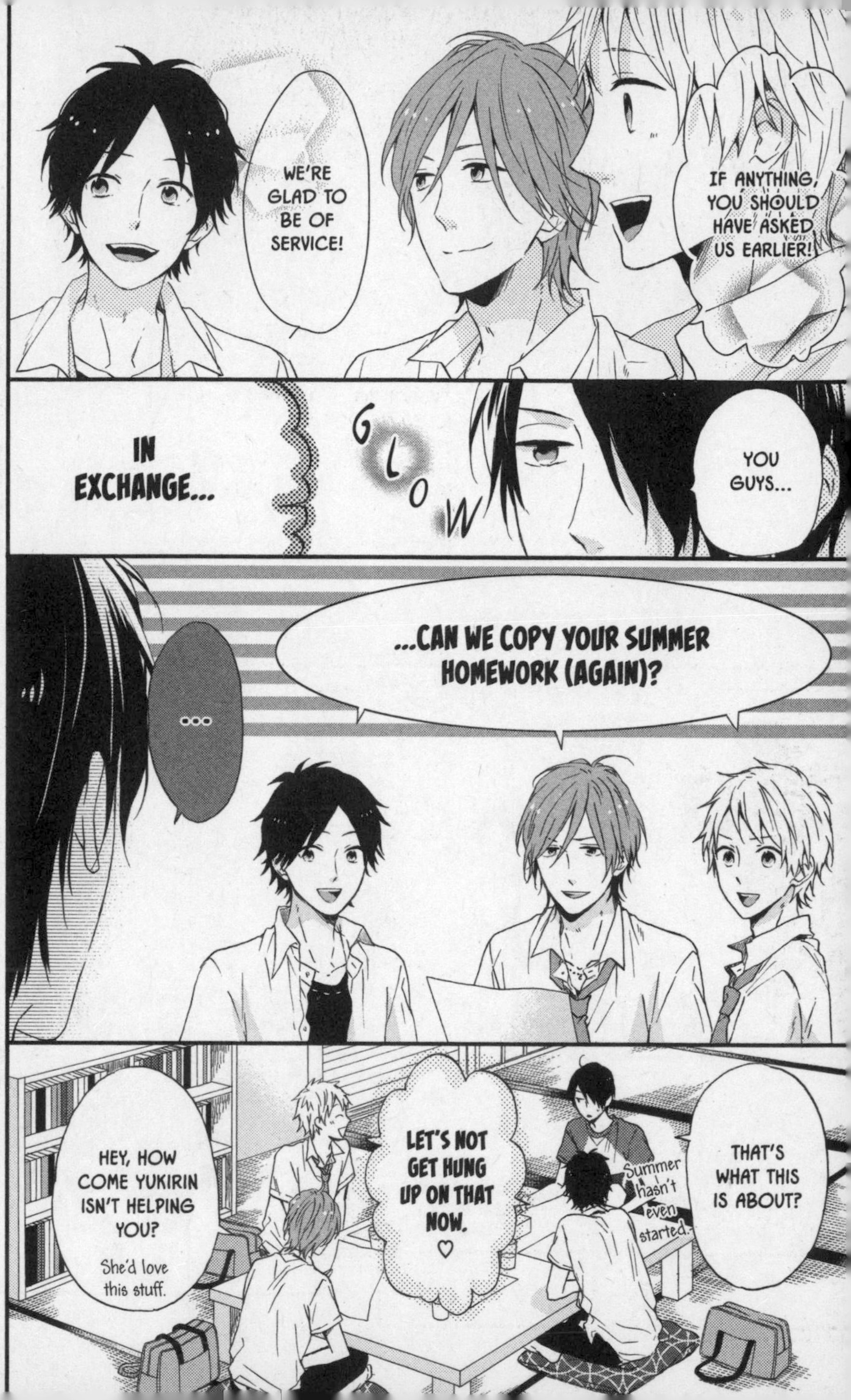
IF ANYTHING, YOU SHOULD HAVE ASKED US EARLIER!
WE'RE GLAD TO BE OF SERVICE!
YOU GUYS...
GLOW
IN EXCHANGE...
...CAN WE COPY YOUR SUMMER HOMEWORK (AGAIN)?
...
THAT'S WHAT THIS IS ABOUT?
Summer hasn't even started.
LET'S NOT GET HUNG UP ON THAT NOW. ♡
HEY, HOW COME YUKIRIN ISN'T HELPING YOU?
She'd love this stuff.

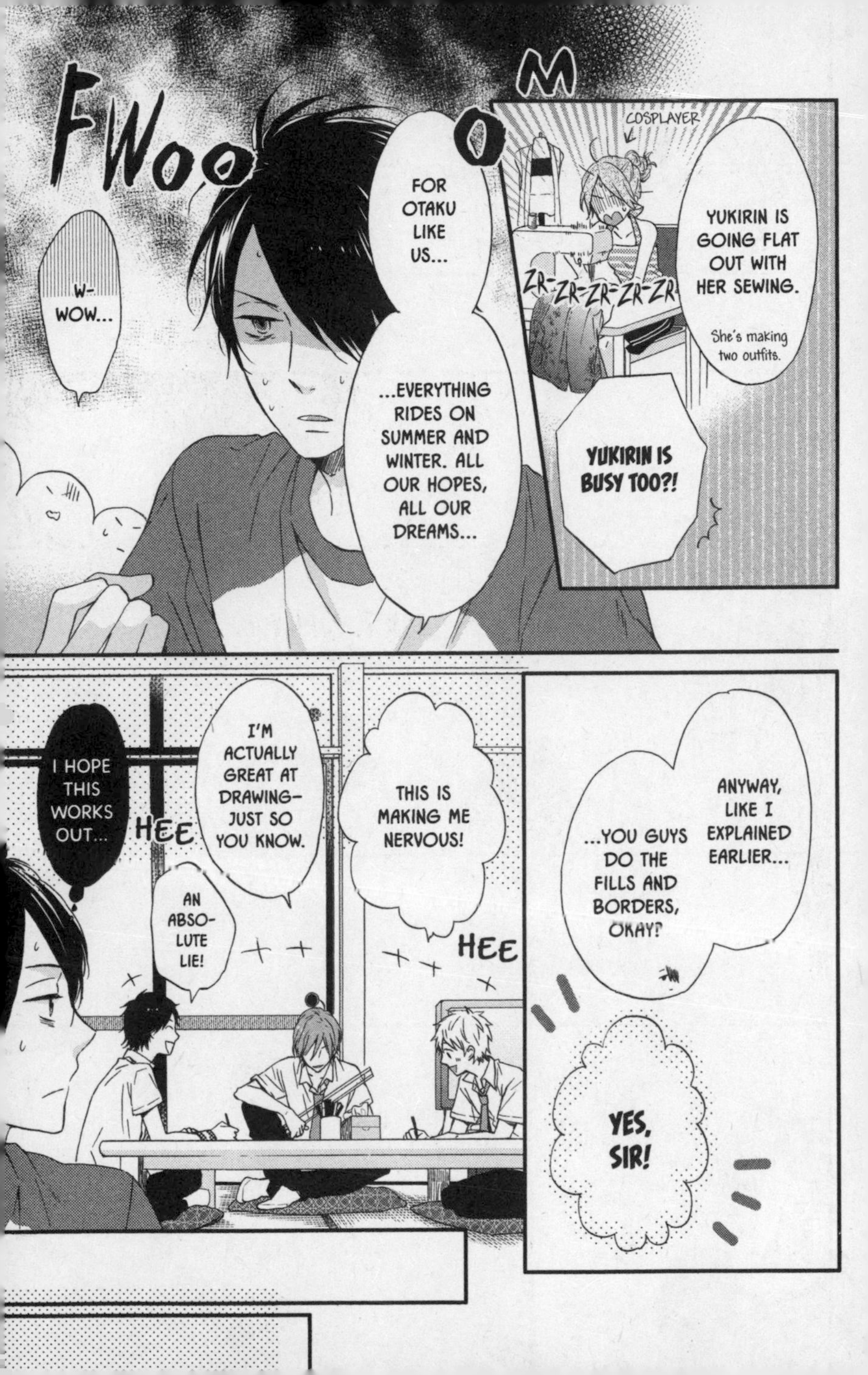
COSPLAYER
YUKIRIN IS GOING FLAT OUT WITH HER SEWING.
She's making two outfits.
ZR-ZR-ZR-ZR-ZR
YUKIRIN IS BUSY TOO?!
FWOOOM
FOR OTAKU LIKE US...
...EVERYTHING RIDES ON SUMMER AND WINTER. ALL OUR HOPES, ALL OUR DREAMS...
W-WOW...
ANYWAY, LIKE I EXPLAINED EARLIER...
...YOU GUYS DO THE FILLS AND BORDERS, OKAY?
YES, SIR!
THIS IS MAKING ME NERVOUS!
HEE
I'M ACTUALLY GREAT AT DRAWING—JUST SO YOU KNOW.
AN ABSO-LUTE LIE!
HEE
I HOPE THIS WORKS OUT...

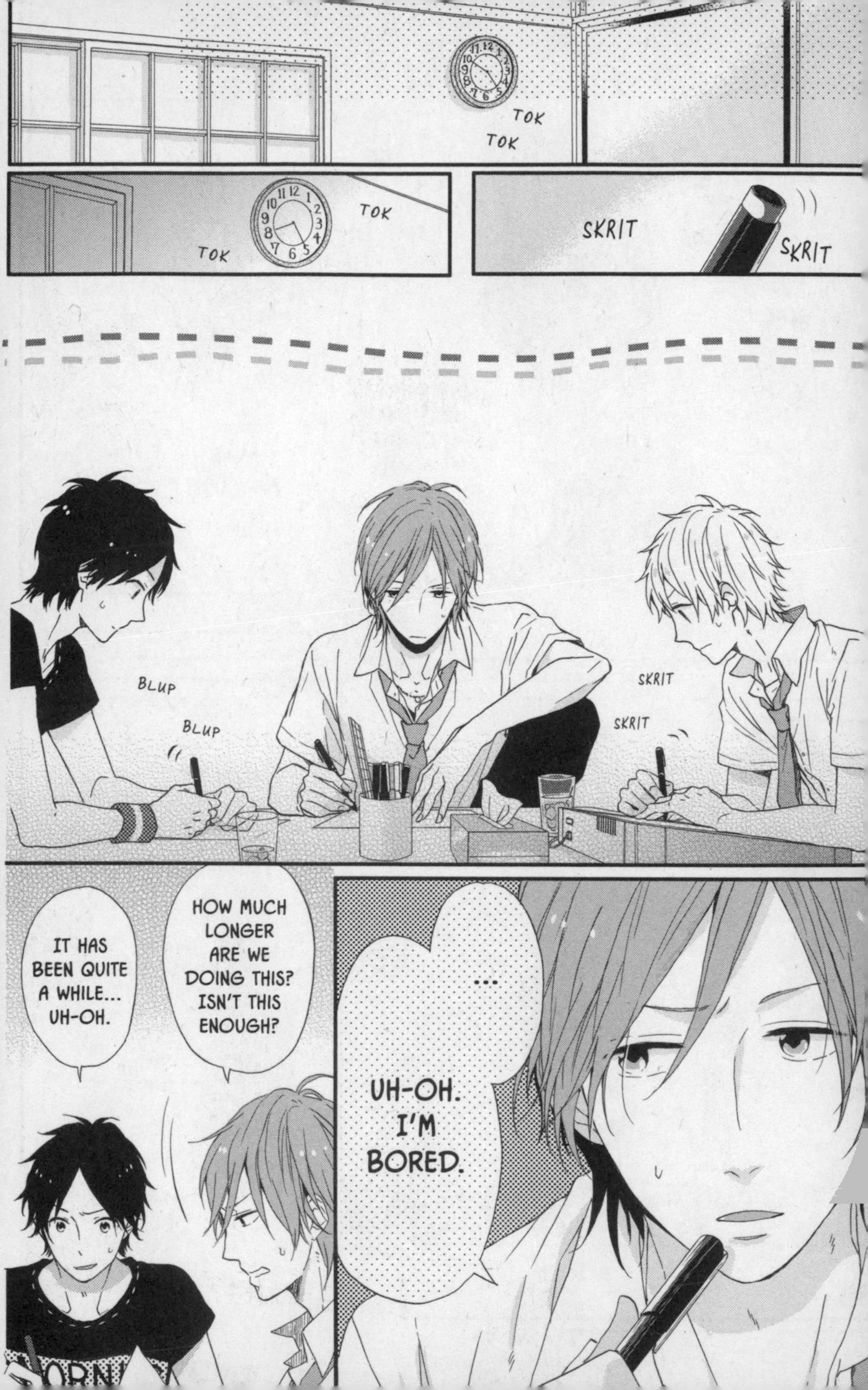
TOK
TOK
SKRIT
SKRIT
TOK
TOK
SKRIT
SKRIT
BLUP
BLUP
...
UH-OH. I'M BORED.
HOW MUCH LONGER ARE WE DOING THIS? ISN'T THIS ENOUGH?
IT HAS BEEN QUITE A WHILE... UH-OH.

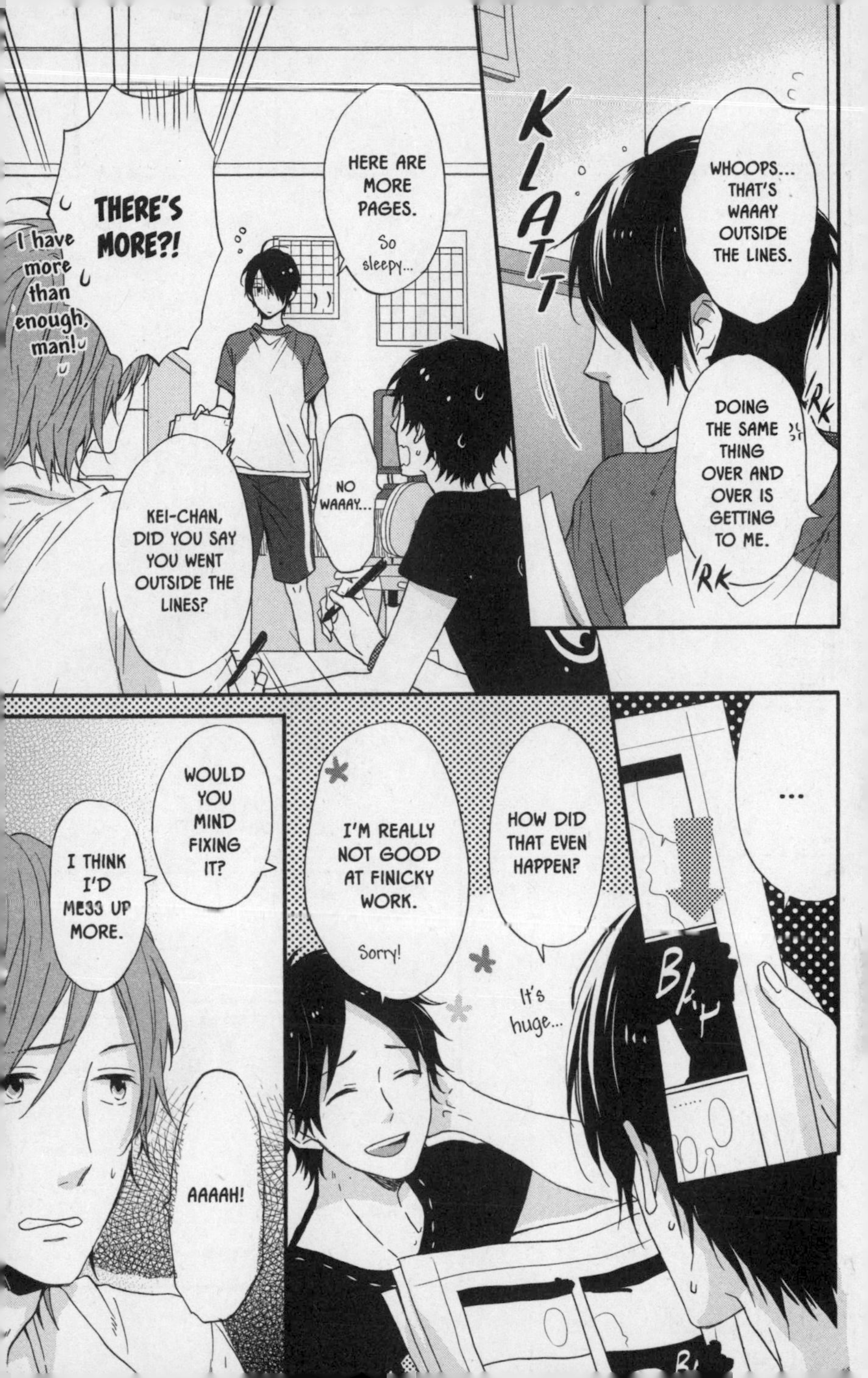
WHOOPS... THAT'S WAAAY OUTSIDE THE LINES.
KLATT
DOING THE SAME THING OVER AND OVER IS GETTING TO ME.
IRK
IRK
HERE ARE MORE PAGES.
So sleepy...
THERE'S MORE?!
I have more than enough, man!
NO WAAAY...
KEI-CHAN, DID YOU SAY YOU WENT OUTSIDE THE LINES?
...
HOW DID THAT EVEN HAPPEN?
It's huge...
I'M REALLY NOT GOOD AT FINICKY WORK.
Sorry!
WOULD YOU MIND FIXING IT?
I THINK I'D MESS UP MORE.
AAAAH!

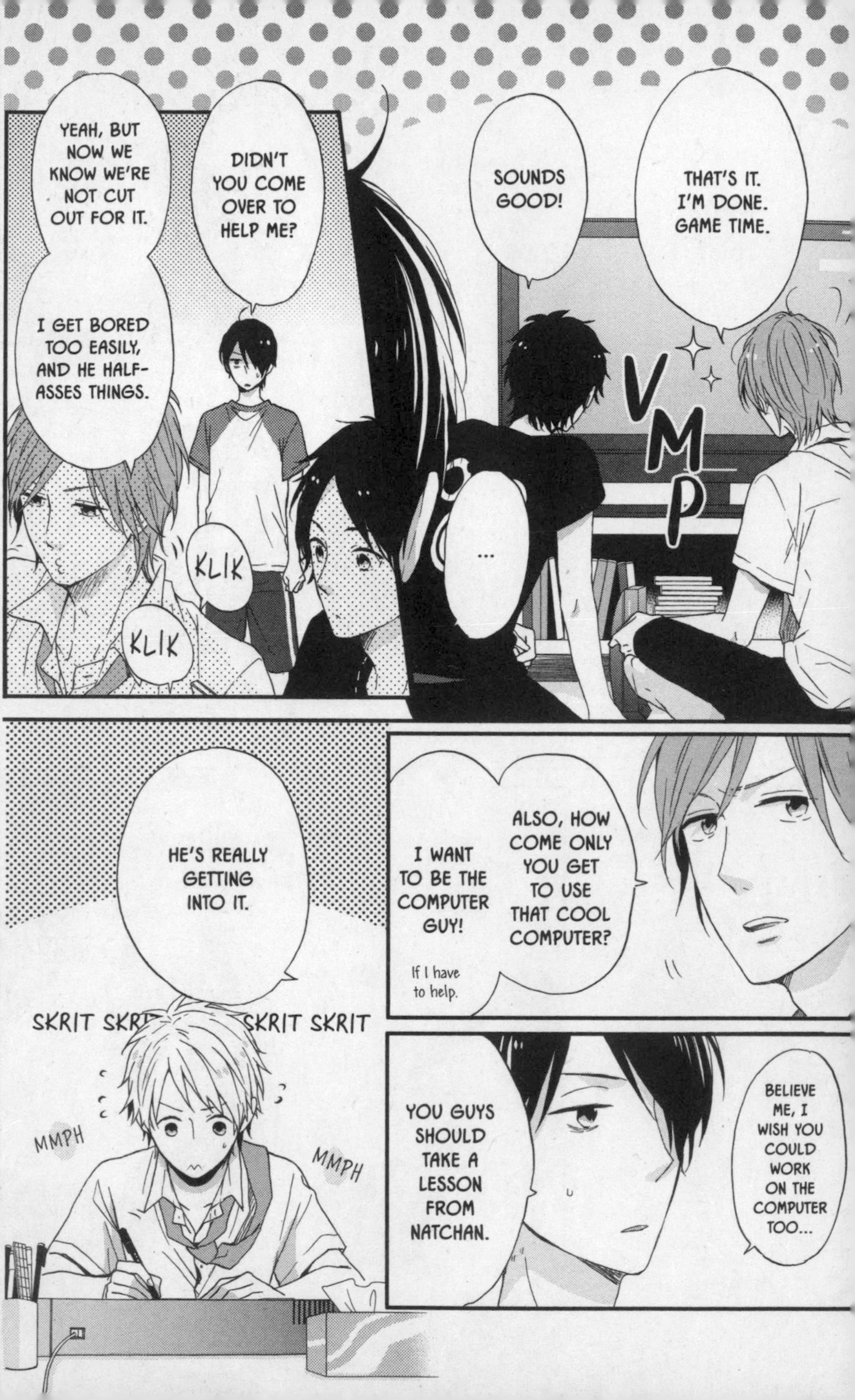
THAT'S IT. I'M DONE. GAME TIME.
SOUNDS GOOD!
VMP
...
DIDN'T YOU COME OVER TO HELP ME?
YEAH, BUT NOW WE KNOW WE'RE NOT CUT OUT FOR IT.
I GET BORED TOO EASILY, AND HE HALF-ASSES THINGS.
KLIK
KLIK
ALSO, HOW COME ONLY YOU GET TO USE THAT COOL COMPUTER?
I WANT TO BE THE COMPUTER GUY!
If I have to help.
BELIEVE ME, I WISH YOU COULD WORK ON THE COMPUTER TOO...
YOU GUYS SHOULD TAKE A LESSON FROM NATCHAN.
HE'S REALLY GETTING INTO IT.
SKRIT SKRIT SKRIT SKRIT
MMPH
MMPH

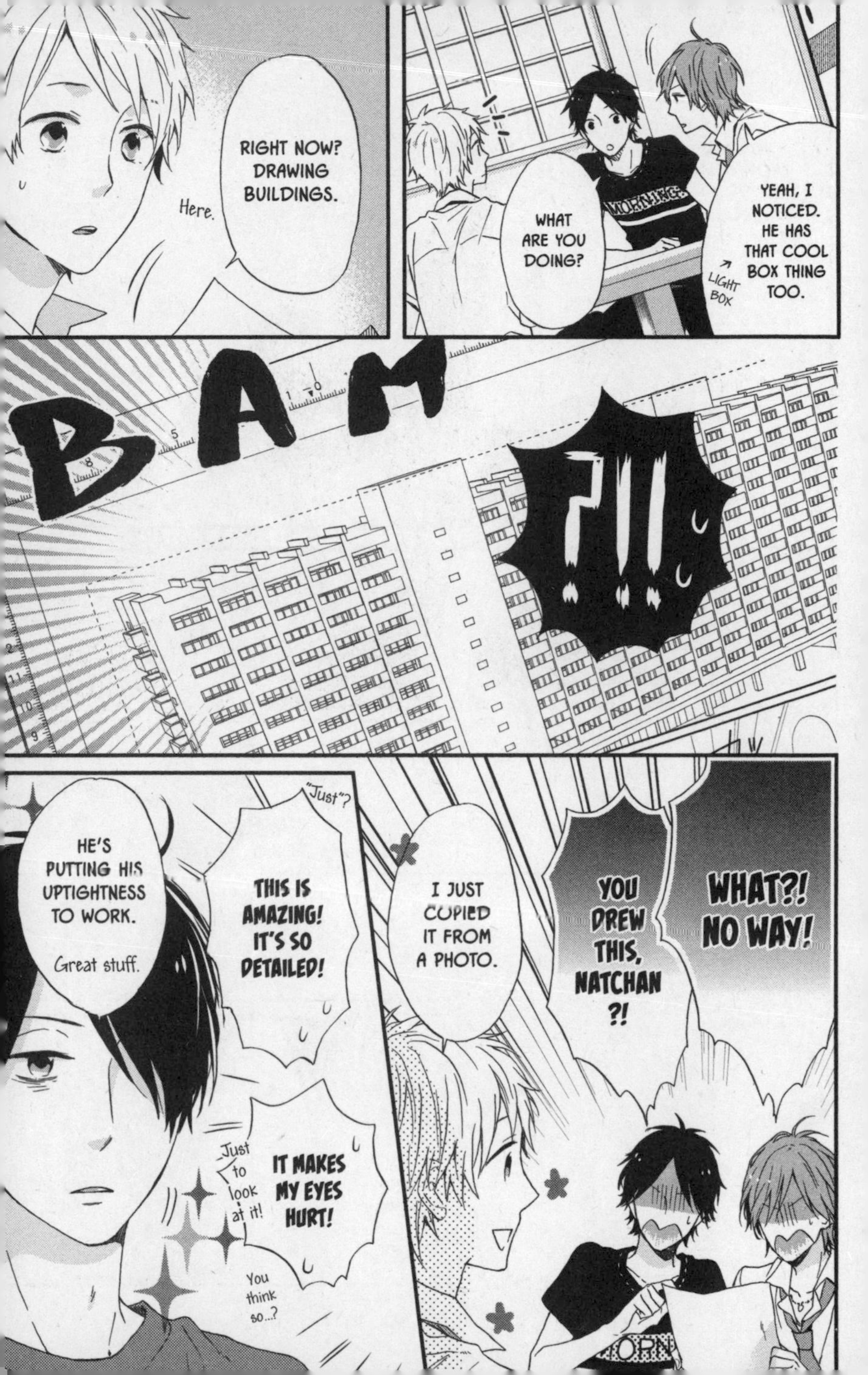
YEAH, I NOTICED. HE HAS THAT COOL BOX THING TOO.
LIGHT BOX
WHAT ARE YOU DOING?
RIGHT NOW? DRAWING BUILDINGS.
Here.
BAM
?!!
WHAT?! NO WAY!
YOU DREW THIS, NATCHAN?!
I JUST COPIED IT FROM A PHOTO.
"Just"?
THIS IS AMAZING! IT'S SO DETAILED!
HE'S PUTTING HIS UPTIGHTNESS TO WORK.
Great stuff.
IT MAKES MY EYES HURT!
Just to look at it!
You think so...?

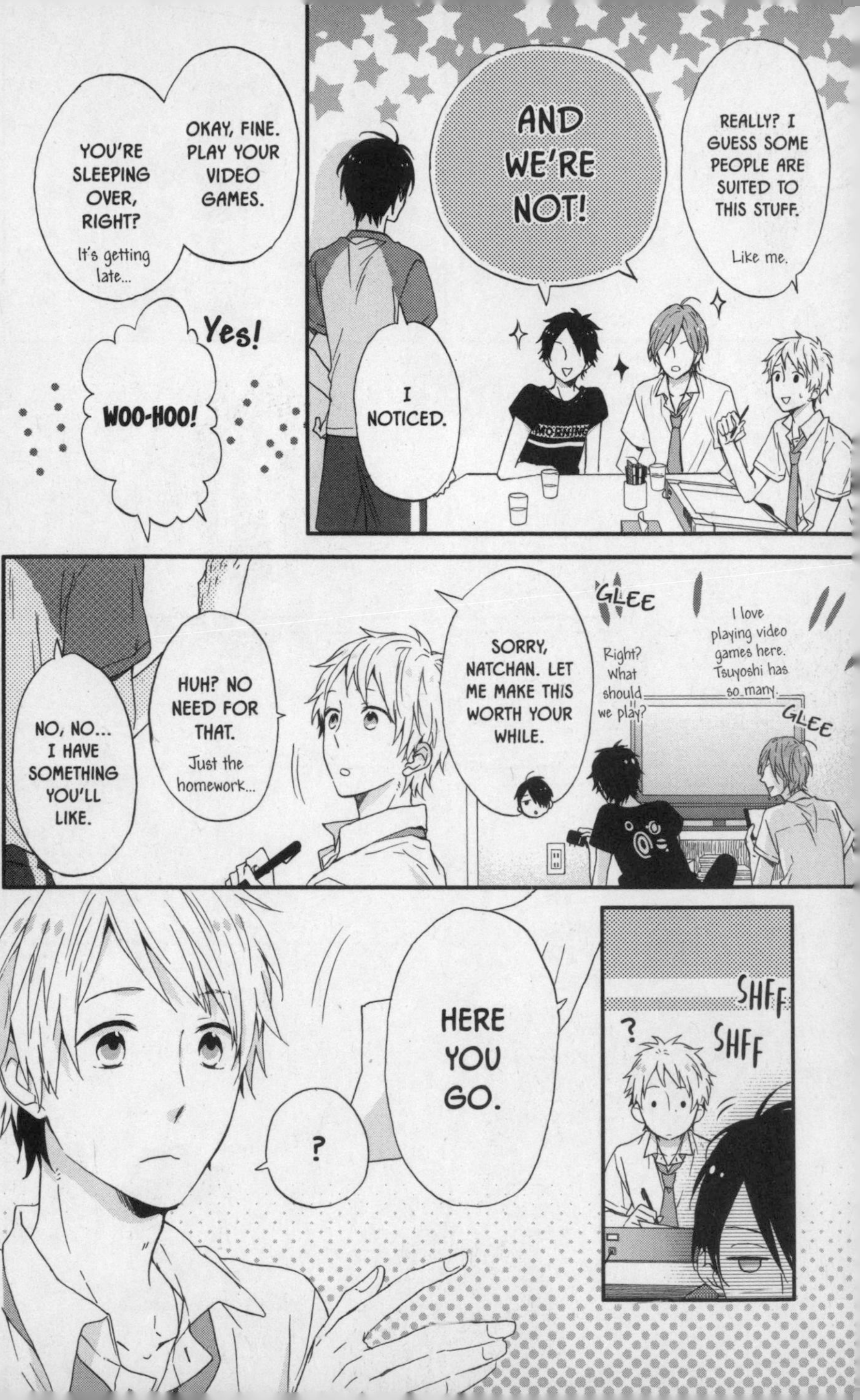
REALLY? I GUESS SOME PEOPLE ARE SUITED TO THIS STUFF.
Like me.
AND WE'RE NOT!
I NOTICED.
OKAY, FINE. PLAY YOUR VIDEO GAMES.
YOU'RE SLEEPING OVER, RIGHT?
It's getting late...
Yes!
WOO-HOO!
GLEE
I love playing video games here. Tsuyoshi has so many.
Right? What should we play?
GLEE
SORRY, NATCHAN. LET ME MAKE THIS WORTH YOUR WHILE.
HUH? NO NEED FOR THAT.
Just the homework...
NO, NO... I HAVE SOMETHING YOU'LL LIKE.
SHFF
SHFF
?
HERE YOU GO.
?

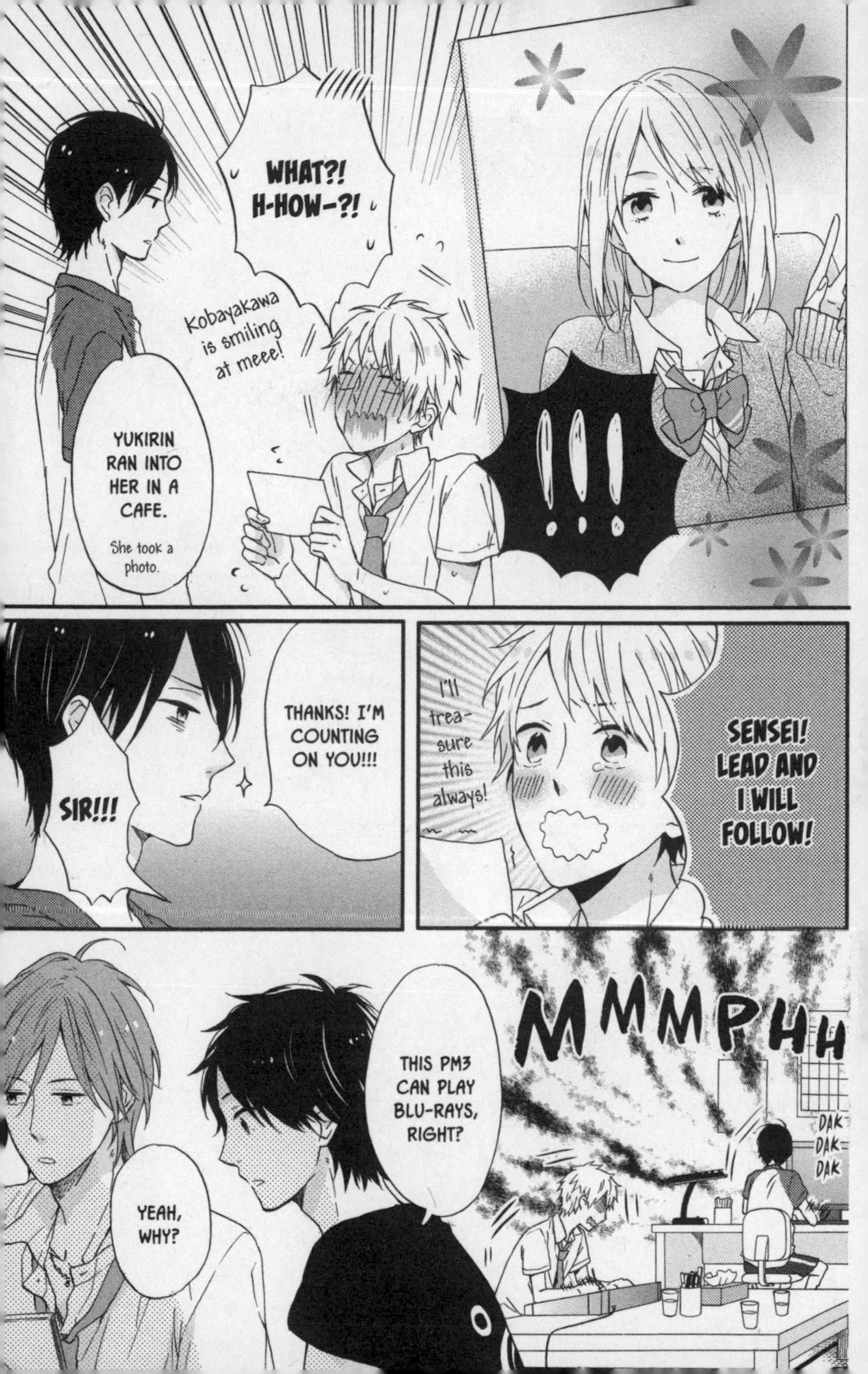
WHAT?! H-HOW-?!
!!!
Kobayakawa is smiling at meee!
YUKIRIN RAN INTO HER IN A CAFE.
She took a photo.
SENSEI! LEAD AND I WILL FOLLOW!
I'll treasure this always!
THANKS! I'M COUNTING ON YOU!!!
SIR!!!
MMMPHH
DAK DAK DAK
THIS PM3 CAN PLAY BLU-RAYS, RIGHT?
YEAH, WHY?

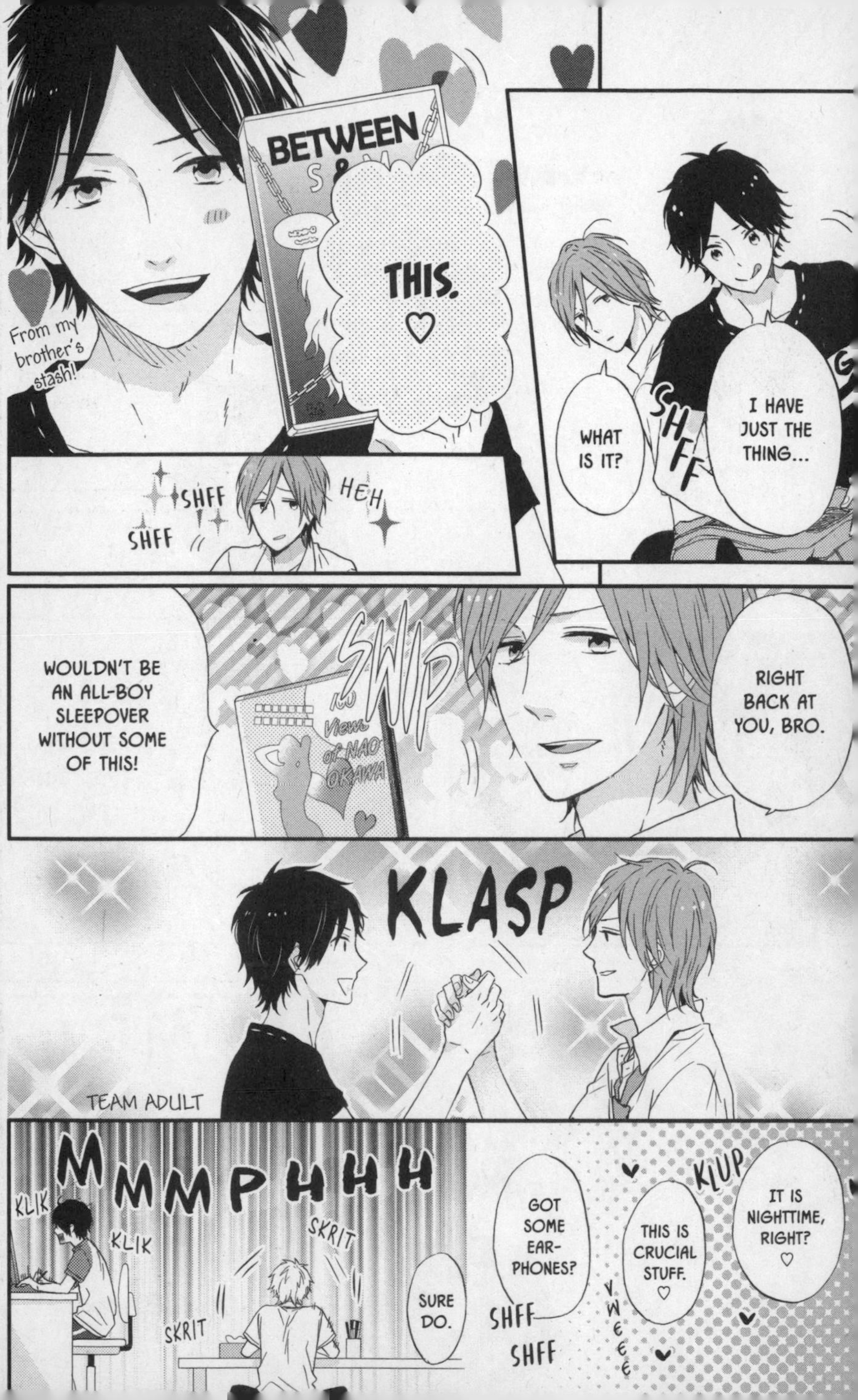
I HAVE JUST THE THING...
SHFF
WHAT IS IT?
BETWEEN
THIS. ♡
From my brother's stash!
HEH
SHFF
SHFF
RIGHT BACK AT YOU, BRO.
SWIP
Views of NAO OKAWA
WOULDN'T BE AN ALL-BOY SLEEPOVER WITHOUT SOME OF THIS!
KLASP
TEAM ADULT
IT IS NIGHTTIME, RIGHT? ♡
KLUP
THIS IS CRUCIAL STUFF. ♡
GOT SOME EAR-PHONES?
VWEEE
SHFF
SHFF
SURE DO.
MMMPHHH
SKRIT
KLIK
KLIK
SKRIT

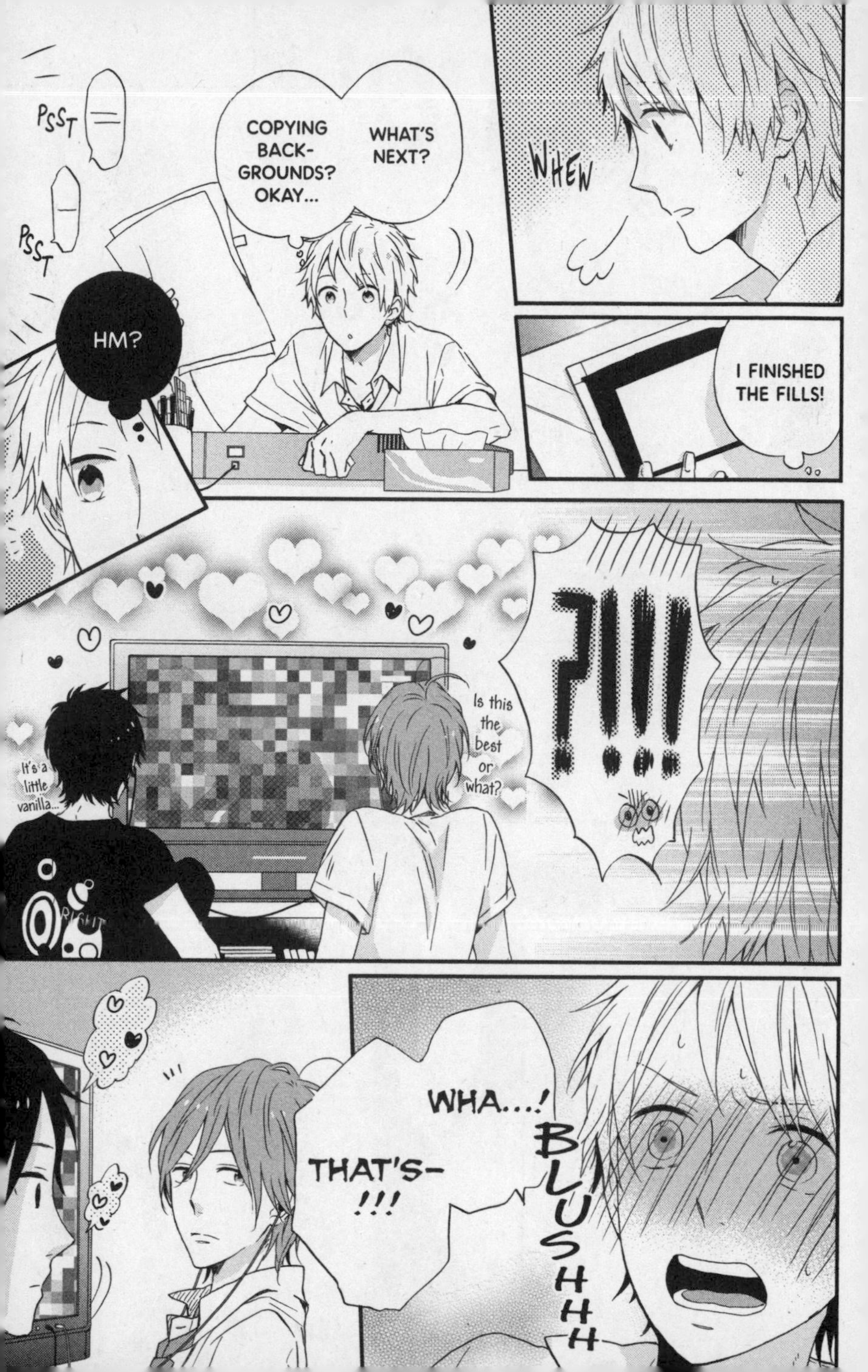
WHEW
I FINISHED THE FILLS!
WHAT'S NEXT?
COPYING BACK-GROUNDS? OKAY...
PSST
PSST
HM?
?!!!
Is this the best or what?
It's a little vanilla...
WHA...!
THAT'S-!!!
BLUSHHH

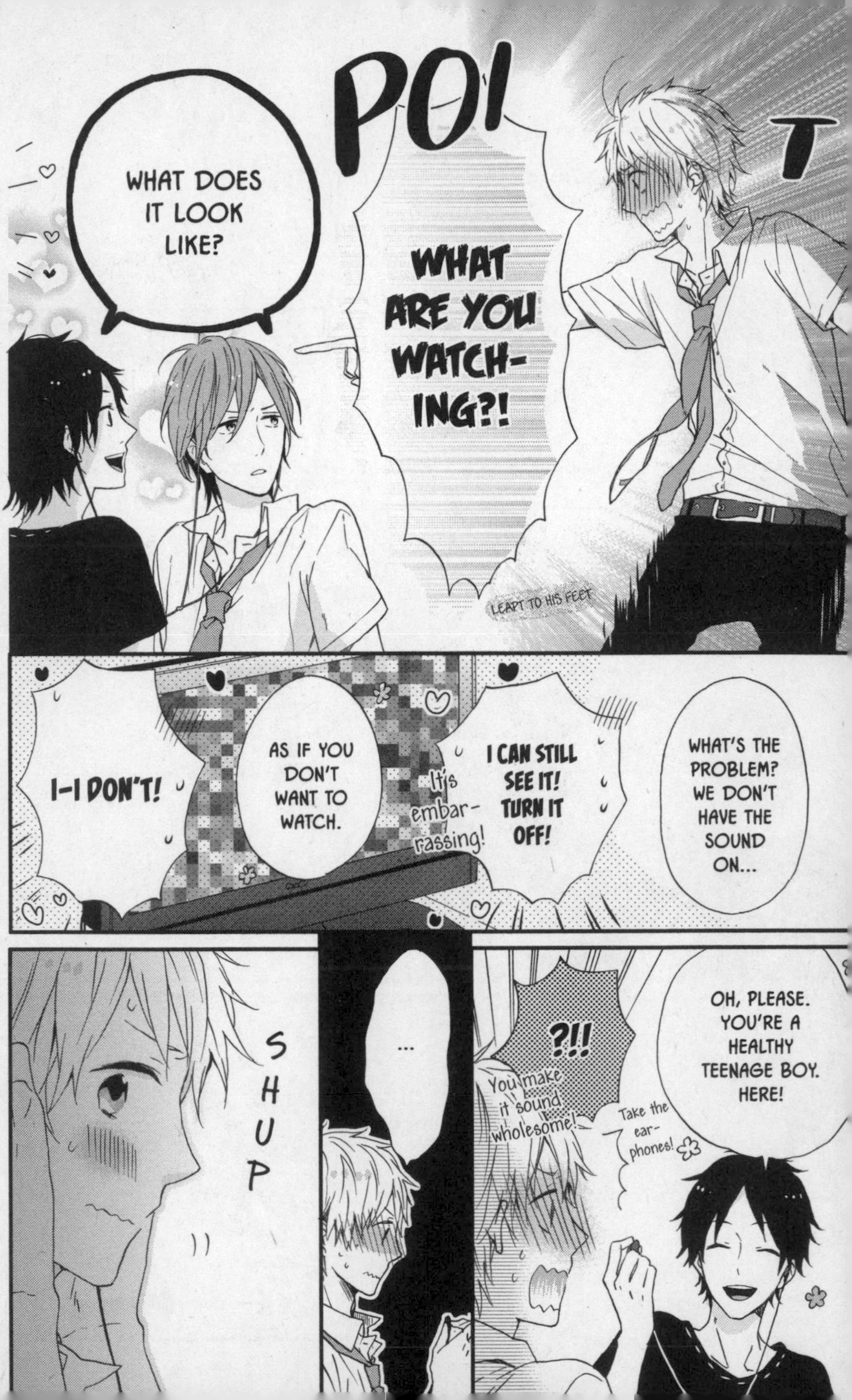
POI T
WHAT ARE YOU WATCH-ING?!
LEAPT TO HIS FEET
WHAT DOES IT LOOK LIKE?
WHAT'S THE PROBLEM? WE DON'T HAVE THE SOUND ON...
I CAN STILL SEE IT! TURN IT OFF!
It's embar-rassing!
AS IF YOU DON'T WANT TO WATCH.
I-I DON'T!
OH, PLEASE. YOU'RE A HEALTHY TEENAGE BOY. HERE!
Take the ear-phones!
?!!
You make it sound wholesome!
...
SHUP

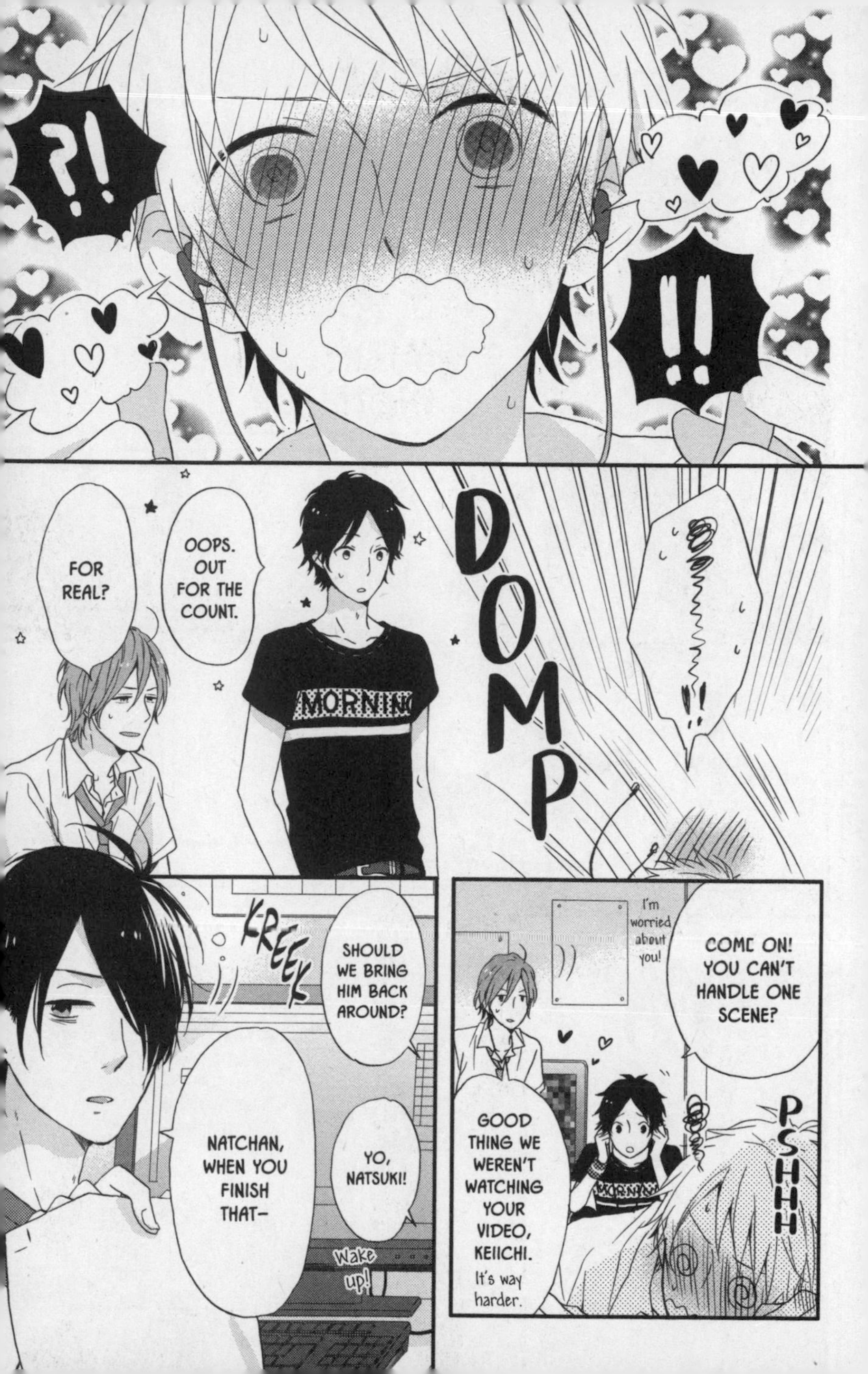
!!
?!
DOMP
!!
OOPS. OUT FOR THE COUNT.
FOR REAL?
COME ON! YOU CAN'T HANDLE ONE SCENE?
I'm worried about you!
PSHHH
GOOD THING WE WEREN'T WATCHING YOUR VIDEO, KEIICHI.
It's way harder.
SHOULD WE BRING HIM BACK AROUND?
KREEK
YO, NATSUKI!
Wake up!
NATCHAN, WHEN YOU FINISH THAT–

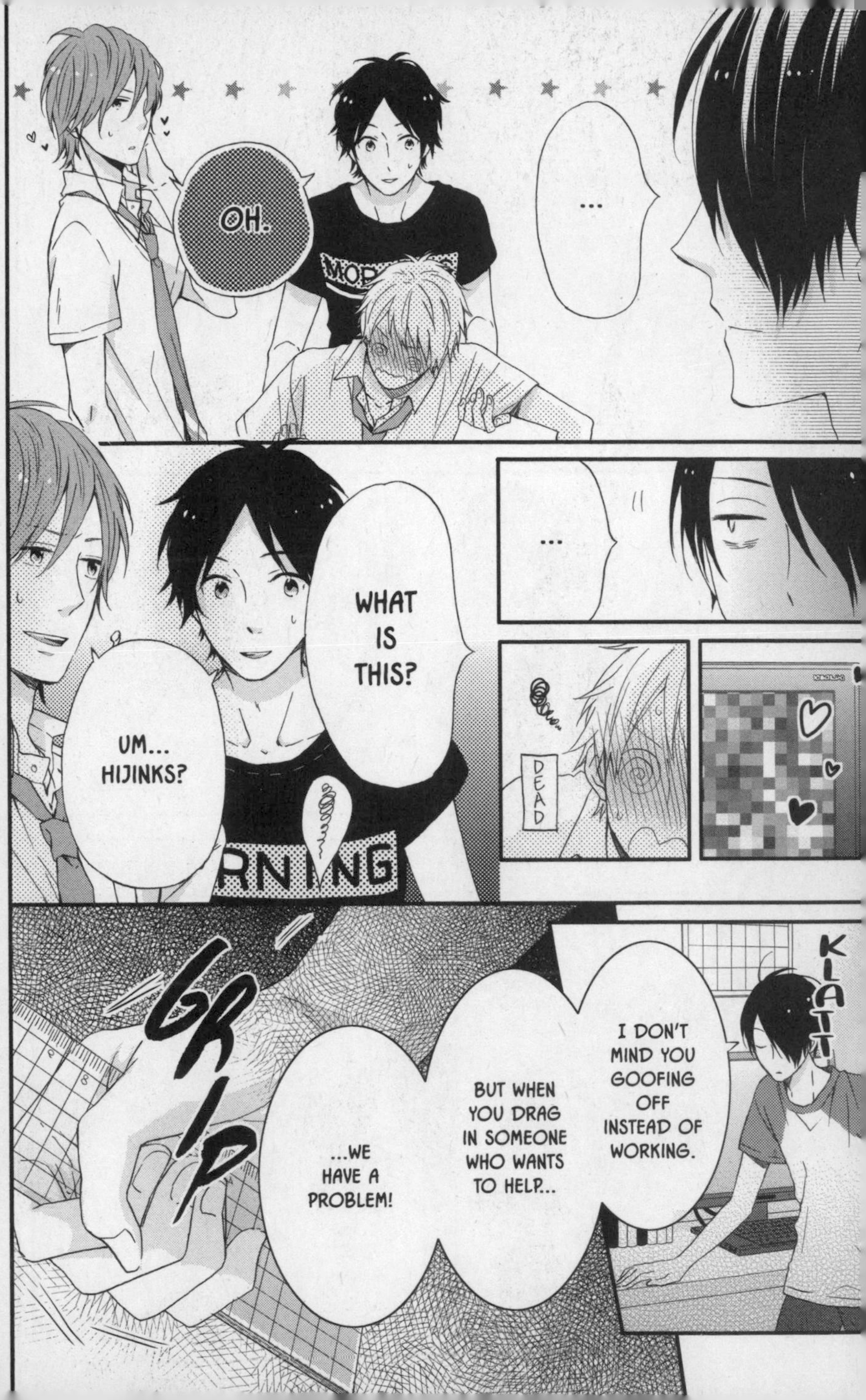
...
OH.
...
DEAD
WHAT IS THIS?
UM... HIJINKS?
KLATT
I DON'T MIND YOU GOOFING OFF INSTEAD OF WORKING.
BUT WHEN YOU DRAG IN SOMEONE WHO WANTS TO HELP...
...WE HAVE A PROBLEM!
GRIP

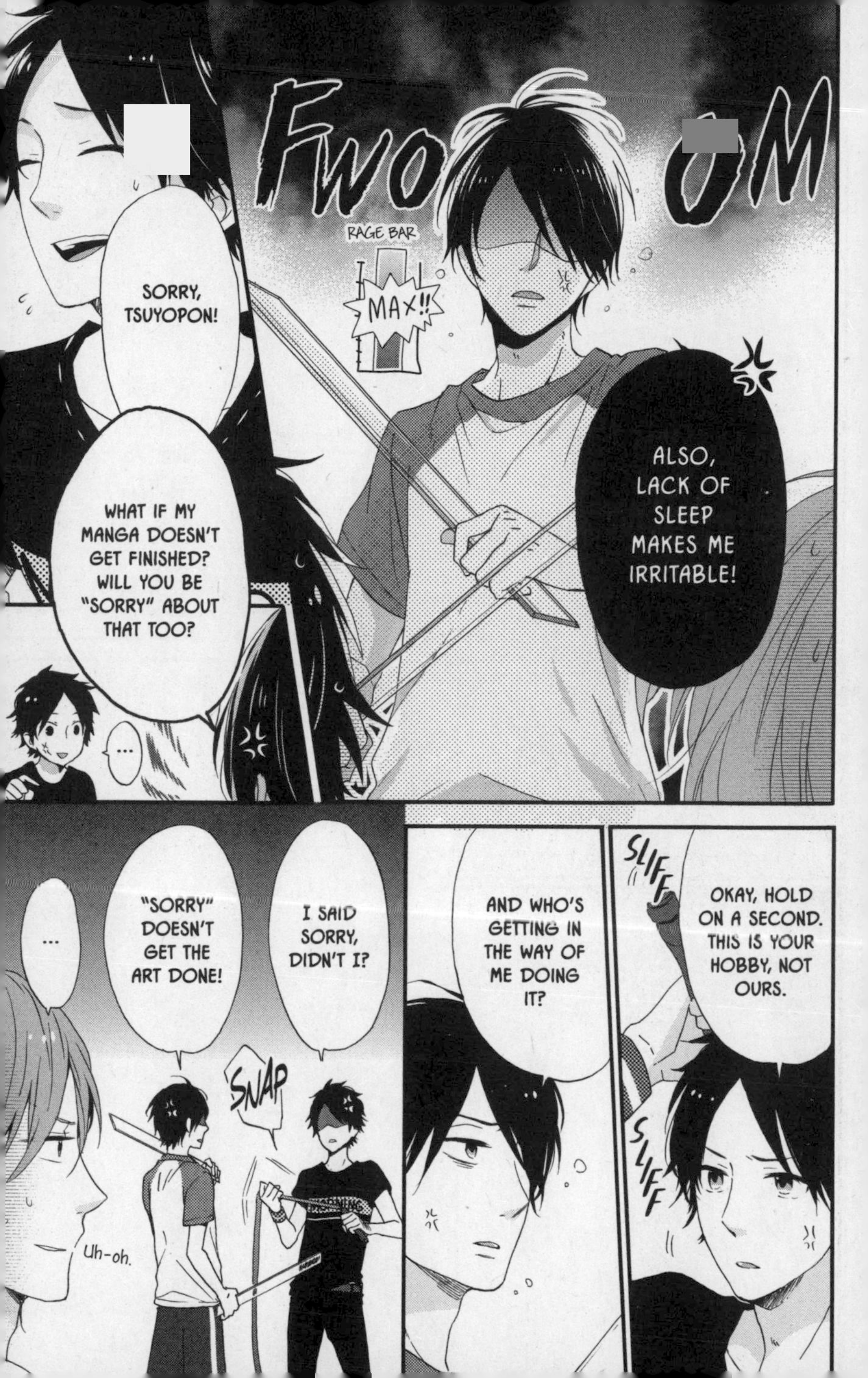
FWO
OM
RAGE BAR
MAX!!
ALSO, LACK OF SLEEP MAKES ME IRRITABLE!
SORRY, TSUYOPON!
WHAT IF MY MANGA DOESN'T GET FINISHED? WILL YOU BE "SORRY" ABOUT THAT TOO?
...
SLIFF
OKAY, HOLD ON A SECOND. THIS IS YOUR HOBBY, NOT OURS.
SLIFF
AND WHO'S GETTING IN THE WAY OF ME DOING IT?
I SAID SORRY, DIDN'T I?
"SORRY" DOESN'T GET THE ART DONE!
...
SNAP
Uh-oh.

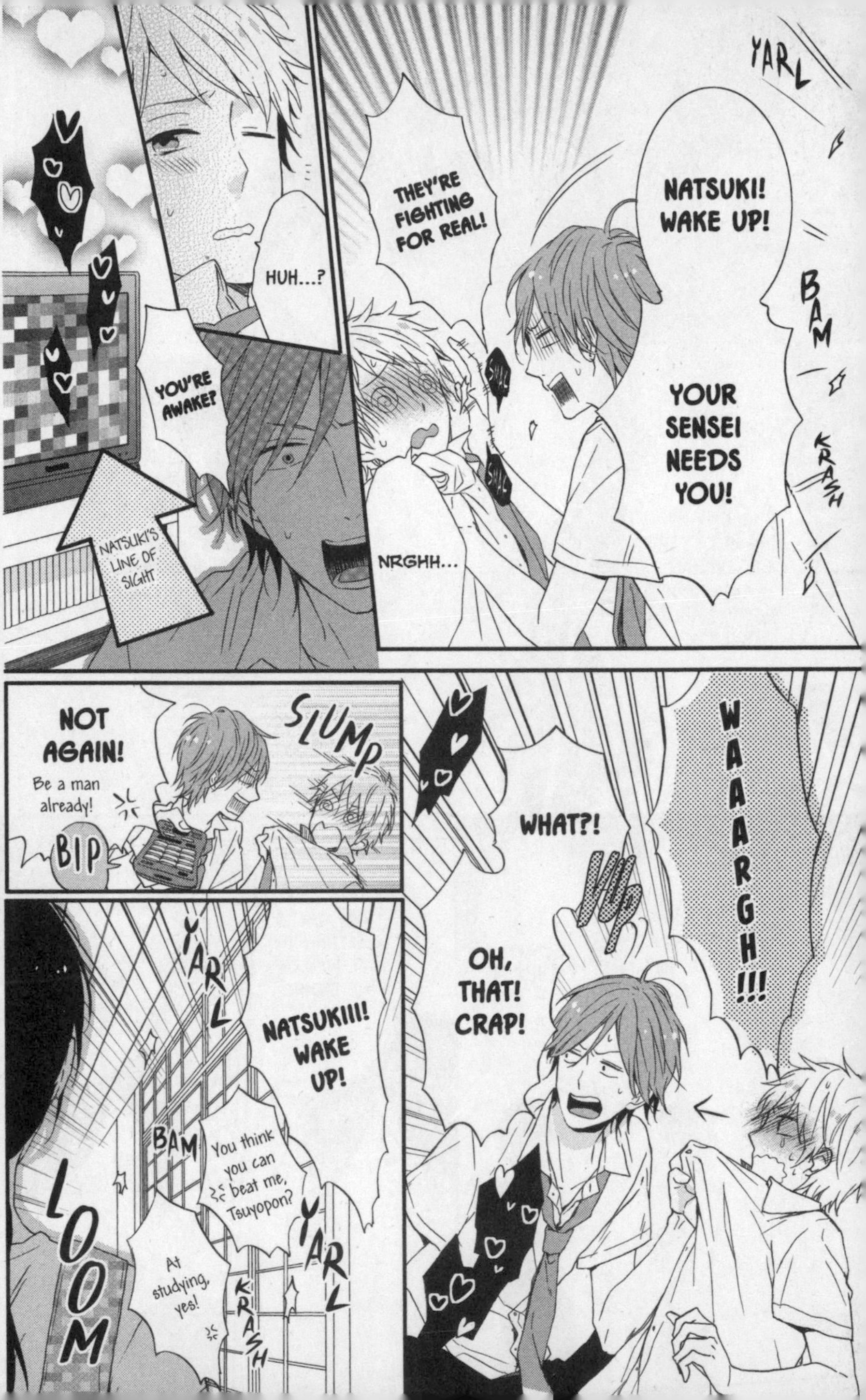
YARL
NATSUKI! WAKE UP!
BAM
YOUR SENSEI NEEDS YOU!
KRASH
THEY'RE FIGHTING FOR REAL!
NRGHH...
HUH...?
YOU'RE AWAKE?
NATSUKI'S LINE OF SIGHT
WAAAARGH!!!
WHAT?!
OH, THAT! CRAP!
SLUMP
NOT AGAIN!
Be a man already!
BIP
YARL
NATSUKIII! WAKE UP!
You think you can beat me, Tsuyopon?
BAM
YARL
At studying, yes!
KRASH
LOOM

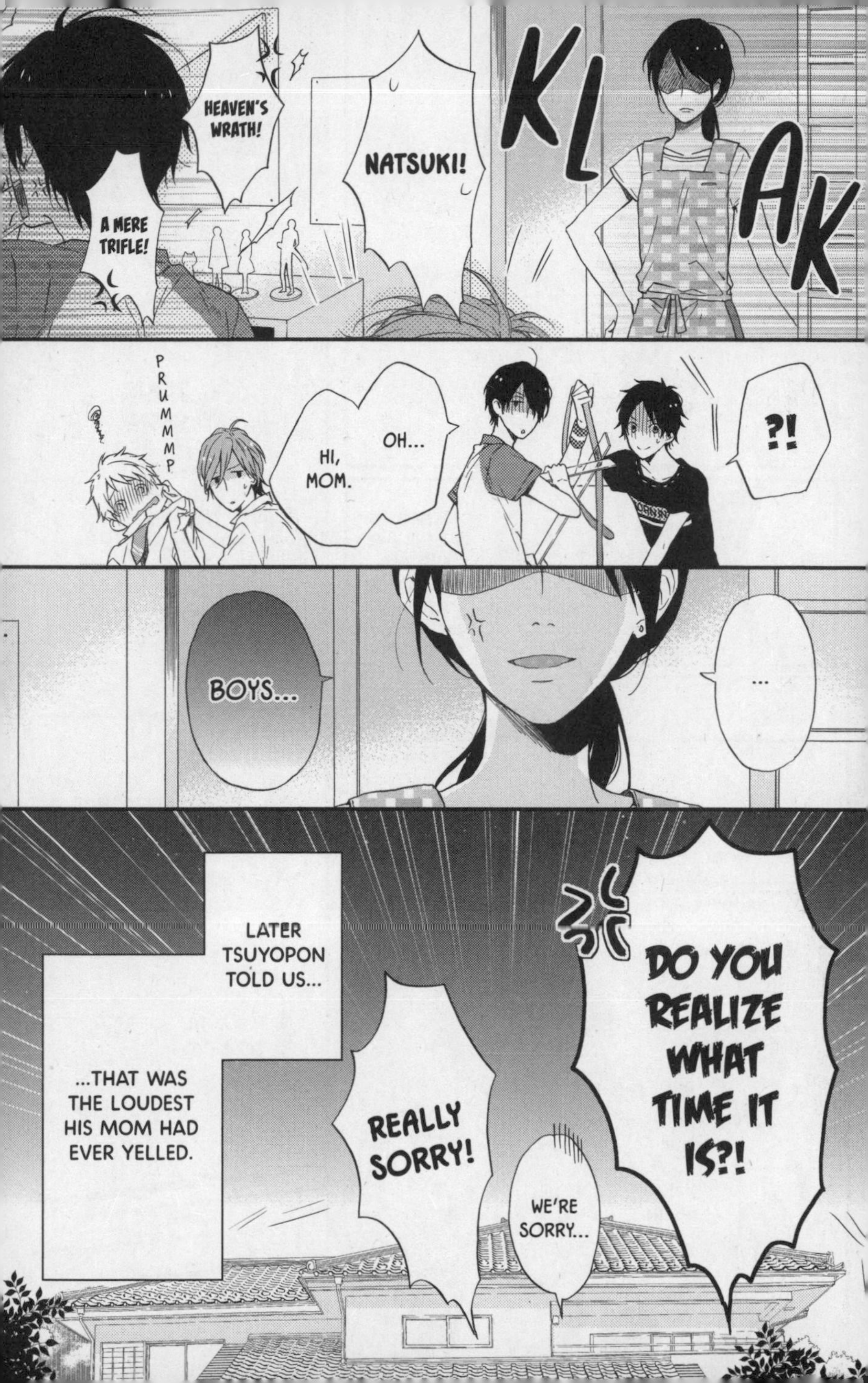
KLAK
NATSUKI!
HEAVEN'S WRATH!
A MERE TRIFLE!
?!
OH...
HI, MOM.
PRUMMMP
...
BOYS...
DO YOU REALIZE WHAT TIME IT IS?!
REALLY SORRY!
WE'RE SORRY...
LATER TSUYOPON TOLD US...
...THAT WAS THE LOUDEST HIS MOM HAD EVER YELLED.

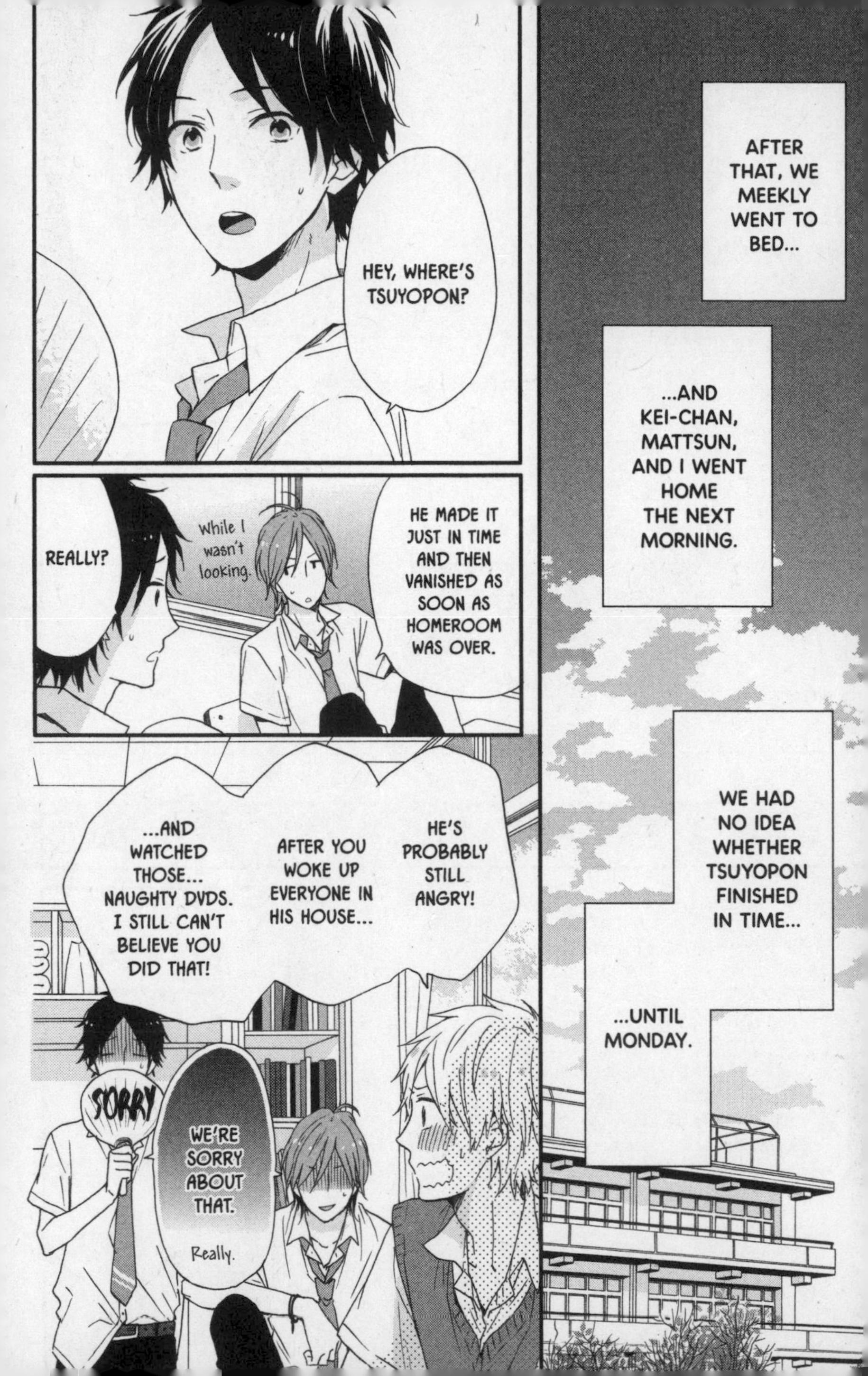
AFTER THAT, WE MEEKLY WENT TO BED...
...AND KEI-CHAN, MATTSUN, AND I WENT HOME THE NEXT MORNING.
WE HAD NO IDEA WHETHER TSUYOPON FINISHED IN TIME...
...UNTIL MONDAY.
HEY, WHERE'S TSUYOPON?
HE MADE IT JUST IN TIME AND THEN VANISHED AS SOON AS HOMEROOM WAS OVER.
While I wasn't looking.
REALLY?
HE'S PROBABLY STILL ANGRY!
AFTER YOU WOKE UP EVERYONE IN HIS HOUSE...
...AND WATCHED THOSE... NAUGHTY DVDS. I STILL CAN'T BELIEVE YOU DID THAT!
SORRY
WE'RE SORRY ABOUT THAT.
Really.

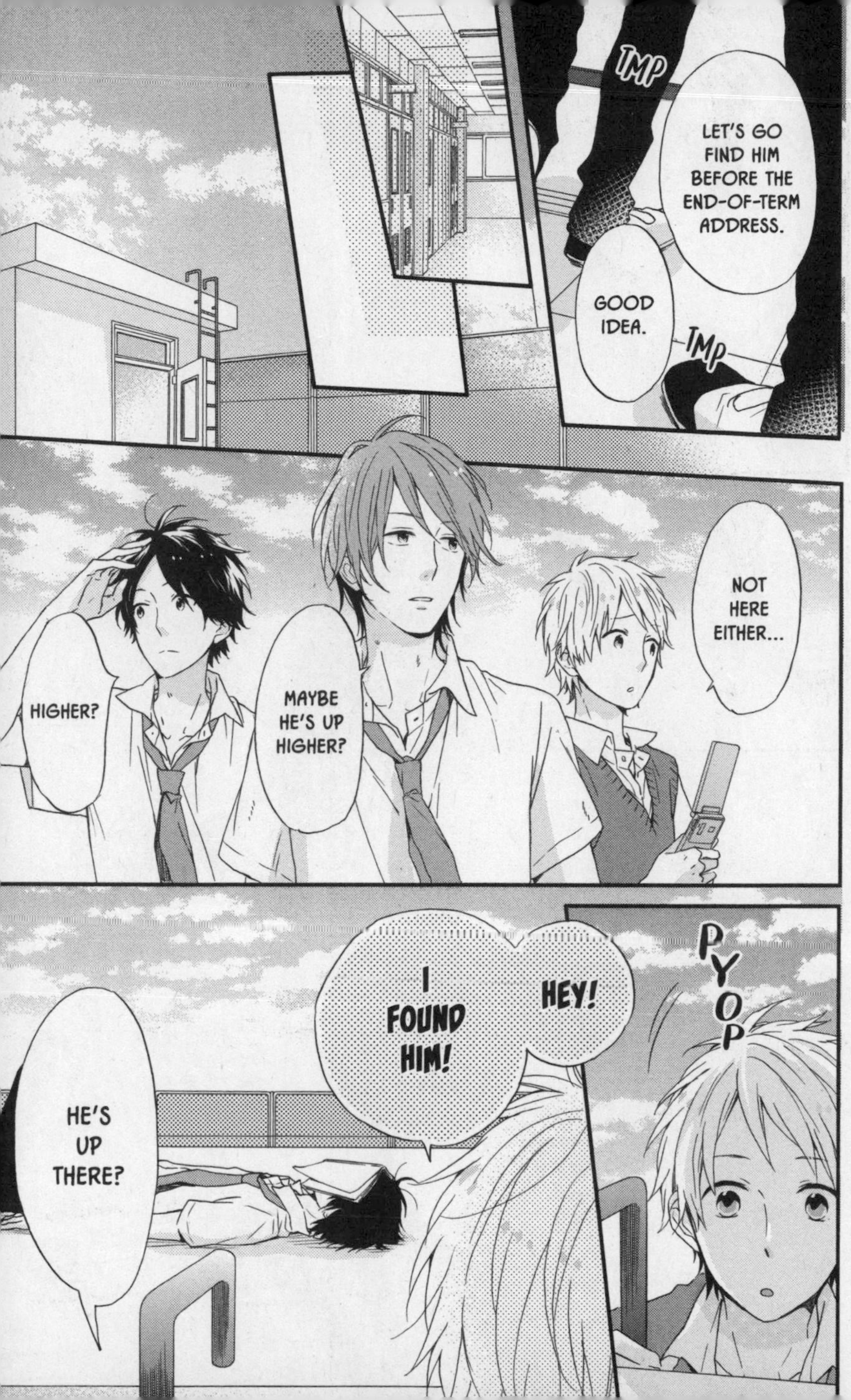
TMP
LET'S GO FIND HIM BEFORE THE END-OF-TERM ADDRESS.
GOOD IDEA.
TMP
NOT HERE EITHER...
MAYBE HE'S UP HIGHER?
HIGHER?
PYOP
HEY!
I FOUND HIM!
HE'S UP THERE?

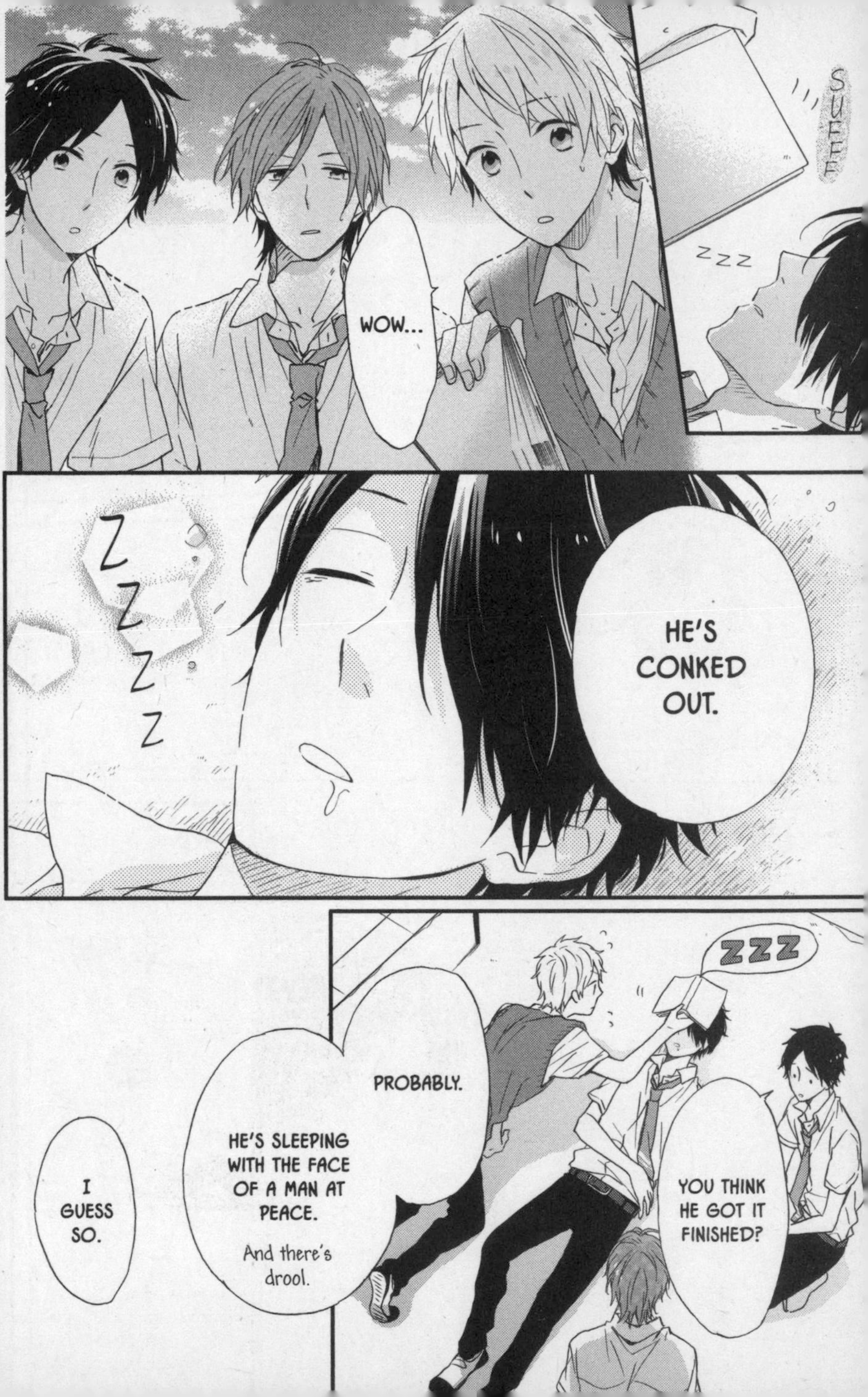
SUFF
ZZZ
WOW...
ZZZZZ
HE'S CONKED OUT.
ZZZ
YOU THINK HE GOT IT FINISHED?
PROBABLY.
HE'S SLEEPING WITH THE FACE OF A MAN AT PEACE.
And there's drool.
I GUESS SO.

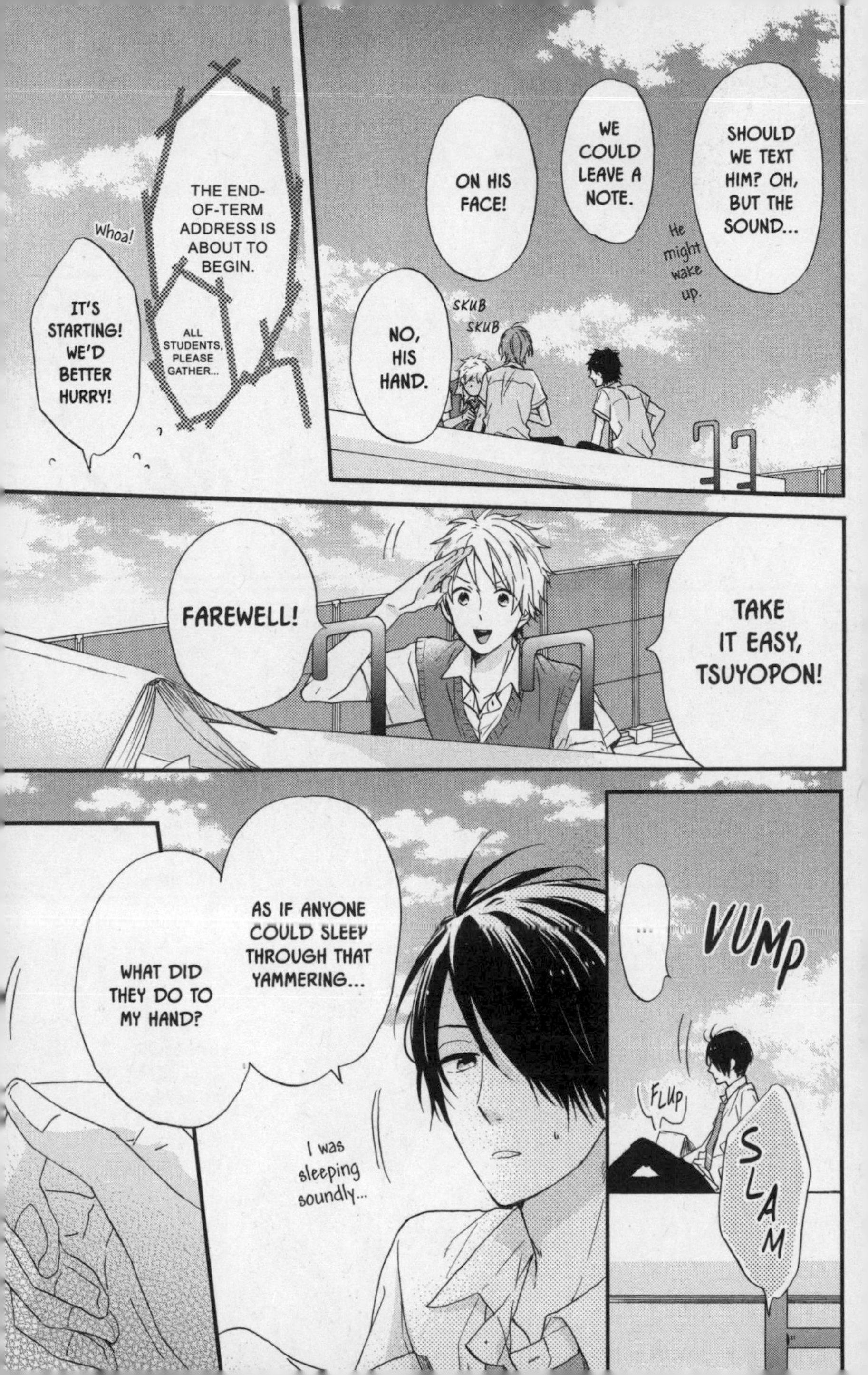
SHOULD WE TEXT HIM? OH, BUT THE SOUND...
He might wake up.
WE COULD LEAVE A NOTE.
ON HIS FACE!
SKUB SKUB
NO, HIS HAND.
THE END-OF-TERM ADDRESS IS ABOUT TO BEGIN.
ALL STUDENTS, PLEASE GATHER...
Whoa!
IT'S STARTING! WE'D BETTER HURRY!
TAKE IT EASY, TSUYOPON!
FAREWELL!
...
VUMP
FLUP
SLAM
AS IF ANYONE COULD SLEEP THROUGH THAT YAMMERING...
WHAT DID THEY DO TO MY HAND?
I was sleeping soundly...

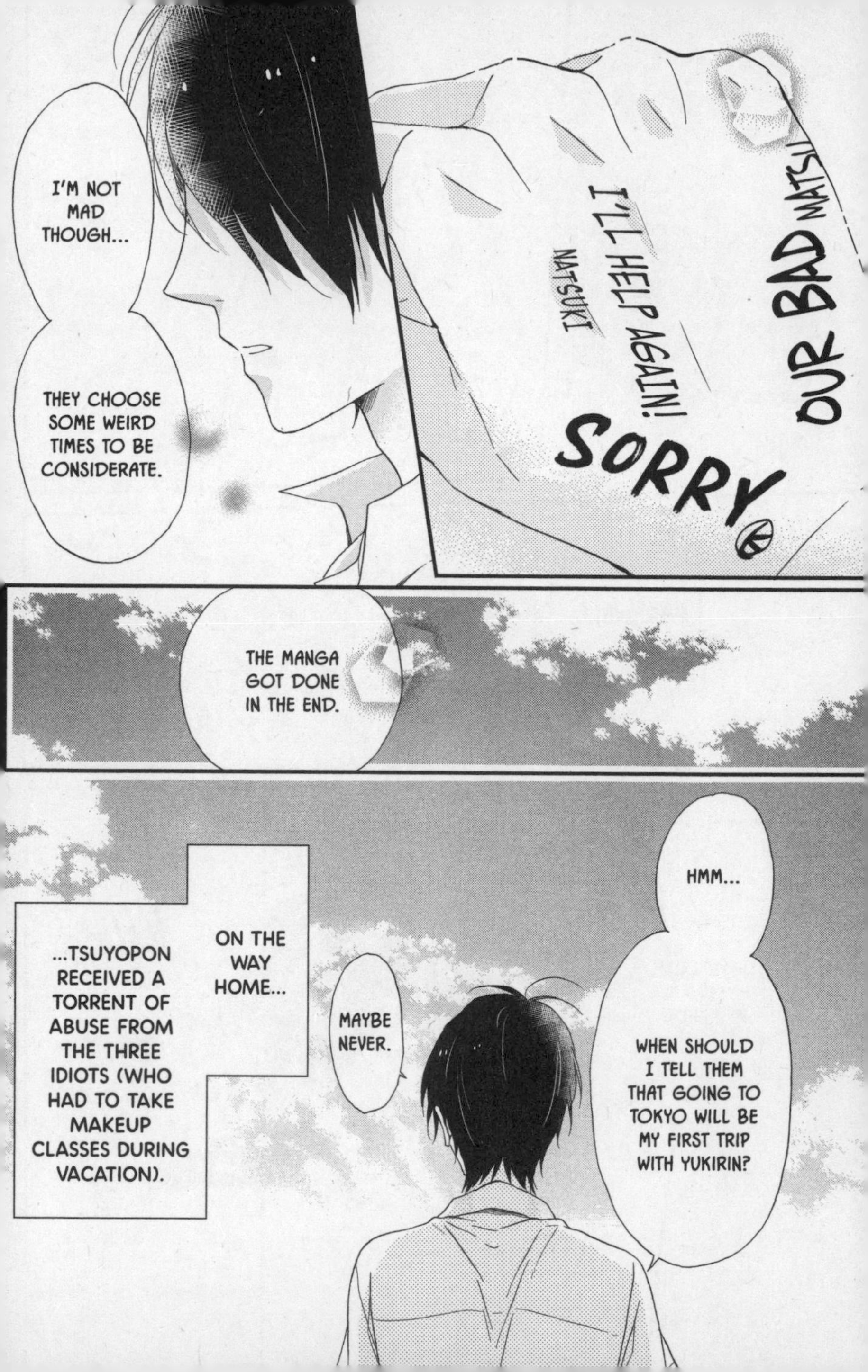
OUR BAD MATSU
I'LL HELP AGAIN! NATSUKI
SORRY
I'M NOT MAD THOUGH...
THEY CHOOSE SOME WEIRD TIMES TO BE CONSIDERATE.
THE MANGA GOT DONE IN THE END.
HMM...
WHEN SHOULD I TELL THEM THAT GOING TO TOKYO WILL BE MY FIRST TRIP WITH YUKIRIN?
MAYBE NEVER.
ON THE WAY HOME...
...TSUYOPON RECEIVED A TORRENT OF ABUSE FROM THE THREE IDIOTS (WHO HAD TO TAKE MAKEUP CLASSES DURING VACATION).

Rainbow
Days

THANK YOU FOR PICKING UP
RAINBOW DAYS VOL. 3!

Hello, I'm Minami Mizuno.
The side story was longer than I expected this time, so my afterword got cut... I can't complain though because I was the one who asked to do a long bonus manga!

When I buy a new manga and find a whole bunch of bonus stuff and comments from the author, I love it, so I spend as much time as I can filling in any white space myself!
What do you think? Maybe it's unnecessary...?
Well, anyway! I choose to believe there are people out there who feel as I do! (*laugh*)

Mind you, when I actually sit down to write behind-the-scenes stories, I don't have any material. I mean, I do! I have funny stories about my amusing assistants, but due to my lack of literary or expressive ability, I can't tell them properly! It's frustrating. One day I hope to write about the struggle of being unable to ink because I'm laughing so hard that my hand shakes (usually thanks to Cozmi). Don't get the wrong idea though! Normally we just concentrate on our work in silence!

Maybe...

← Continued on p. 78!

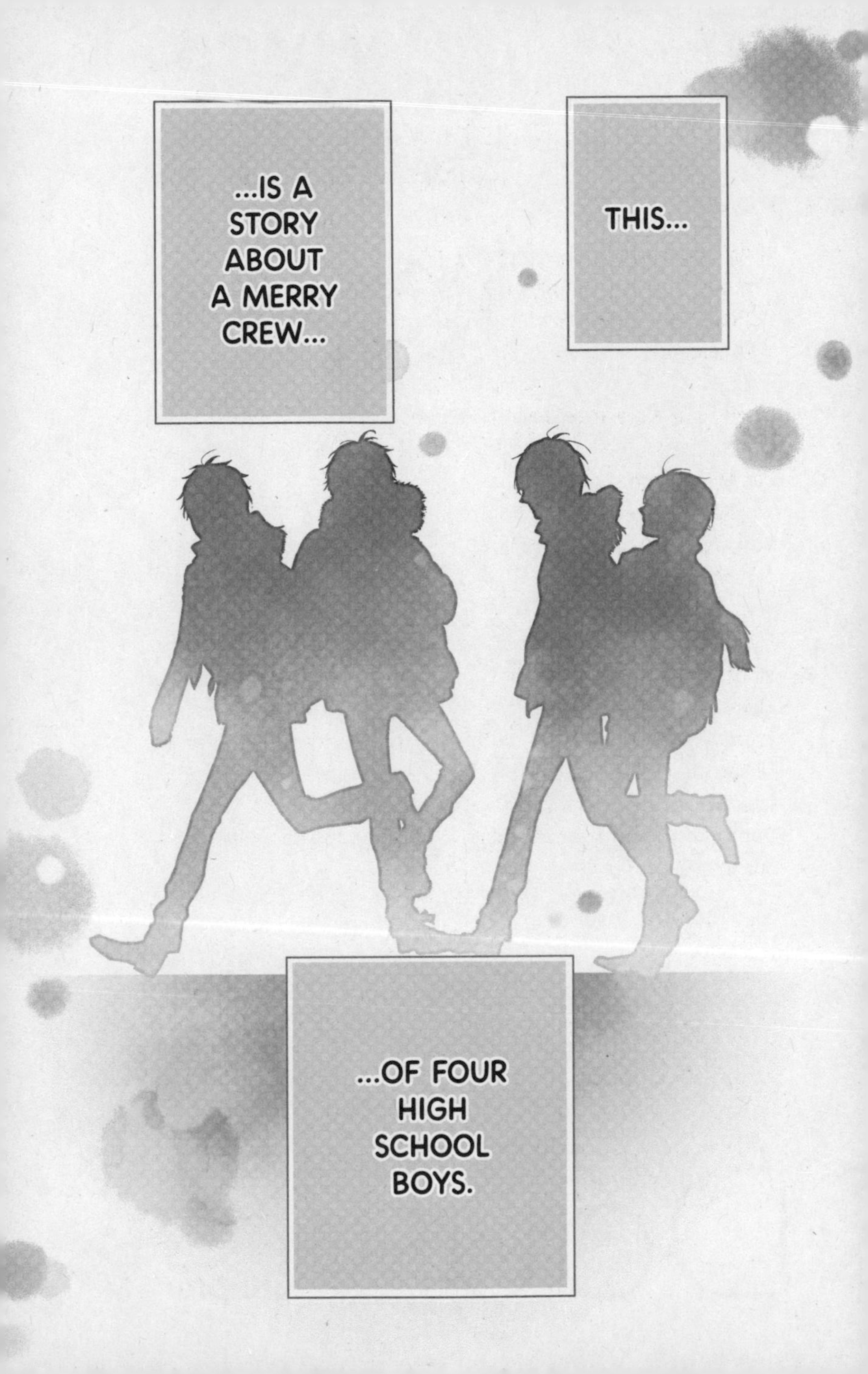
THIS...
...IS A STORY ABOUT A MERRY CREW...
...OF FOUR HIGH SCHOOL BOYS.

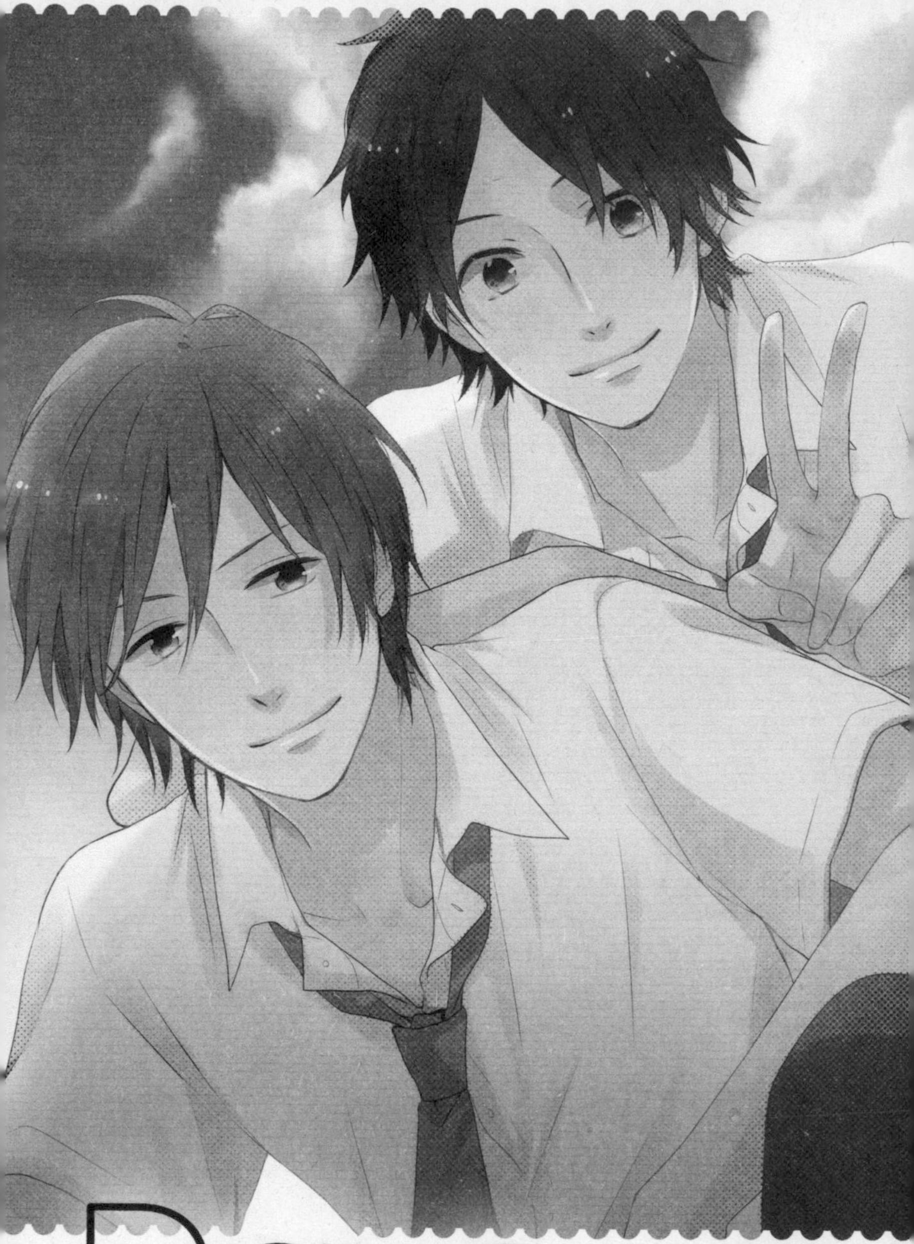

Days

Chapter 6

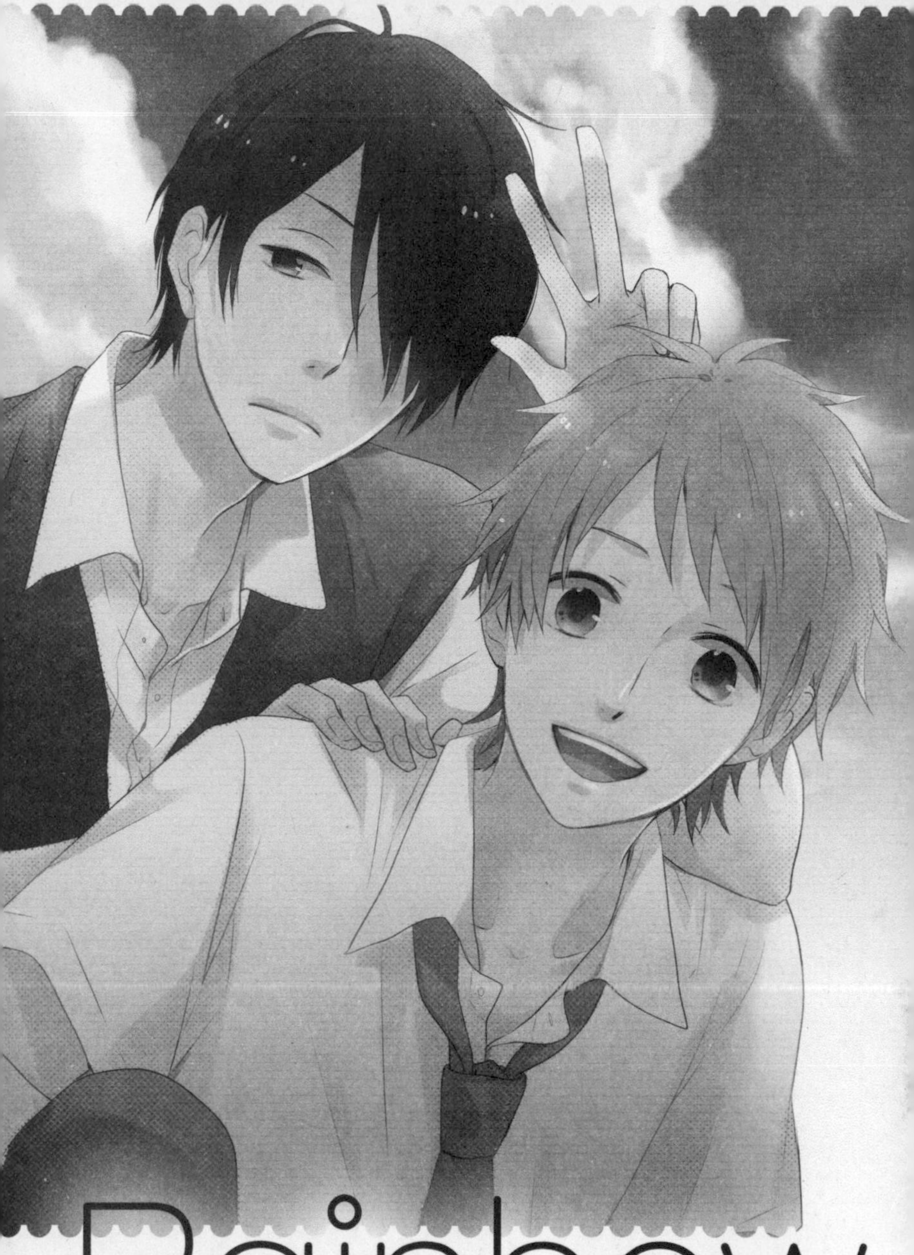

Rainbow

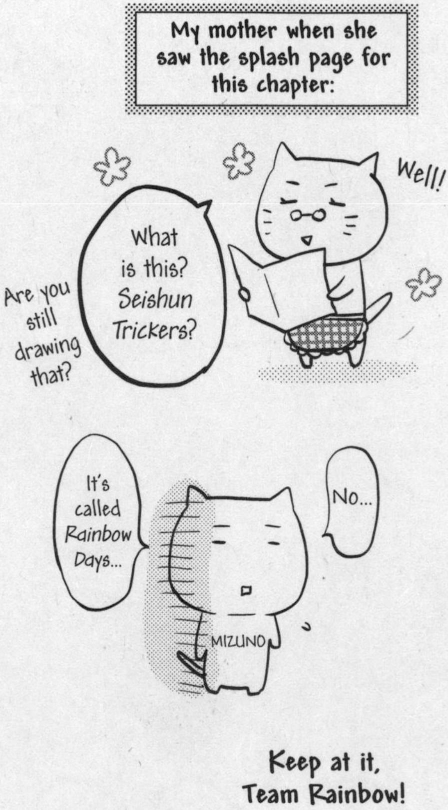
My mother when she saw the splash page for this chapter:
Well!
What is this? Seishun Trickers?
Are you still drawing that?
No...
It's called Rainbow Days...
MIZUNO
Keep at it, Team Rainbow!

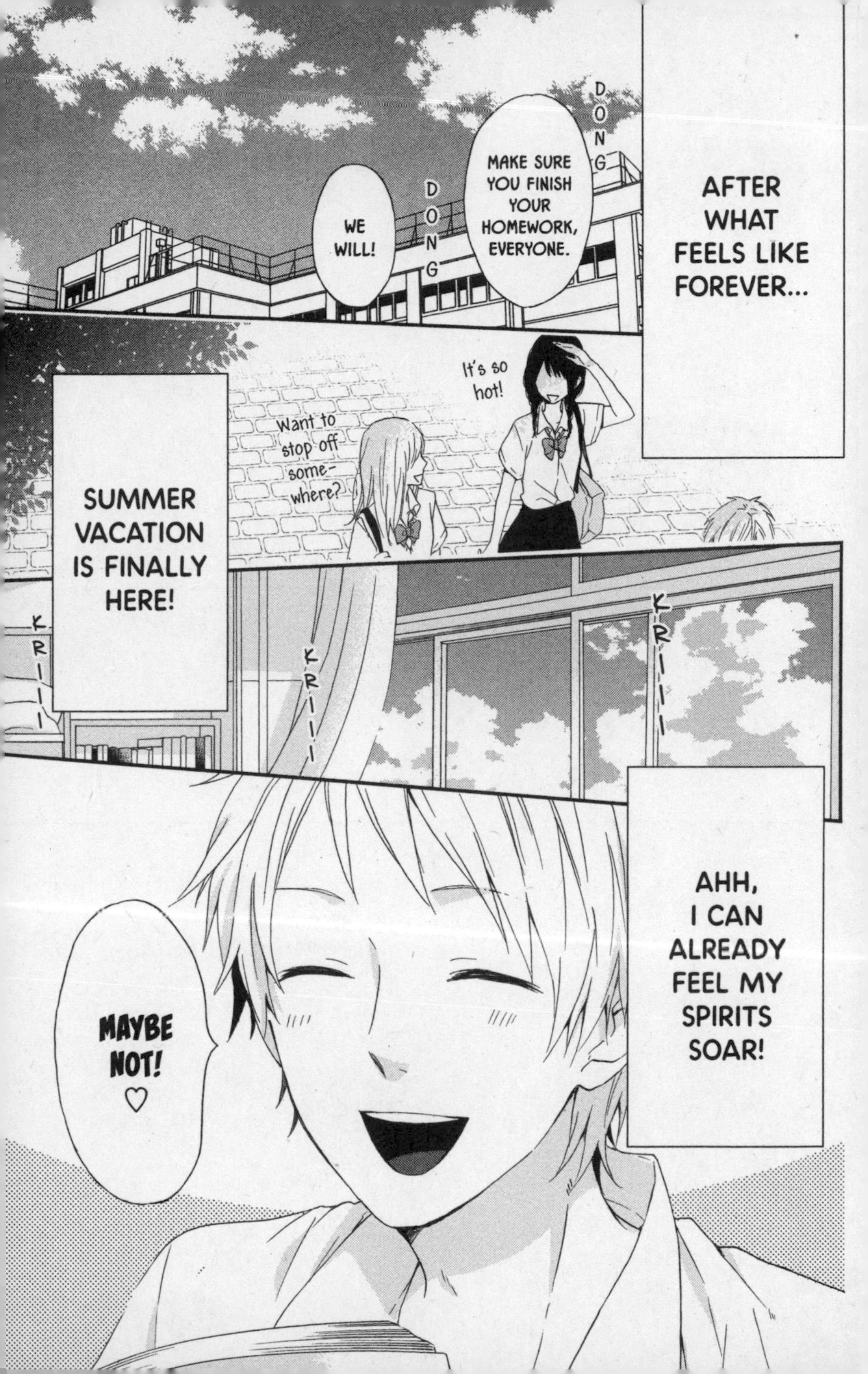
AFTER WHAT FEELS LIKE FOREVER...
DONG
MAKE SURE YOU FINISH YOUR HOMEWORK, EVERYONE.
DONG
WE WILL!
It's so hot!
Want to stop off some-where?
SUMMER VACATION IS FINALLY HERE!
KRIII
KRIII
KRIII
AHH, I CAN ALREADY FEEL MY SPIRITS SOAR!
MAYBE NOT! ♡

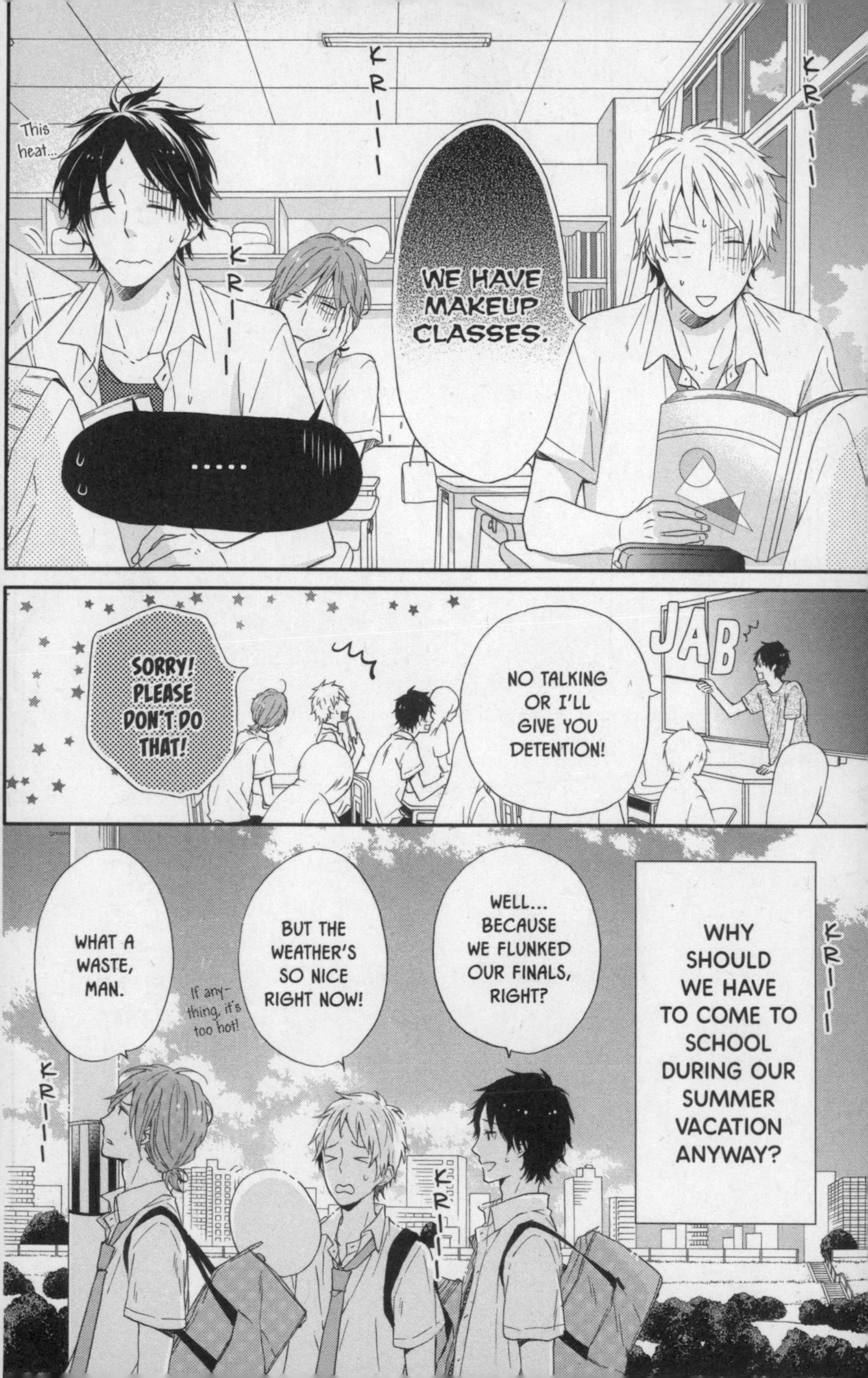
KRIII
WE HAVE MAKEUP CLASSES.
KRIII
This heat...
KRIII
......
JAB
NO TALKING OR I'LL GIVE YOU DETENTION!
SORRY! PLEASE DON'T DO THAT!
WHY SHOULD WE HAVE TO COME TO SCHOOL DURING OUR SUMMER VACATION ANYWAY?
KRIII
WELL... BECAUSE WE FLUNKED OUR FINALS, RIGHT?
KRIII
BUT THE WEATHER'S SO NICE RIGHT NOW!
If anything, it's too hot!
WHAT A WASTE, MAN.
KRIII

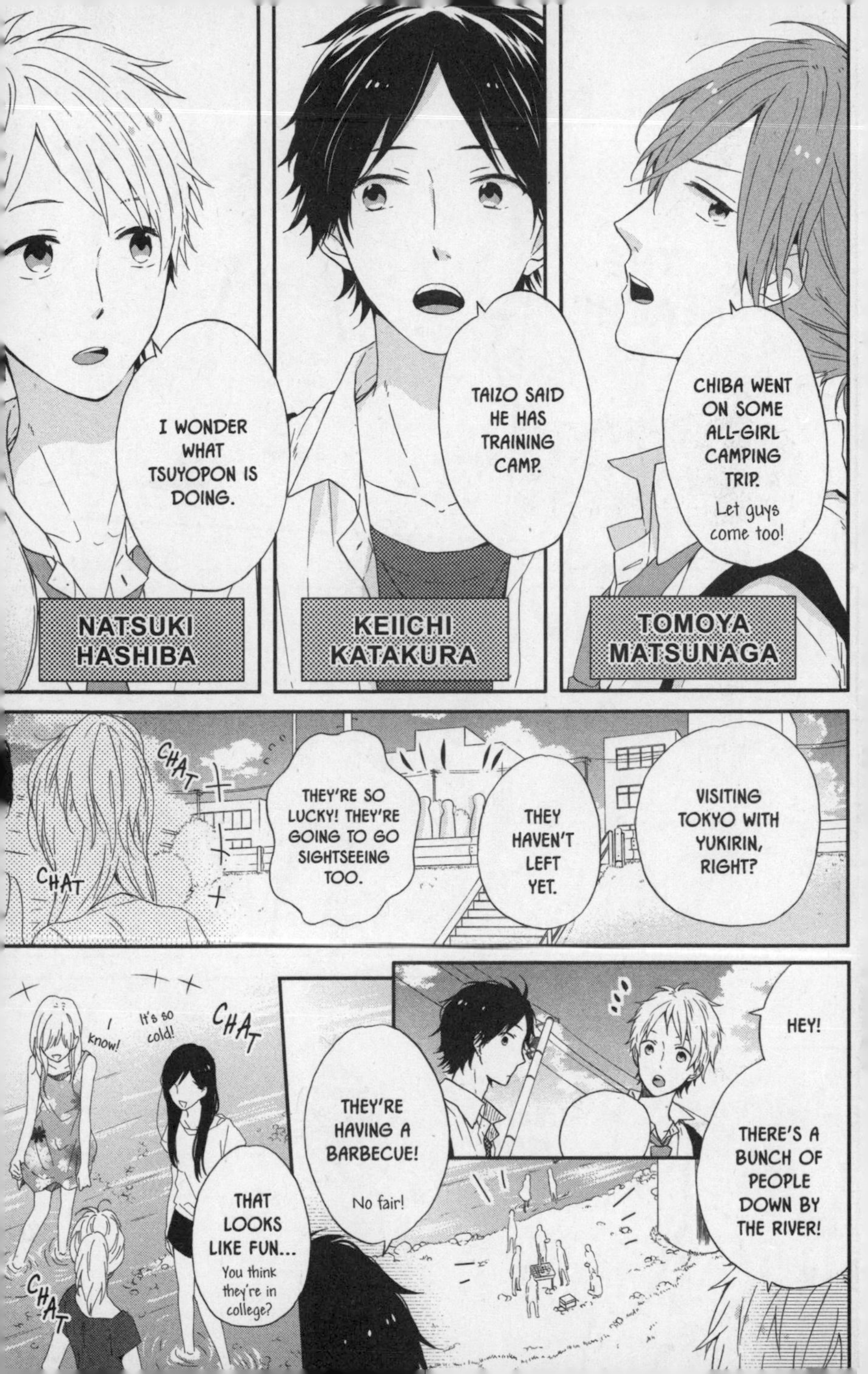
CHIBA WENT ON SOME ALL-GIRL CAMPING TRIP.
Let guys come too!
TOMOYA MATSUNAGA
TAIZO SAID HE HAS TRAINING CAMP.
KEIICHI KATAKURA
I WONDER WHAT TSUYOPON IS DOING.
NATSUKI HASHIBA
VISITING TOKYO WITH YUKIRIN, RIGHT?
THEY HAVEN'T LEFT YET.
THEY'RE SO LUCKY! THEY'RE GOING TO GO SIGHTSEEING TOO.
CHAT
CHAT
HEY!
THERE'S A BUNCH OF PEOPLE DOWN BY THE RIVER!
THEY'RE HAVING A BARBECUE!
No fair!
CHAT
It's so cold!
I know!
THAT LOOKS LIKE FUN...
You think they're in college?
CHAT

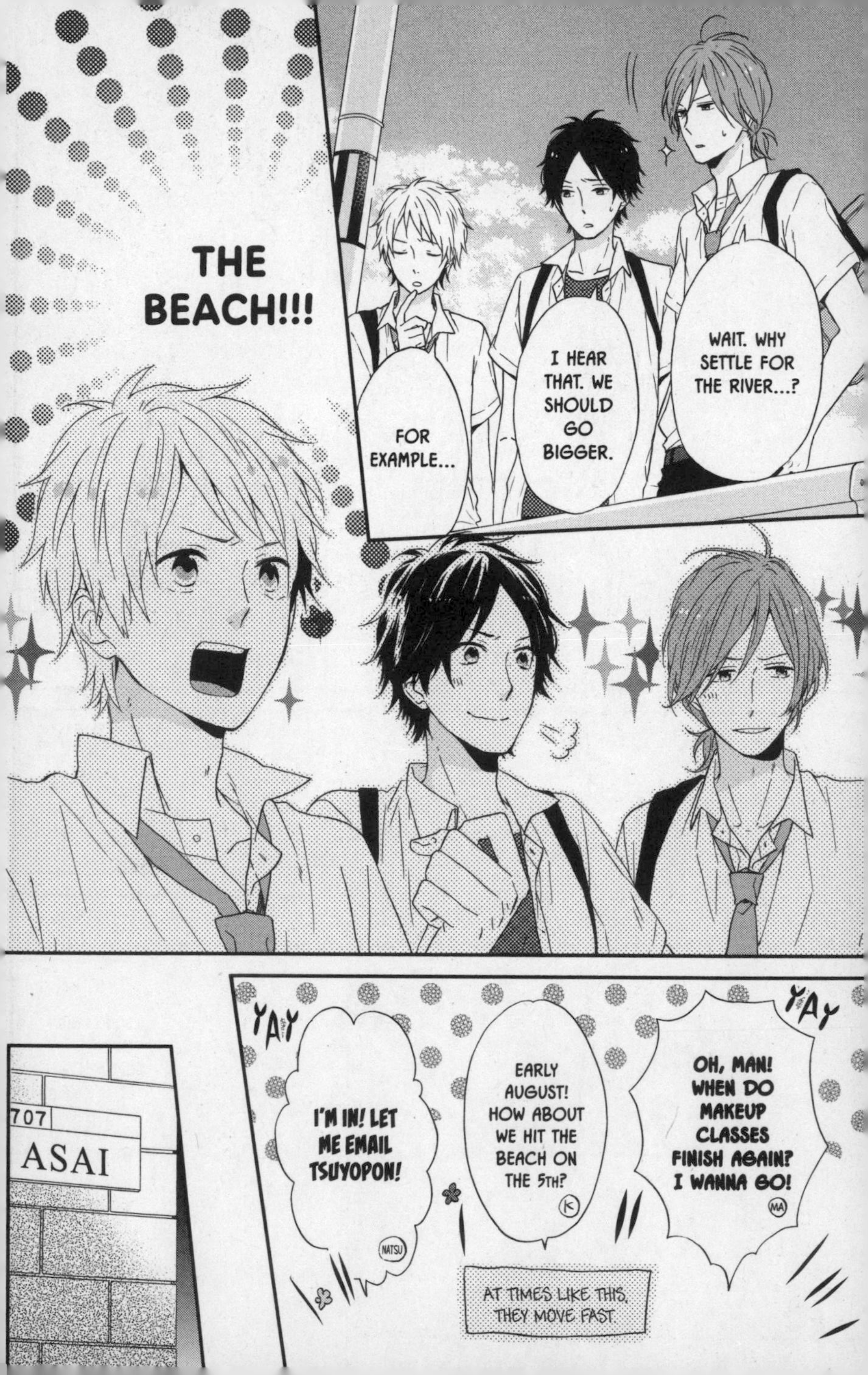
WAIT. WHY SETTLE FOR THE RIVER...?
I HEAR THAT. WE SHOULD GO BIGGER.
FOR EXAMPLE...
THE BEACH!!!
YAY
OH, MAN! WHEN DO MAKEUP CLASSES FINISH AGAIN? I WANNA GO!
MA
EARLY AUGUST! HOW ABOUT WE HIT THE BEACH ON THE 5TH?
K
I'M IN! LET ME EMAIL TSUYOPON!
NATSU
YAY
AT TIMES LIKE THIS, THEY MOVE FAST.
707
ASAI

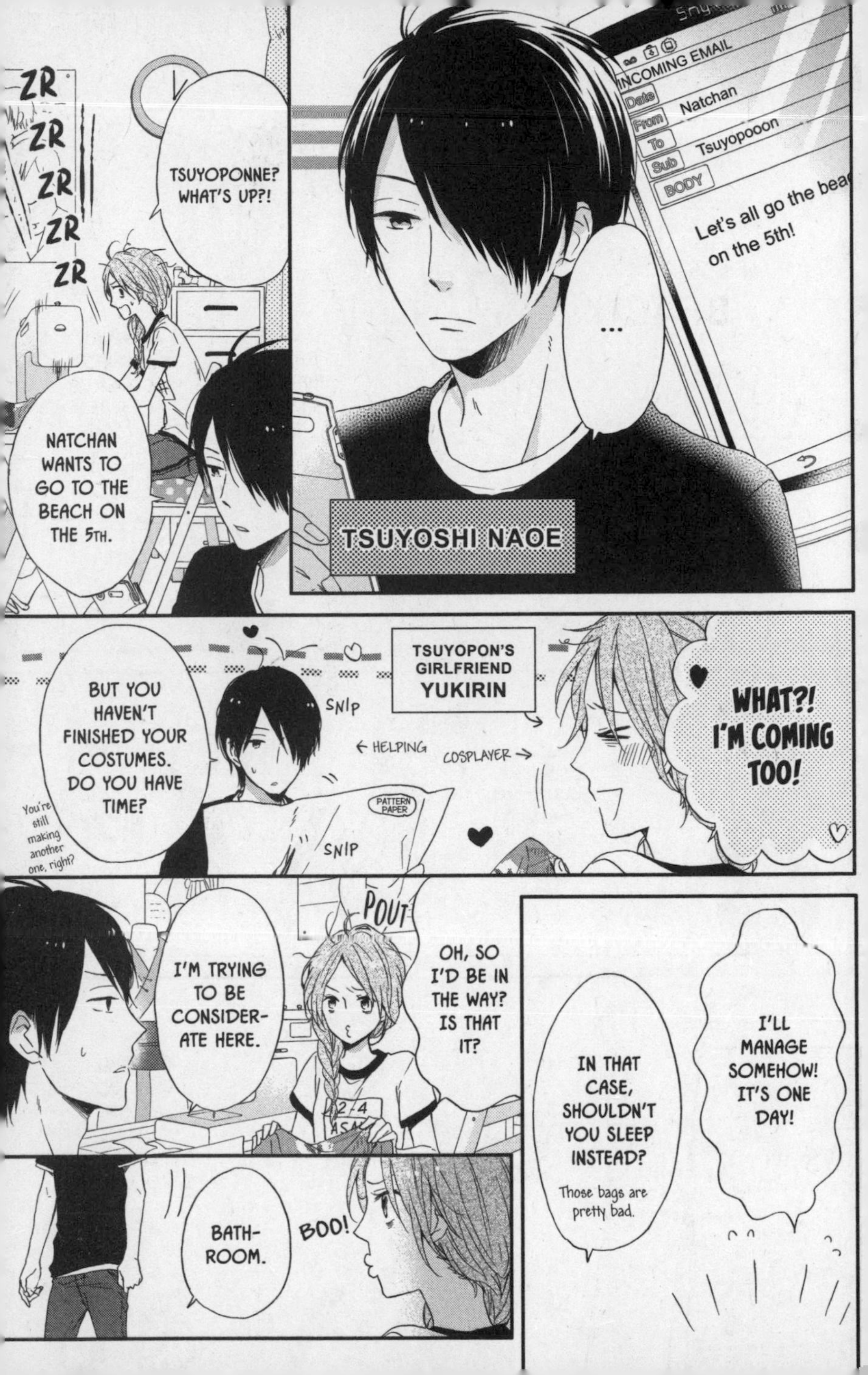
INCOMING EMAIL
Date
From Natchan
To
Sub Tsuyopooon
BODY
Let's all go the bea
on the 5th!
...
TSUYOSHI NAOE
TSUYOPONNE? WHAT'S UP?!
ZR ZR ZR ZR ZR
NATCHAN WANTS TO GO TO THE BEACH ON THE 5TH.
WHAT?! I'M COMING TOO!
TSUYOPON'S GIRLFRIEND YUKIRIN
COSPLAYER
HELPING
SNIP
PATTERN PAPER
BUT YOU HAVEN'T FINISHED YOUR COSTUMES. DO YOU HAVE TIME?
You're still making another one, right?
SNIP
I'LL MANAGE SOMEHOW! IT'S ONE DAY!
IN THAT CASE, SHOULDN'T YOU SLEEP INSTEAD?
Those bags are pretty bad.
POUT
OH, SO I'D BE IN THE WAY? IS THAT IT?
I'M TRYING TO BE CONSIDER-ATE HERE.
BOO!
BATH-ROOM.

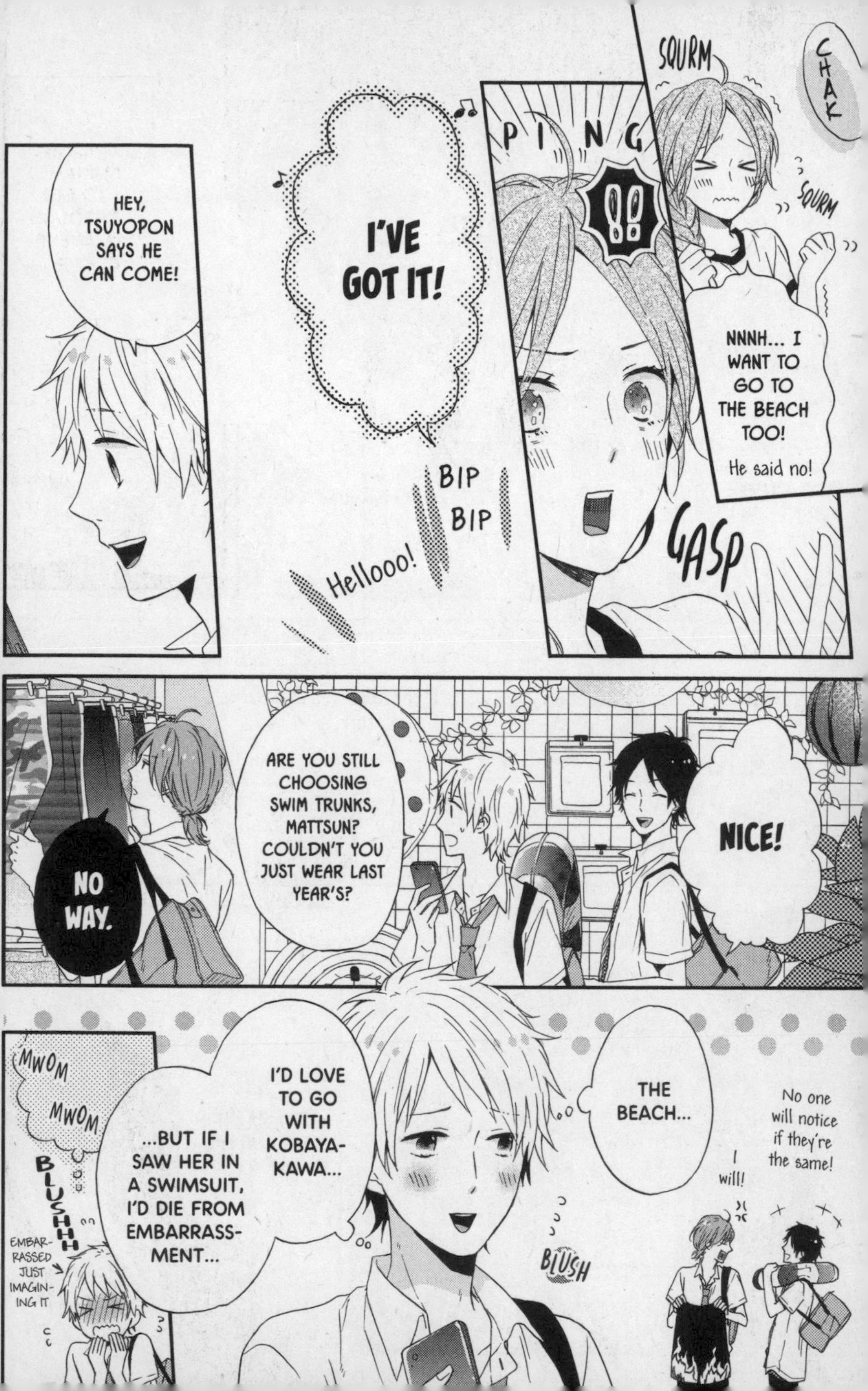
CHAK
SQURM
SQURM
NNNH... I WANT TO GO TO THE BEACH TOO!
He said no!
PING
!!
GASP
I'VE GOT IT!
BIP BIP
Hellooo!
HEY, TSUYOPON SAYS HE CAN COME!
NICE!
ARE YOU STILL CHOOSING SWIM TRUNKS, MATTSUN? COULDN'T YOU JUST WEAR LAST YEAR'S?
NO WAY.
No one will notice if they're the same!
I will!
THE BEACH...
BLUSH
I'D LOVE TO GO WITH KOBAYA-KAWA...
...BUT IF I SAW HER IN A SWIMSUIT, I'D DIE FROM EMBARRASS-MENT...
MWOM MWOM
BLUSHHH
EMBAR-RASSED JUST IMAGIN-ING IT

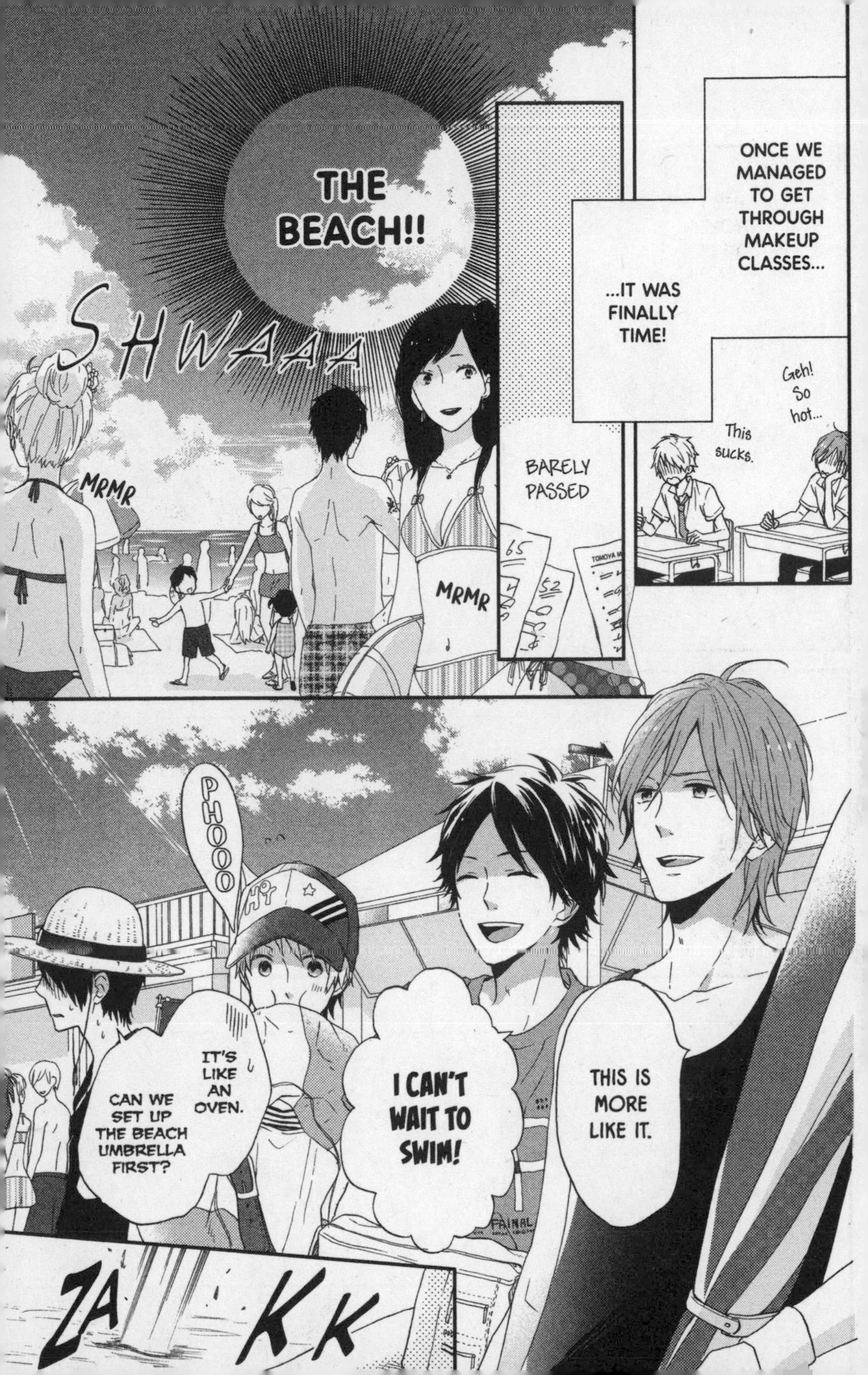
ONCE WE MANAGED TO GET THROUGH MAKEUP CLASSES...
Geh! So hot...
This sucks.
...IT WAS FINALLY TIME!
BARELY PASSED
THE BEACH!!
SHWAAA
MRMR
MRMR
THIS IS MORE LIKE IT.
I CAN'T WAIT TO SWIM!
PHOOO
IT'S LIKE AN OVEN.
CAN WE SET UP THE BEACH UMBRELLA FIRST?
ZAKK

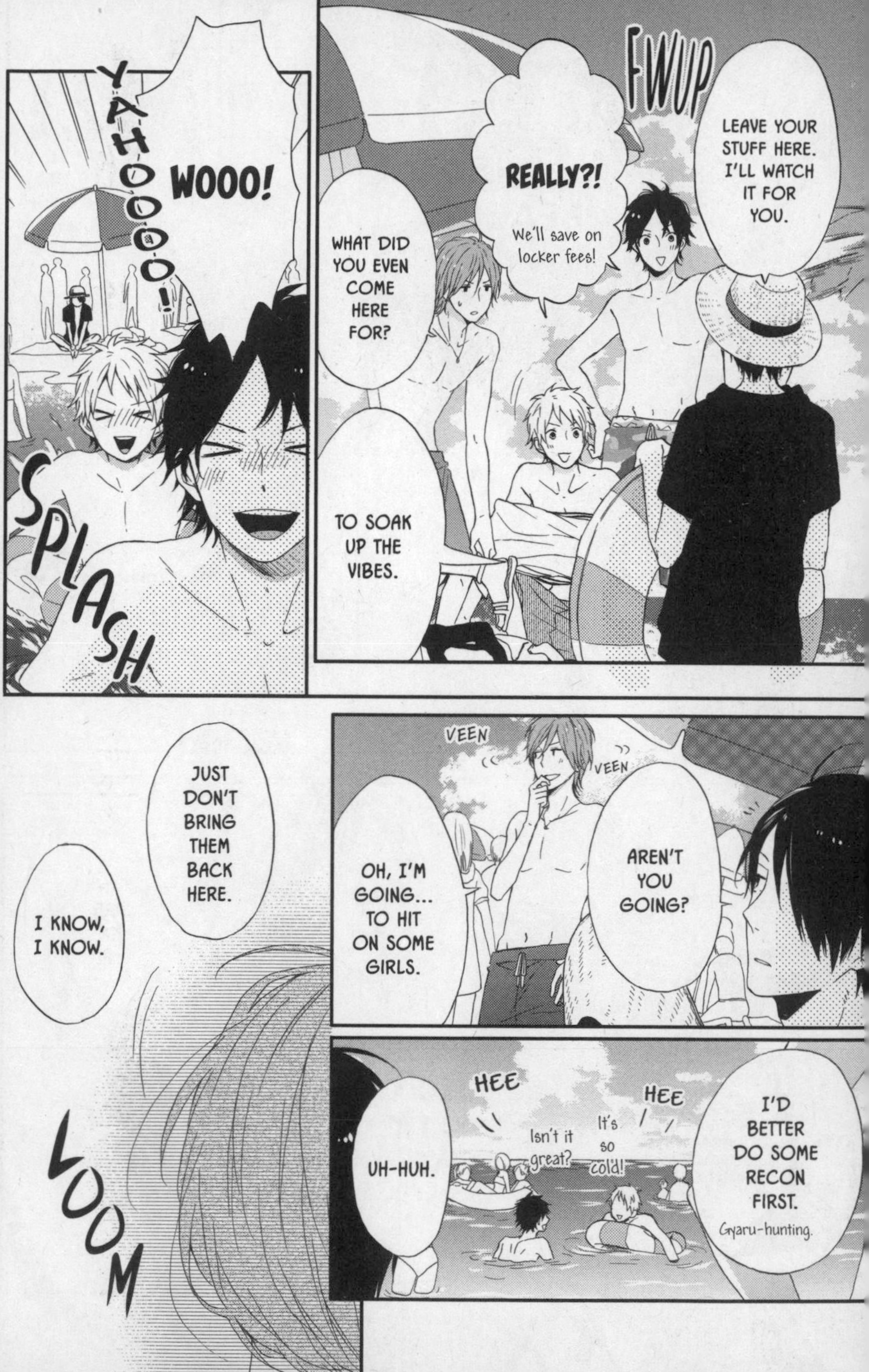
FWUP
LEAVE YOUR STUFF HERE. I'LL WATCH IT FOR YOU.
REALLY?!
We'll save on locker fees!
WHAT DID YOU EVEN COME HERE FOR?
TO SOAK UP THE VIBES.
YAHOOOOOO!
WOOO!
SPLASH
VEEN
VEEN
AREN'T YOU GOING?
OH, I'M GOING... TO HIT ON SOME GIRLS.
I'D BETTER DO SOME RECON FIRST.
Gyaru-hunting.
HEE
HEE
It's so cold!
Isn't it great?
UH-HUH.
JUST DON'T BRING THEM BACK HERE.
I KNOW, I KNOW.
VOOM

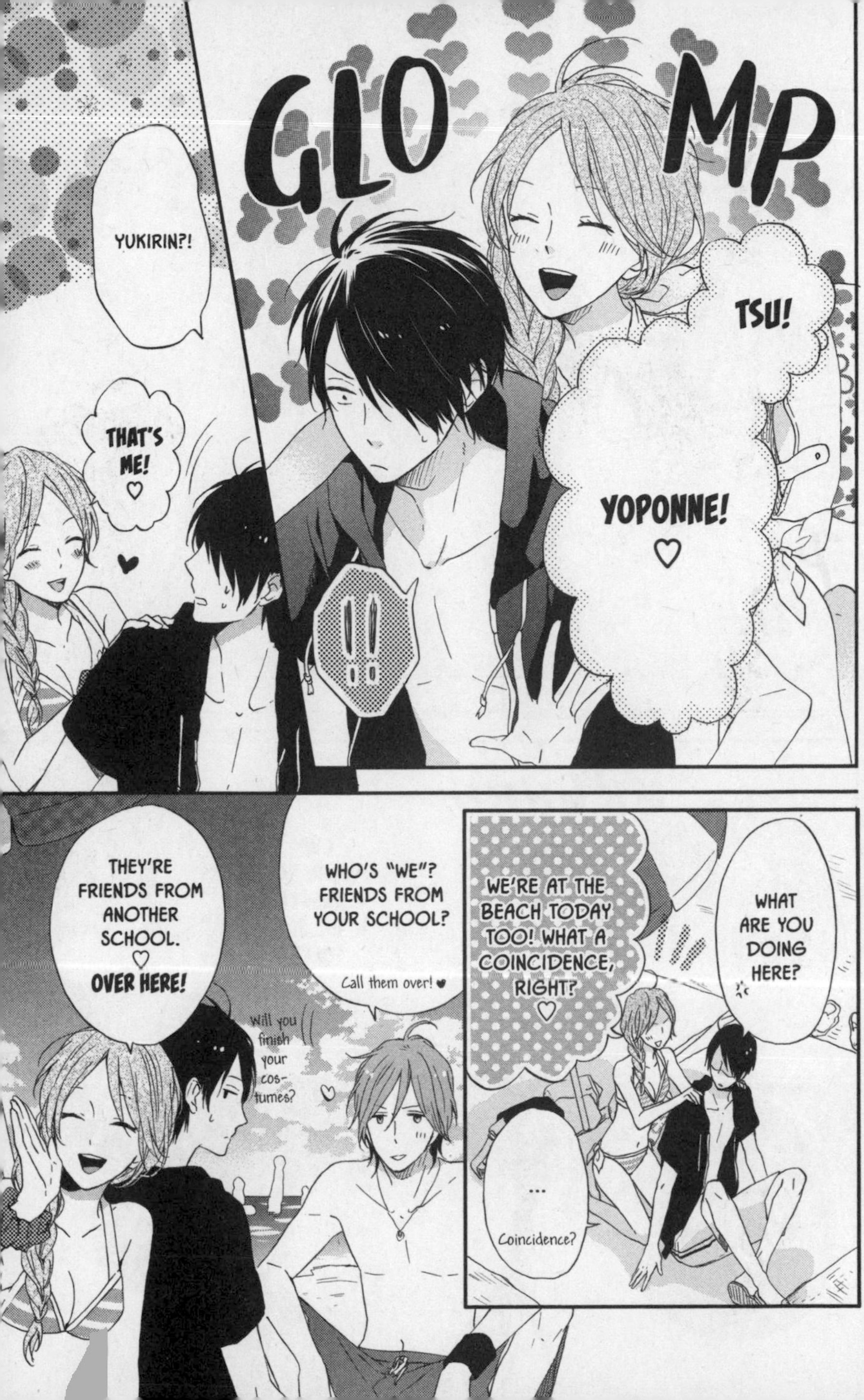
GLOMP
TSU!
YOPONNE! ♡
!!
YUKIRIN?!
THAT'S ME! ♡
WHAT ARE YOU DOING HERE?
WE'RE AT THE BEACH TODAY TOO! WHAT A COINCIDENCE, RIGHT? ♡
...
Coincidence?
WHO'S "WE"? FRIENDS FROM YOUR SCHOOL?
Call them over!
THEY'RE FRIENDS FROM ANOTHER SCHOOL. ♡ OVER HERE!
Will you finish your cos-tumes?

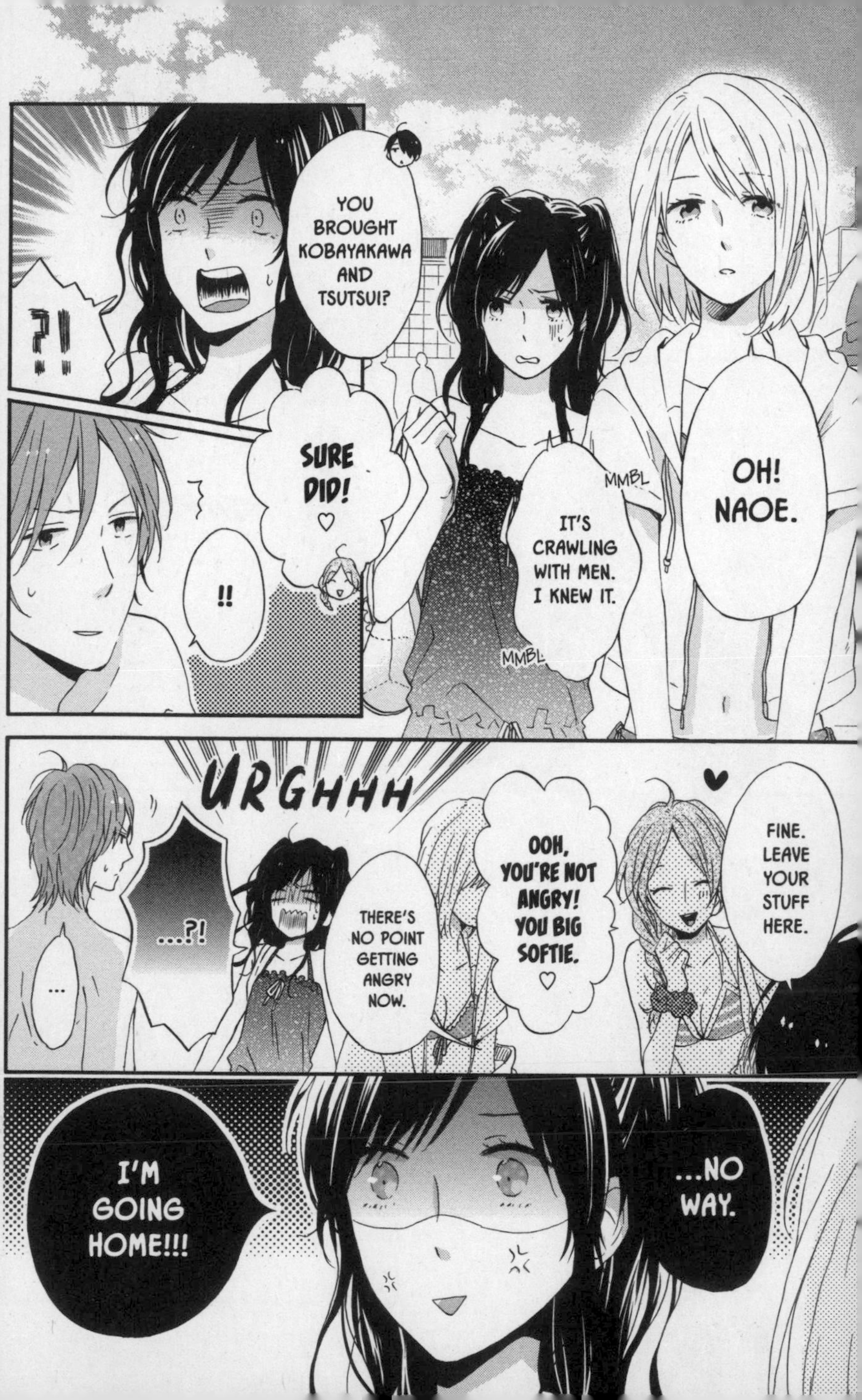
OH! NAOE.
MMBL
IT'S CRAWLING WITH MEN. I KNEW IT.
MMBL
?!
YOU BROUGHT KOBAYAKAWA AND TSUTSUI?
SURE DID! ♡
!!
FINE. LEAVE YOUR STUFF HERE.
OOH, YOU'RE NOT ANGRY! YOU BIG SOFTIE. ♡
THERE'S NO POINT GETTING ANGRY NOW.
URGHHH
...?!
...
...NO WAY.
I'M GOING HOME!!!

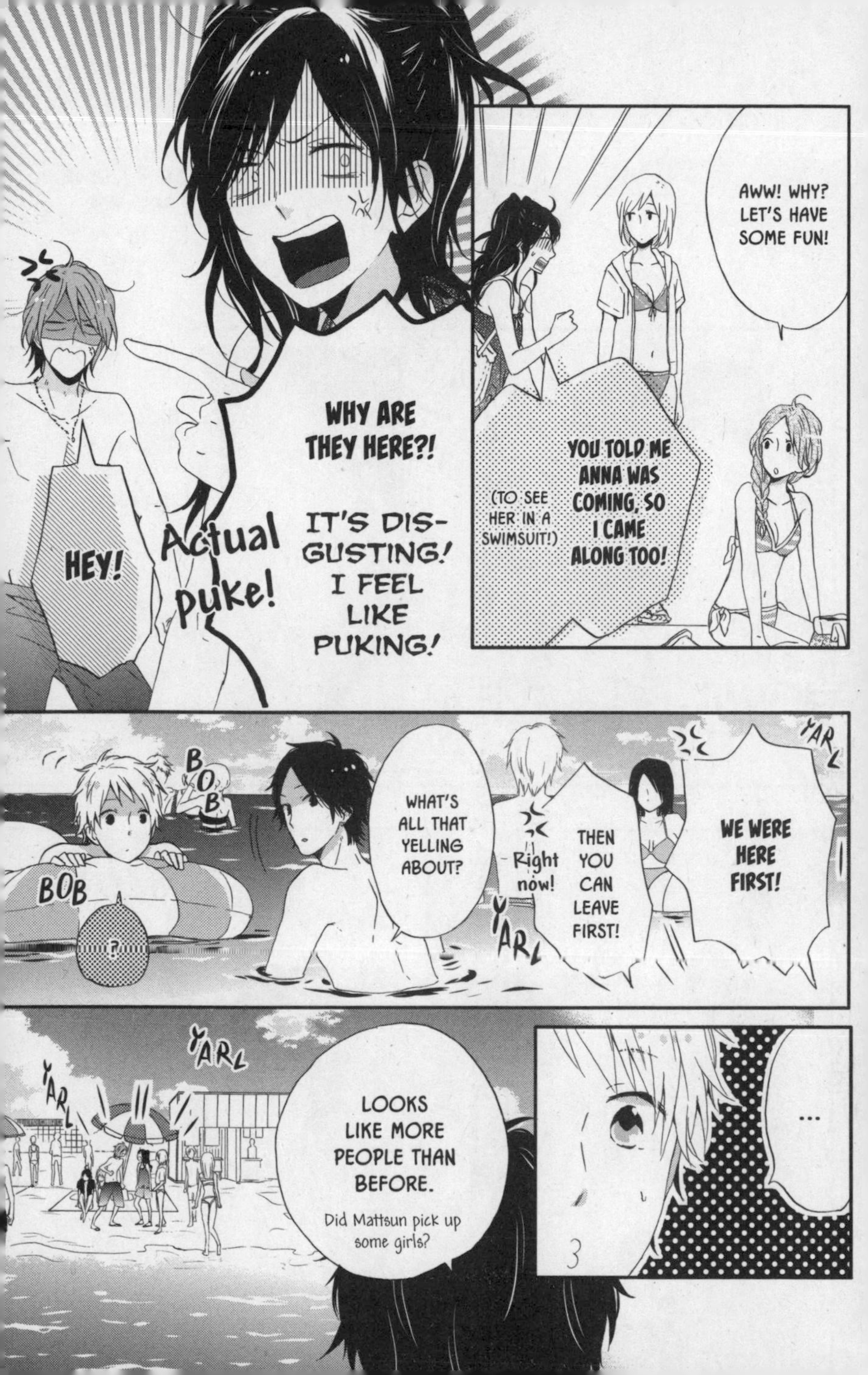
AWW! WHY? LET'S HAVE SOME FUN!
YOU TOLD ME ANNA WAS COMING, SO I CAME ALONG TOO!
(TO SEE HER IN A SWIMSUIT!)
WHY ARE THEY HERE?!
IT'S DIS-GUSTING! I FEEL LIKE PUKING!
Actual puke!
HEY!
YARL
WE WERE HERE FIRST!
THEN YOU CAN LEAVE FIRST!
Right now!
YARL
WHAT'S ALL THAT YELLING ABOUT?
BOB
BOB
?
...
YARL
YARL
LOOKS LIKE MORE PEOPLE THAN BEFORE.
Did Mattsun pick up some girls?

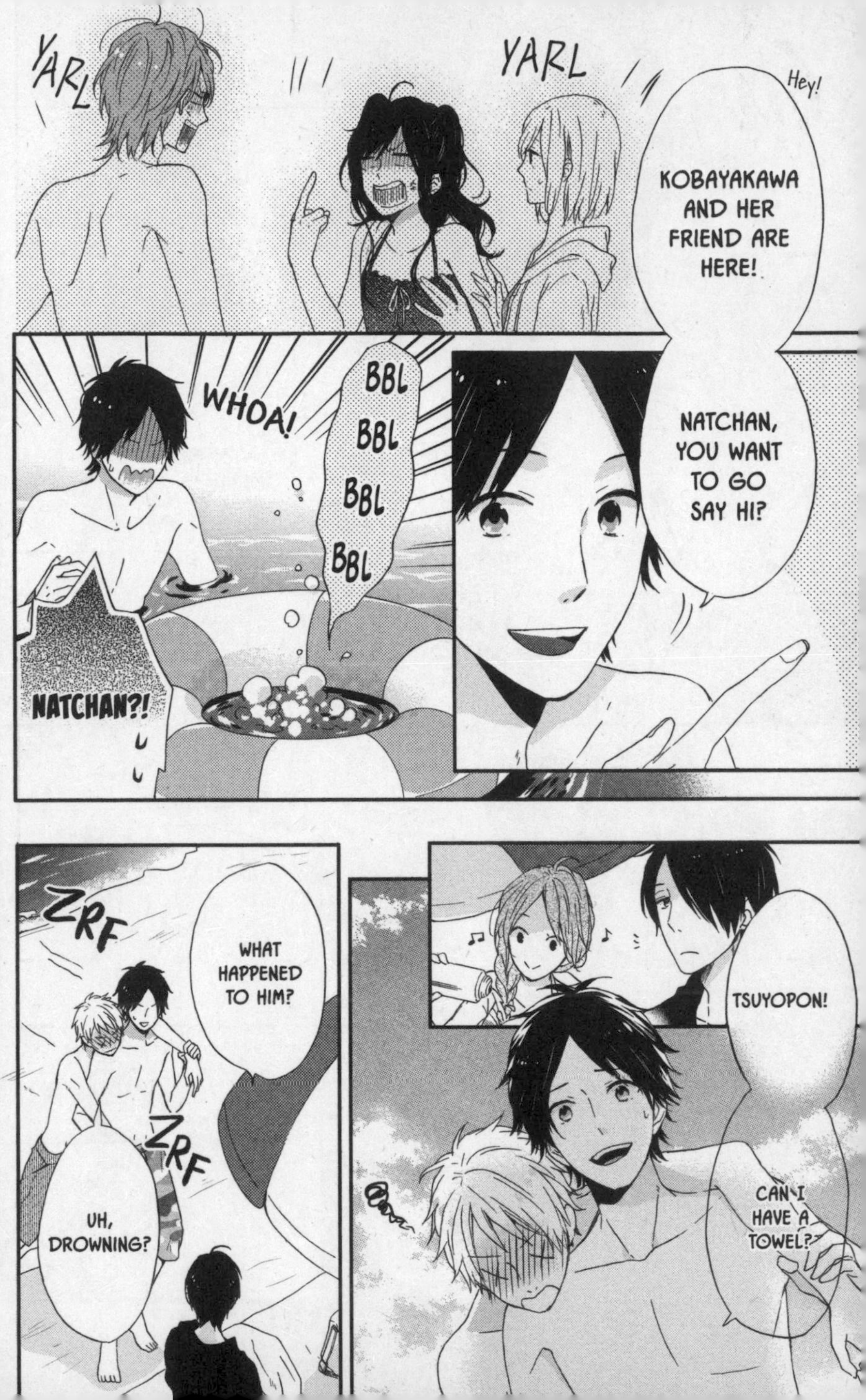
Hey!
KOBAYAKAWA AND HER FRIEND ARE HERE!
YARL
YARL
NATCHAN, YOU WANT TO GO SAY HI?
BBL BBL BBL BBL
WHOA!
NATCHAN?!
TSUYOPON!
CAN I HAVE A TOWEL?
WHAT HAPPENED TO HIM?
ZRF
ZRF
UH, DROWNING?

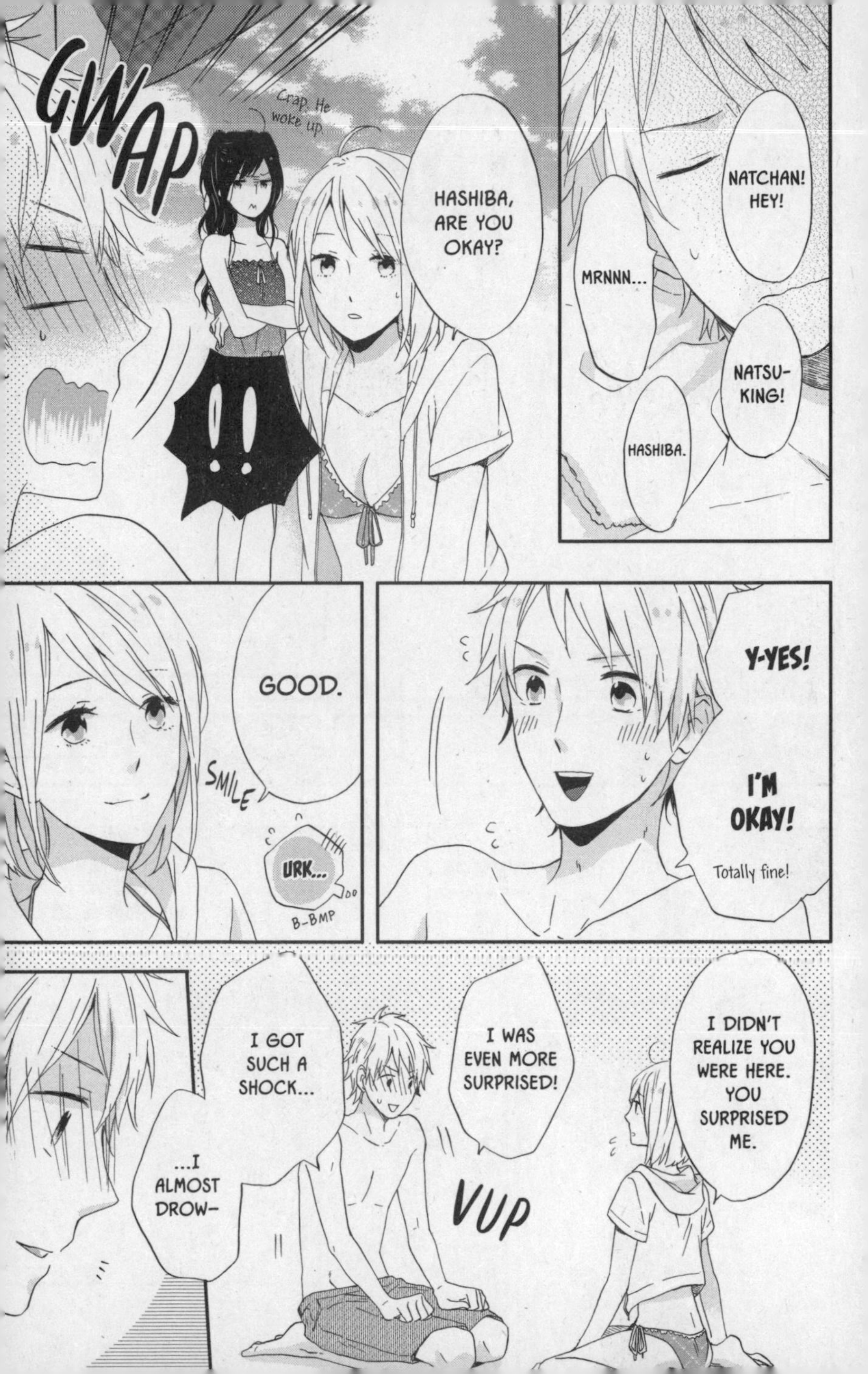
NATCHAN! HEY!
MRNNN...
NATSU-KING!
HASHIBA.
HASHIBA, ARE YOU OKAY?
Crap. He woke up.
GWAP
!!
Y-YES!
I'M OKAY!
Totally fine!
GOOD.
SMILE
URK...
B-BMP
I DIDN'T REALIZE YOU WERE HERE. YOU SURPRISED ME.
I WAS EVEN MORE SURPRISED!
I GOT SUCH A SHOCK...
VUP
...I ALMOST DROW-

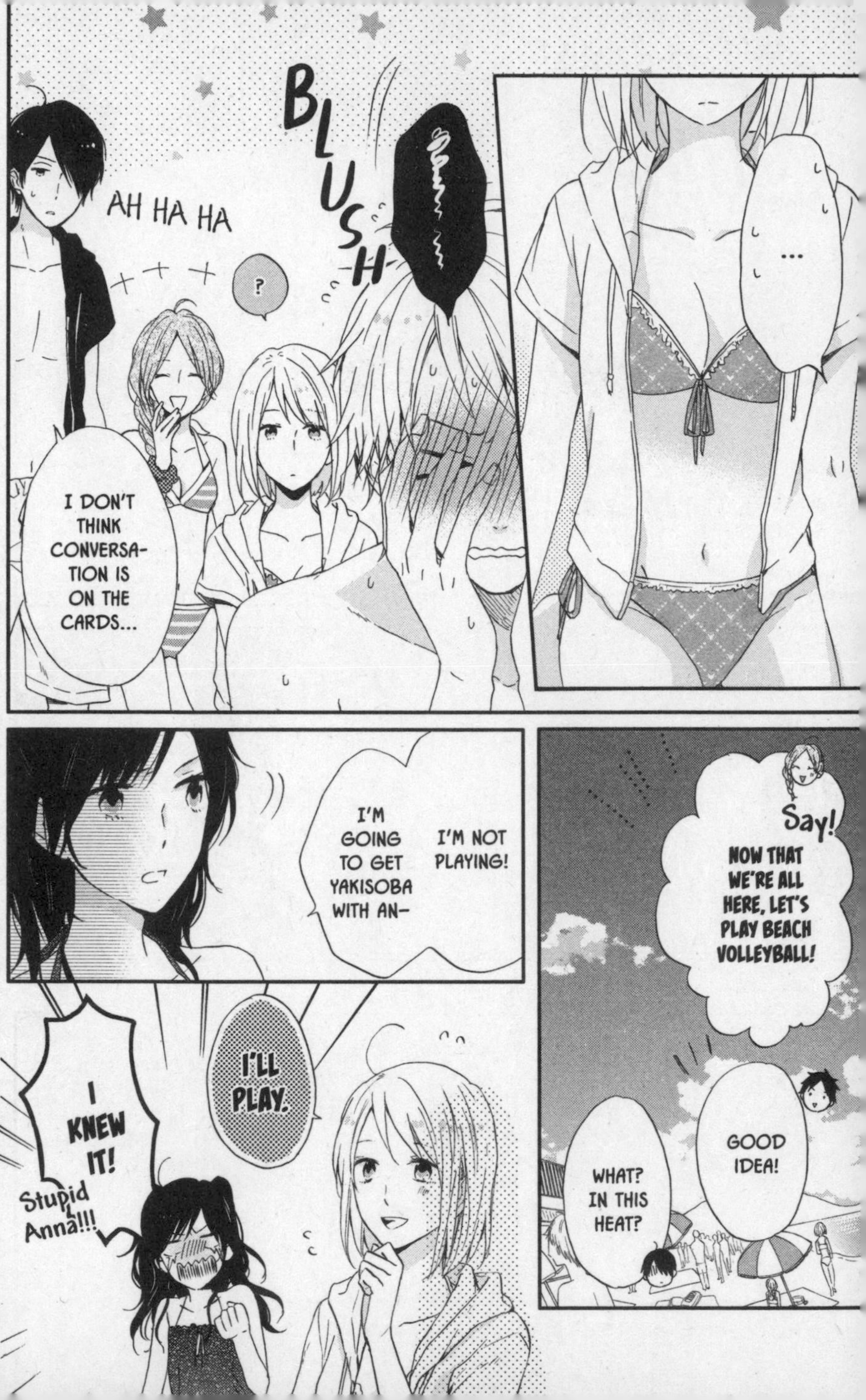
...
BLUSH
?
AH HA HA
I DON'T THINK CONVERSA-TION IS ON THE CARDS...
Say!
NOW THAT WE'RE ALL HERE, LET'S PLAY BEACH VOLLEYBALL!
GOOD IDEA!
WHAT? IN THIS HEAT?
I'M NOT PLAYING!
I'M GOING TO GET YAKISOBA WITH AN–
I'LL PLAY.
I KNEW IT!
Stupid Anna!!!

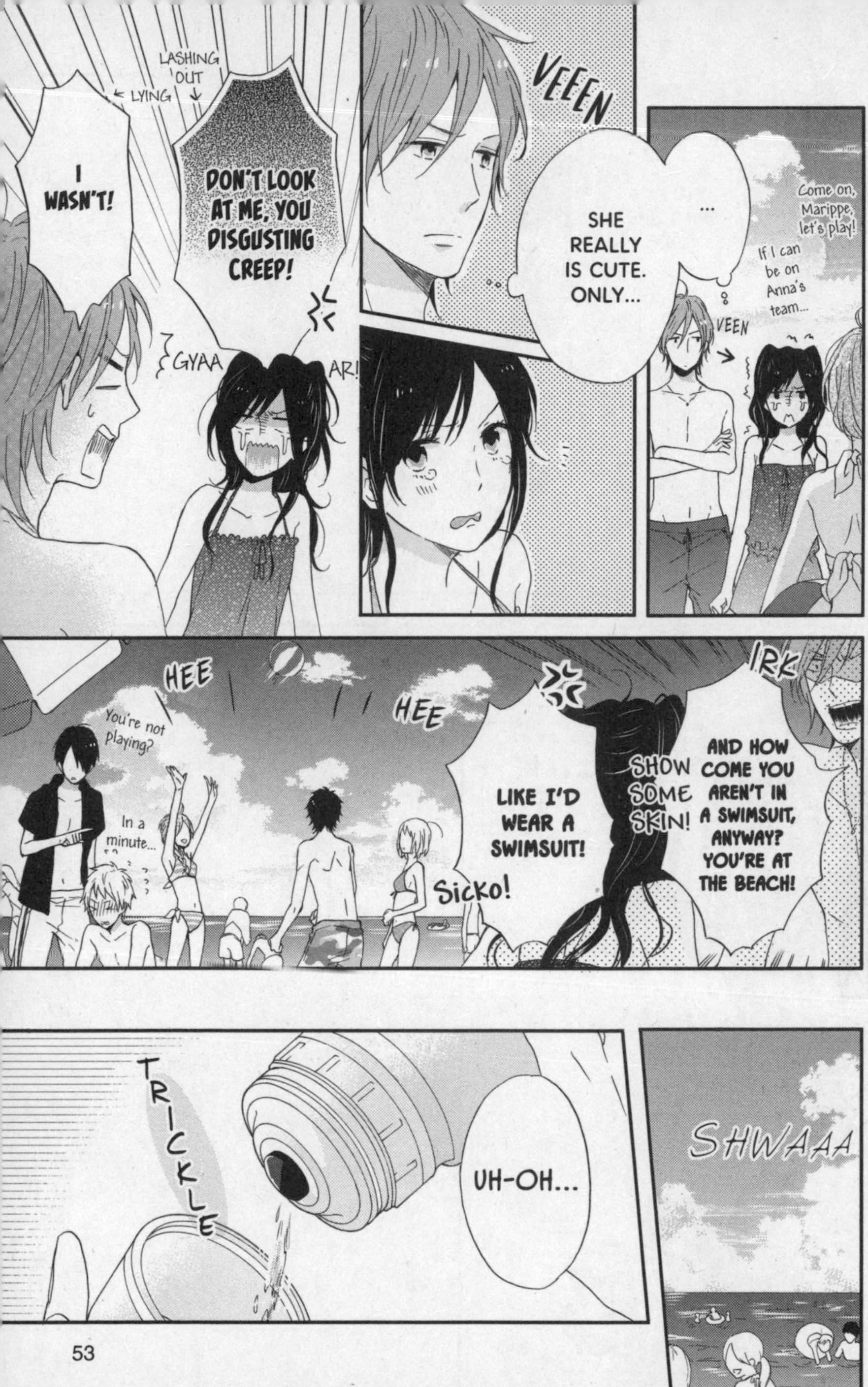
Come on, Marippe, let's play!
If I can be on Anna's team...
VEEN
...
VEEEN
SHE REALLY IS CUTE. ONLY...
DON'T LOOK AT ME, YOU DISGUSTING CREEP!
GYAA AR!
I WASN'T!
LASHING OUT
LYING
IRK
AND HOW COME YOU AREN'T IN A SWIMSUIT, ANYWAY? YOU'RE AT THE BEACH!
SHOW SOME SKIN!
LIKE I'D WEAR A SWIMSUIT!
Sicko!
HEE
HEE
You're not playing?
In a minute...
SHWAAA
UH-OH...
TRICKLE

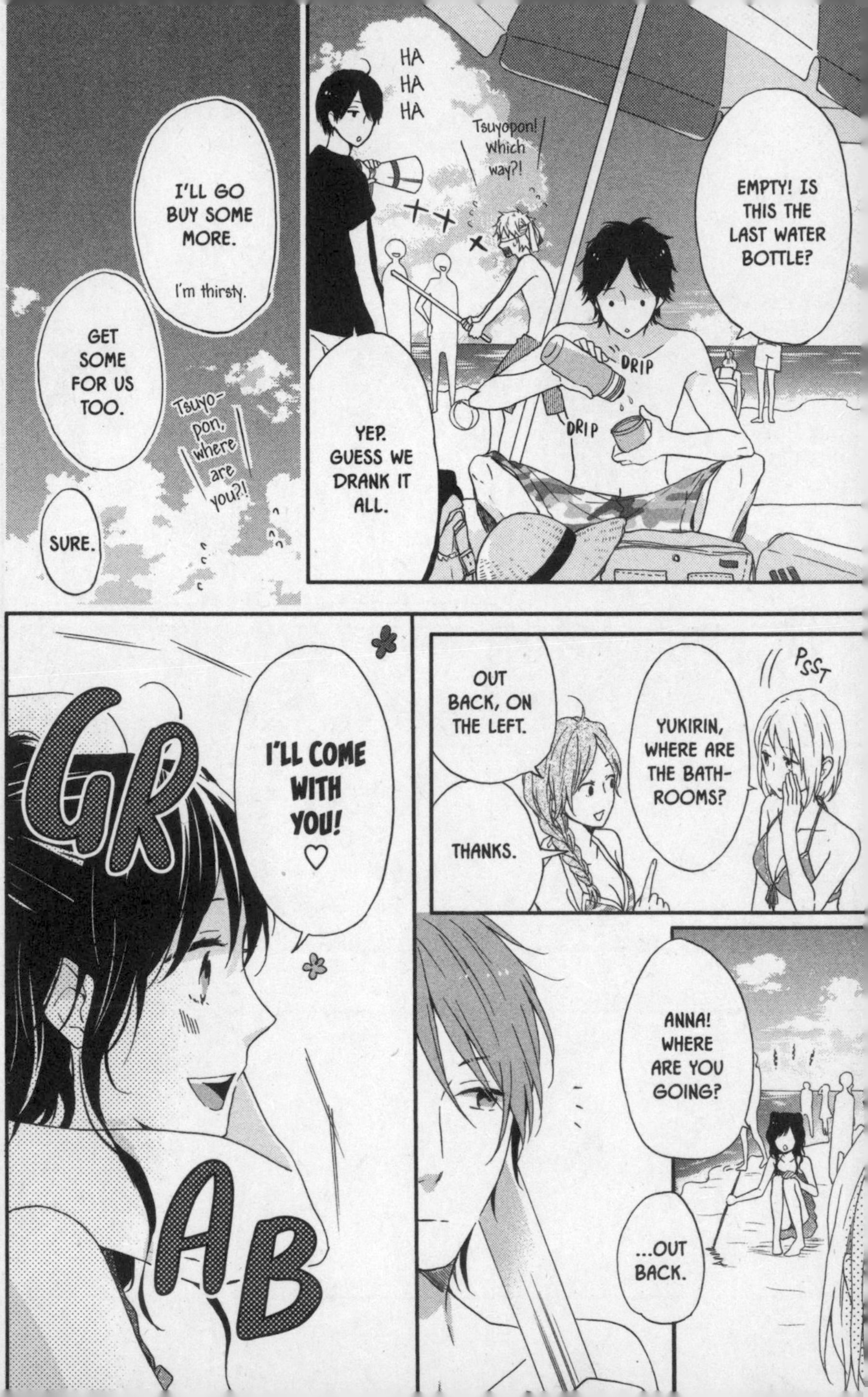
EMPTY! IS THIS THE LAST WATER BOTTLE?
HA HA HA
Tsuyopon! Which way?!
DRIP
DRIP
YEP. GUESS WE DRANK IT ALL.
I'LL GO BUY SOME MORE.
I'm thirsty.
GET SOME FOR US TOO.
Tsuyo-pon, where are you?!
SURE.
PSST
YUKIRIN, WHERE ARE THE BATH-ROOMS?
OUT BACK, ON THE LEFT.
THANKS.
ANNA! WHERE ARE YOU GOING?
...OUT BACK.
I'LL COME WITH YOU! ♡
GRAB

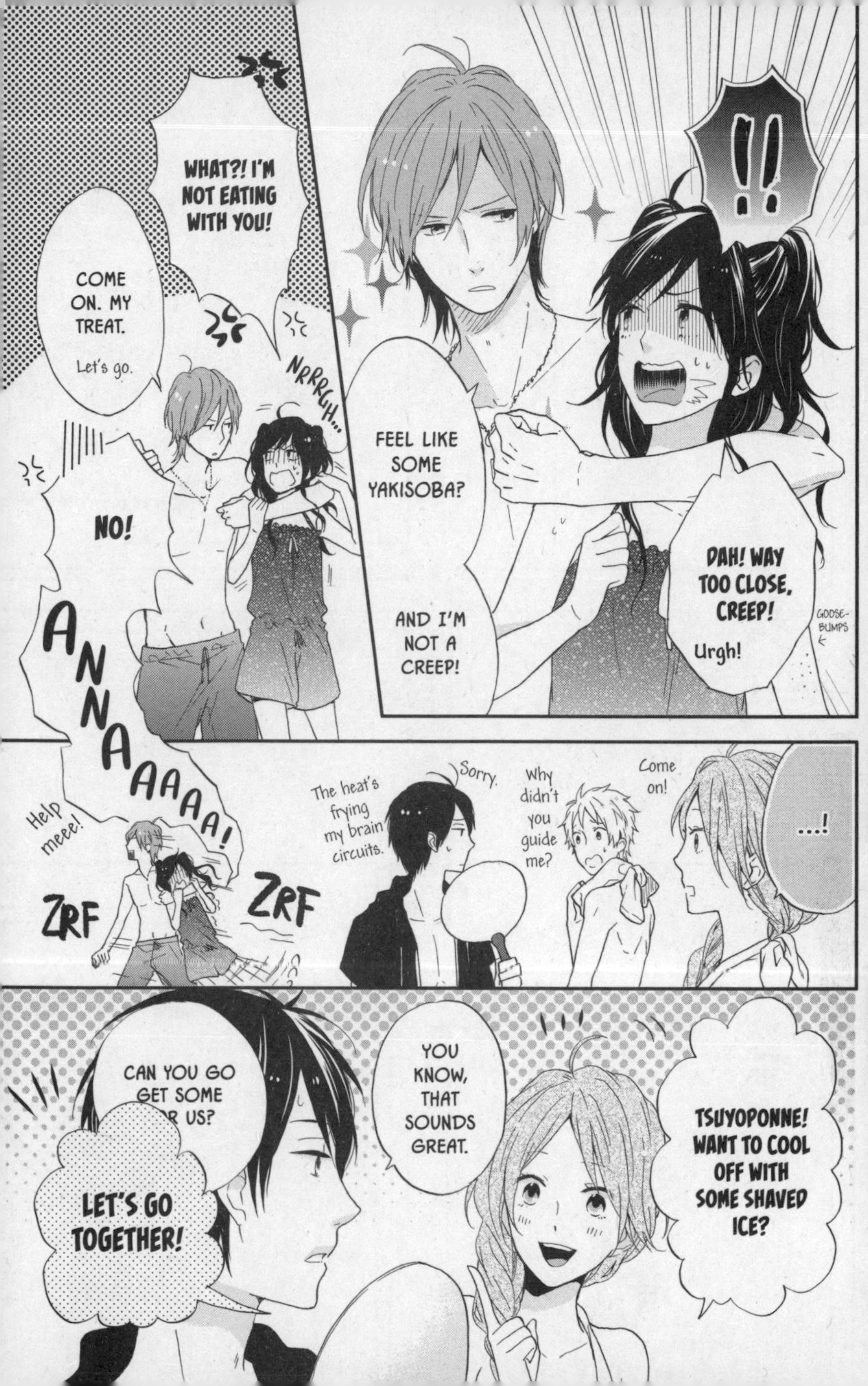
!!
FEEL LIKE SOME YAKISOBA?
DAH! WAY TOO CLOSE, CREEP!
Urgh!
GOOSE-BUMPS
AND I'M NOT A CREEP!
WHAT?! I'M NOT EATING WITH YOU!
COME ON. MY TREAT.
Let's go.
NRRRGH...
NO!
ANNAAAAAA!
Help meee!
ZRF
ZRF
...!
Come on!
Why didn't you guide me?
Sorry.
The heat's frying my brain circuits.
TSUYOPONNE! WANT TO COOL OFF WITH SOME SHAVED ICE?
YOU KNOW, THAT SOUNDS GREAT.
CAN YOU GO GET SOME
R US?
LET'S GO TOGETHER!

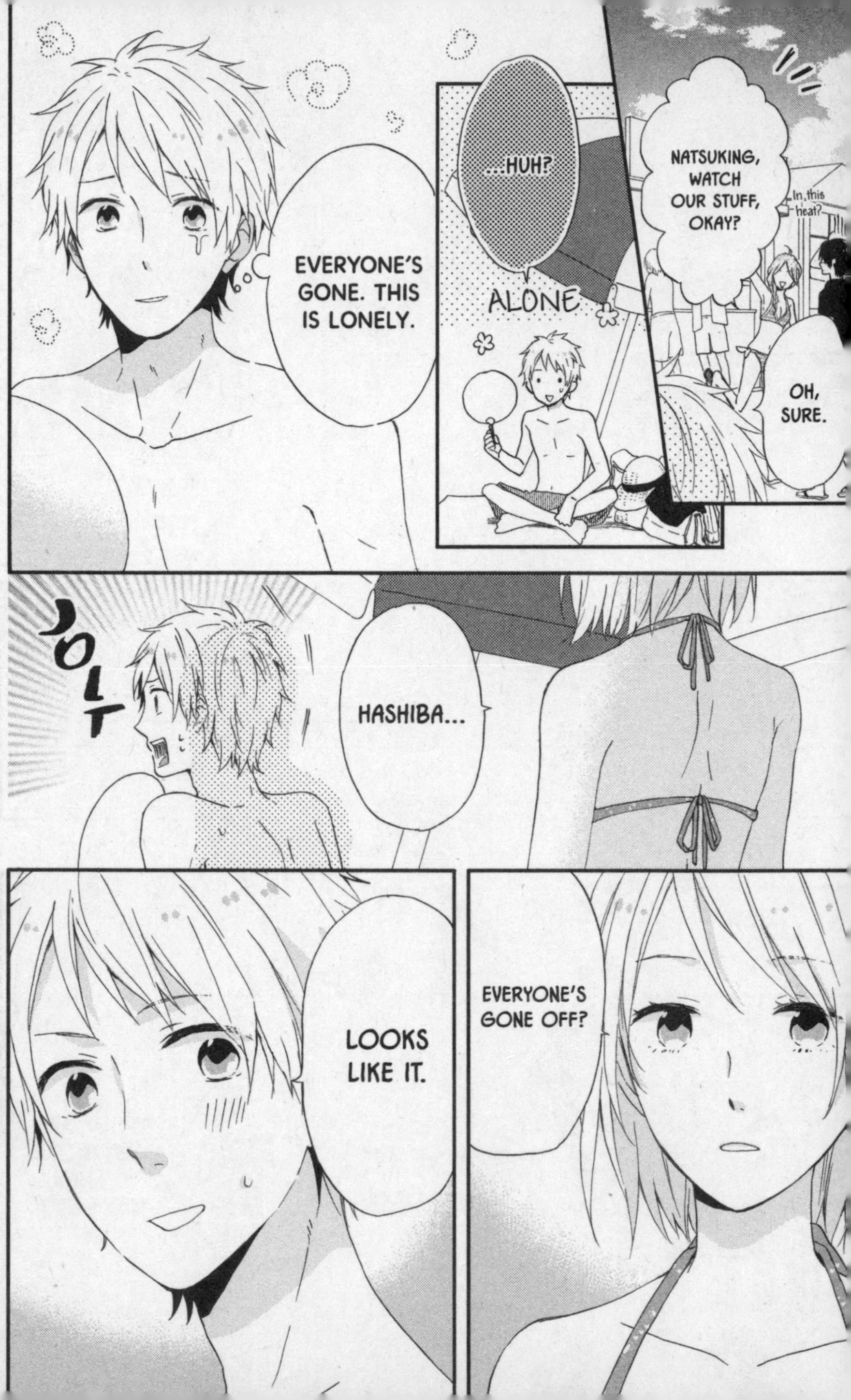
NATSUKING, WATCH OUR STUFF, OKAY?
In this heat?
OH, SURE.
...HUH?
ALONE
EVERYONE'S GONE. THIS IS LONELY.
HASHIBA...
JOLT
EVERYONE'S GONE OFF?
LOOKS LIKE IT.

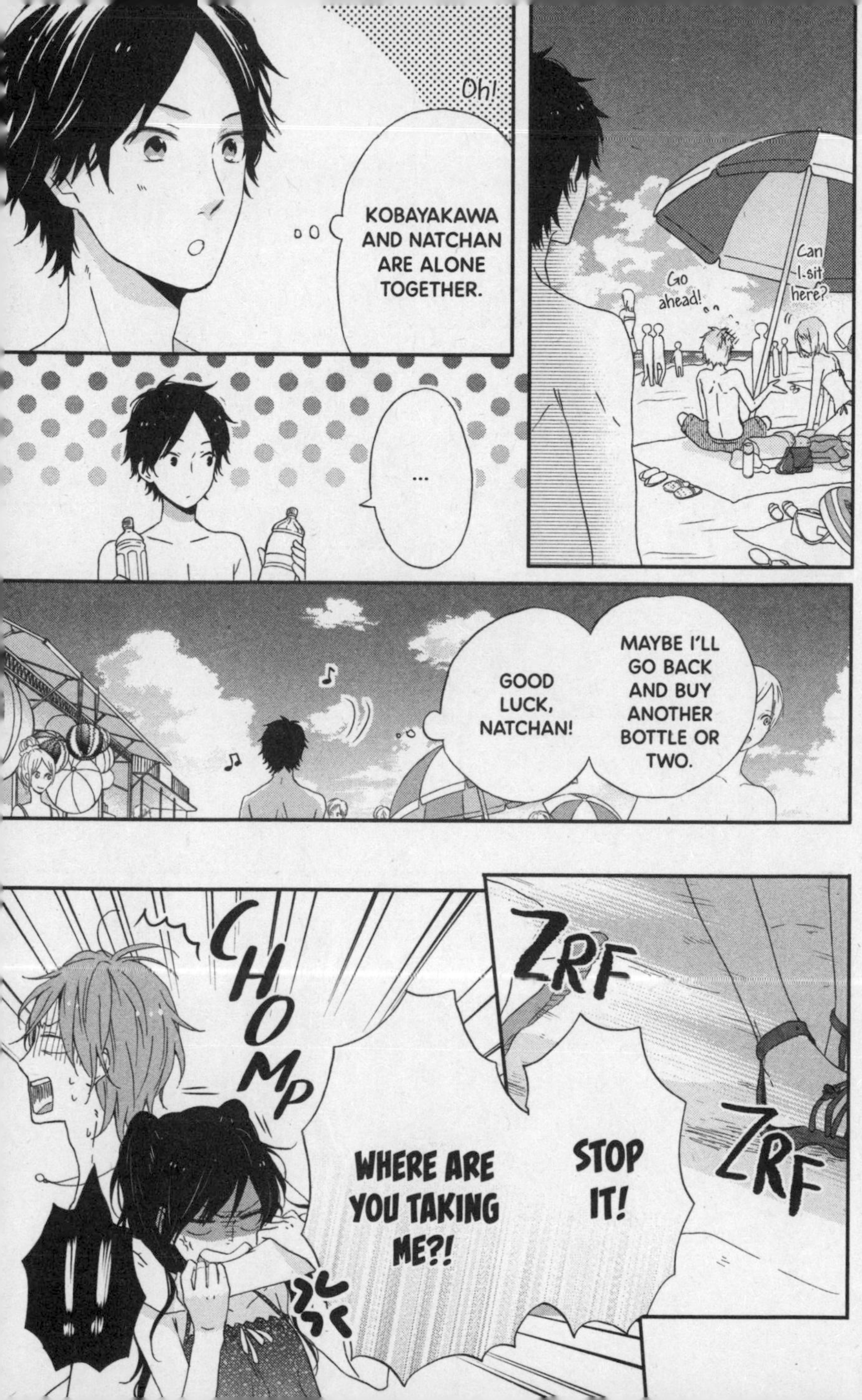
Can I sit here?
Go ahead!
Oh!
KOBAYAKAWA AND NATCHAN ARE ALONE TOGETHER.
...
MAYBE I'LL GO BACK AND BUY ANOTHER BOTTLE OR TWO.
GOOD LUCK, NATCHAN!
ZRF
ZRF
STOP IT!
CHOMP
WHERE ARE YOU TAKING ME?!

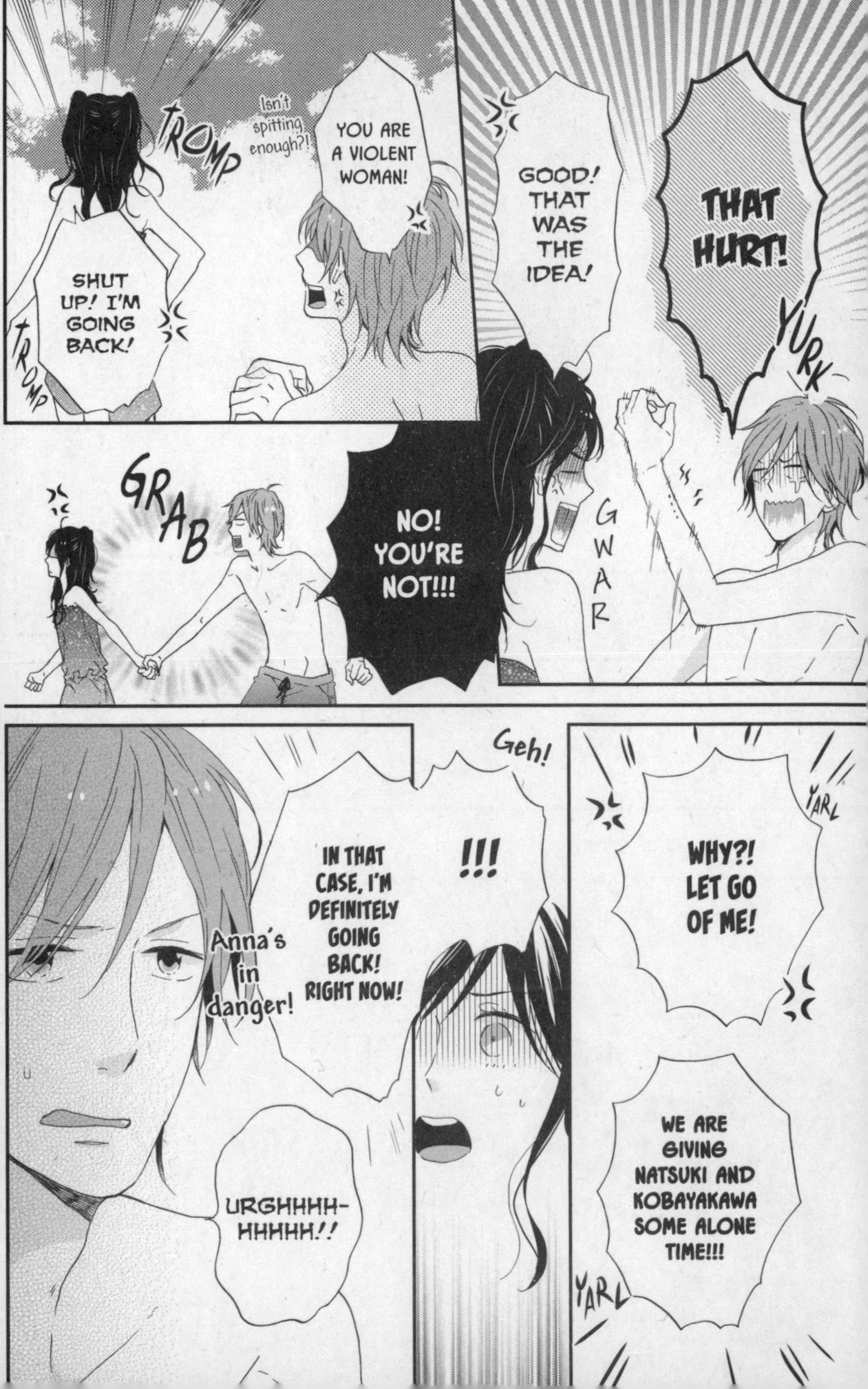
THAT HURT!
YURK
GOOD! THAT WAS THE IDEA!
GWAR
YOU ARE A VIOLENT WOMAN!
Isn't spitting enough?!
TROMP
SHUT UP! I'M GOING BACK!
TROMP
NO! YOU'RE NOT!!!
GRAB
WHY?! LET GO OF ME!
YARL
WE ARE GIVING NATSUKI AND KOBAYAKAWA SOME ALONE TIME!!!
YARL
Geh!
!!!
IN THAT CASE, I'M DEFINITELY GOING BACK! RIGHT NOW!
Anna's in danger!
URGHHHH-HHHHH!!

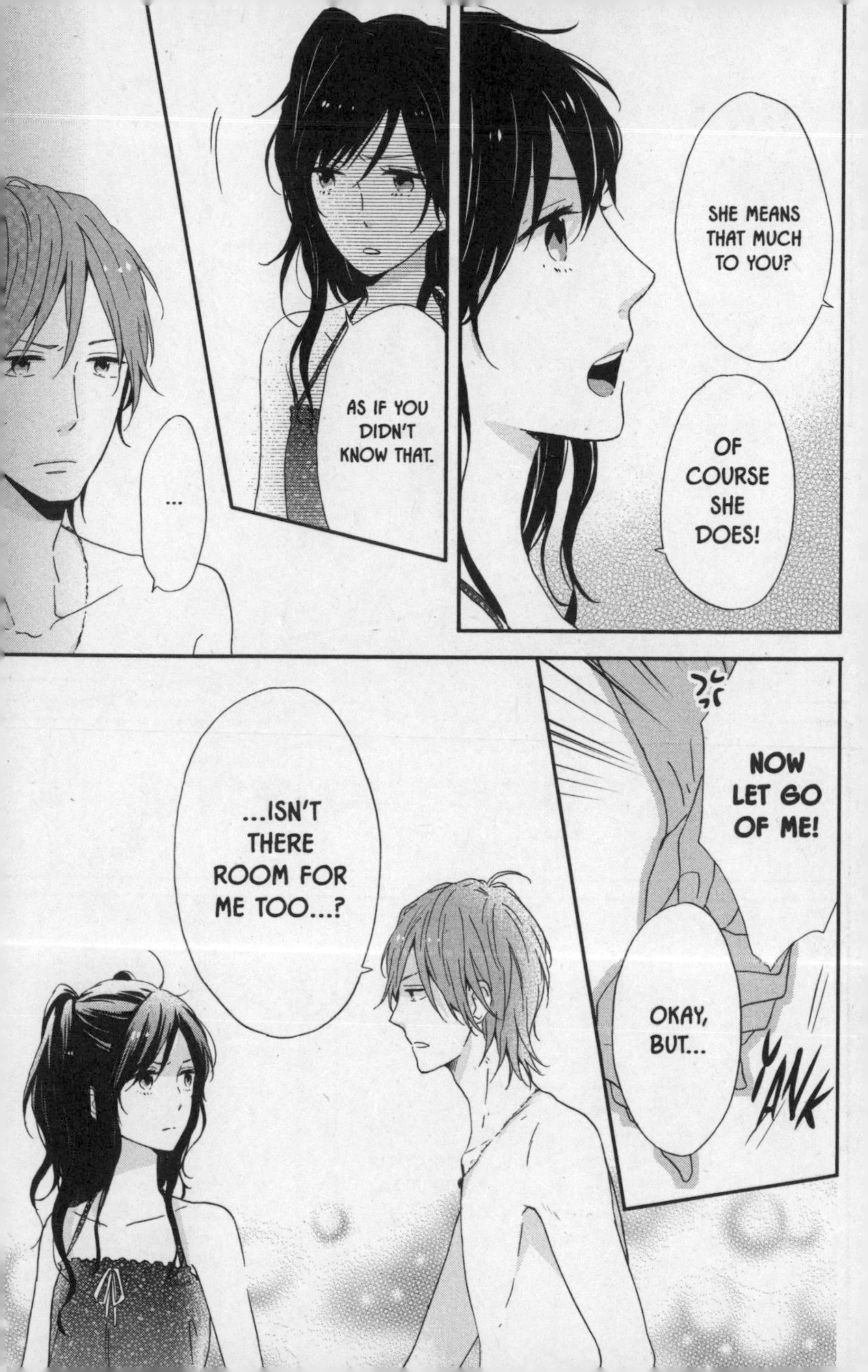
SHE MEANS THAT MUCH TO YOU?
OF COURSE SHE DOES!
AS IF YOU DIDN'T KNOW THAT.
...
NOW LET GO OF ME!
YANK
OKAY, BUT...
...ISN'T THERE ROOM FOR ME TOO...?

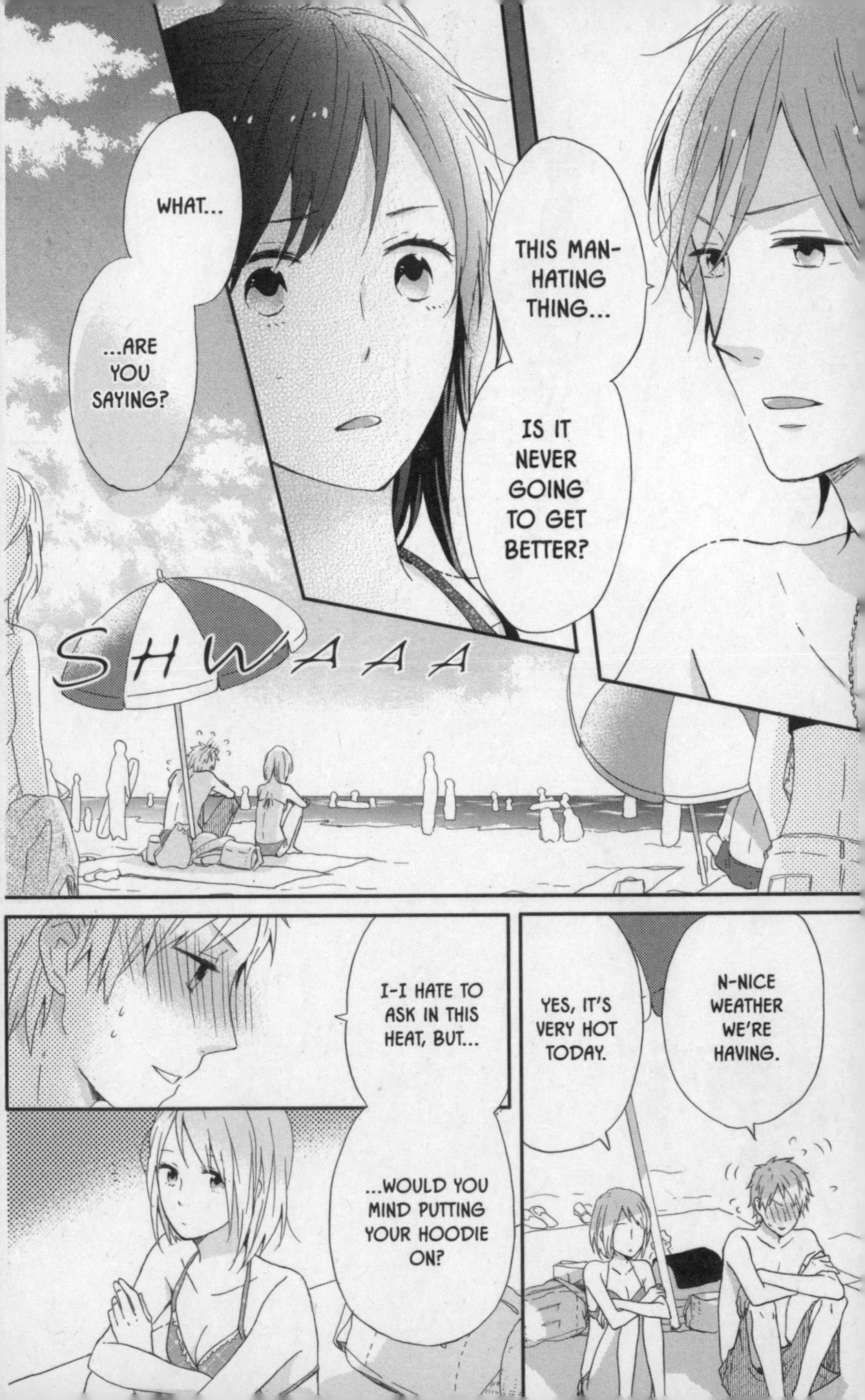
THIS MAN-HATING THING...
IS IT NEVER GOING TO GET BETTER?
WHAT...
...ARE YOU SAYING?
SHWAAA
N-NICE WEATHER WE'RE HAVING.
YES, IT'S VERY HOT TODAY.
I-I HATE TO ASK IN THIS HEAT, BUT...
...WOULD YOU MIND PUTTING YOUR HOODIE ON?

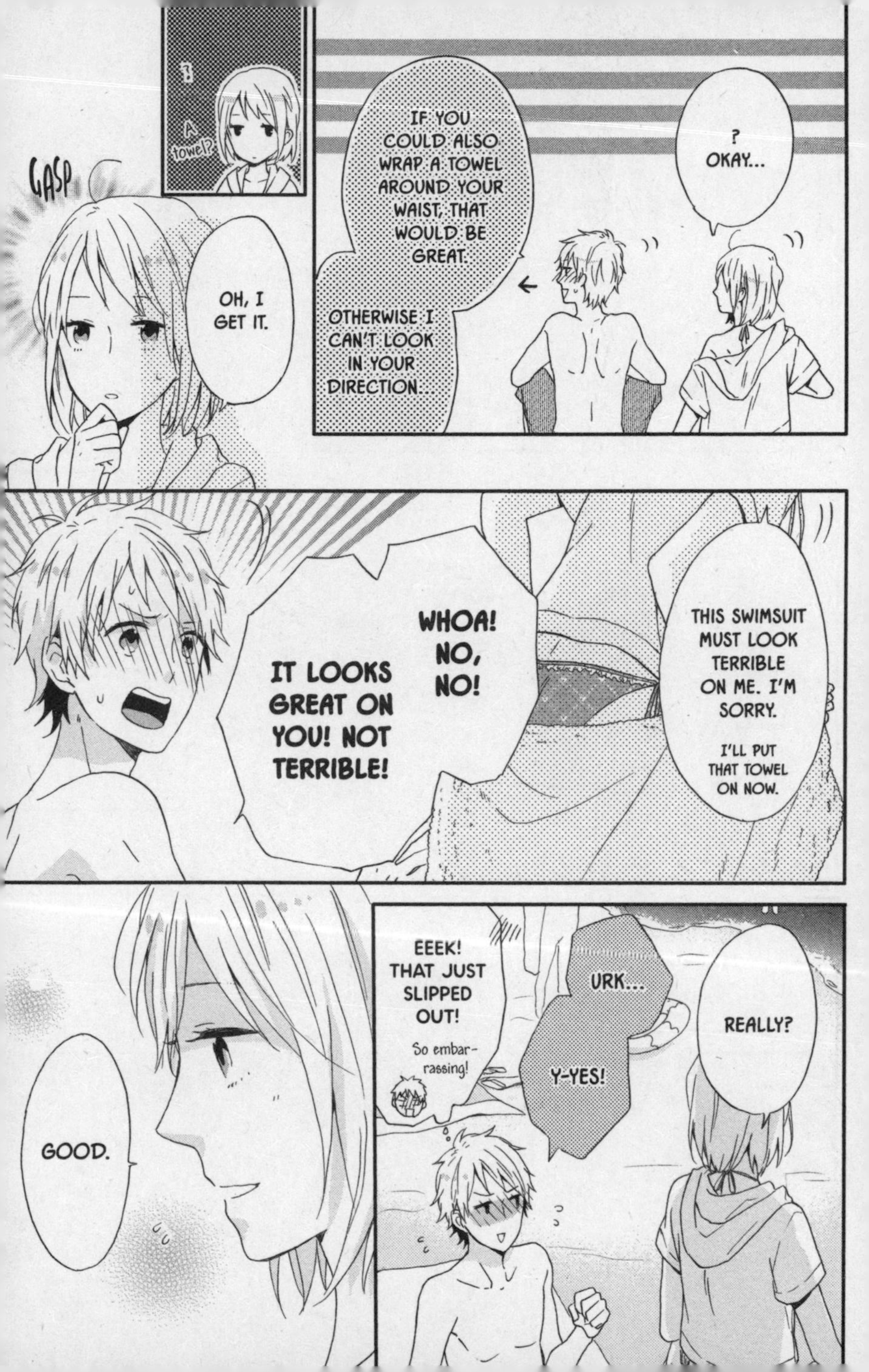
? OKAY...
IF YOU COULD ALSO WRAP A TOWEL AROUND YOUR WAIST, THAT WOULD BE GREAT.
OTHERWISE I CAN'T LOOK IN YOUR DIRECTION...
?
A towel?
GASP
OH, I GET IT.
THIS SWIMSUIT MUST LOOK TERRIBLE ON ME. I'M SORRY.
I'LL PUT THAT TOWEL ON NOW.
WHOA! NO, NO!
IT LOOKS GREAT ON YOU! NOT TERRIBLE!
REALLY?
URK...
Y-YES!
EEEK! THAT JUST SLIPPED OUT!
So embar-rassing!
GOOD.

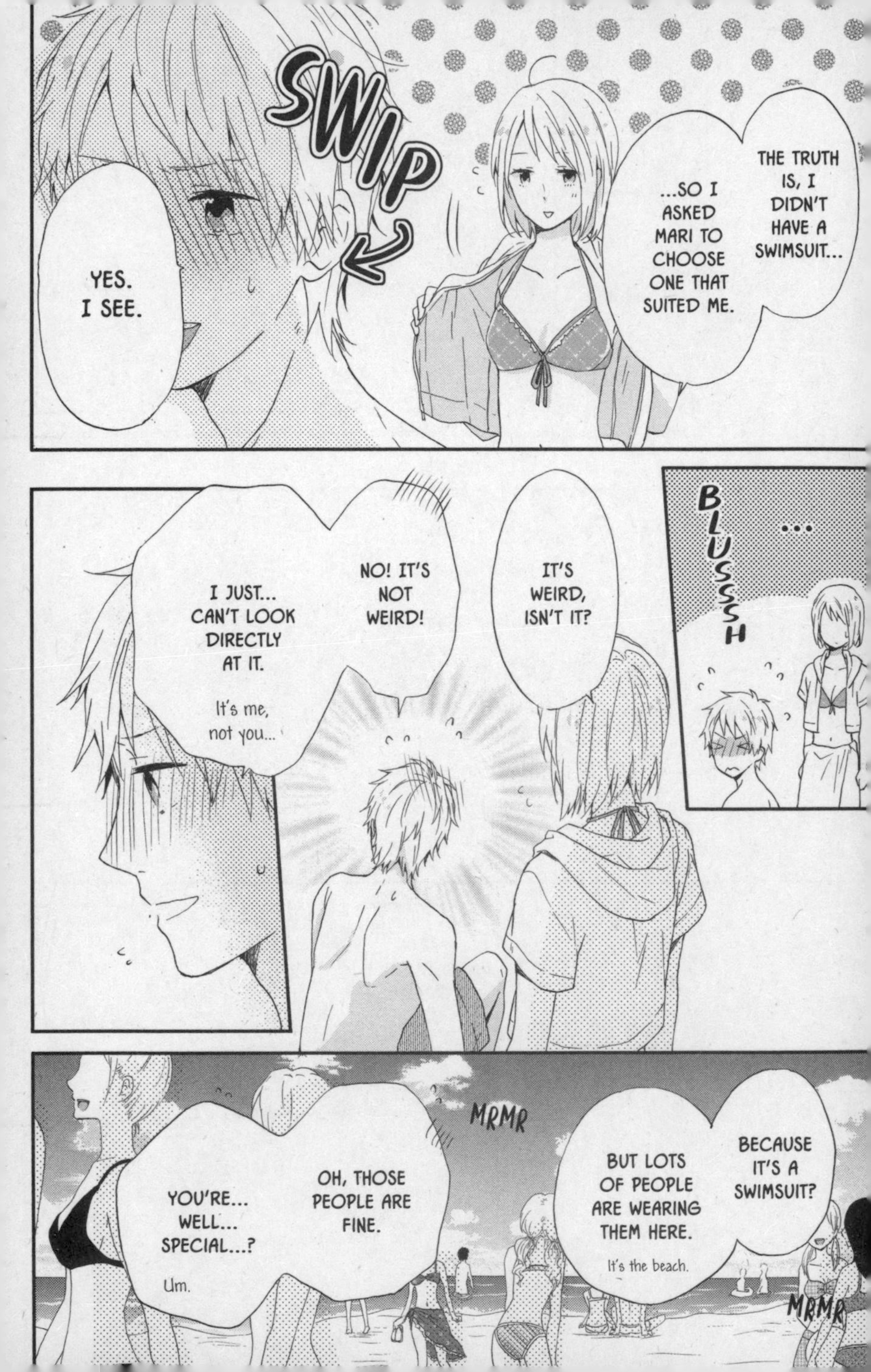
THE TRUTH IS, I DIDN'T HAVE A SWIMSUIT...
...SO I ASKED MARI TO CHOOSE ONE THAT SUITED ME.
SWIP
YES. I SEE.
...
BLUSSSH
IT'S WEIRD, ISN'T IT?
NO! IT'S NOT WEIRD!
I JUST... CAN'T LOOK DIRECTLY AT IT.
It's me, not you...
BECAUSE IT'S A SWIMSUIT?
BUT LOTS OF PEOPLE ARE WEARING THEM HERE.
It's the beach.
MRMR
MRMR
OH, THOSE PEOPLE ARE FINE.
YOU'RE... WELL... SPECIAL...?
Um.

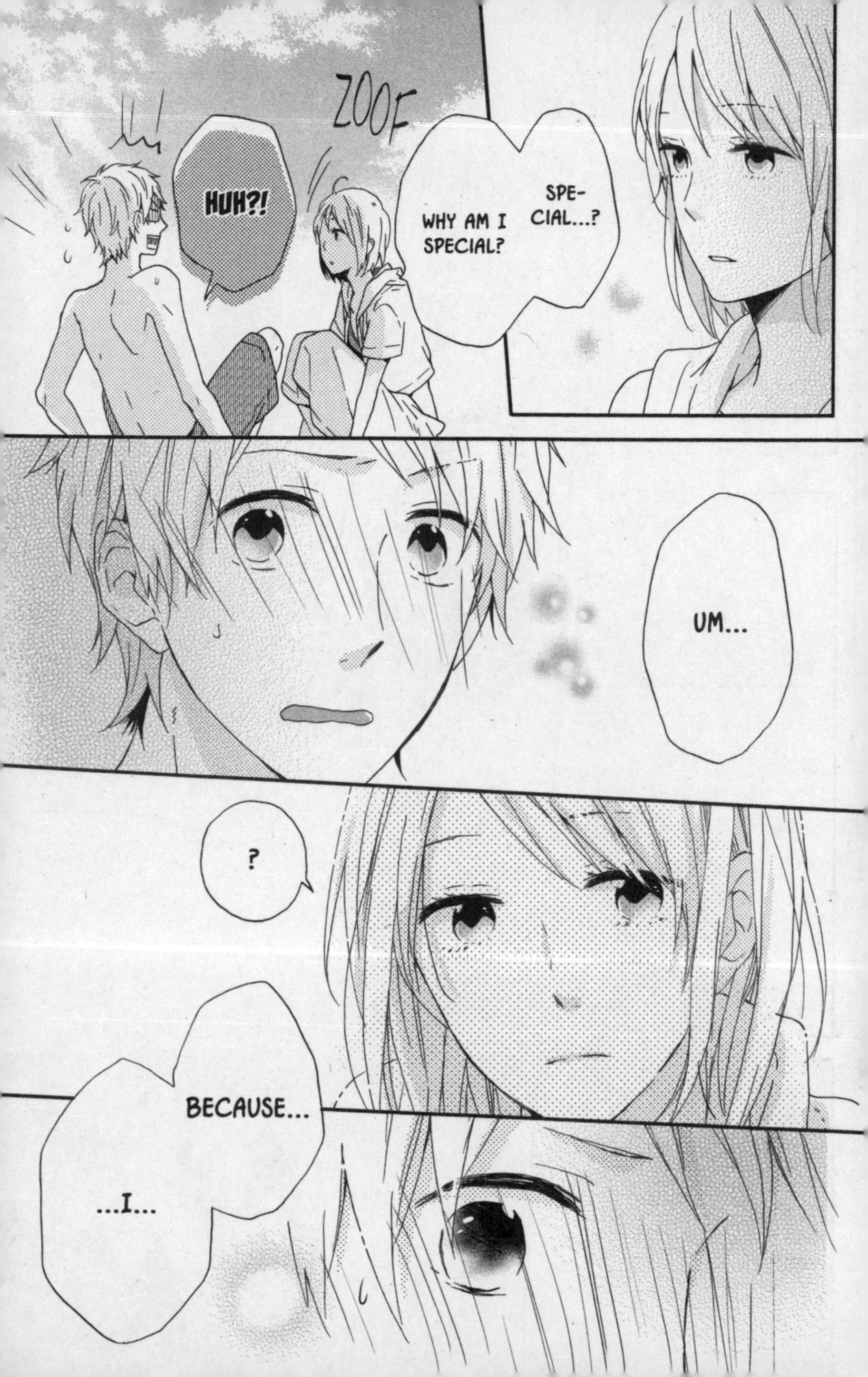
SPE-CIAL...?
WHY AM I SPECIAL?
ZOOF
HUH?!
UM...
?
BECAUSE...
...I...

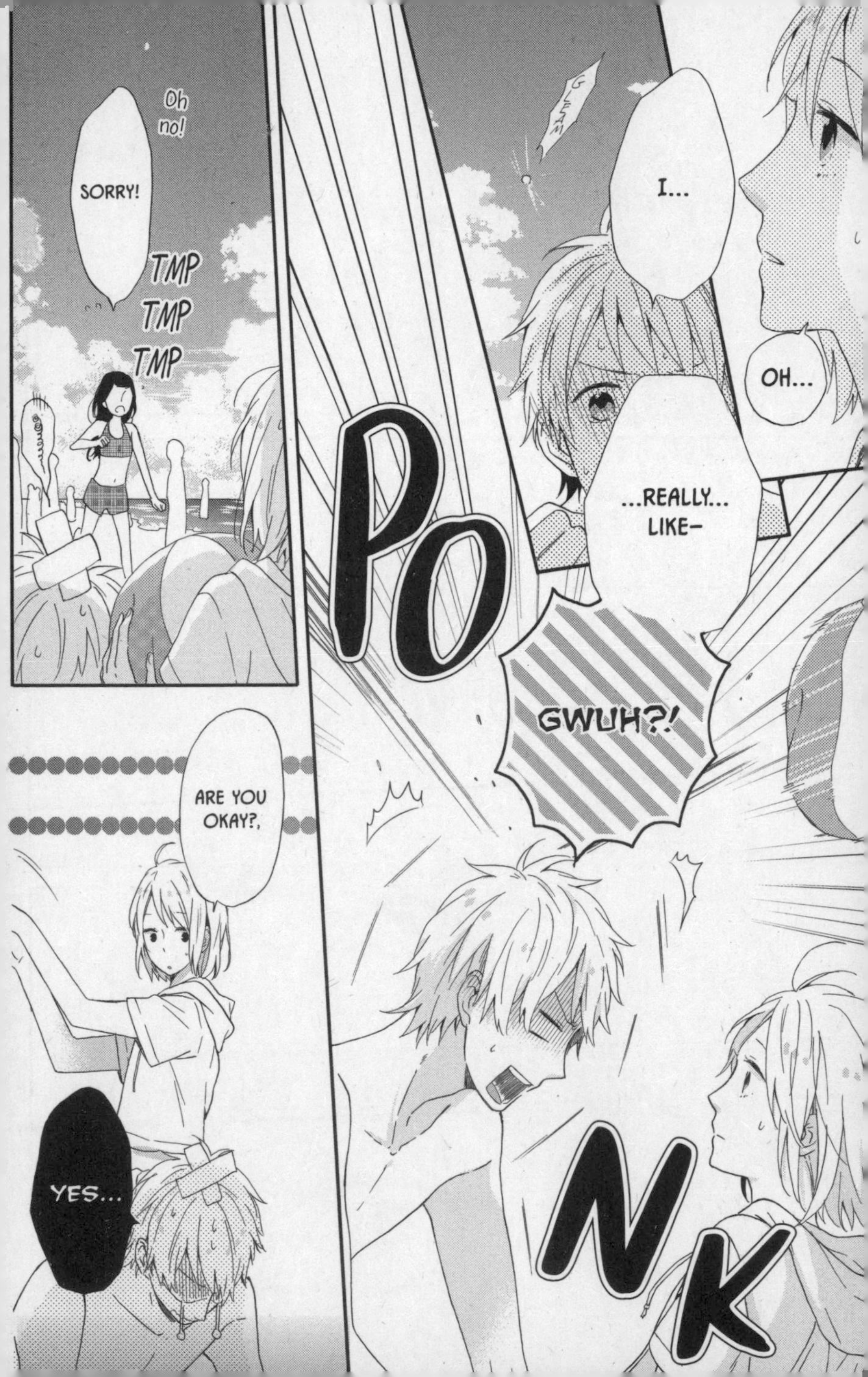
GLEAM
I...
OH...
...REALLY... LIKE–
PO
GWUH?!
NK
Oh no!
SORRY!
TMP TMP TMP
ARE YOU OKAY?,
YES...

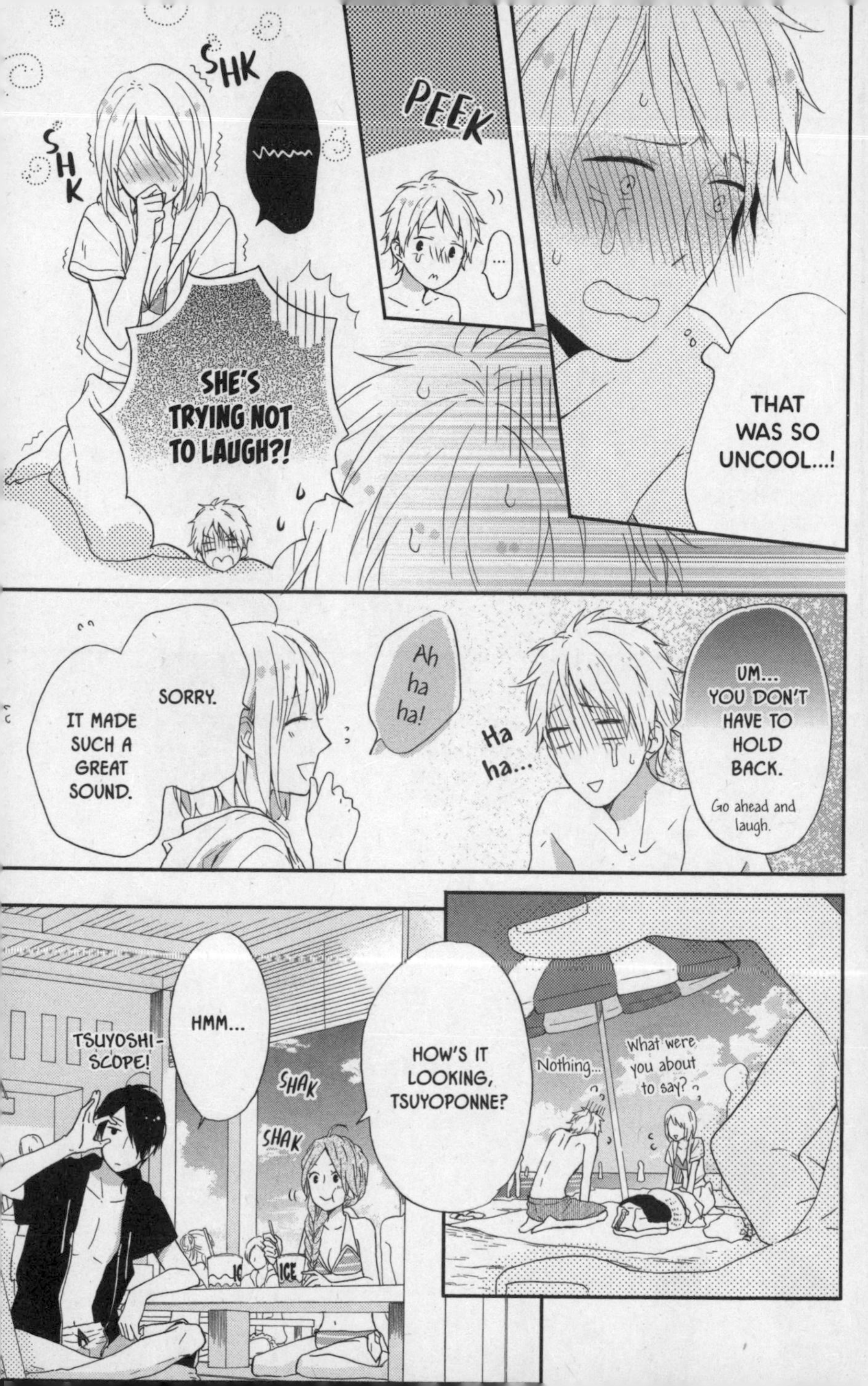
THAT WAS SO UNCOOL...!
PEEK
...
SHK
SHK
SHE'S TRYING NOT TO LAUGH?!
UM... YOU DON'T HAVE TO HOLD BACK.
Go ahead and laugh.
Ha ha...
Ah ha ha!
SORRY.
IT MADE SUCH A GREAT SOUND.
What were you about to say?
Nothing...
HOW'S IT LOOKING, TSUYOPONNE?
SHAK
SHAK
ICE
HMM...
TSUYOSHI-SCOPE!

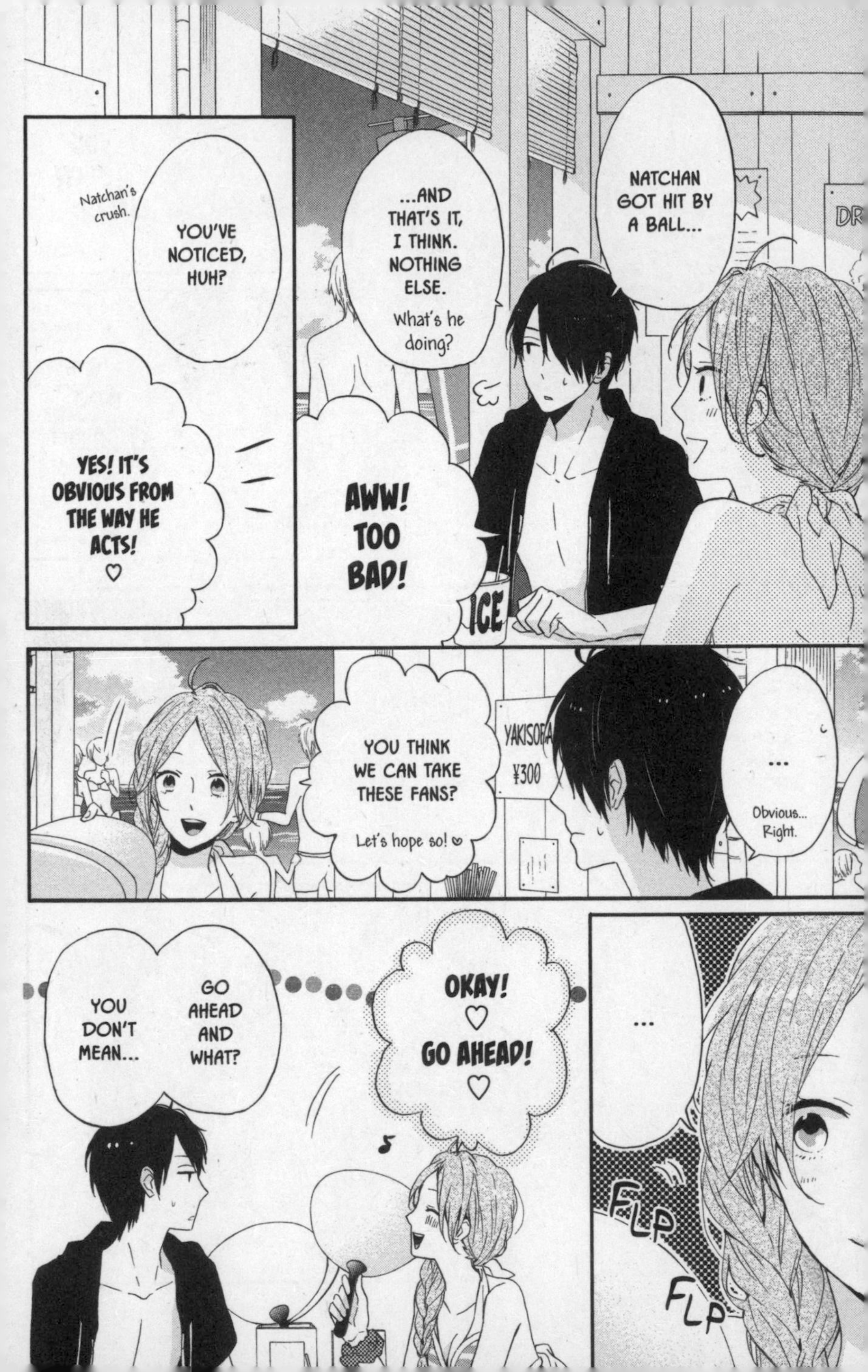

NATCHAN GOT HIT BY A BALL...
...AND THAT'S IT, I THINK. NOTHING ELSE.
What's he doing?
AWW! TOO BAD!
ICE
Natchan's crush.
YOU'VE NOTICED, HUH?
YES! IT'S OBVIOUS FROM THE WAY HE ACTS! ♡
...
Obvious... Right.
YAKISOBA ¥300
YOU THINK WE CAN TAKE THESE FANS?
Let's hope so!
...
FLP
FLP
OKAY! ♡ GO AHEAD! ♡
GO AHEAD AND WHAT?
YOU DON'T MEAN...

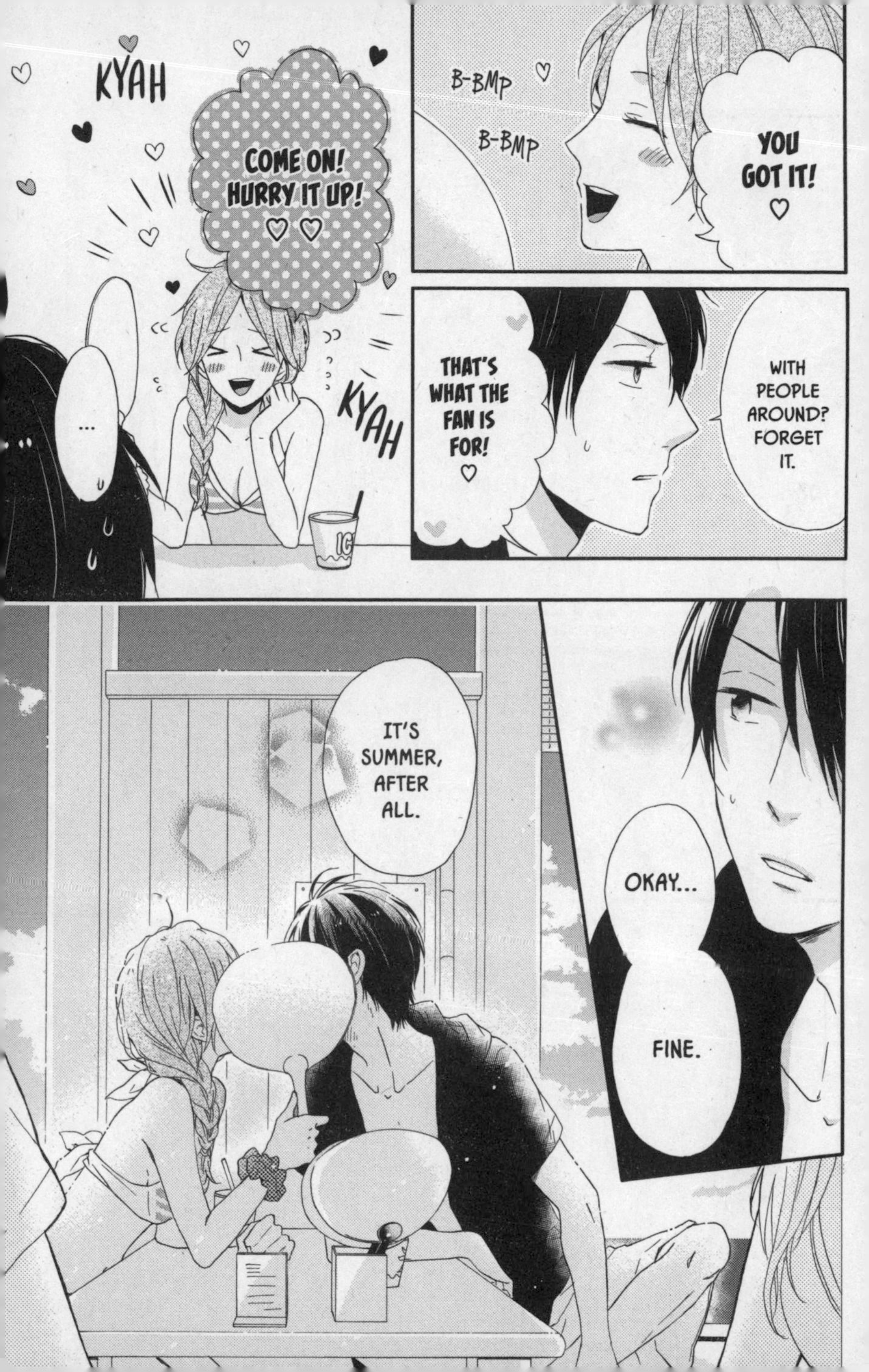
B-BMP
B-BMP
YOU GOT IT! ♡
WITH PEOPLE AROUND? FORGET IT.
THAT'S WHAT THE FAN IS FOR! ♡
KYAH
COME ON! HURRY IT UP! ♡ ♡
...
KYAH
OKAY...
FINE.
IT'S SUMMER, AFTER ALL.

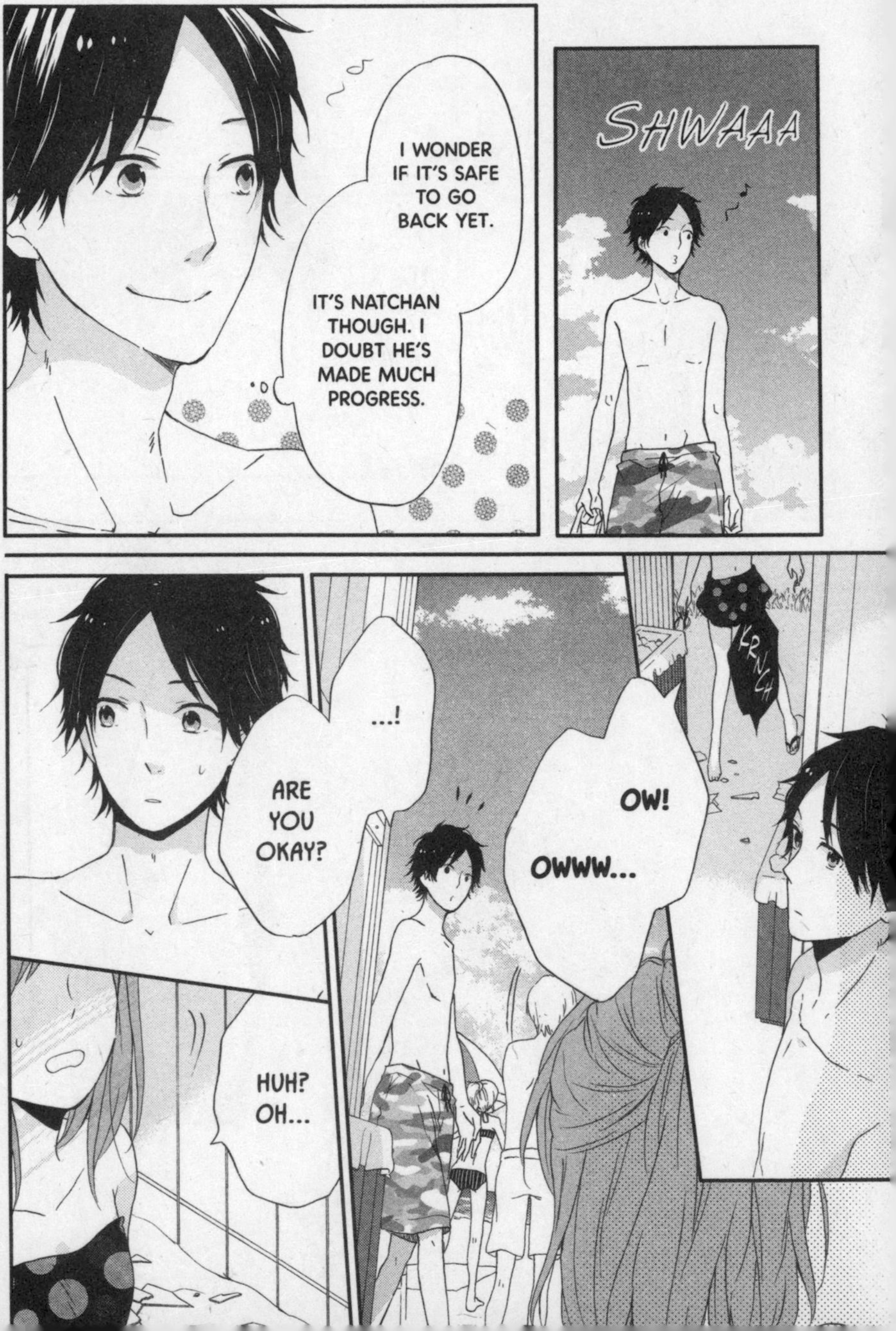
SHWAAA
I WONDER IF IT'S SAFE TO GO BACK YET.
IT'S NATCHAN THOUGH. I DOUBT HE'S MADE MUCH PROGRESS.
KRNCH
OW!
OWWW...
...!
ARE YOU OKAY?
HUH? OH...

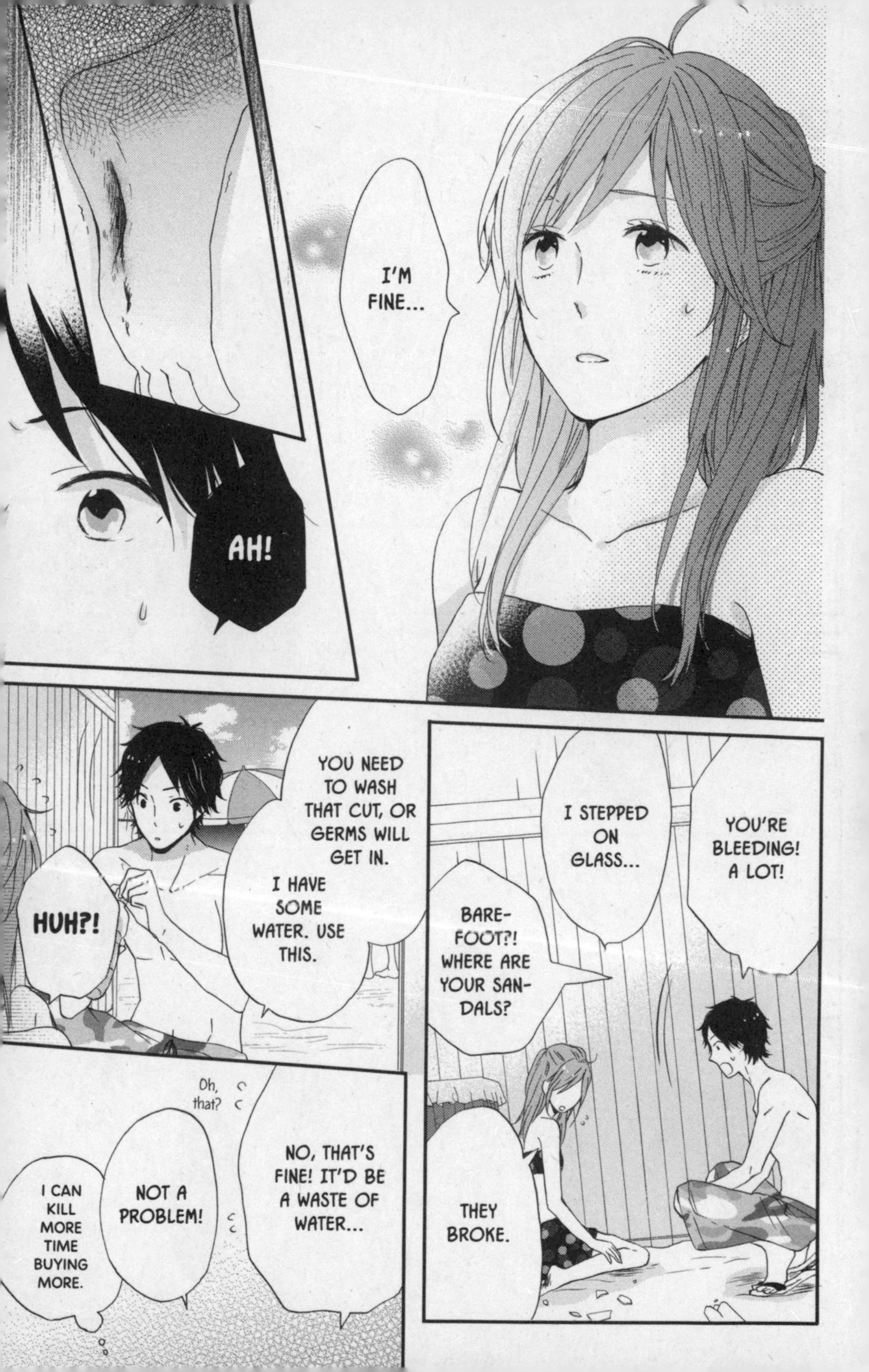

I'M FINE...
AH!
YOU'RE BLEEDING! A LOT!
I STEPPED ON GLASS...
BARE-FOOT?! WHERE ARE YOUR SAN-DALS?
THEY BROKE.
YOU NEED TO WASH THAT CUT, OR GERMS WILL GET IN.
I HAVE SOME WATER. USE THIS.
HUH?!
NO, THAT'S FINE! IT'D BE A WASTE OF WATER...
Oh, that?
NOT A PROBLEM!
I CAN KILL MORE TIME BUYING MORE.

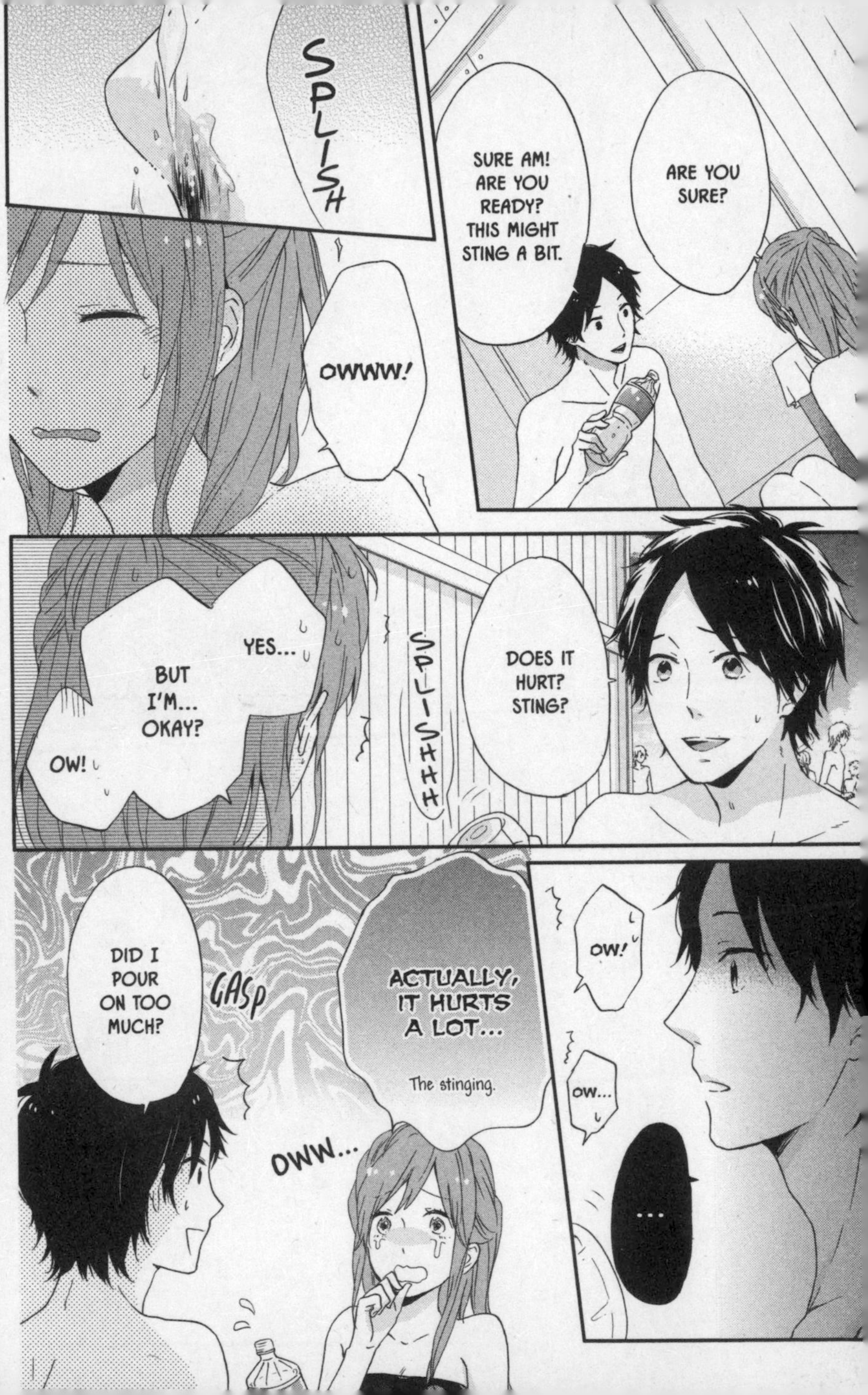
ARE YOU SURE?
SURE AM! ARE YOU READY? THIS MIGHT STING A BIT.
SPLISH
OWWW!
DOES IT HURT? STING?
SPLISHHH
YES... BUT I'M... OKAY?
OW!
OW!
OW...
...
ACTUALLY, IT HURTS A LOT...
The stinging.
DID I POUR ON TOO MUCH?
GASP
OWW...

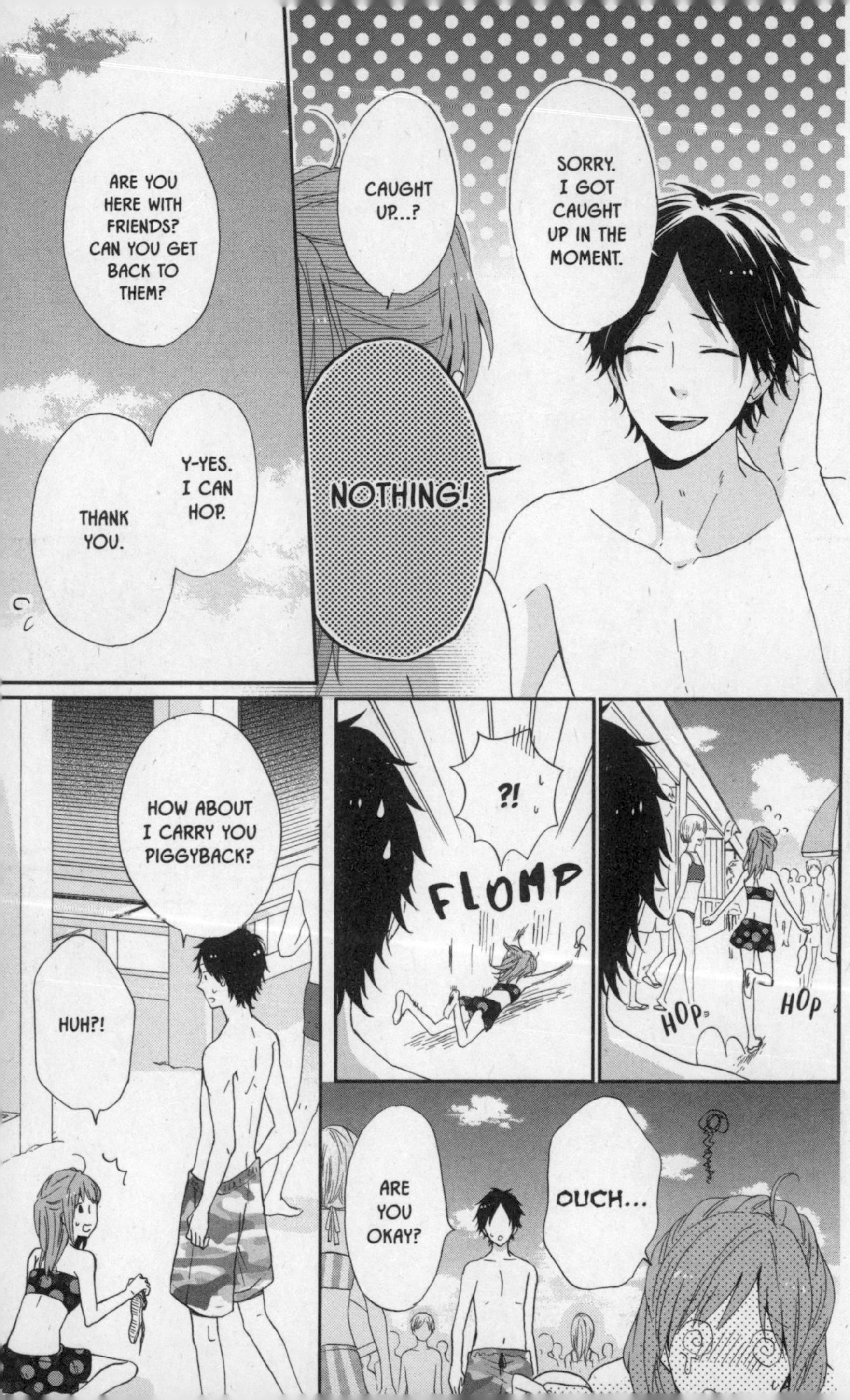
SORRY. I GOT CAUGHT UP IN THE MOMENT.
CAUGHT UP...?
NOTHING!
ARE YOU HERE WITH FRIENDS? CAN YOU GET BACK TO THEM?
Y-YES. I CAN HOP.
THANK YOU.
HOP
HOP
?!
FLOMP
OUCH...
ARE YOU OKAY?
HOW ABOUT I CARRY YOU PIGGYBACK?
HUH?!

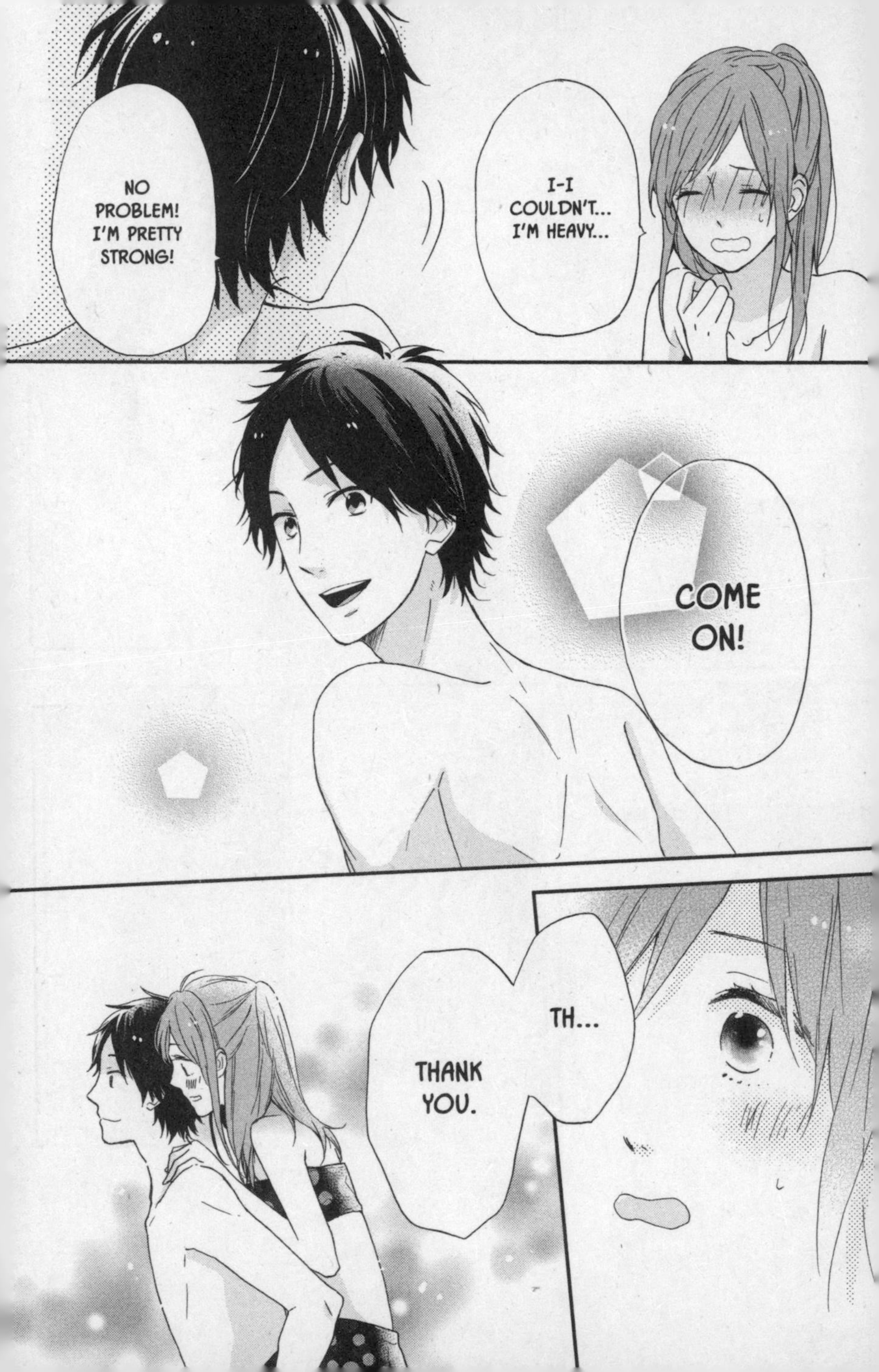
I-I COULDN'T... I'M HEAVY...
NO PROBLEM! I'M PRETTY STRONG!
COME ON!
TH...
THANK YOU.

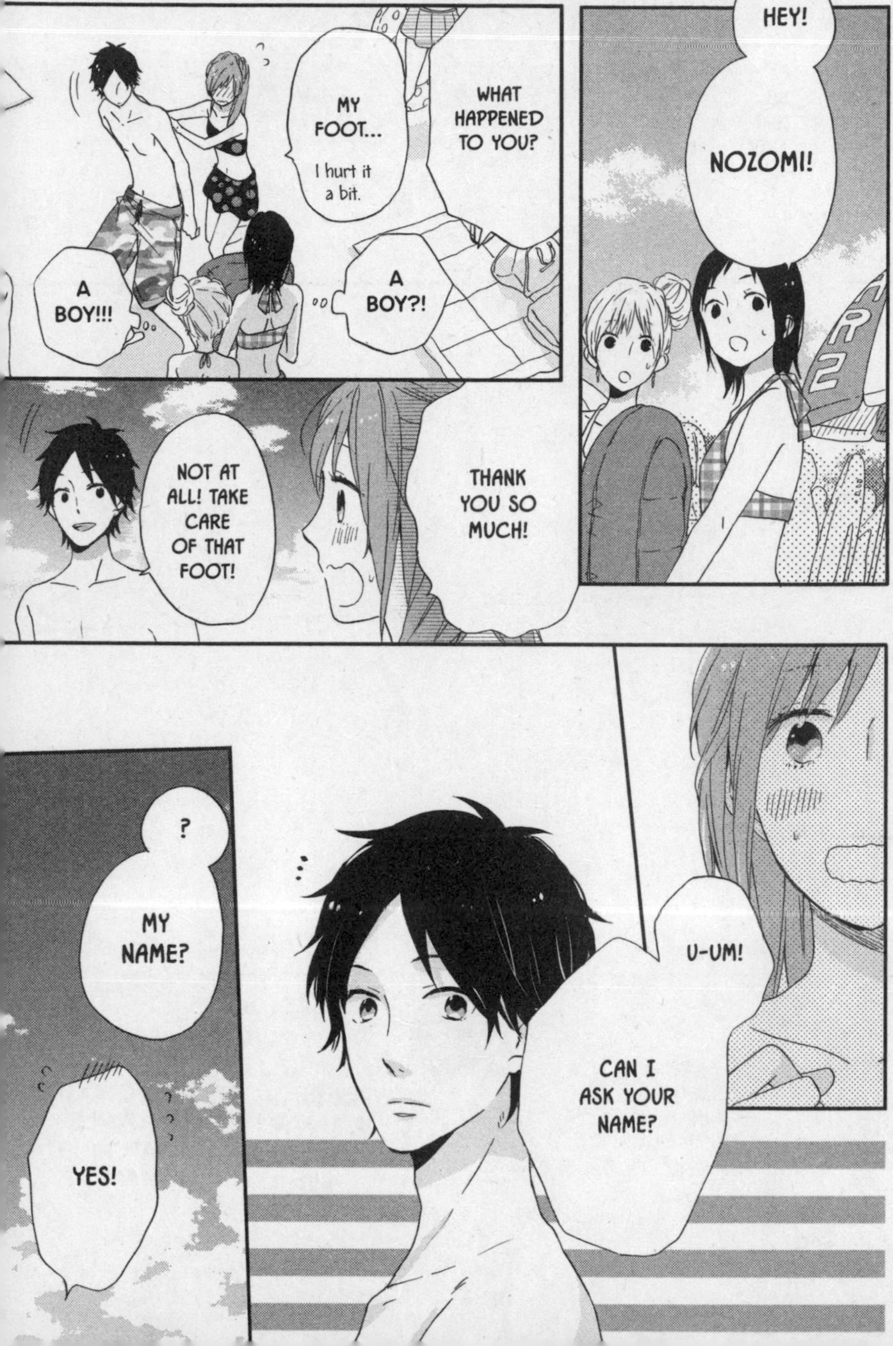
HEY!
NOZOMI!
WHAT HAPPENED TO YOU?
MY FOOT... I hurt it a bit.
A BOY?!
A BOY!!!
THANK YOU SO MUCH!
NOT AT ALL! TAKE CARE OF THAT FOOT!
U-UM!
CAN I ASK YOUR NAME?
?
MY NAME?
YES!

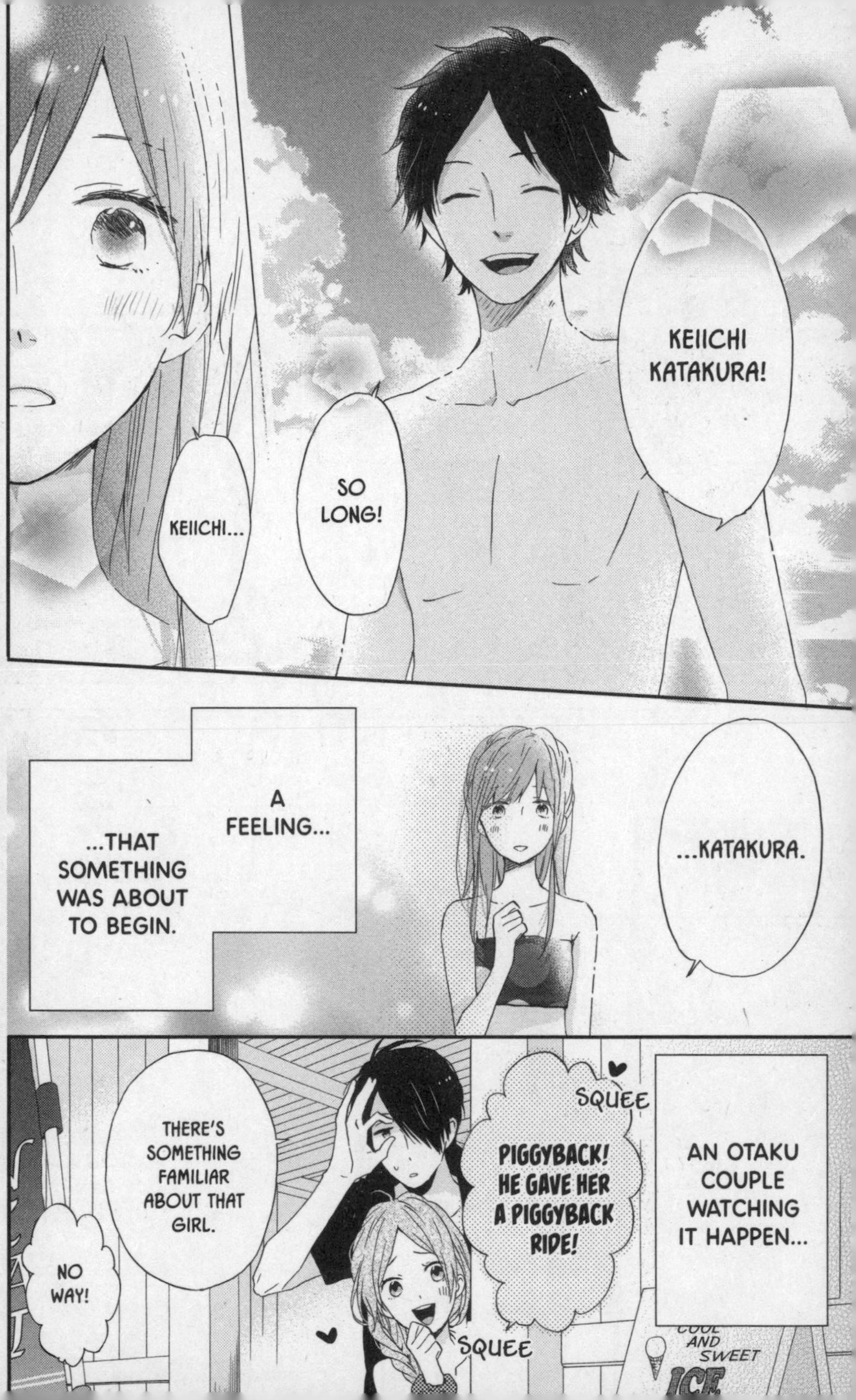
KEIICHI KATAKURA!
SO LONG!
KEIICHI...
...KATAKURA.
A FEELING...
...THAT SOMETHING WAS ABOUT TO BEGIN.
AN OTAKU COUPLE WATCHING IT HAPPEN...
SQUEE
PIGGYBACK! HE GAVE HER A PIGGYBACK RIDE!
SQUEE
THERE'S SOMETHING FAMILIAR ABOUT THAT GIRL.
NO WAY!
COOL AND SWEET

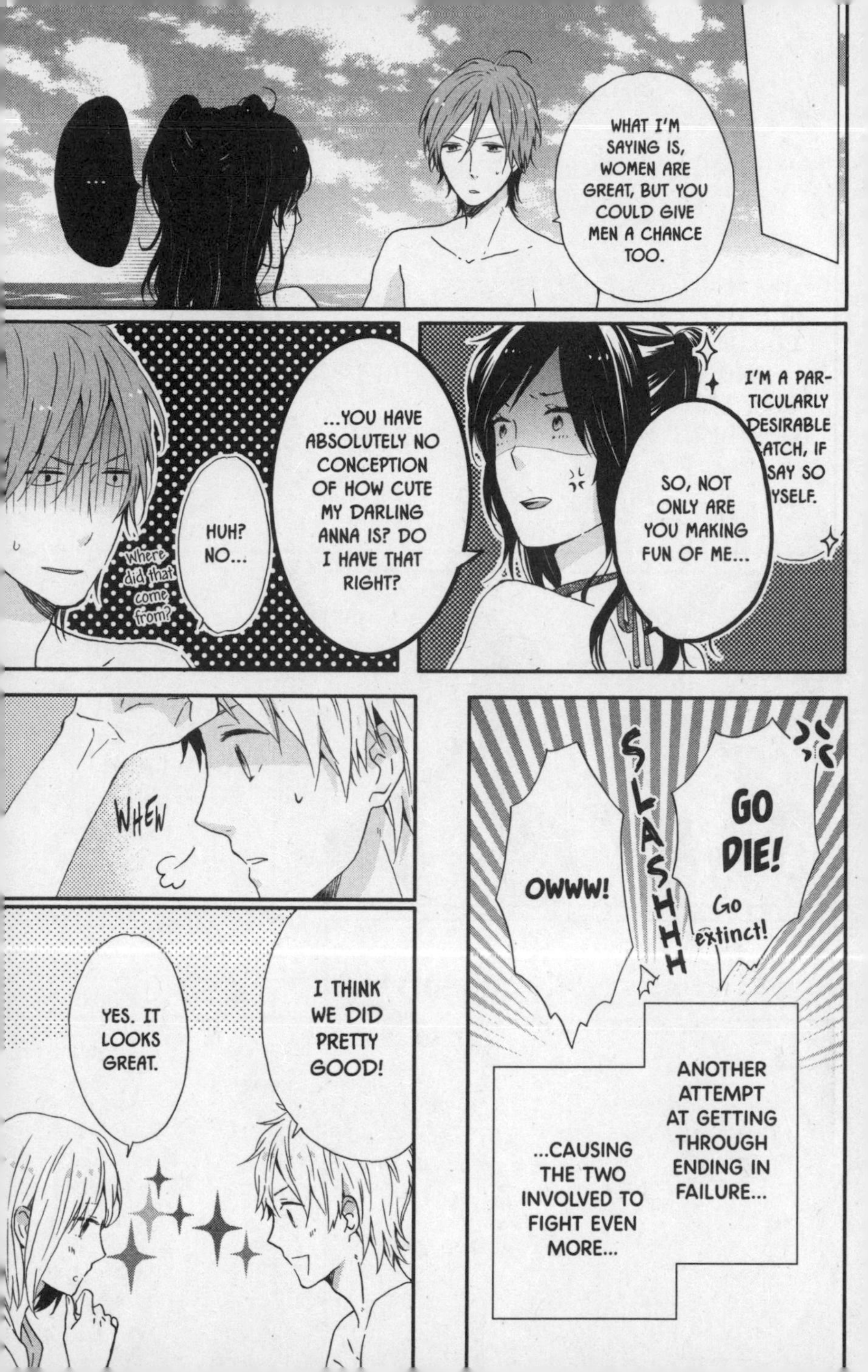
WHAT I'M SAYING IS, WOMEN ARE GREAT, BUT YOU COULD GIVE MEN A CHANCE TOO.
...
I'M A PARTICULARLY DESIRABLE CATCH, IF SAY SO YSELF.
SO, NOT ONLY ARE YOU MAKING FUN OF ME...
...YOU HAVE ABSOLUTELY NO CONCEPTION OF HOW CUTE MY DARLING ANNA IS? DO I HAVE THAT RIGHT?
HUH? NO...
Where did that come from?
GO DIE!
Go extinct!
SLASHHH
OWWW!
ANOTHER ATTEMPT AT GETTING THROUGH ENDING IN FAILURE...
...CAUSING THE TWO INVOLVED TO FIGHT EVEN MORE...
WHEW
I THINK WE DID PRETTY GOOD!
YES. IT LOOKS GREAT.

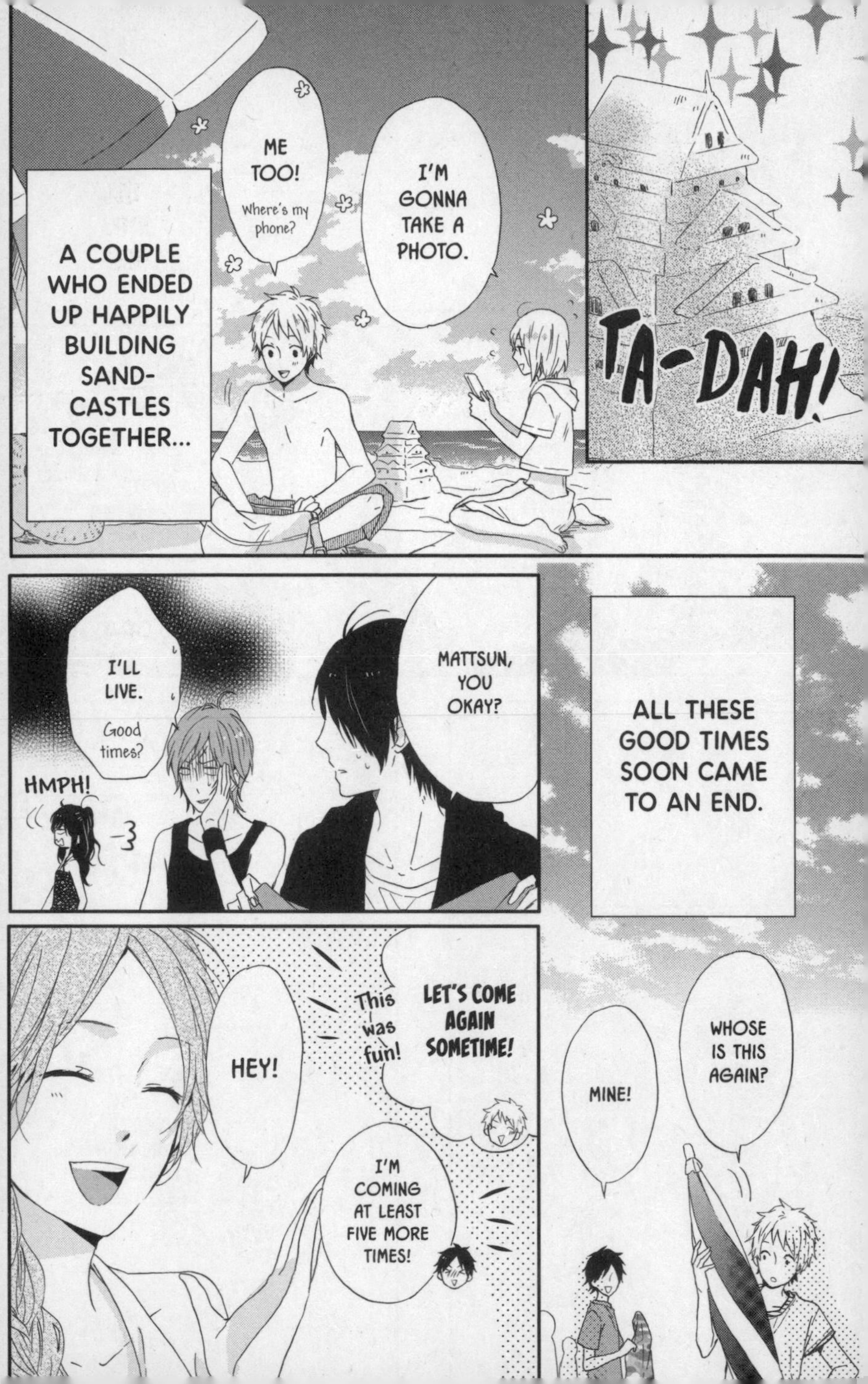
TA-DAH!
I'M GONNA TAKE A PHOTO.
ME TOO!
Where's my phone?
A COUPLE WHO ENDED UP HAPPILY BUILDING SAND-CASTLES TOGETHER...
ALL THESE GOOD TIMES SOON CAME TO AN END.
WHOSE IS THIS AGAIN?
MINE!
MATTSUN, YOU OKAY?
I'LL LIVE.
Good times?
HMPH!
LET'S COME AGAIN SOMETIME!
This was fun!
HEY!
I'M COMING AT LEAST FIVE MORE TIMES!

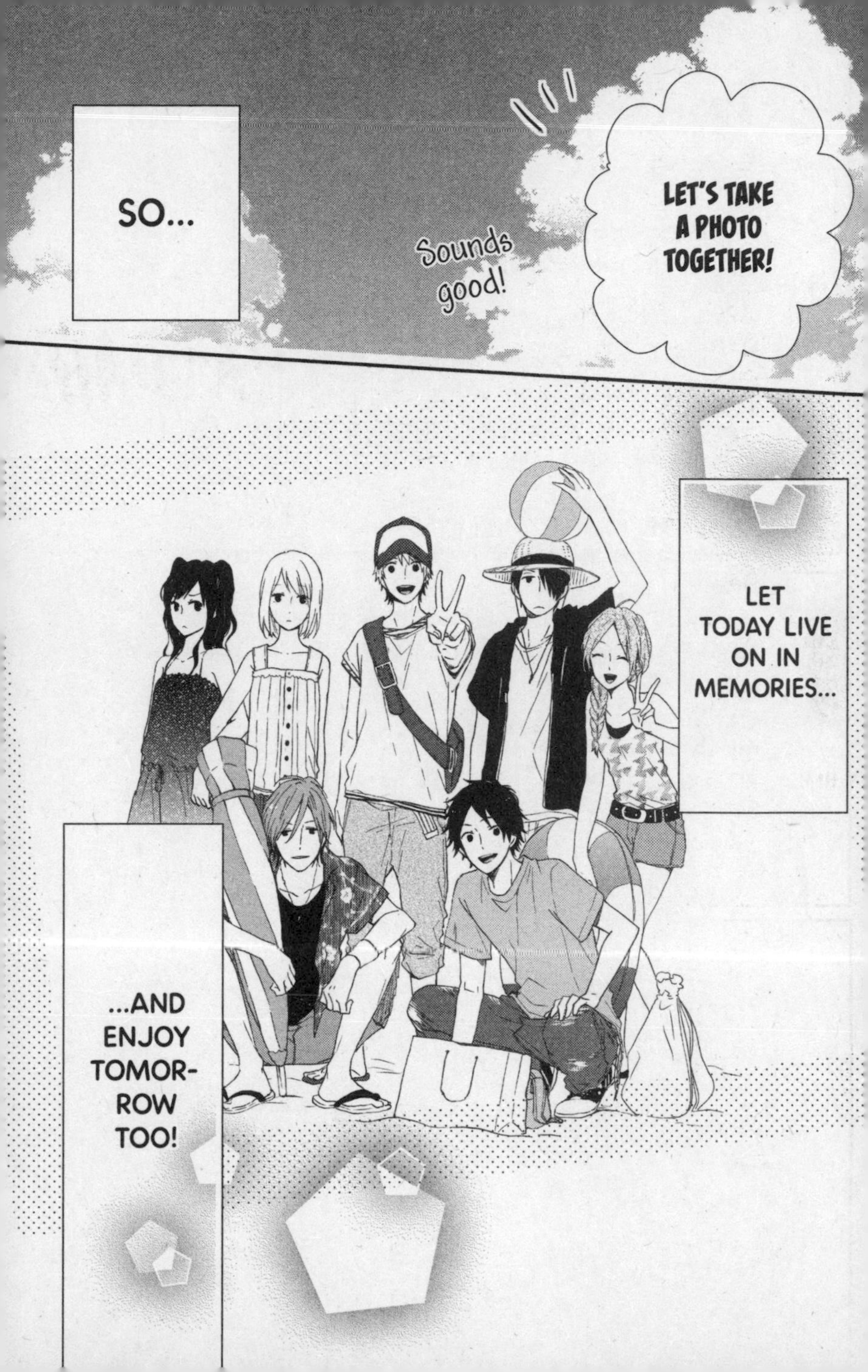
LET'S TAKE A PHOTO TOGETHER!
Sounds good!
SO...
LET TODAY LIVE ON IN MEMORIES...
...AND ENJOY TOMOR-ROW TOO!

②

Now, since we're at volume 3, the cover illustration is Kei-chan, but to be honest I was torn between him and Tsuyopon. Kei-chan gets his turn in volume 4...
But even before the story was picked up as a series, I had a dream: "I want to draw one character per volume for the cover illustrations in the order they appear!" Well, I've stuck to that, and I've been drawing the covers without caring what the contents were. I don't think that will change in the future.

To begin with, I'm super-happy that there's an "in the future"!
Drawing a series for the main magazine again is like a dream come true!
And it's all thanks to all my readers! Thank you so much!
Mind you, I was surprised that I got the call right after *Komatsu-san* finished...! (*laugh*)

And so, the beach chapter turned into a kind of prologue, or maybe not (vague). You know, I really enjoyed drawing those swimsuits—the girls', I mean! Maybe I should've let them wear cuter ones...
Another regret! Well, I'll have another chance!

← Continued on p. 190.

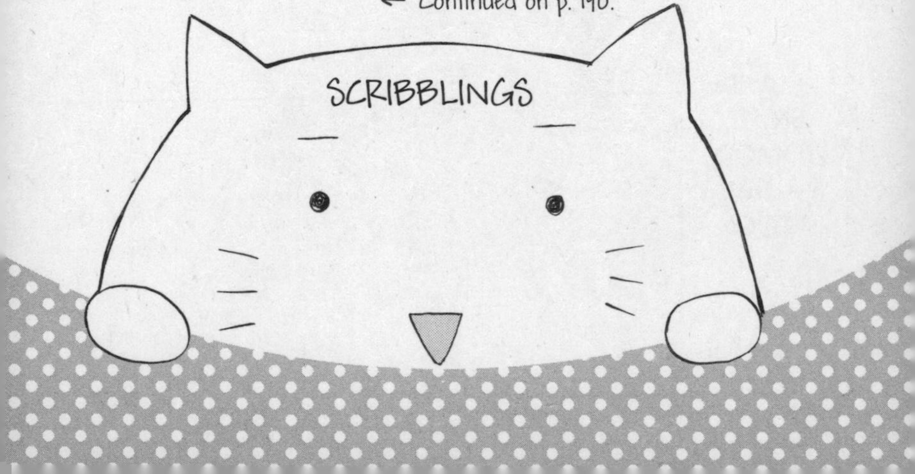
SCRIBBLINGS

THIS IS A STORY ABOUT SOME BOYS...

...AND THEIR DAYS FILLED WITH WORK, PLAY...

...AND LOVE.

BUSY AS THEY ARE, THEY ALWAYS FIND TIME FOR FUN.

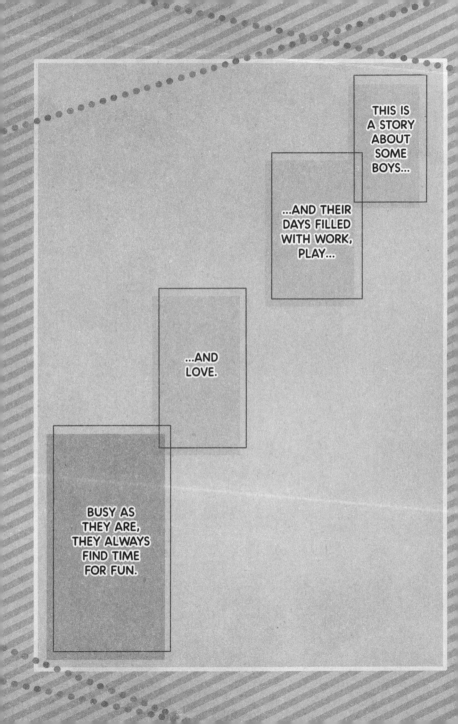

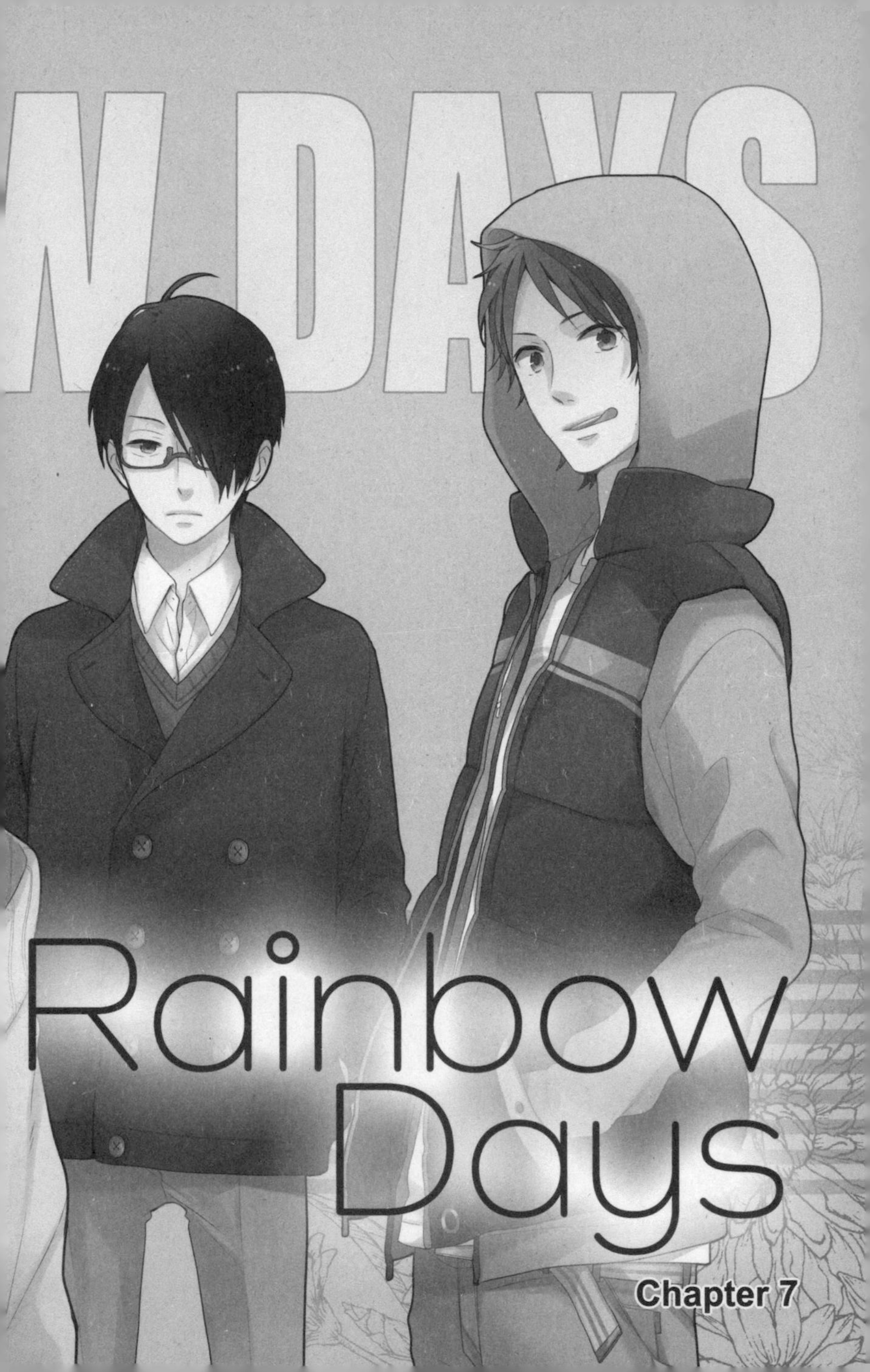
Rainbow Days
Chapter 7

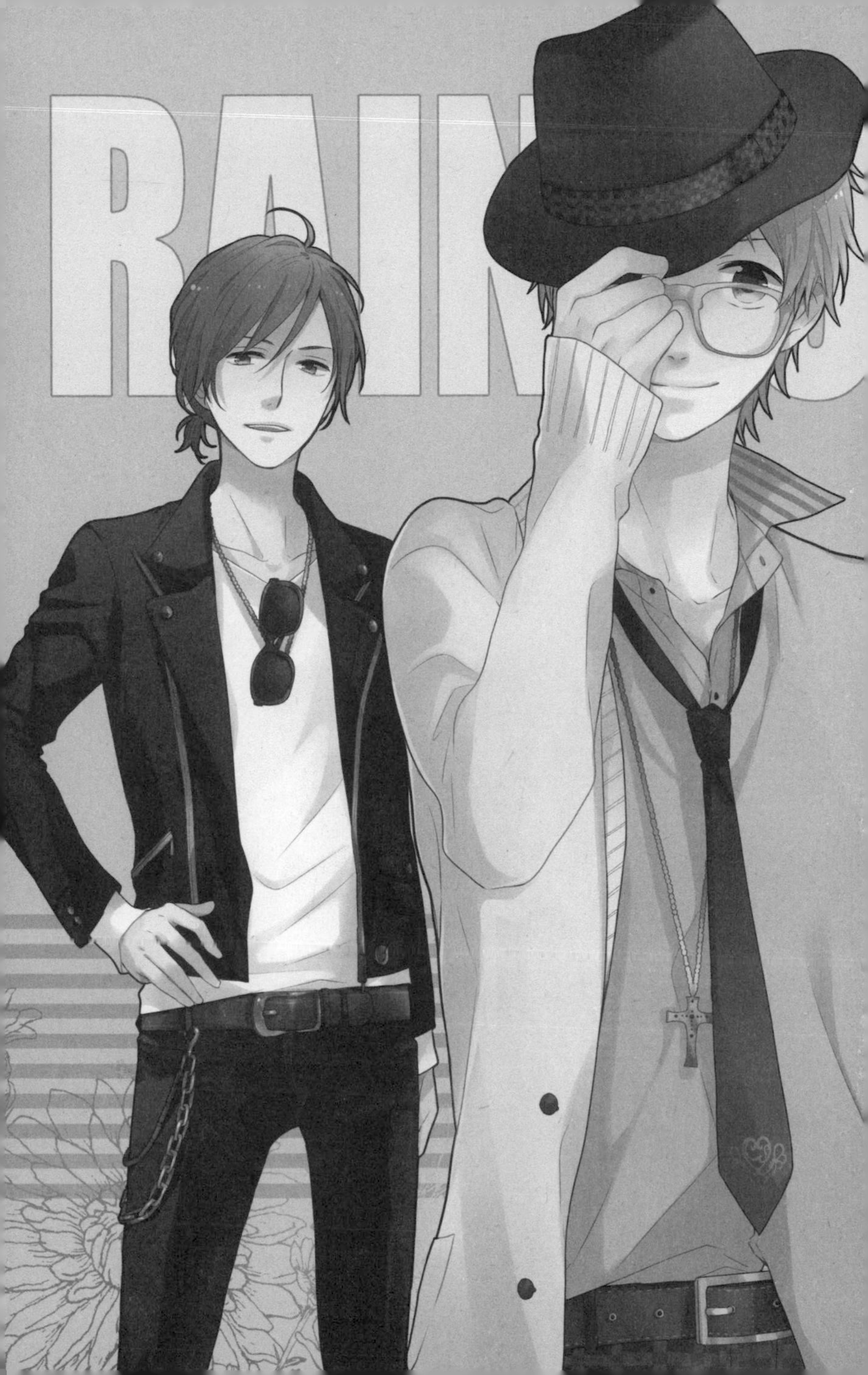
RAI

Rainbow
Days

■ ■ ■ ■ ■ ■ ■

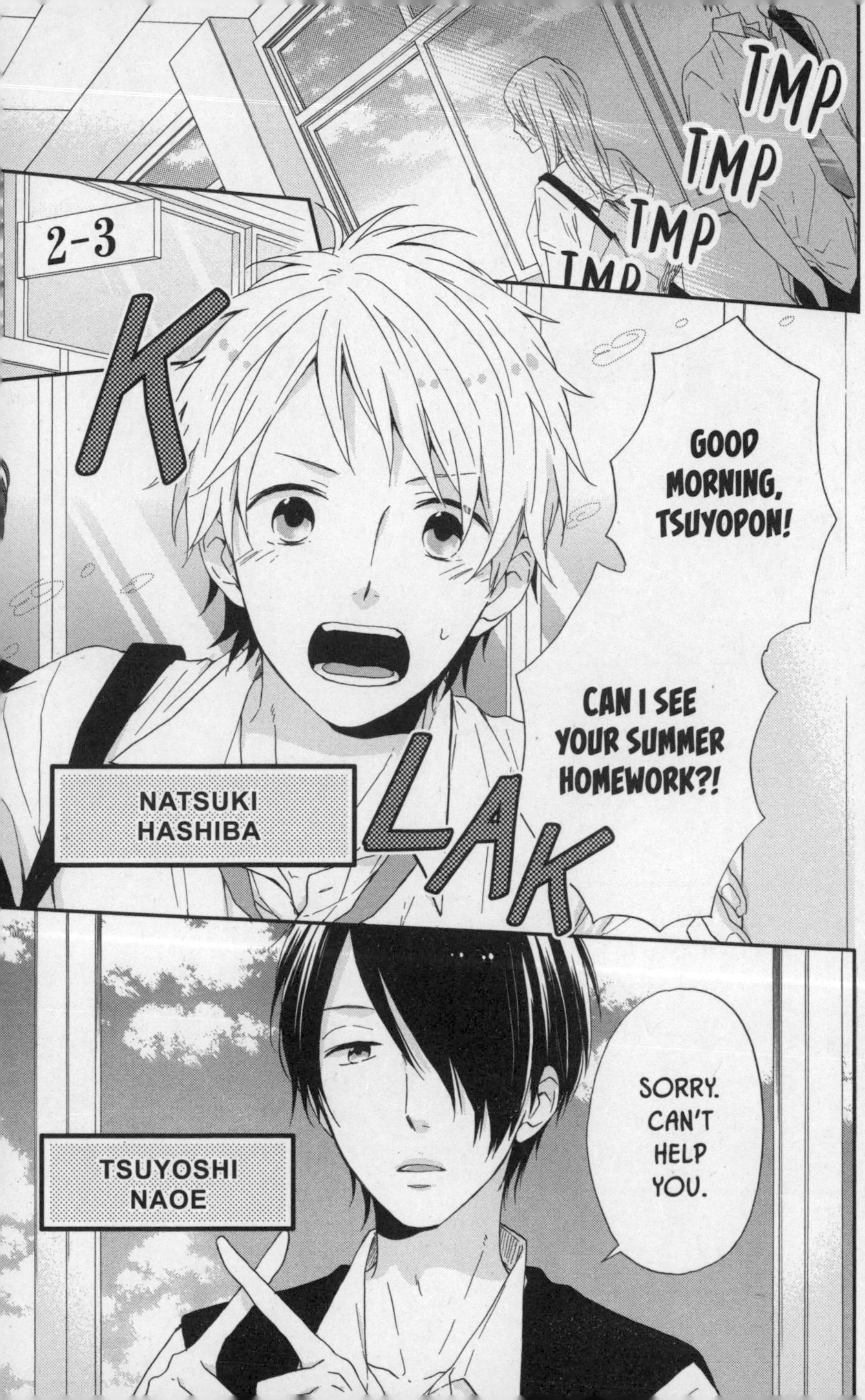
TMP
TMP
TMP
TMP
2-3
GOOD MORNING, TSUYOPON!
CAN I SEE YOUR SUMMER HOMEWORK?!
KLAK
NATSUKI HASHIBA
SORRY. CAN'T HELP YOU.
TSUYOSHI NAOE

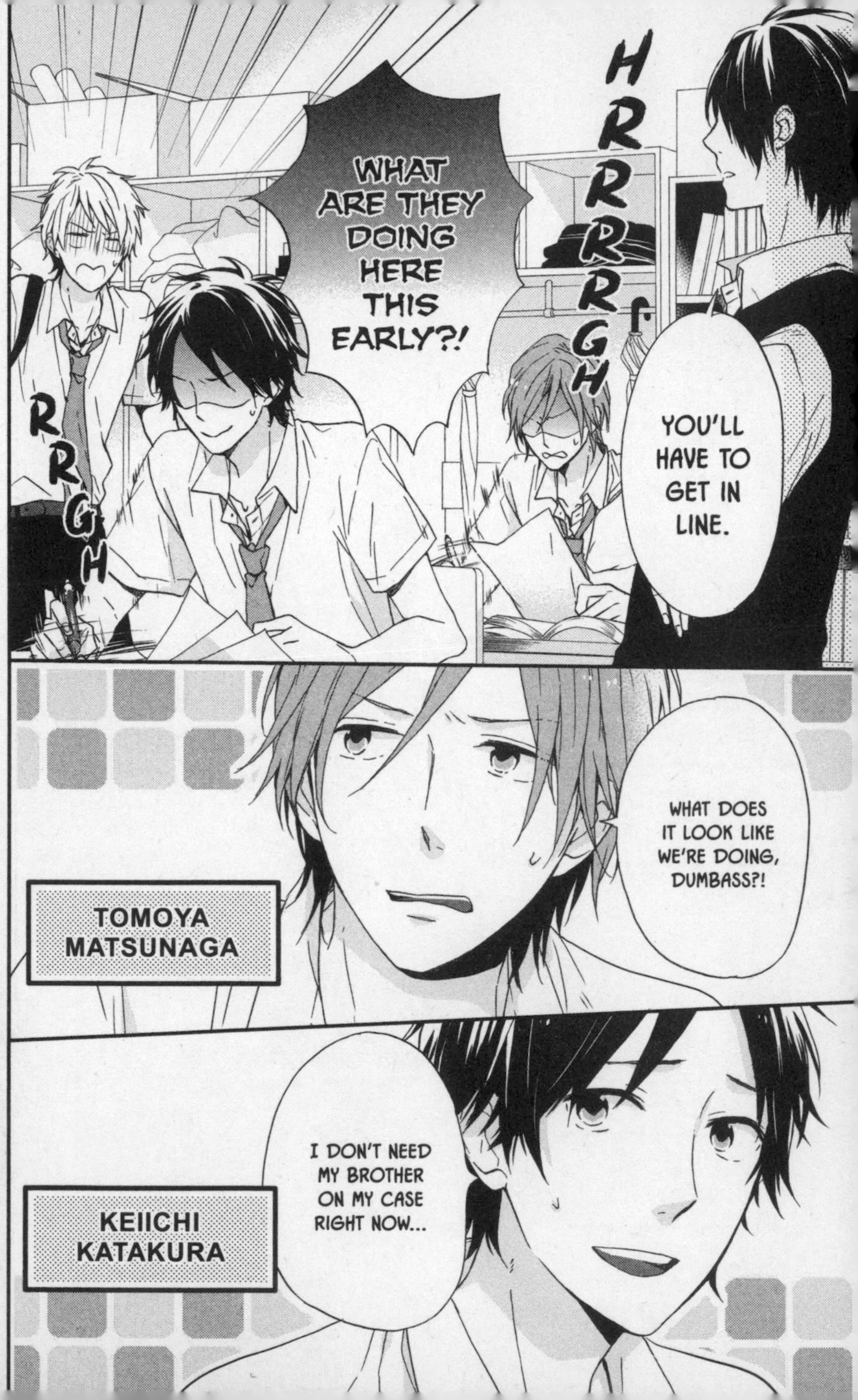
HRRRRRGH
YOU'LL HAVE TO GET IN LINE.
WHAT ARE THEY DOING HERE THIS EARLY?!
RRGH
WHAT DOES IT LOOK LIKE WE'RE DOING, DUMBASS?!
TOMOYA MATSUNAGA
I DON'T NEED MY BROTHER ON MY CASE RIGHT NOW...
KEIICHI KATAKURA

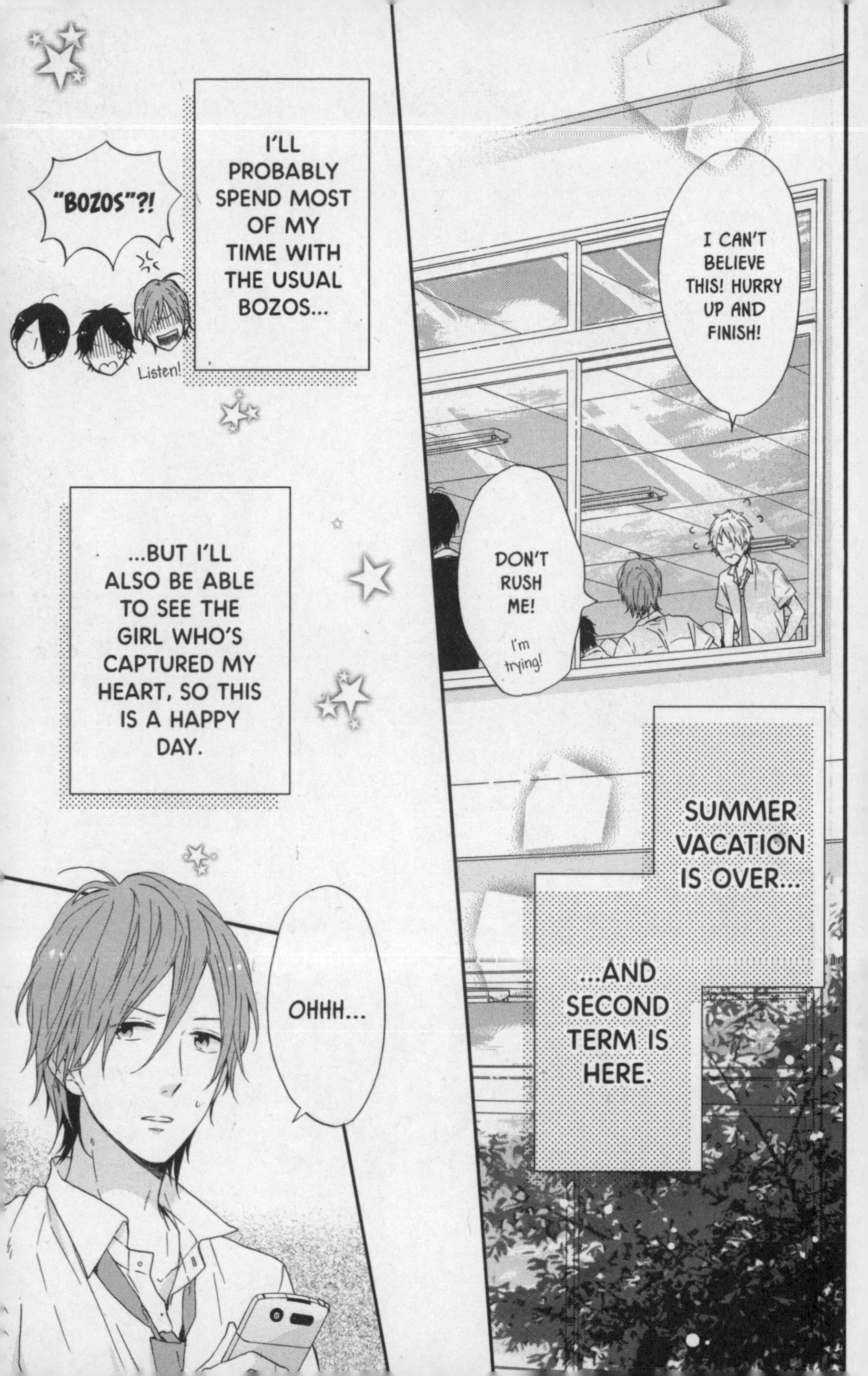
I CAN'T BELIEVE THIS! HURRY UP AND FINISH!
DON'T RUSH ME!
I'm trying!
SUMMER VACATION IS OVER...
...AND SECOND TERM IS HERE.
I'LL PROBABLY SPEND MOST OF MY TIME WITH THE USUAL BOZOS...
"BOZOS"?!
Listen!
...BUT I'LL ALSO BE ABLE TO SEE THE GIRL WHO'S CAPTURED MY HEART, SO THIS IS A HAPPY DAY.
OHHH...

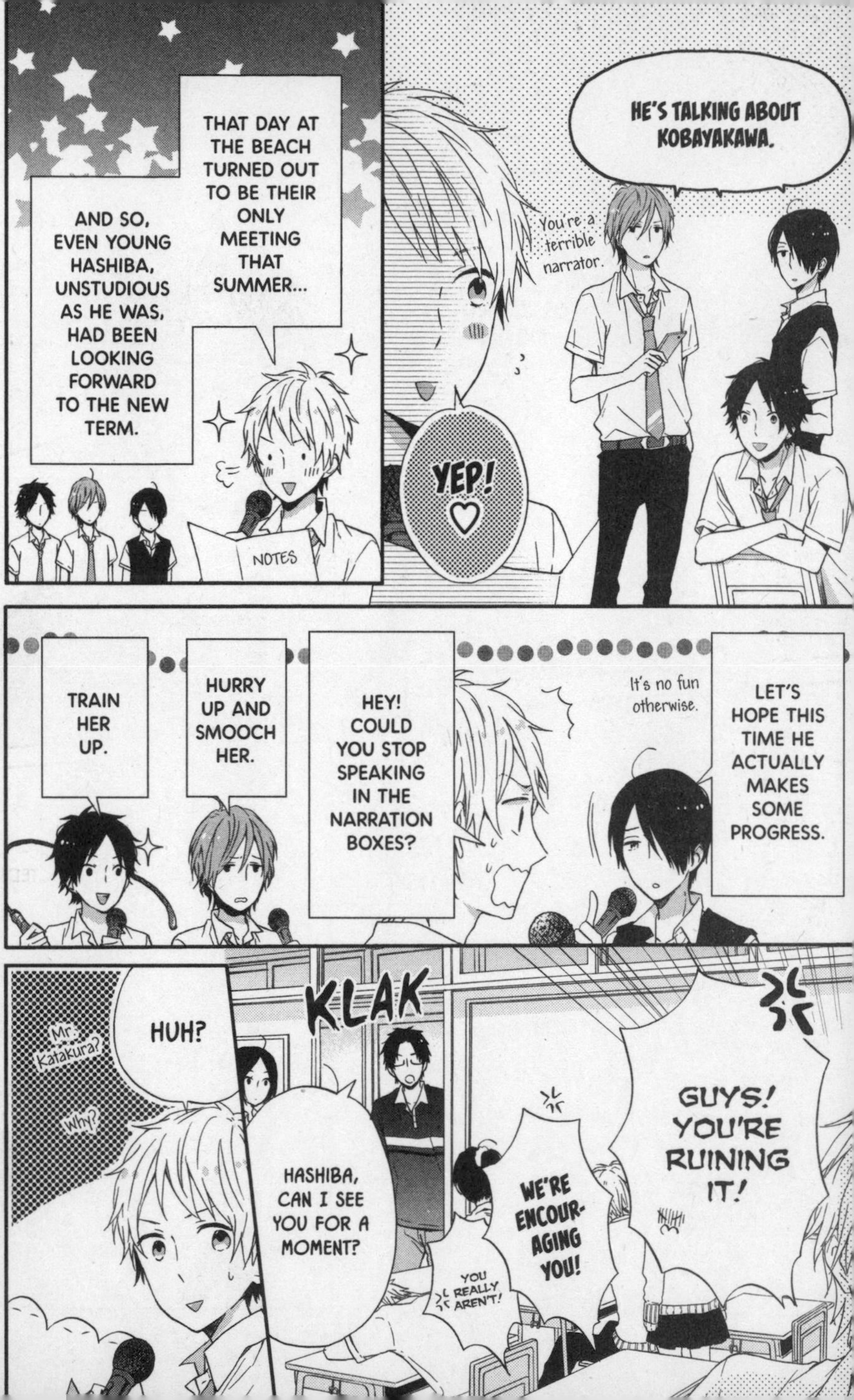
HE'S TALKING ABOUT KOBAYAKAWA.
You're a terrible narrator.
YEP! ♡
THAT DAY AT THE BEACH TURNED OUT TO BE THEIR ONLY MEETING THAT SUMMER...
AND SO, EVEN YOUNG HASHIBA, UNSTUDIOUS AS HE WAS, HAD BEEN LOOKING FORWARD TO THE NEW TERM.
NOTES
LET'S HOPE THIS TIME HE ACTUALLY MAKES SOME PROGRESS.
It's no fun otherwise.
HEY! COULD YOU STOP SPEAKING IN THE NARRATION BOXES?
HURRY UP AND SMOOCH HER.
TRAIN HER UP.
KLAK
GUYS! YOU'RE RUINING IT!
WE'RE ENCOUR-AGING YOU!
YOU REALLY AREN'T!
HASHIBA, CAN I SEE YOU FOR A MOMENT?
HUH?
Mr. Katakura?
Why?

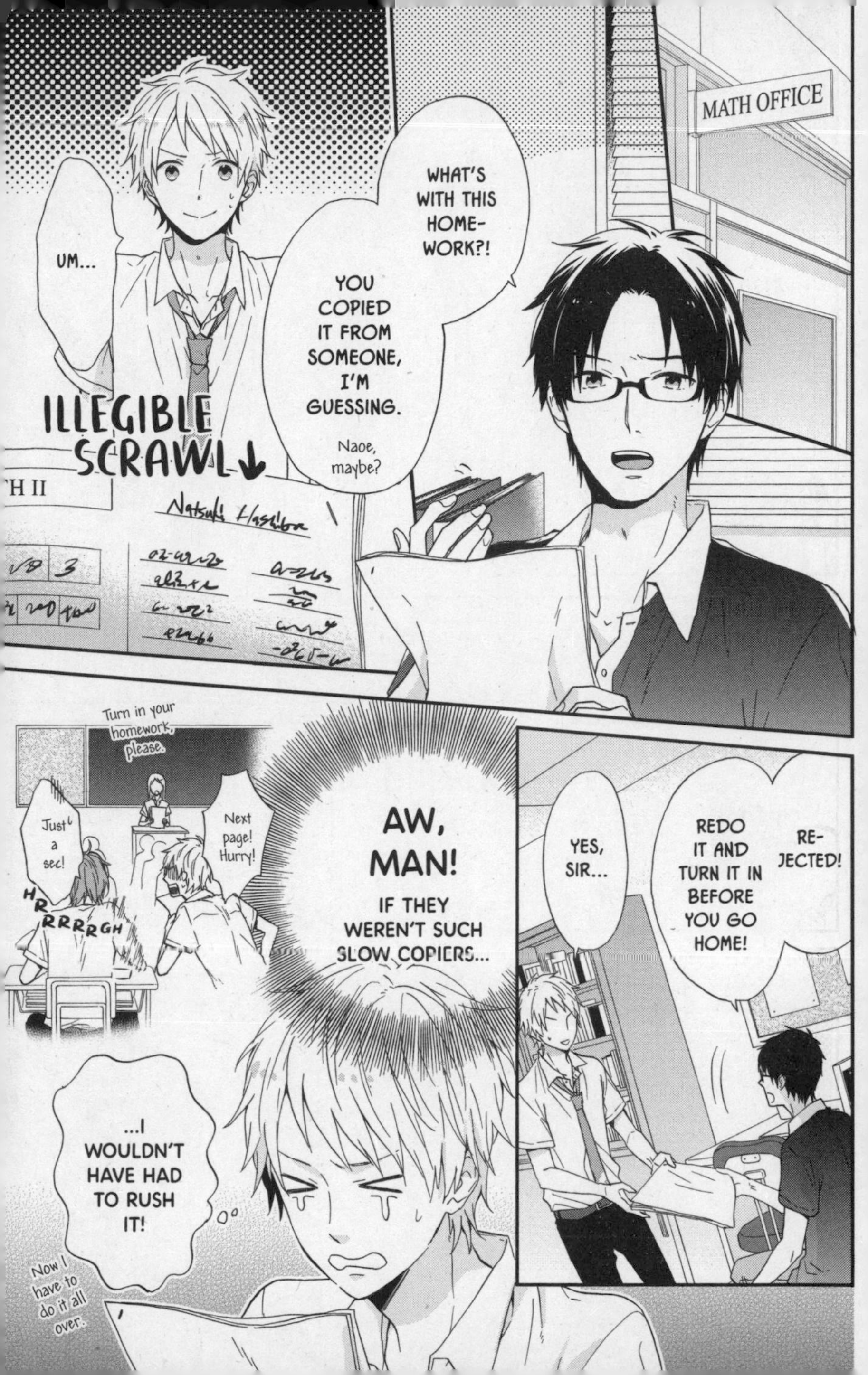
MATH OFFICE
WHAT'S WITH THIS HOME-WORK?!
YOU COPIED IT FROM SOMEONE, I'M GUESSING.
Naoe, maybe?
UM...
ILLEGIBLE SCRAWL↓
RE-JECTED!
REDO IT AND TURN IT IN BEFORE YOU GO HOME!
YES, SIR...
AW, MAN!
IF THEY WEREN'T SUCH SLOW COPIERS...
Turn in your homework, please.
Next page! Hurry!
Just a sec!
HRRRRRGH
...I WOULDN'T HAVE HAD TO RUSH IT!
Now I have to do it all over.

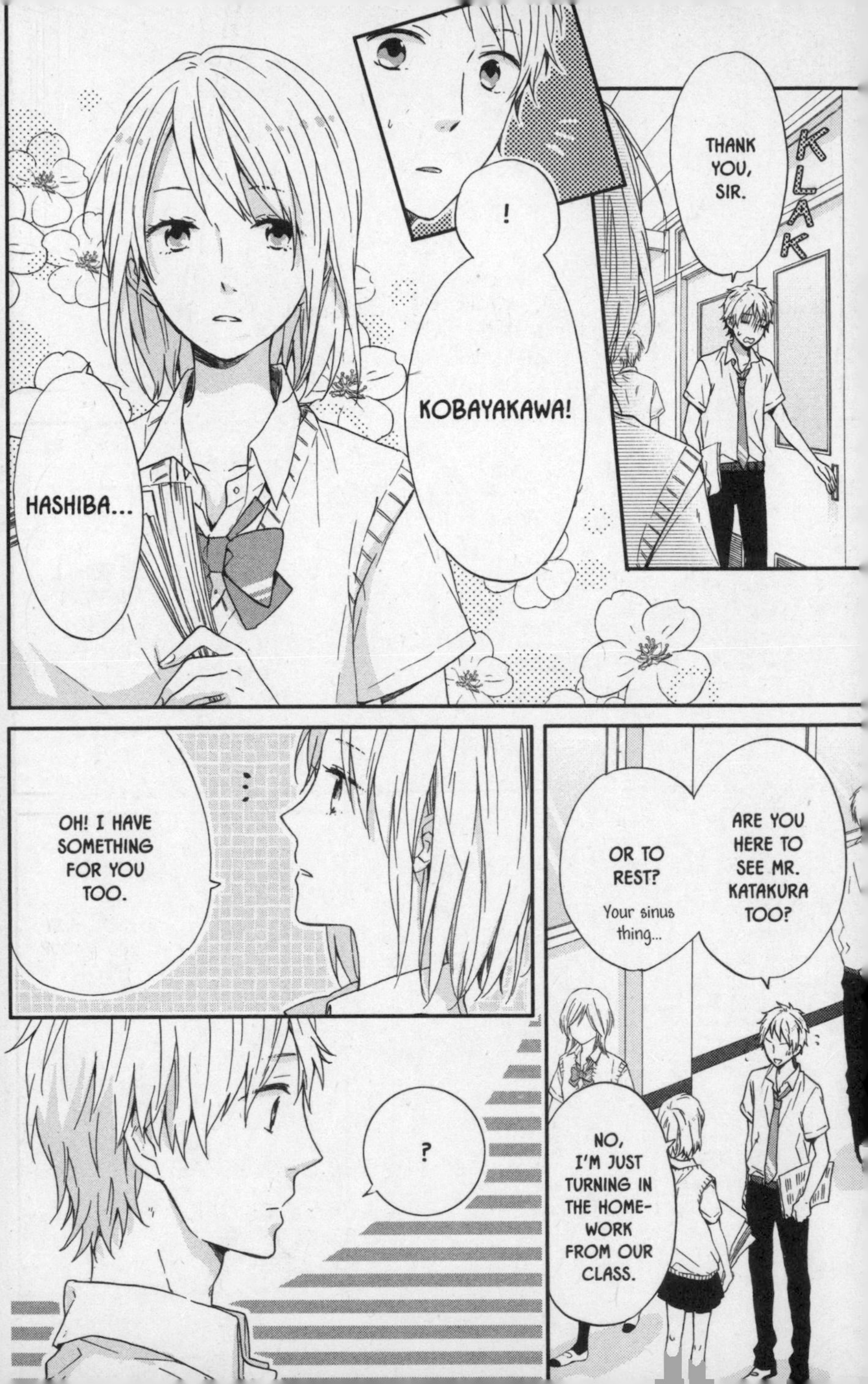
THANK YOU, SIR.
KLAK
!
KOBAYAKAWA!
HASHIBA...
ARE YOU HERE TO SEE MR. KATAKURA TOO?
OR TO REST?
Your sinus thing...
NO, I'M JUST TURNING IN THE HOME-WORK FROM OUR CLASS.
...
OH! I HAVE SOMETHING FOR YOU TOO.
?

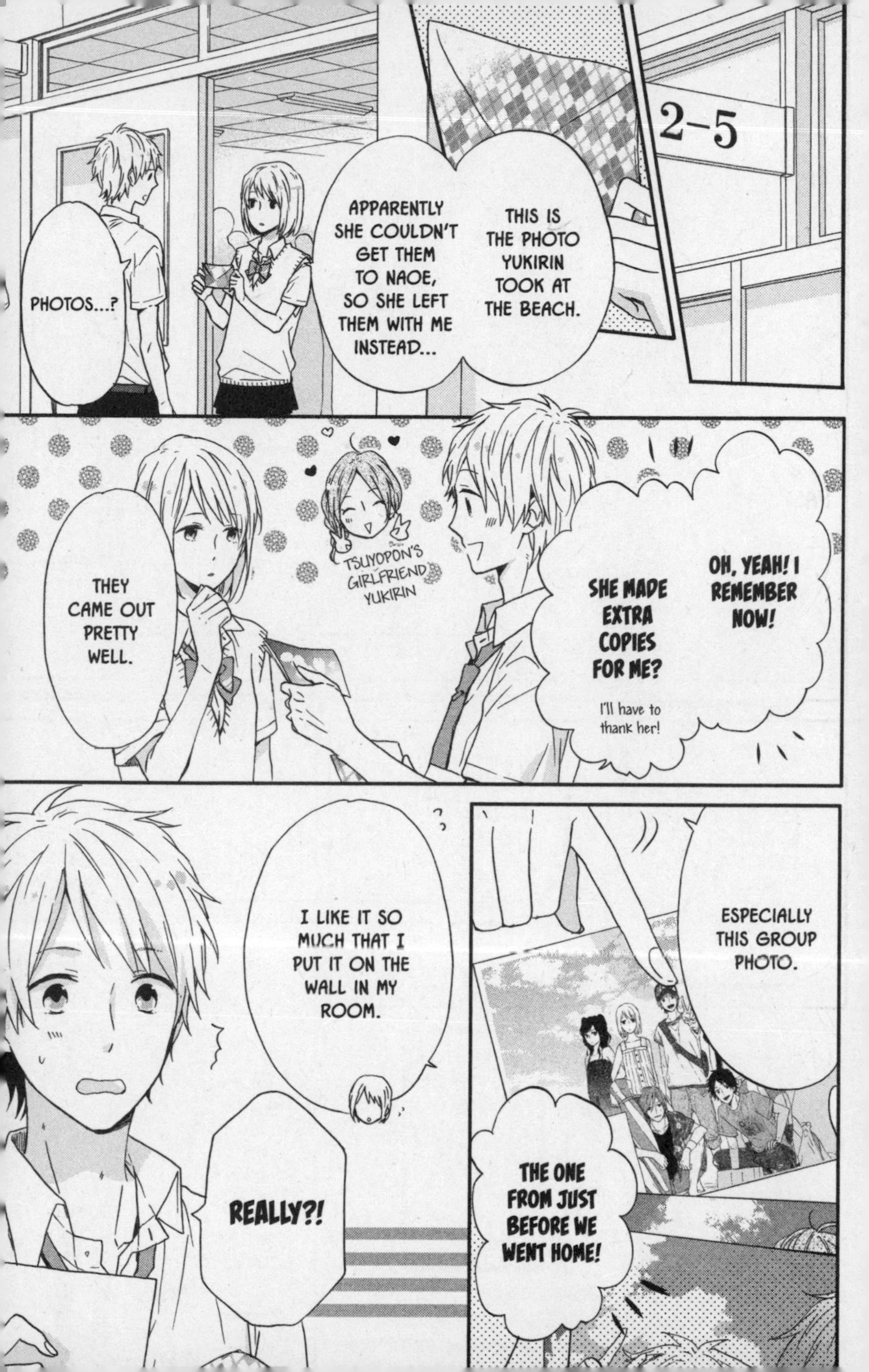
2-5
THIS IS THE PHOTO YUKIRIN TOOK AT THE BEACH.
APPARENTLY SHE COULDN'T GET THEM TO NAOE, SO SHE LEFT THEM WITH ME INSTEAD...
PHOTOS...?
OH, YEAH! I REMEMBER NOW!
SHE MADE EXTRA COPIES FOR ME?
I'll have to thank her!
TSUYOPON'S GIRLFRIEND YUKIRIN
THEY CAME OUT PRETTY WELL.
ESPECIALLY THIS GROUP PHOTO.
THE ONE FROM JUST BEFORE WE WENT HOME!
I LIKE IT SO MUCH THAT I PUT IT ON THE WALL IN MY ROOM.
REALLY?!

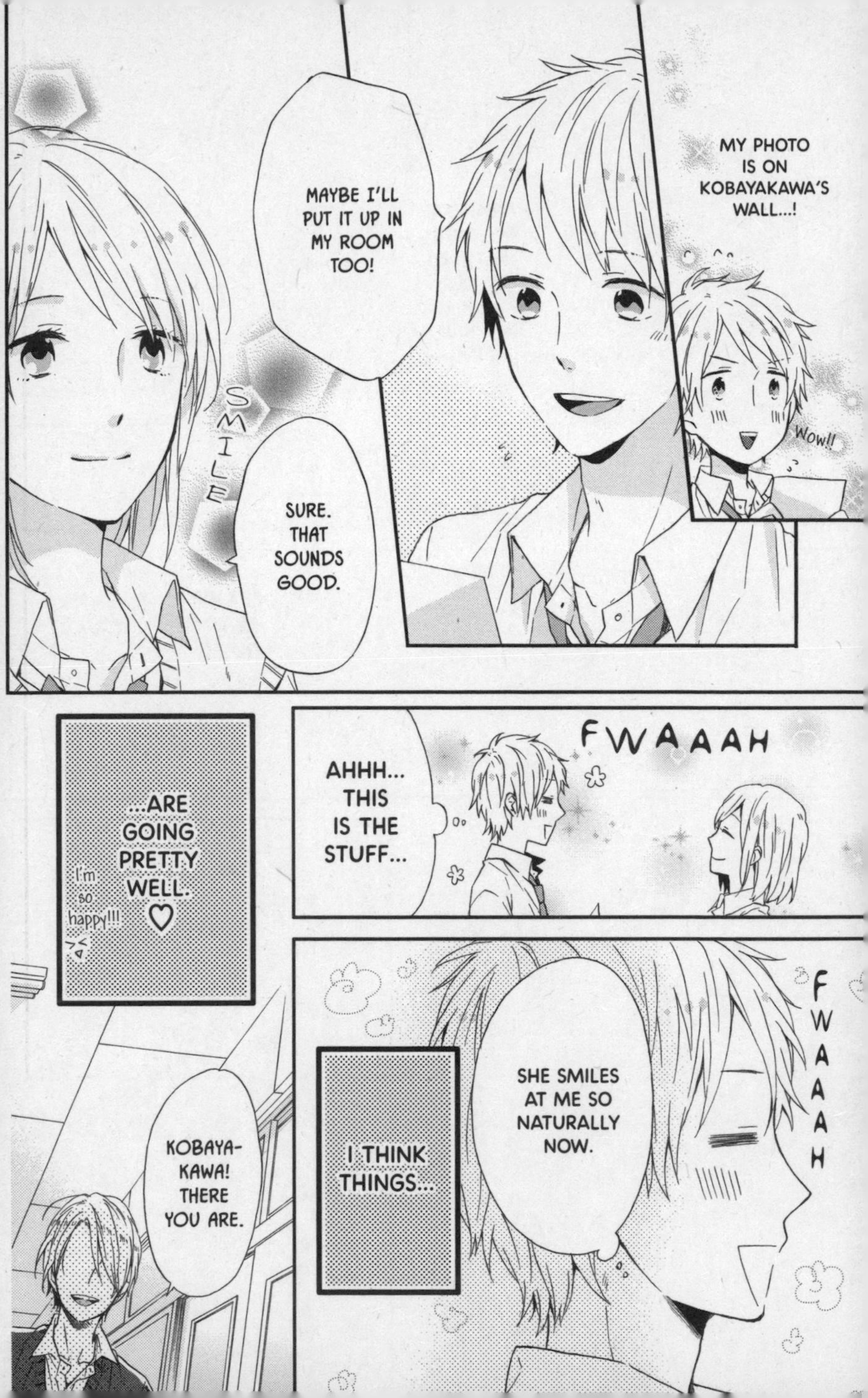
MY PHOTO IS ON KOBAYAKAWA'S WALL...!
WOW!!
MAYBE I'LL PUT IT UP IN MY ROOM TOO!
SMILE
SURE. THAT SOUNDS GOOD.
FWAAAH
AHHH... THIS IS THE STUFF...
FWAAAH
SHE SMILES AT ME SO NATURALLY NOW.
I THINK THINGS...
...ARE GOING PRETTY WELL. ♡
I'm so happy!!!
KOBAYA-KAWA! THERE YOU ARE.

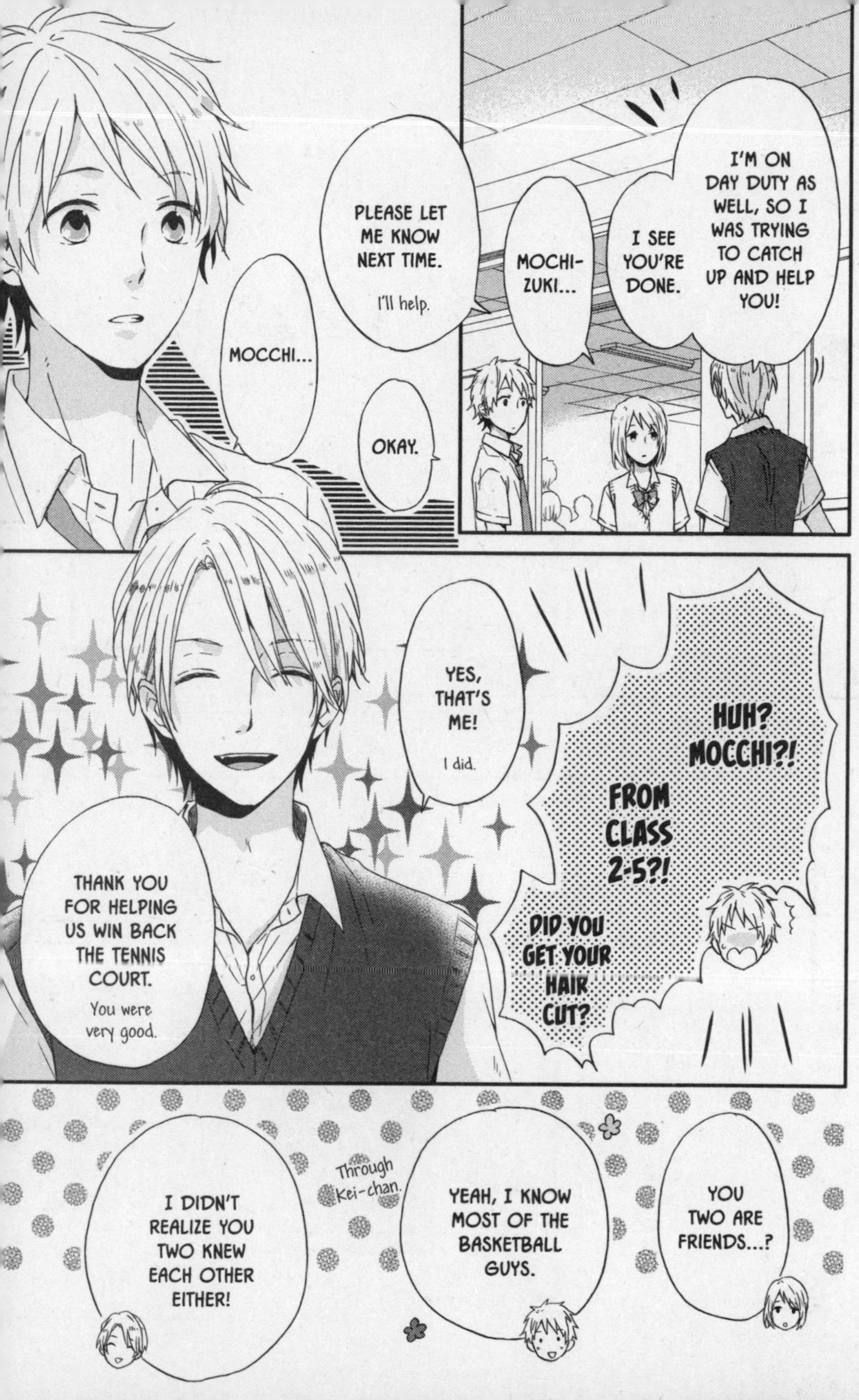
I'M ON DAY DUTY AS WELL, SO I WAS TRYING TO CATCH UP AND HELP YOU!
I SEE YOU'RE DONE.
MOCHI-ZUKI...
PLEASE LET ME KNOW NEXT TIME.
I'll help.
OKAY.
MOCCHI...
HUH? MOCCHI?!
FROM CLASS 2-5?!
DID YOU GET YOUR HAIR CUT?
YES, THAT'S ME!
I did.
THANK YOU FOR HELPING US WIN BACK THE TENNIS COURT.
You were very good.
YOU TWO ARE FRIENDS...?
YEAH, I KNOW MOST OF THE BASKETBALL GUYS.
Through Kei-chan.
I DIDN'T REALIZE YOU TWO KNEW EACH OTHER EITHER!

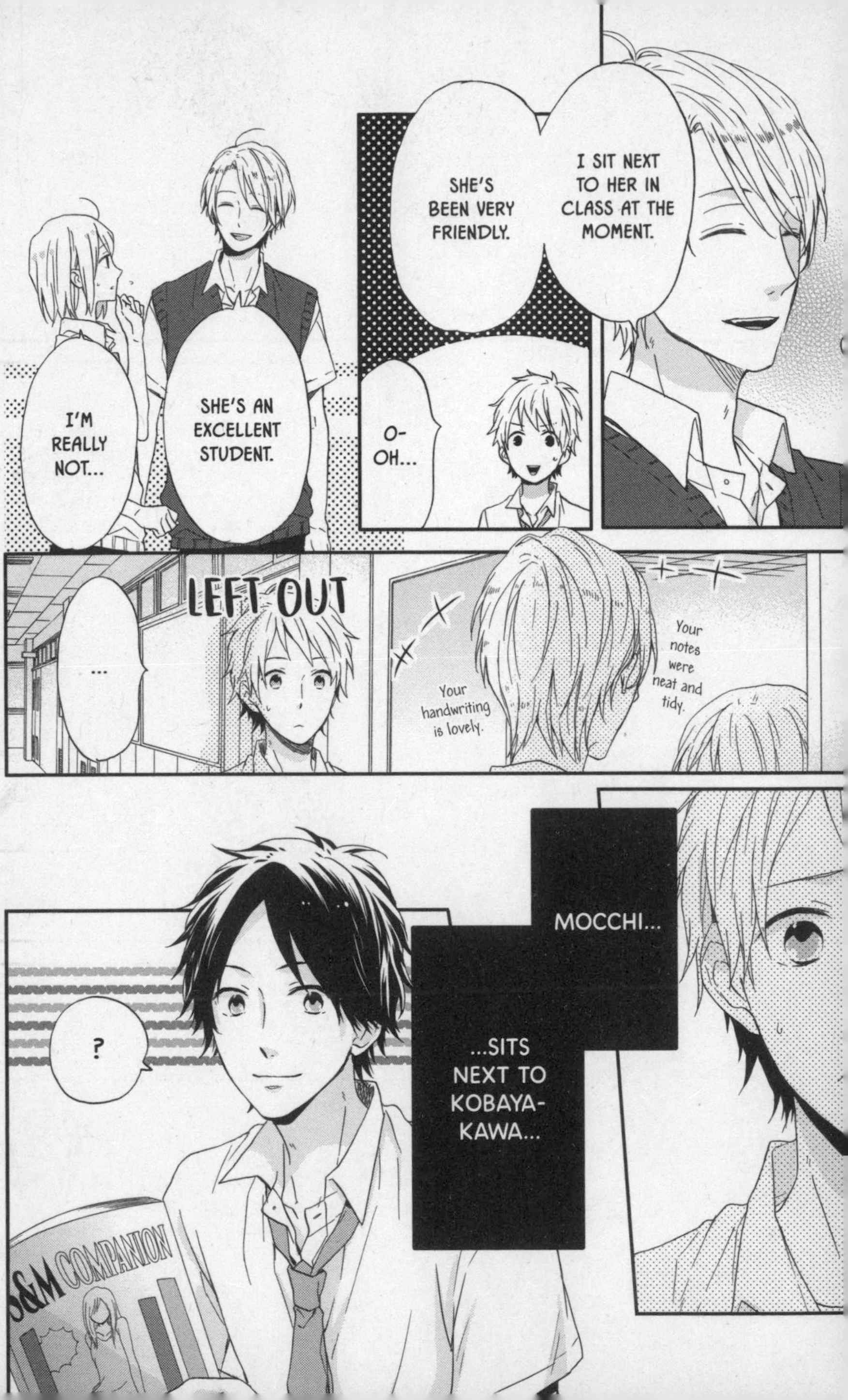
I SIT NEXT TO HER IN CLASS AT THE MOMENT.
SHE'S BEEN VERY FRIENDLY.
O-OH...
SHE'S AN EXCELLENT STUDENT.
I'M REALLY NOT...
Your notes were neat and tidy.
Your handwriting is lovely.
LEFT OUT
...
MOCCHI...
...SITS NEXT TO KOBAYA-KAWA...
?
COMPANION

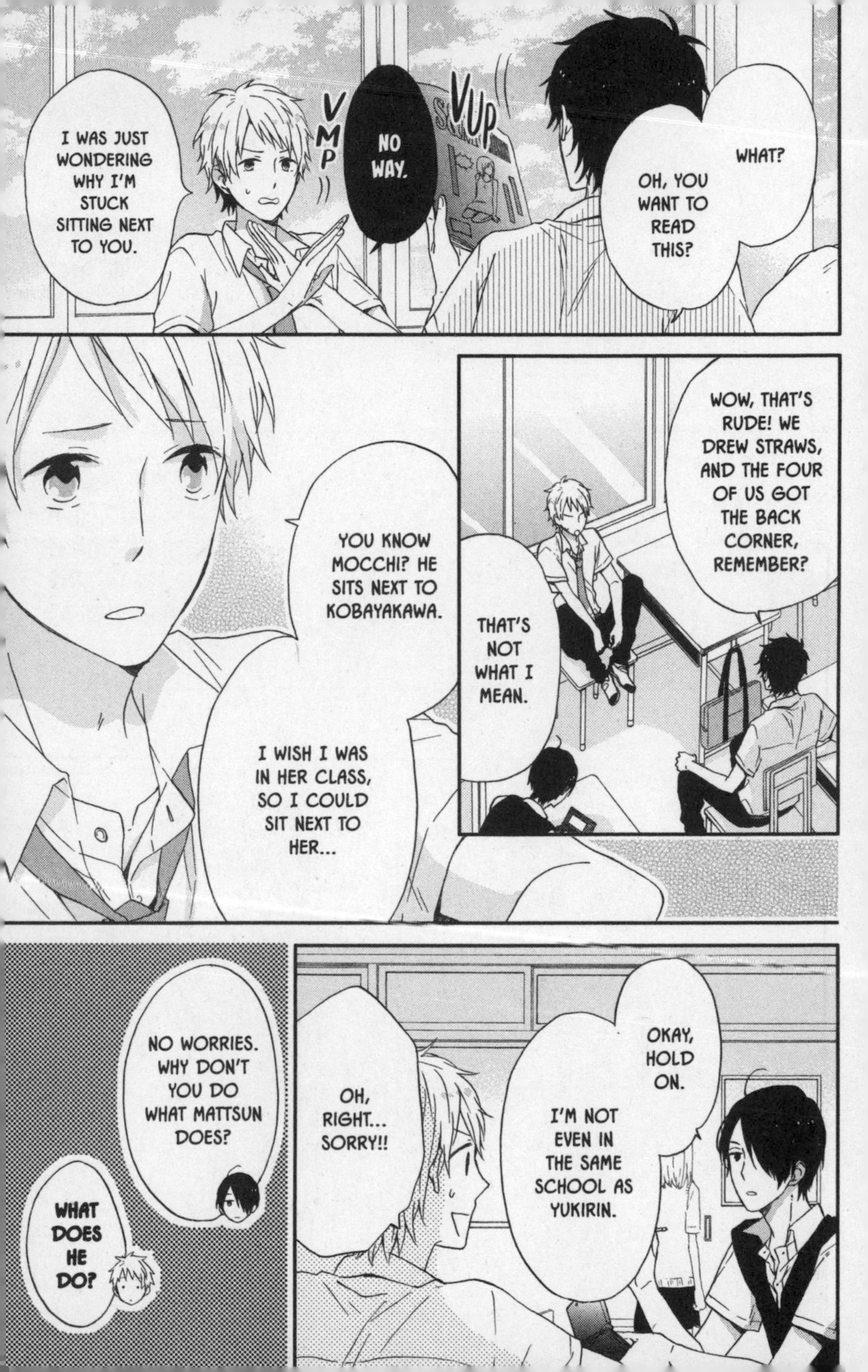
VUP
WHAT?
OH, YOU WANT TO READ THIS?
NO WAY.
VMP
I WAS JUST WONDERING WHY I'M STUCK SITTING NEXT TO YOU.
WOW, THAT'S RUDE! WE DREW STRAWS, AND THE FOUR OF US GOT THE BACK CORNER, REMEMBER?
THAT'S NOT WHAT I MEAN.
YOU KNOW MOCCHI? HE SITS NEXT TO KOBAYAKAWA.
I WISH I WAS IN HER CLASS, SO I COULD SIT NEXT TO HER...
OKAY, HOLD ON.
I'M NOT EVEN IN THE SAME SCHOOL AS YUKIRIN.
OH, RIGHT... SORRY!!
NO WORRIES. WHY DON'T YOU DO WHAT MATTSUN DOES?
WHAT DOES HE DO?

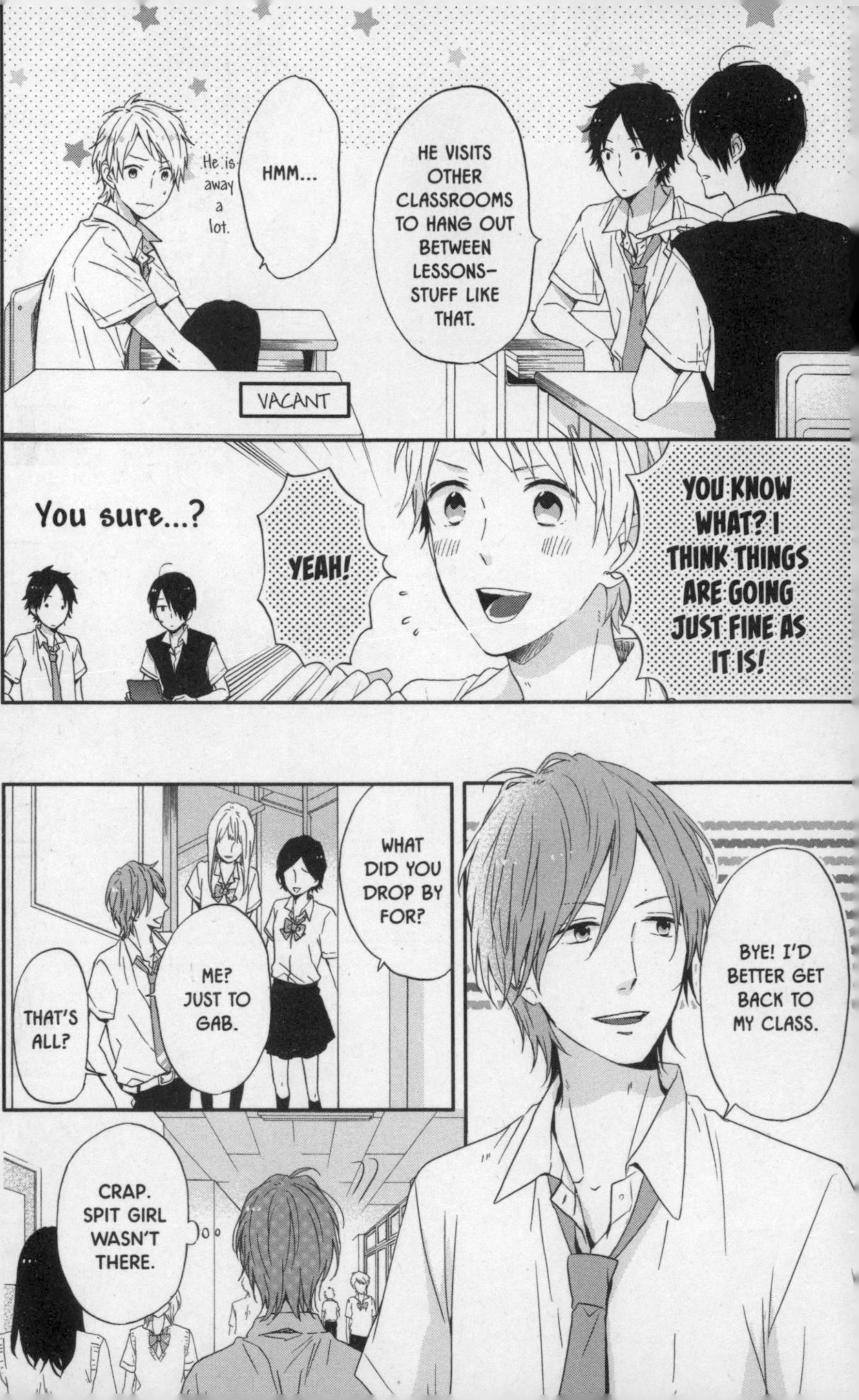
HE VISITS OTHER CLASSROOMS TO HANG OUT BETWEEN LESSONS— STUFF LIKE THAT.
HMM...
He is away a lot.
VACANT
YOU KNOW WHAT? I THINK THINGS ARE GOING JUST FINE AS IT IS!
YEAH!
You sure...?
BYE! I'D BETTER GET BACK TO MY CLASS.
WHAT DID YOU DROP BY FOR?
ME? JUST TO GAB.
THAT'S ALL?
CRAP. SPIT GIRL WASN'T THERE.

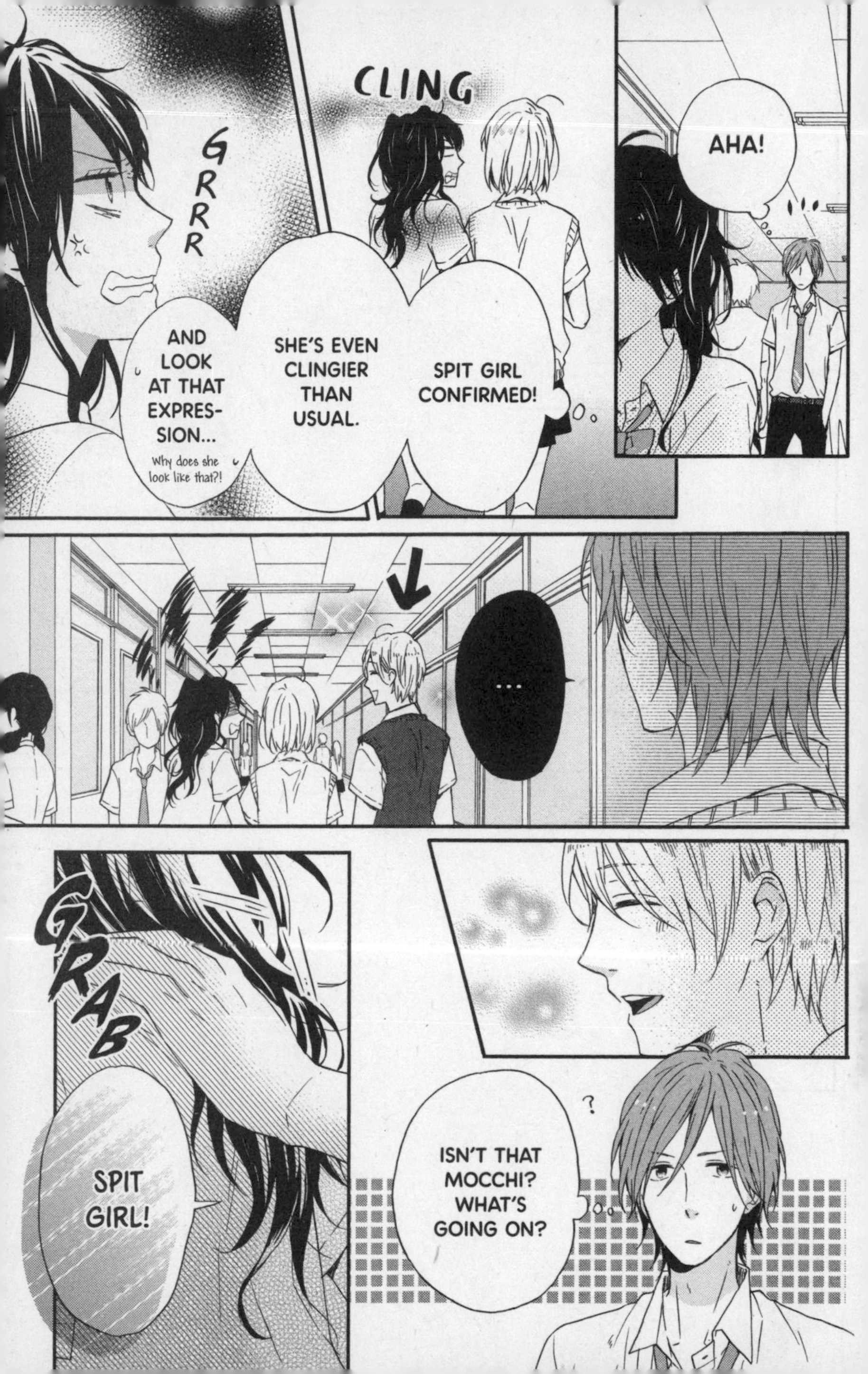
AHA!
CLING
GRRR
SPIT GIRL CONFIRMED!
SHE'S EVEN CLINGIER THAN USUAL.
AND LOOK AT THAT EXPRES- SION...
Why does she look like that?!
...
?
ISN'T THAT MOCCHI? WHAT'S GOING ON?
GRAB
SPIT GIRL!

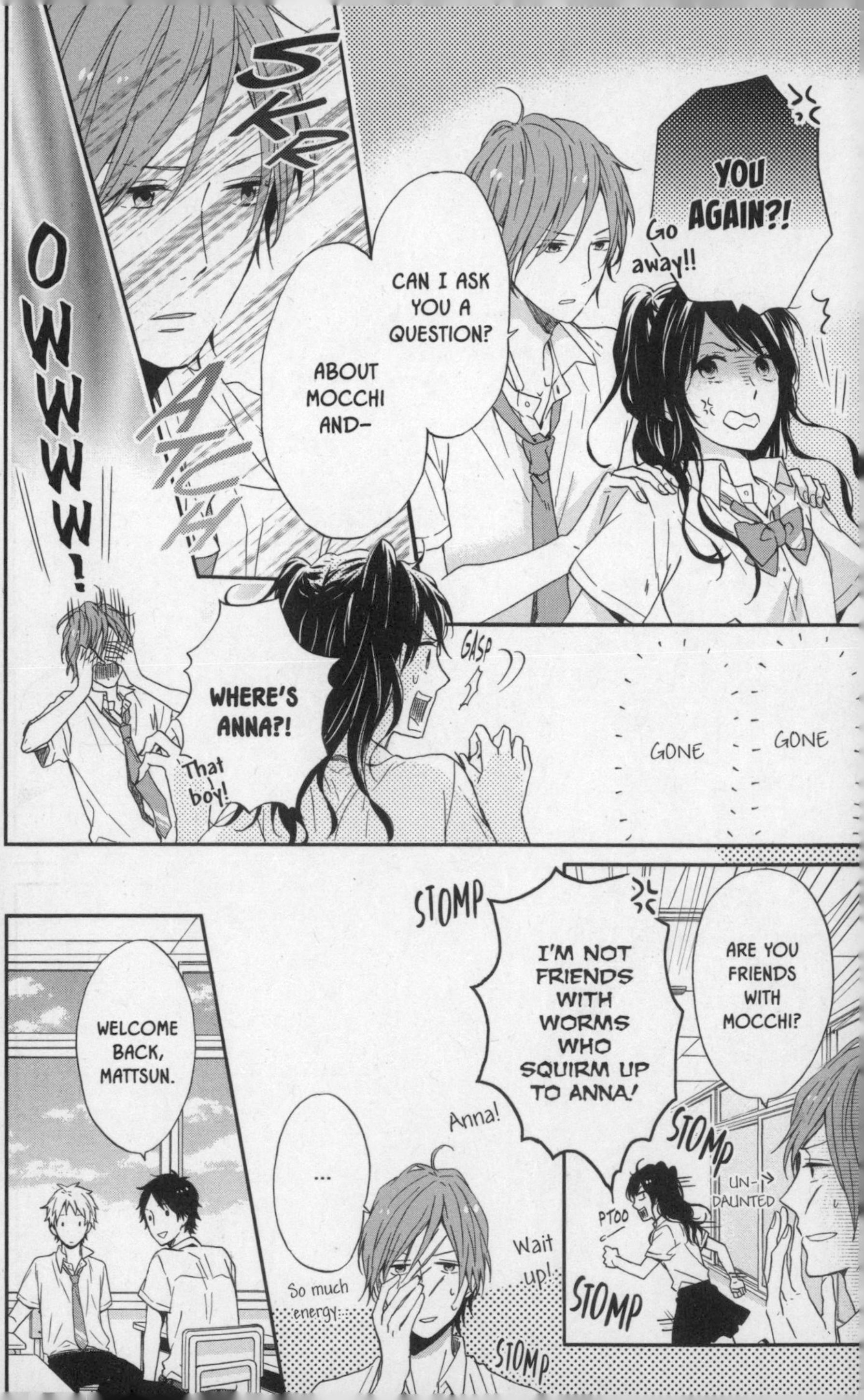
YOU AGAIN?!
Go away!!
CAN I ASK YOU A QUESTION?
ABOUT MOCCHI AND-
SKR
AACH
OWWWW!
GONE
GONE
GASP
WHERE'S ANNA?!
That boy!
ARE YOU FRIENDS WITH MOCCHI?
UN-DAUNTED
STOMP
I'M NOT FRIENDS WITH WORMS WHO SQUIRM UP TO ANNA!
STOMP
PTOO
STOMP
Anna!
Wait up!
...
So much energy...
STOMP
WELCOME BACK, MATTSUN.

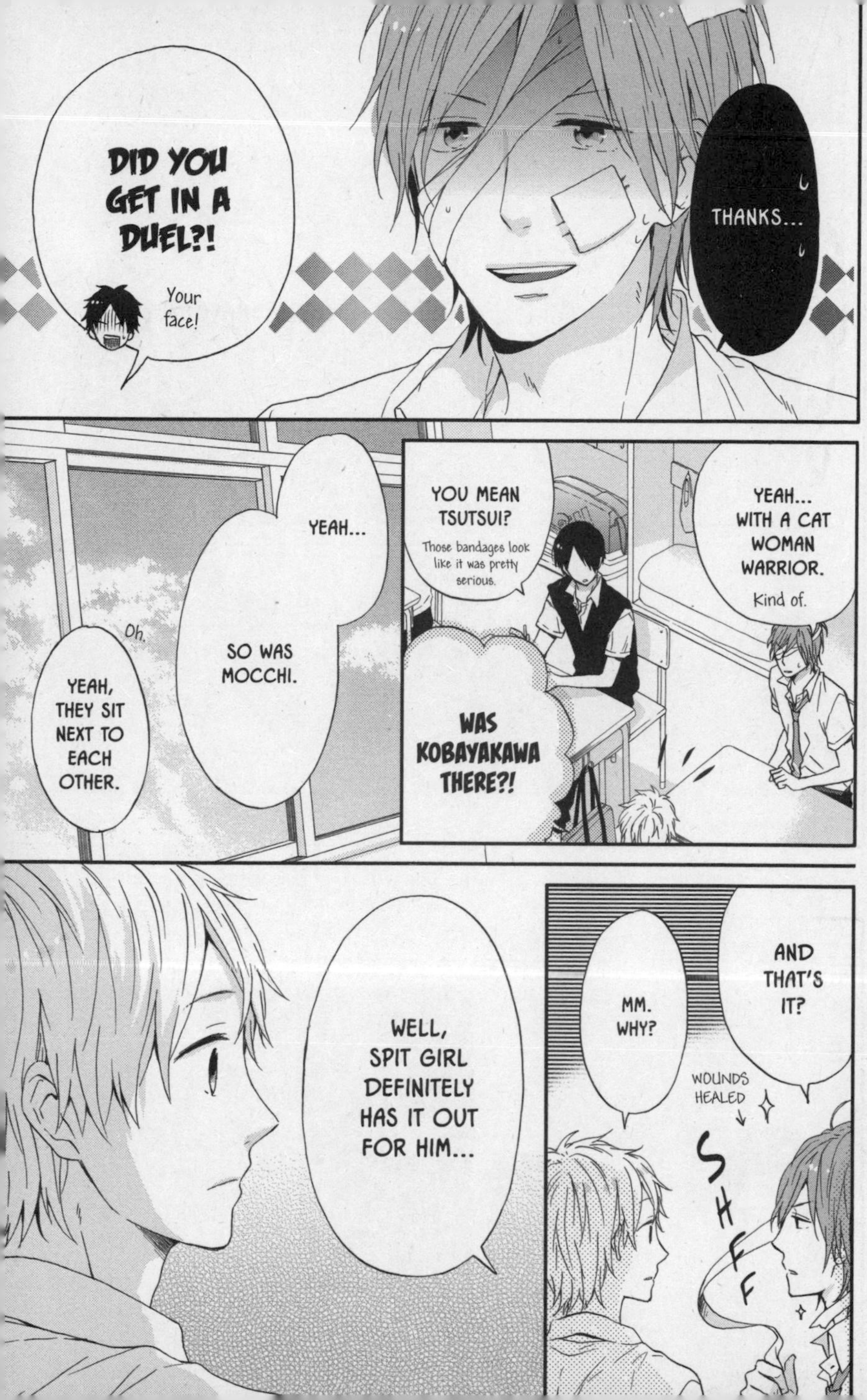
DID YOU GET IN A DUEL?!
Your face!
THANKS...
YEAH... WITH A CAT WOMAN WARRIOR.
Kind of.
YOU MEAN TSUTSUI?
Those bandages look like it was pretty serious.
WAS KOBAYAKAWA THERE?!
YEAH...
SO WAS MOCCHI.
Oh.
YEAH, THEY SIT NEXT TO EACH OTHER.
AND THAT'S IT?
MM. WHY?
WOUNDS HEALED
SHFF
WELL, SPIT GIRL DEFINITELY HAS IT OUT FOR HIM...

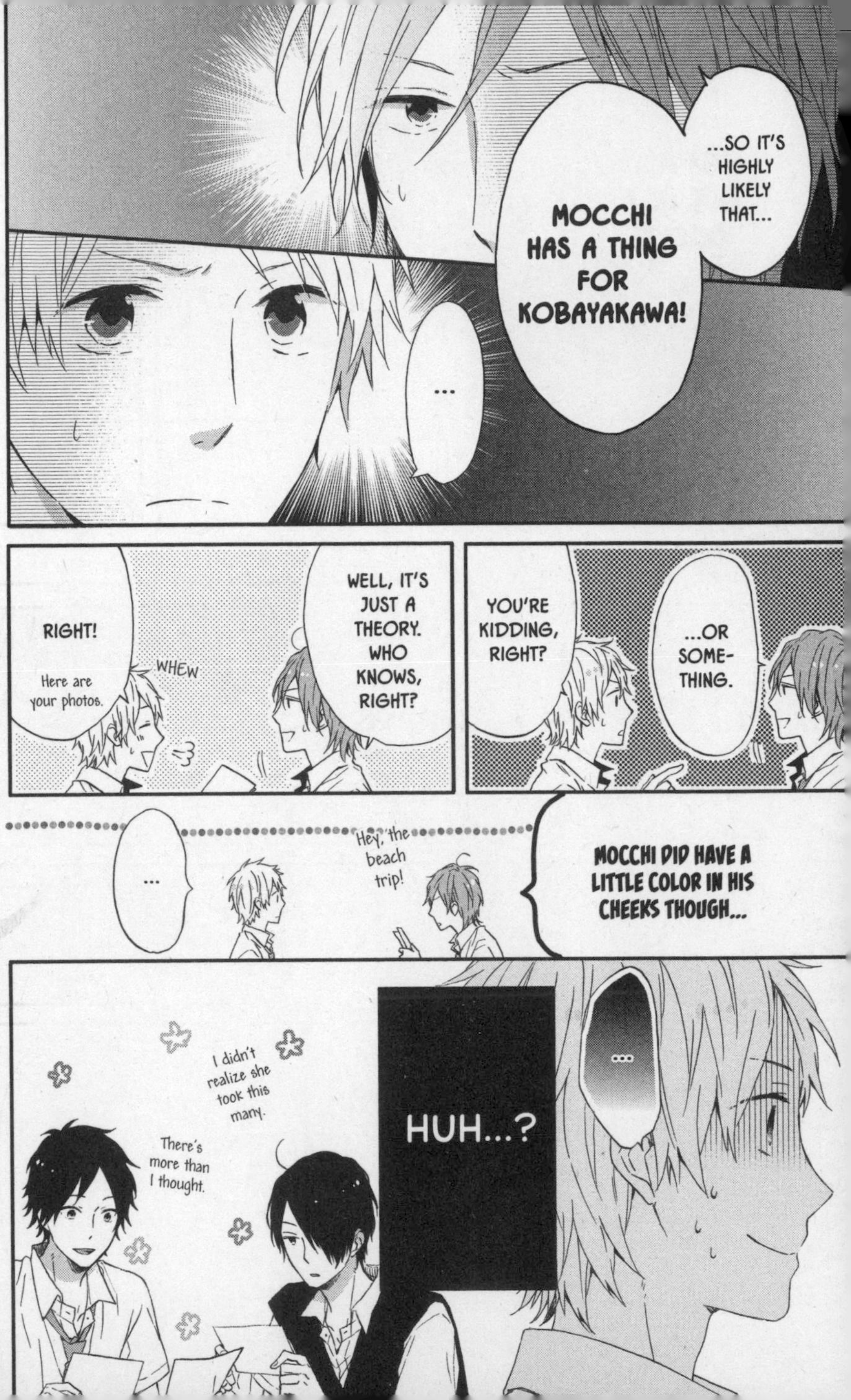
...SO IT'S HIGHLY LIKELY THAT...
MOCCHI HAS A THING FOR KOBAYAKAWA!
...
...OR SOME-THING.
YOU'RE KIDDING, RIGHT?
WELL, IT'S JUST A THEORY. WHO KNOWS, RIGHT?
WHEW
RIGHT!
Here are your photos.
MOCCHI DID HAVE A LITTLE COLOR IN HIS CHEEKS THOUGH...
Hey, the beach trip!
...
...
HUH...?
I didn't realize she took this many.
There's more than I thought.

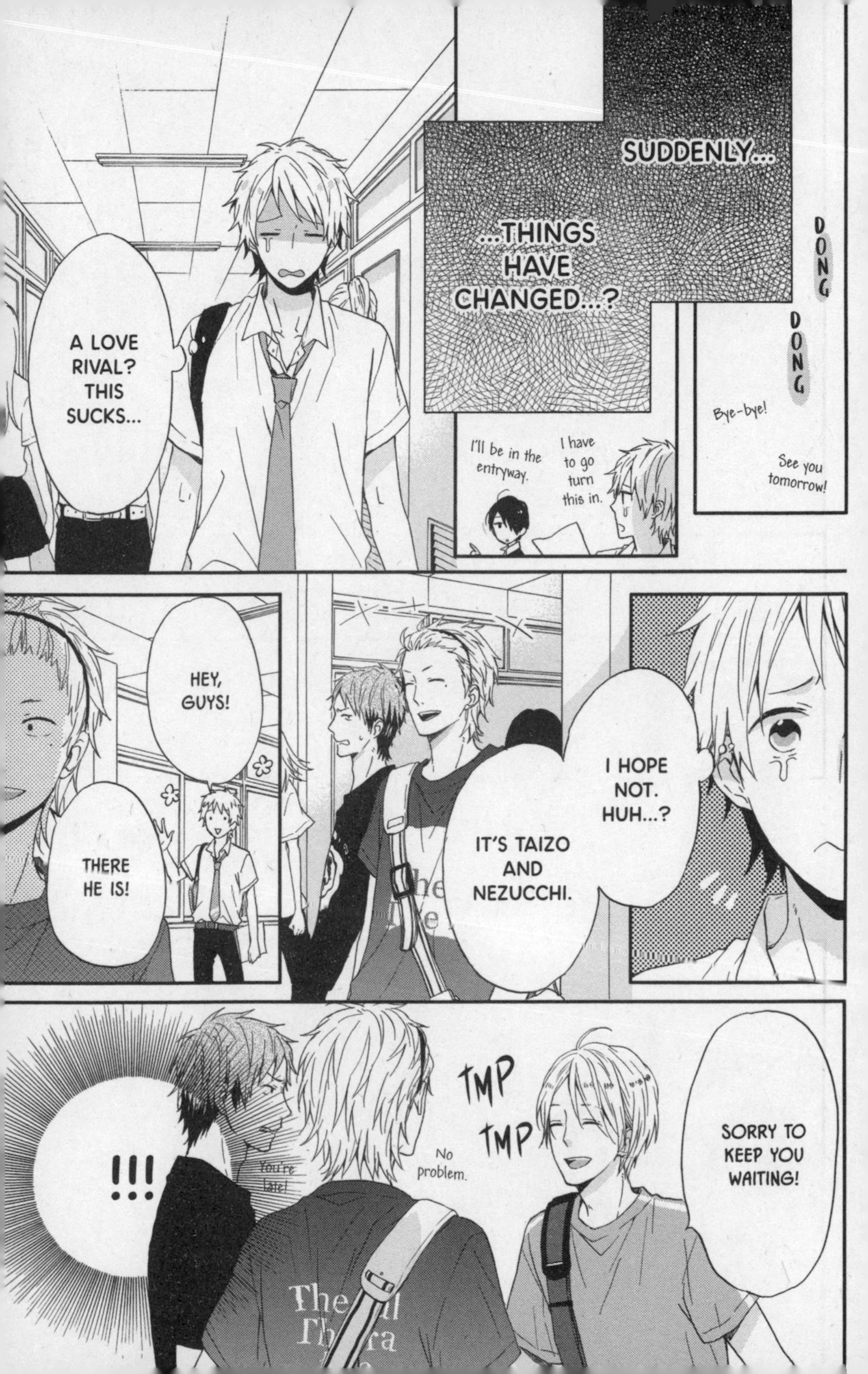
DONG
DONG
Bye-bye!
See you tomorrow!
SUDDENLY...
...THINGS HAVE CHANGED...?
I have to go turn this in.
I'll be in the entryway.
A LOVE RIVAL? THIS SUCKS...
I HOPE NOT. HUH...?
IT'S TAIZO AND NEZUCCHI.
HEY, GUYS!
THERE HE IS!
SORRY TO KEEP YOU WAITING!
TMP
TMP
No problem.
You're late!
!!!

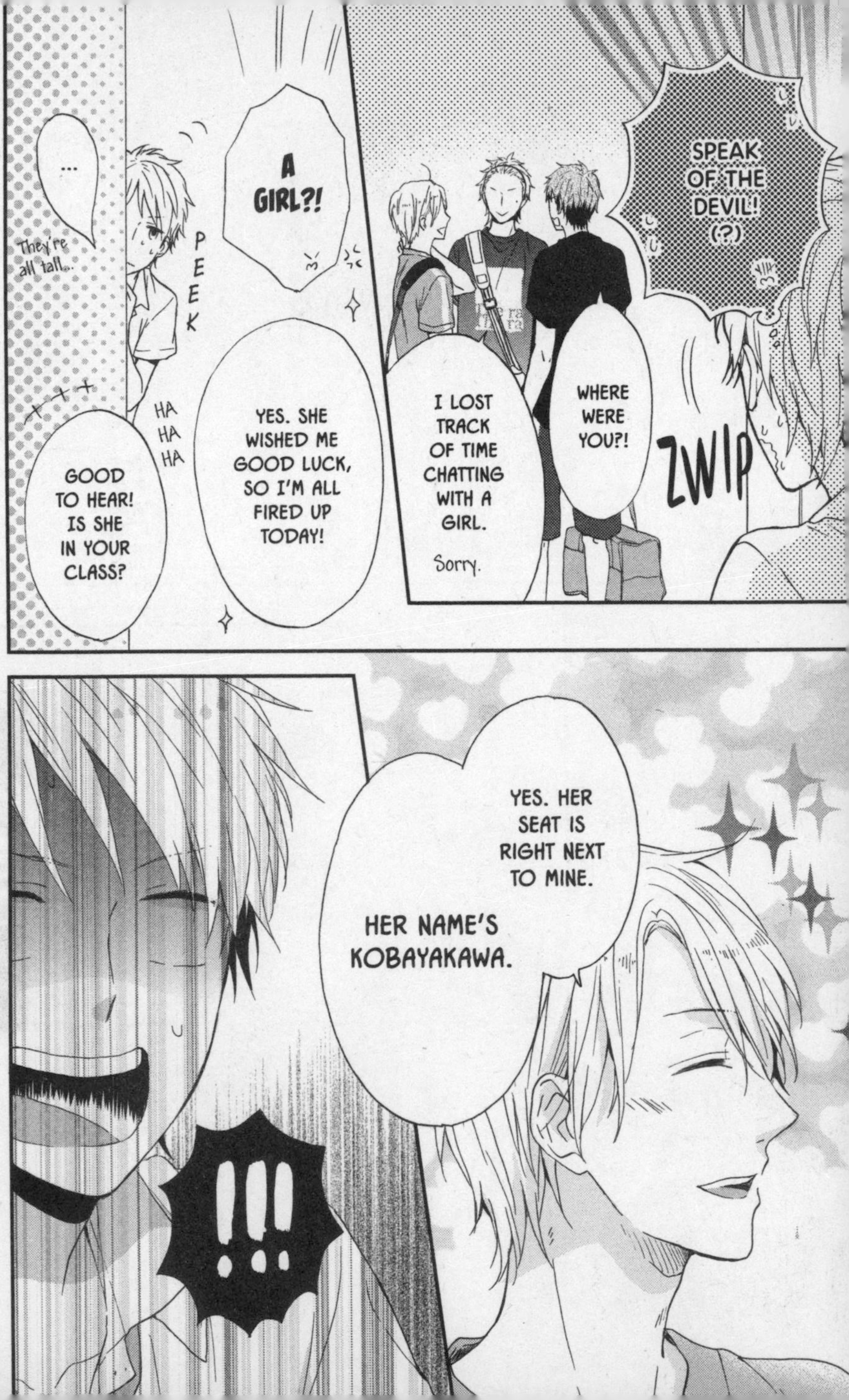
SPEAK OF THE DEVIL! (?)
ZWIP
WHERE WERE YOU?!
I LOST TRACK OF TIME CHATTING WITH A GIRL.
Sorry.
A GIRL?!
PEEK
...
They're all tall...
YES. SHE WISHED ME GOOD LUCK, SO I'M ALL FIRED UP TODAY!
HA HA HA
GOOD TO HEAR! IS SHE IN YOUR CLASS?
YES. HER SEAT IS RIGHT NEXT TO MINE.
HER NAME'S KOBAYAKAWA.
!!!

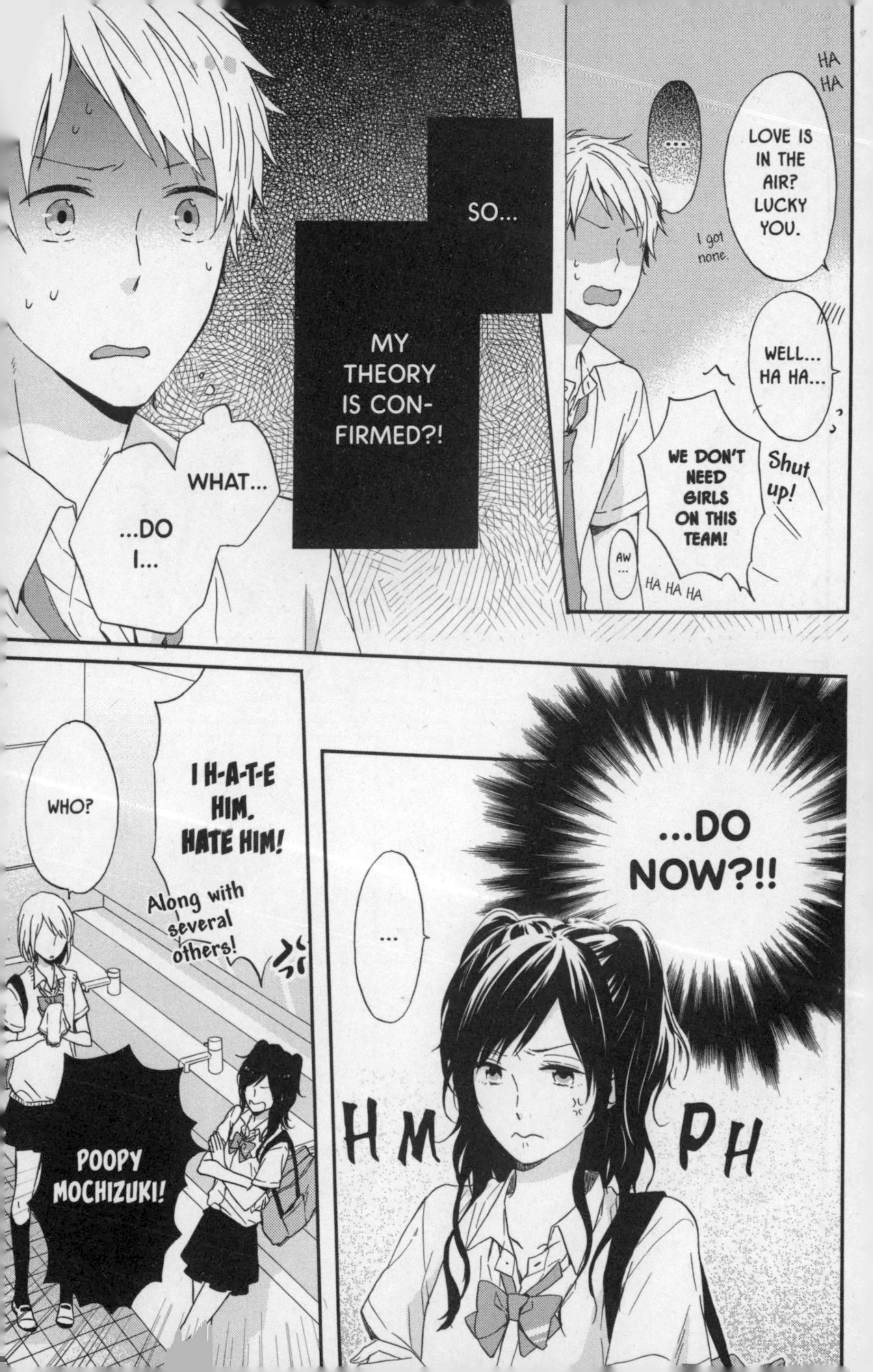

HA HA
...
LOVE IS IN THE AIR? LUCKY YOU.
I got none.
WELL... HA HA...
Shut up!
WE DON'T NEED GIRLS ON THIS TEAM!
AW...
HA HA HA
SO...
MY THEORY IS CON-FIRMED?!
WHAT...
...DO I...
...DO NOW?!!
...
HMPH
I H-A-T-E HIM. HATE HIM!
Along with several others!
WHO?
POOPY MOCHIZUKI!

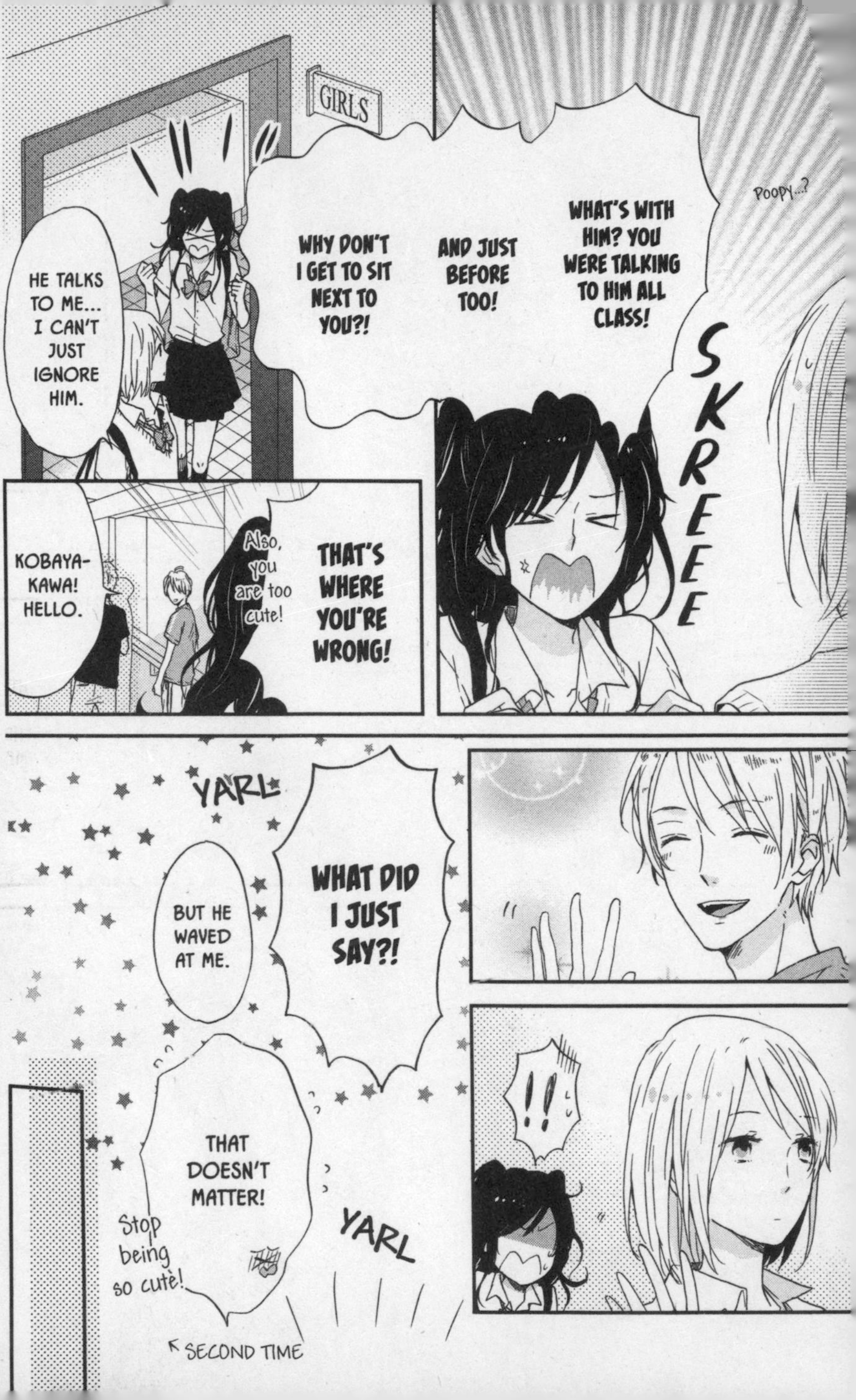
Poopy...?
WHAT'S WITH HIM? YOU WERE TALKING TO HIM ALL CLASS!
AND JUST BEFORE TOO!
WHY DON'T I GET TO SIT NEXT TO YOU?!
SKREEE
GIRLS
HE TALKS TO ME... I CAN'T JUST IGNORE HIM.
THAT'S WHERE YOU'RE WRONG!
Also, you are too cute!
KOBAYA-KAWA! HELLO.
!!
YARL
WHAT DID I JUST SAY?!
BUT HE WAVED AT ME.
YARL
THAT DOESN'T MATTER!
Stop being so cute!
SECOND TIME

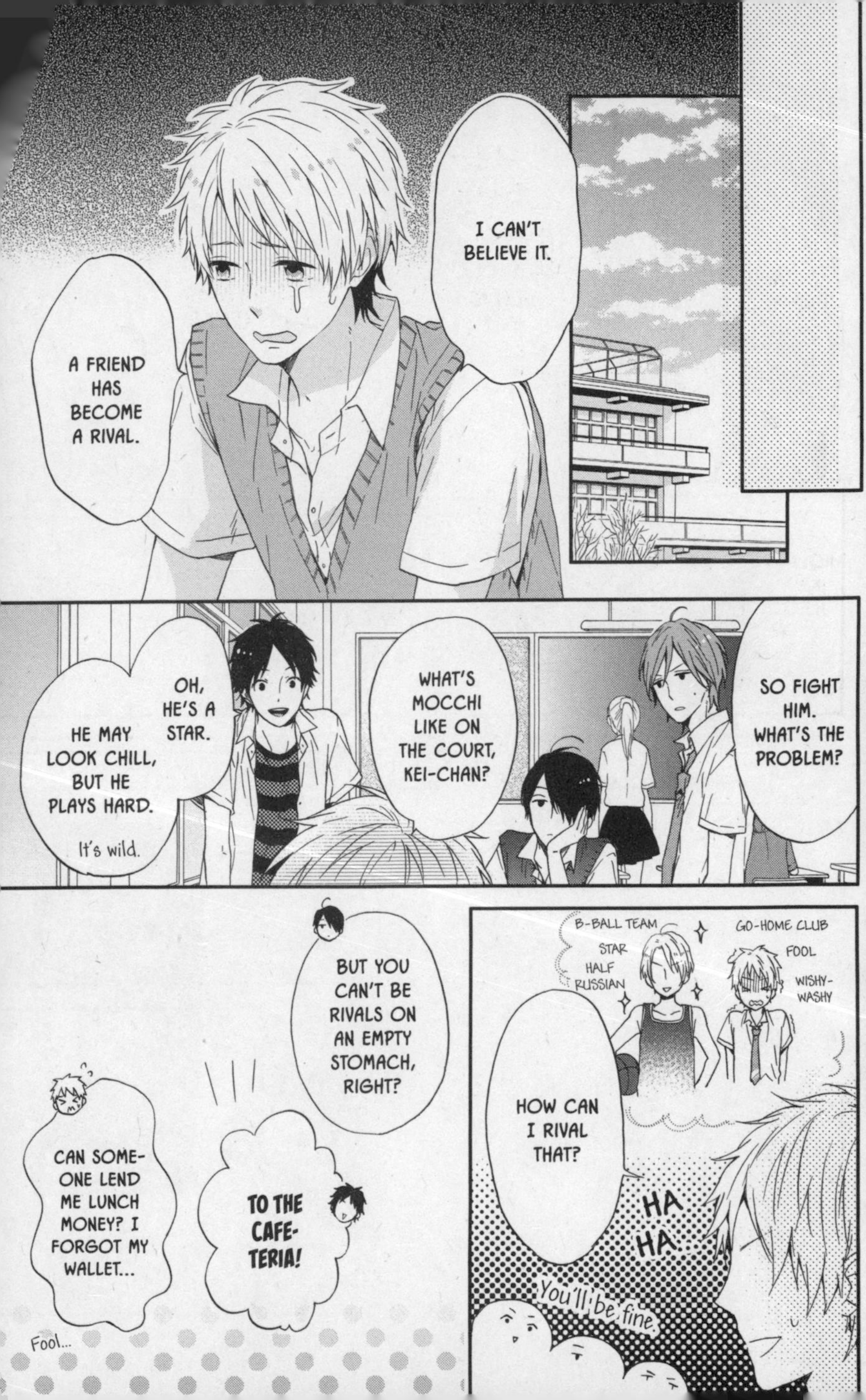
I CAN'T BELIEVE IT.
A FRIEND HAS BECOME A RIVAL.
SO FIGHT HIM. WHAT'S THE PROBLEM?
WHAT'S MOCCHI LIKE ON THE COURT, KEI-CHAN?
OH, HE'S A STAR.
HE MAY LOOK CHILL, BUT HE PLAYS HARD.
It's wild.
GO-HOME CLUB
FOOL
WISHY-WASHY
B-BALL TEAM
STAR
HALF RUSSIAN
HOW CAN I RIVAL THAT?
HA HA
You'll be fine.
BUT YOU CAN'T BE RIVALS ON AN EMPTY STOMACH, RIGHT?
TO THE CAFETERIA!
CAN SOMEONE LEND ME LUNCH MONEY? I FORGOT MY WALLET...
Fool...

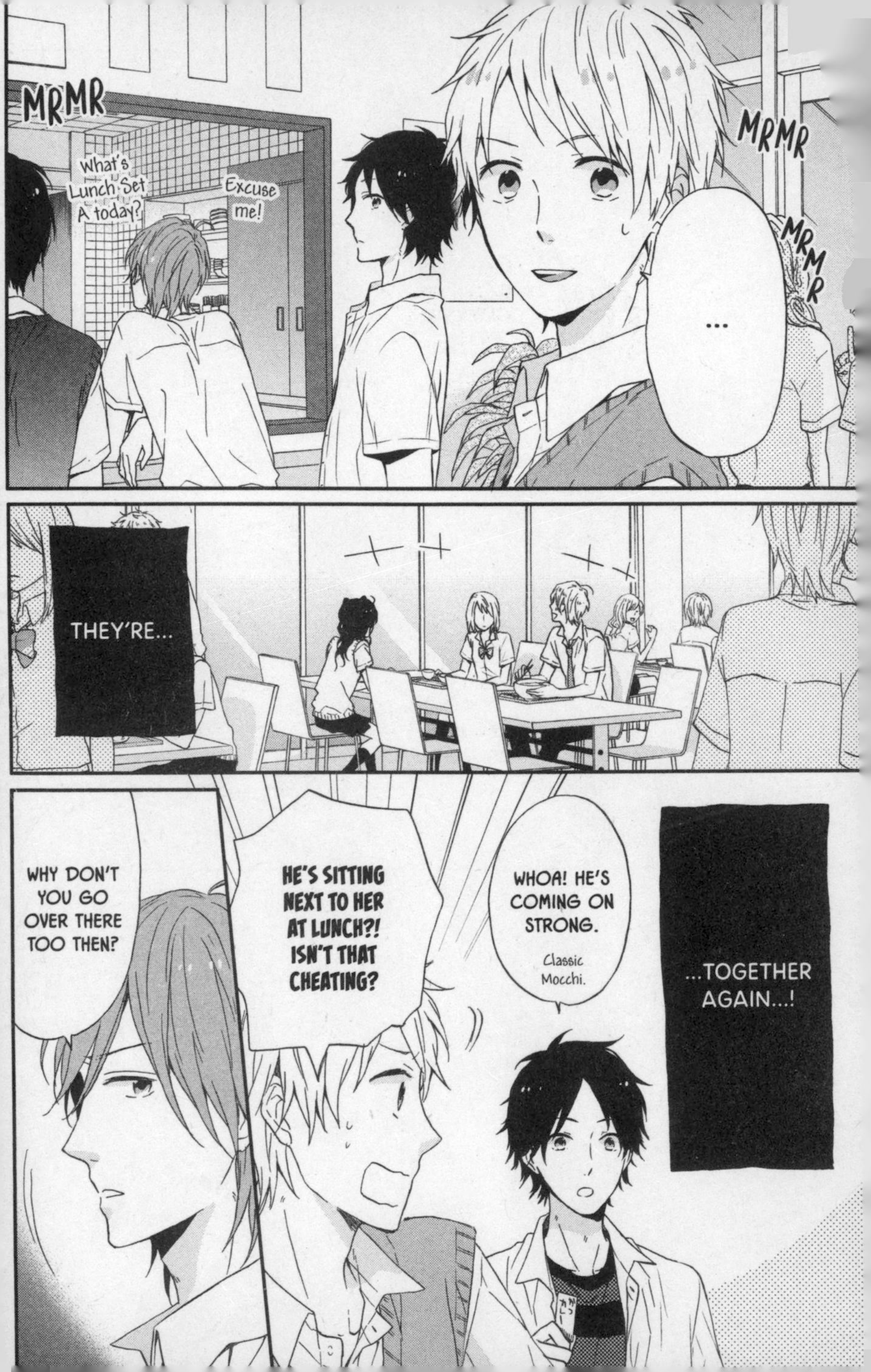
MRMR
MRMR
...
Excuse me!
What's Lunch Set A today?
MRMR
THEY'RE...
...TOGETHER AGAIN...!
WHOA! HE'S COMING ON STRONG.
Classic Mocchi.
HE'S SITTING NEXT TO HER AT LUNCH?! ISN'T THAT CHEATING?
WHY DON'T YOU GO OVER THERE TOO THEN?

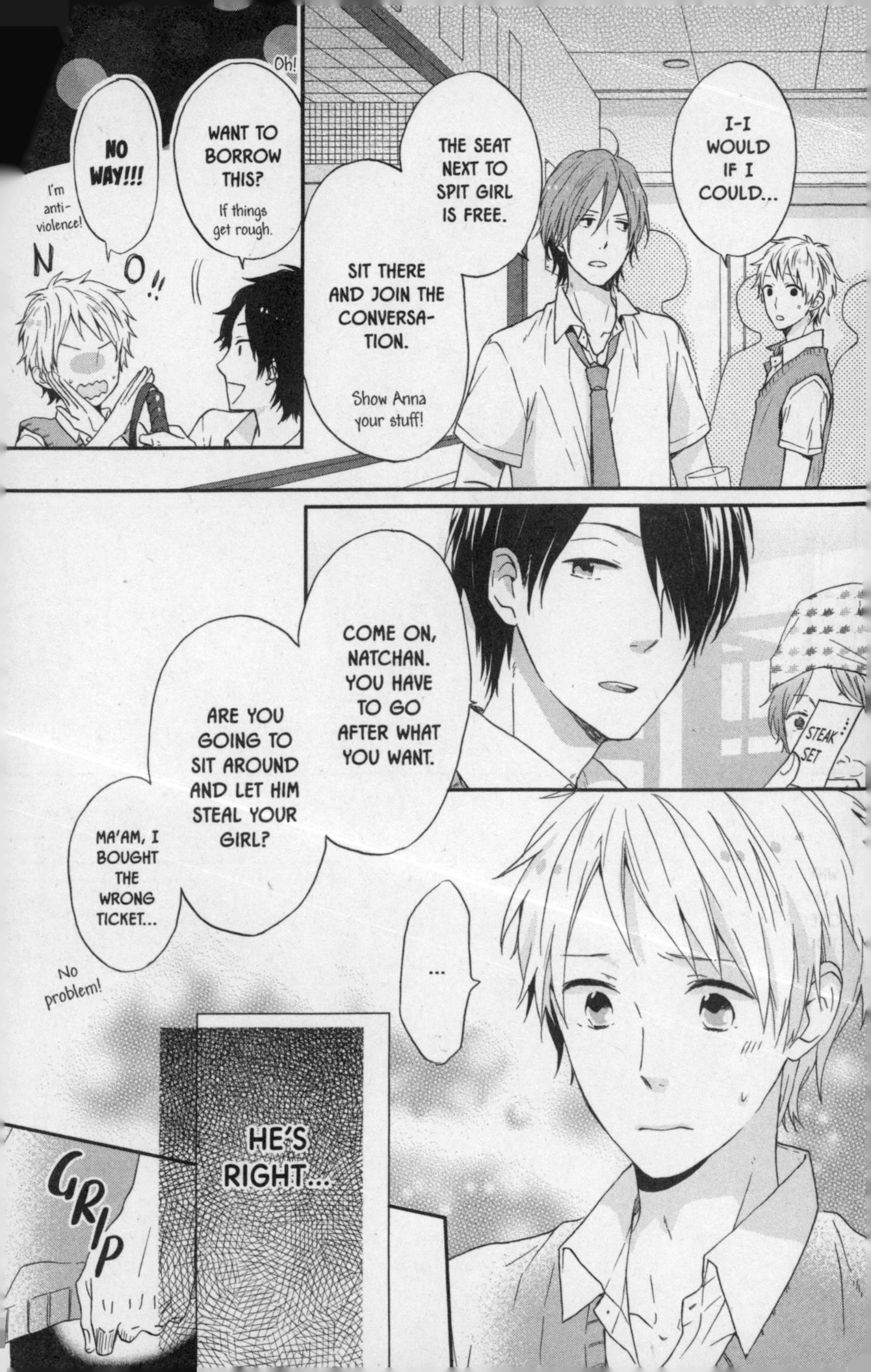
I-I WOULD IF I COULD...
THE SEAT NEXT TO SPIT GIRL IS FREE.
SIT THERE AND JOIN THE CONVERSATION.
Show Anna your stuff!
Oh!
WANT TO BORROW THIS?
If things get rough.
NO WAY!!!
I'm anti-violence!
NO!!
COME ON, NATCHAN. YOU HAVE TO GO AFTER WHAT YOU WANT.
ARE YOU GOING TO SIT AROUND AND LET HIM STEAL YOUR GIRL?
STEAK SET
MA'AM, I BOUGHT THE WRONG TICKET...
No problem!
...
HE'S RIGHT...
GRIP

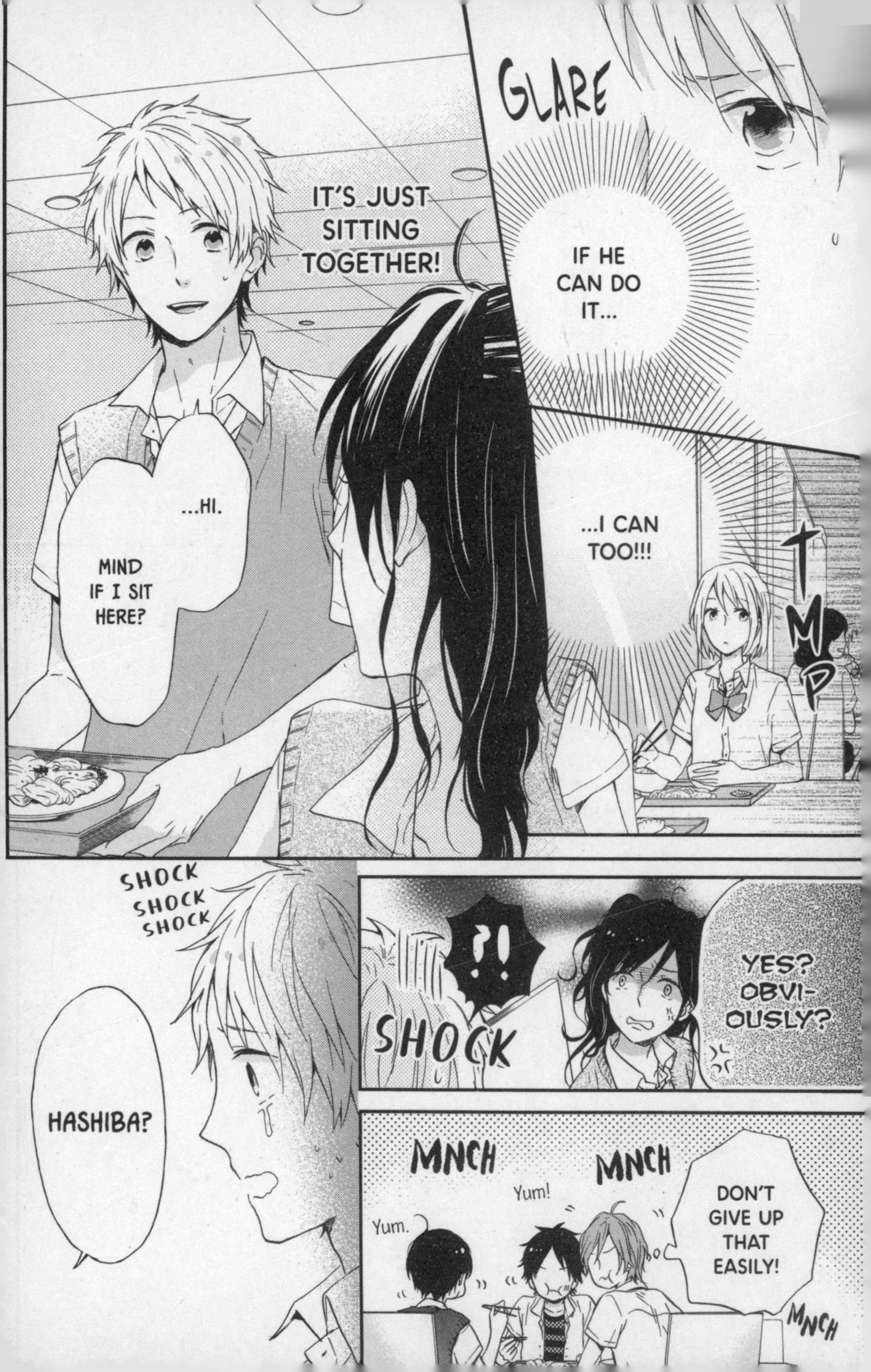
GLARE
IF HE CAN DO IT...
...I CAN TOO!!!
TMP
IT'S JUST SITTING TOGETHER!
...HI.
MIND IF I SIT HERE?
?!
SHOCK
YES? OBVI-OUSLY?
MNCH
MNCH
Yum!
Yum.
DON'T GIVE UP THAT EASILY!
MNCH
SHOCK SHOCK SHOCK
HASHIBA?

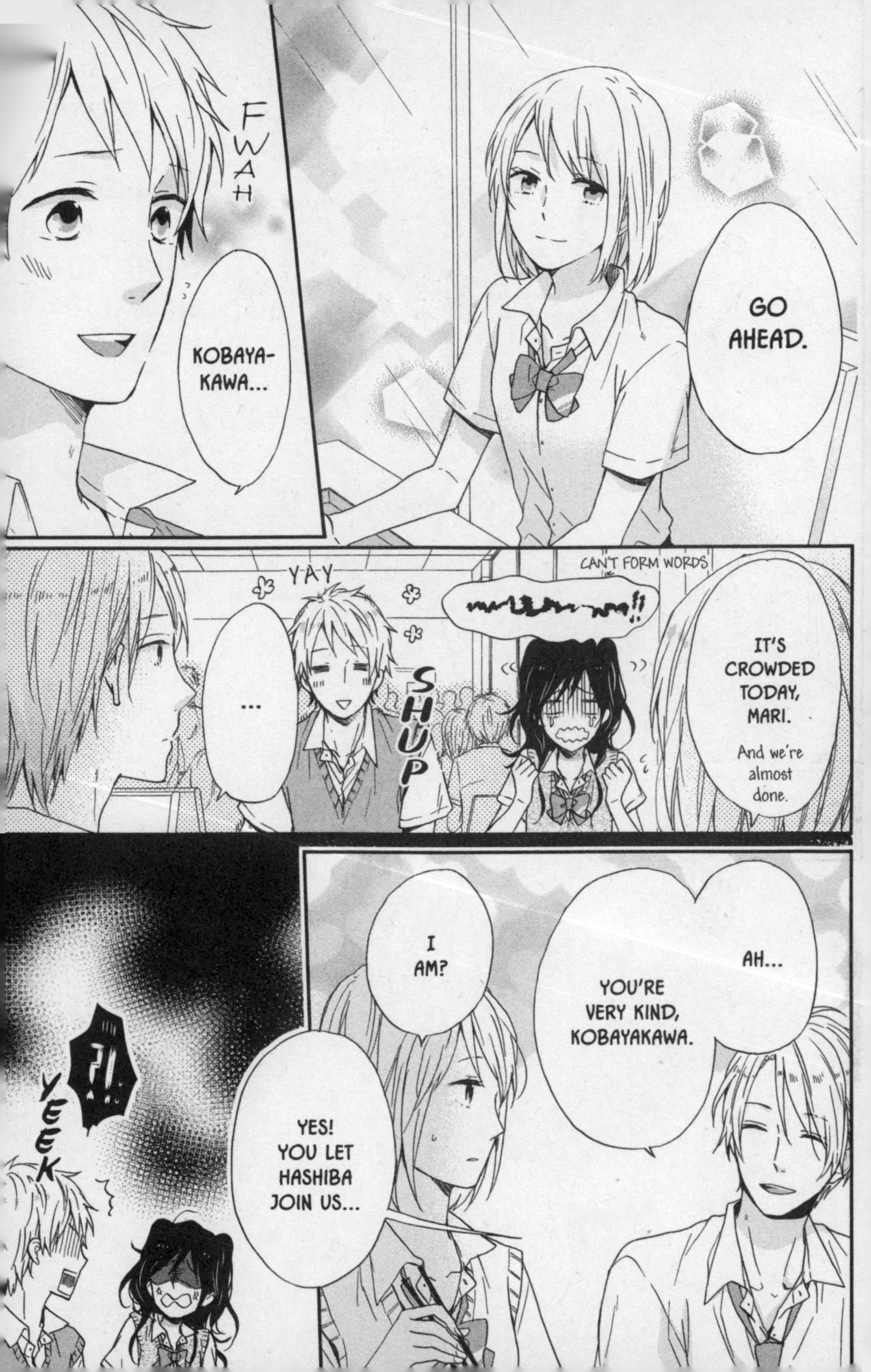
GO AHEAD.
FWAH
KOBAYA-KAWA...
IT'S CROWDED TODAY, MARI.
And we're almost done.
CAN'T FORM WORDS
SHUP
YAY
...
AH...
YOU'RE VERY KIND, KOBAYAKAWA.
I AM?
YES! YOU LET HASHIBA JOIN US...
?!
YEEK

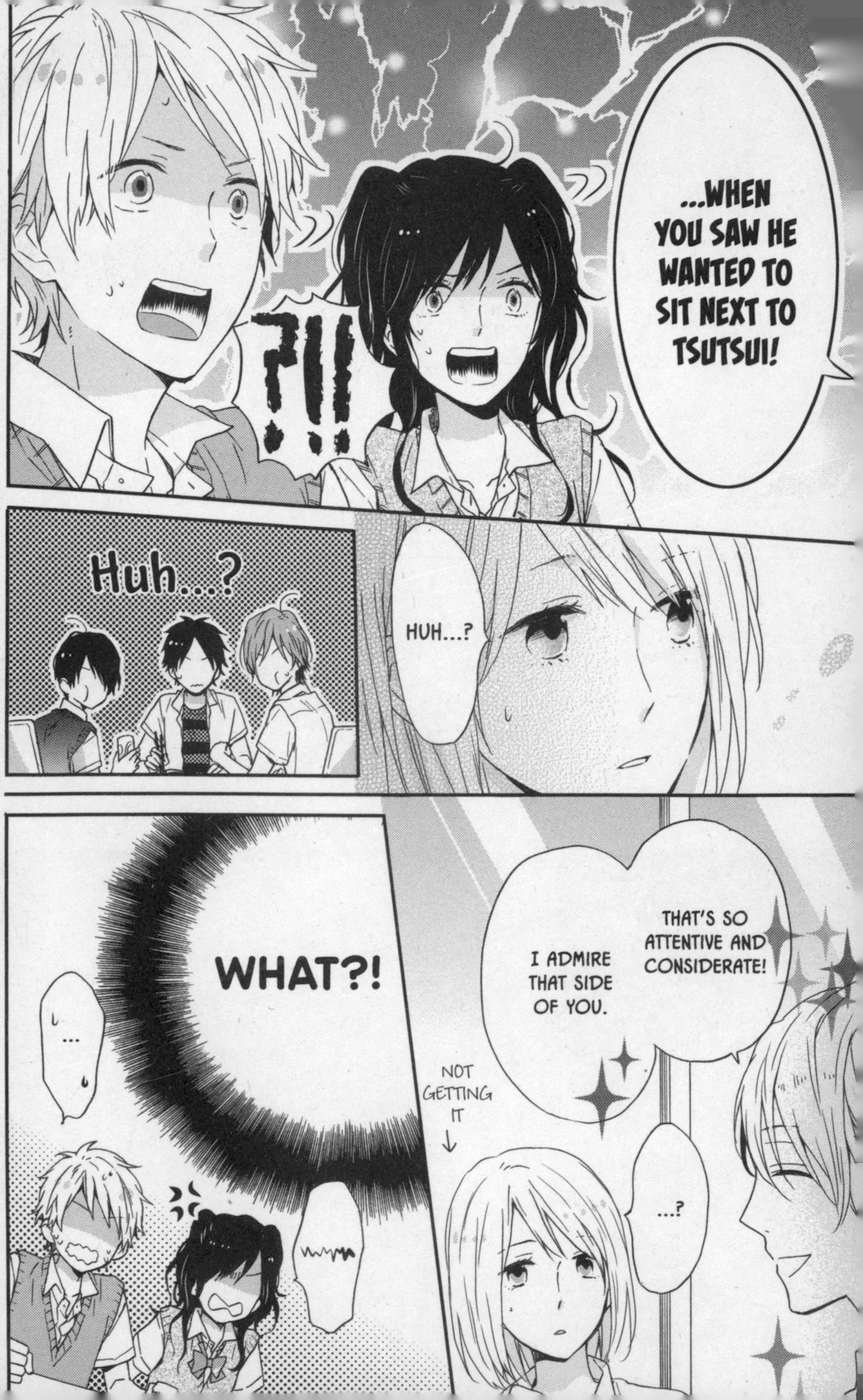
...WHEN YOU SAW HE WANTED TO SIT NEXT TO TSUTSUI!
?!!
HUH...?
Huh...?
THAT'S SO ATTENTIVE AND CONSIDERATE!
I ADMIRE THAT SIDE OF YOU.
NOT GETTING IT
...?
WHAT?!
...

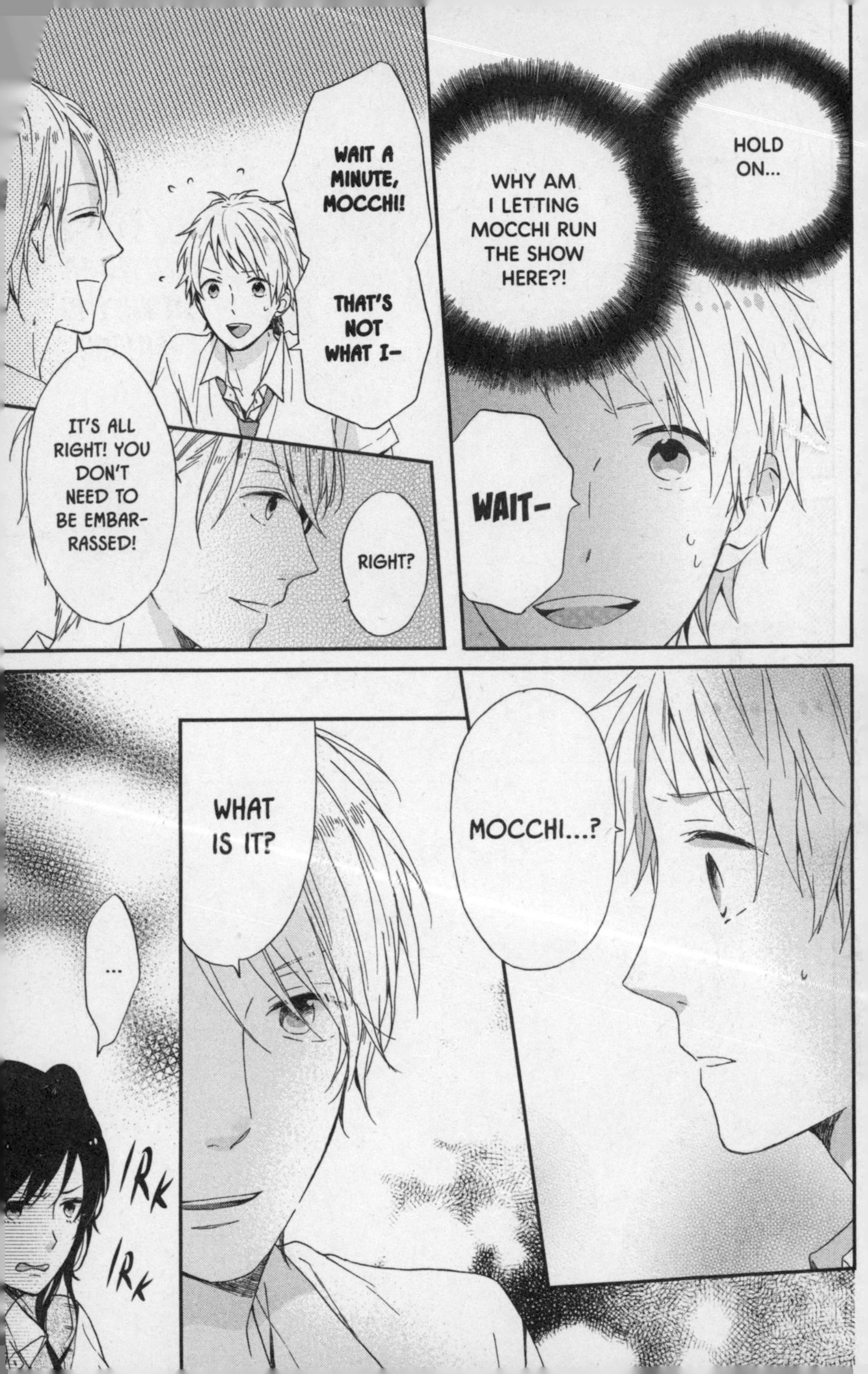
HOLD ON...
WHY AM I LETTING MOCCHI RUN THE SHOW HERE?!
WAIT-
WAIT A MINUTE, MOCCHI!
THAT'S NOT WHAT I-
IT'S ALL RIGHT! YOU DON'T NEED TO BE EMBAR-RASSED!
RIGHT?
MOCCHI...?
WHAT IS IT?
...
IRK
IRK

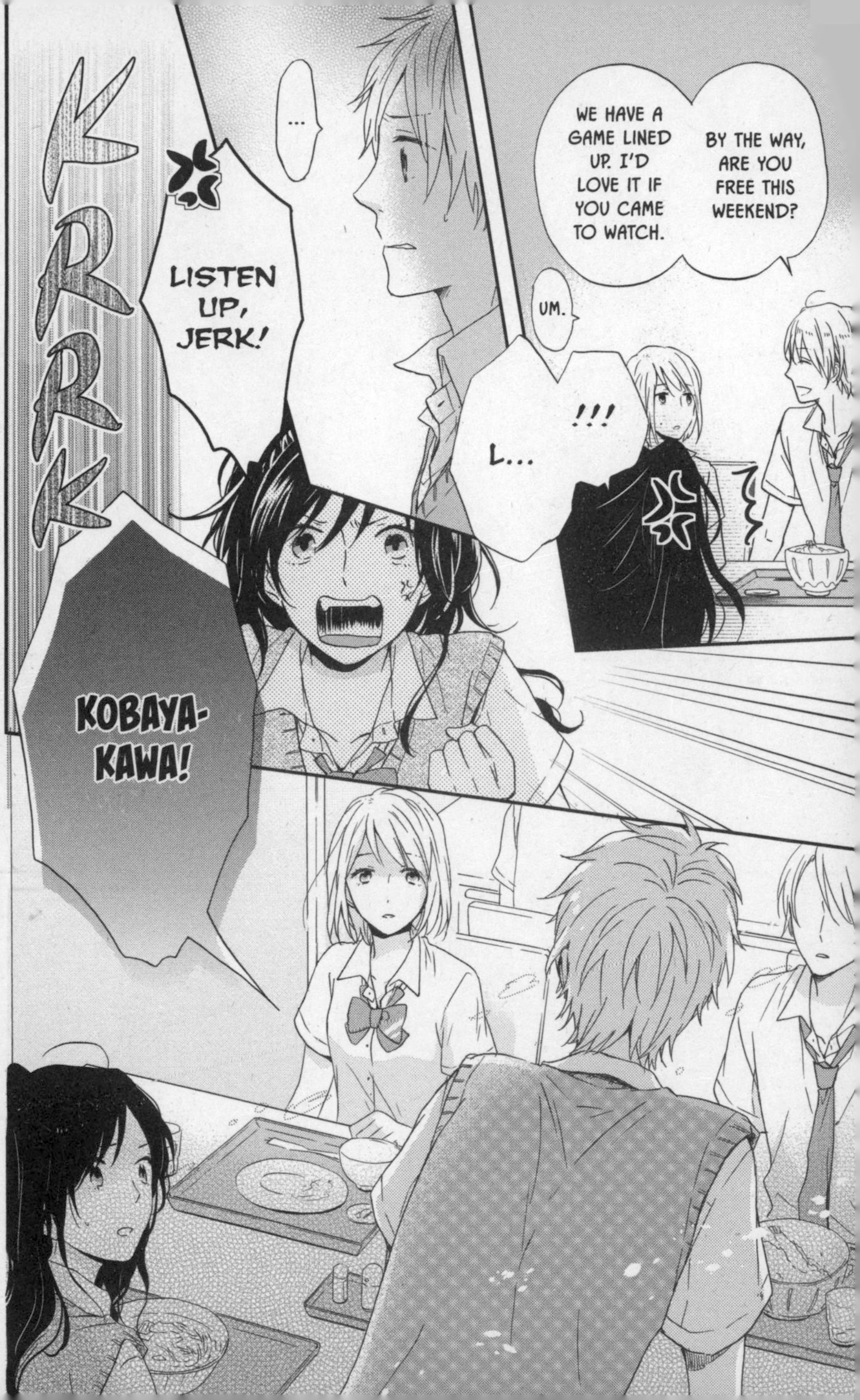
BY THE WAY, ARE YOU FREE THIS WEEKEND?
WE HAVE A GAME LINED UP. I'D LOVE IT IF YOU CAME TO WATCH.
UM.
!!!
L...
...
LISTEN UP, JERK!
KRRK
KOBAYA-KAWA!

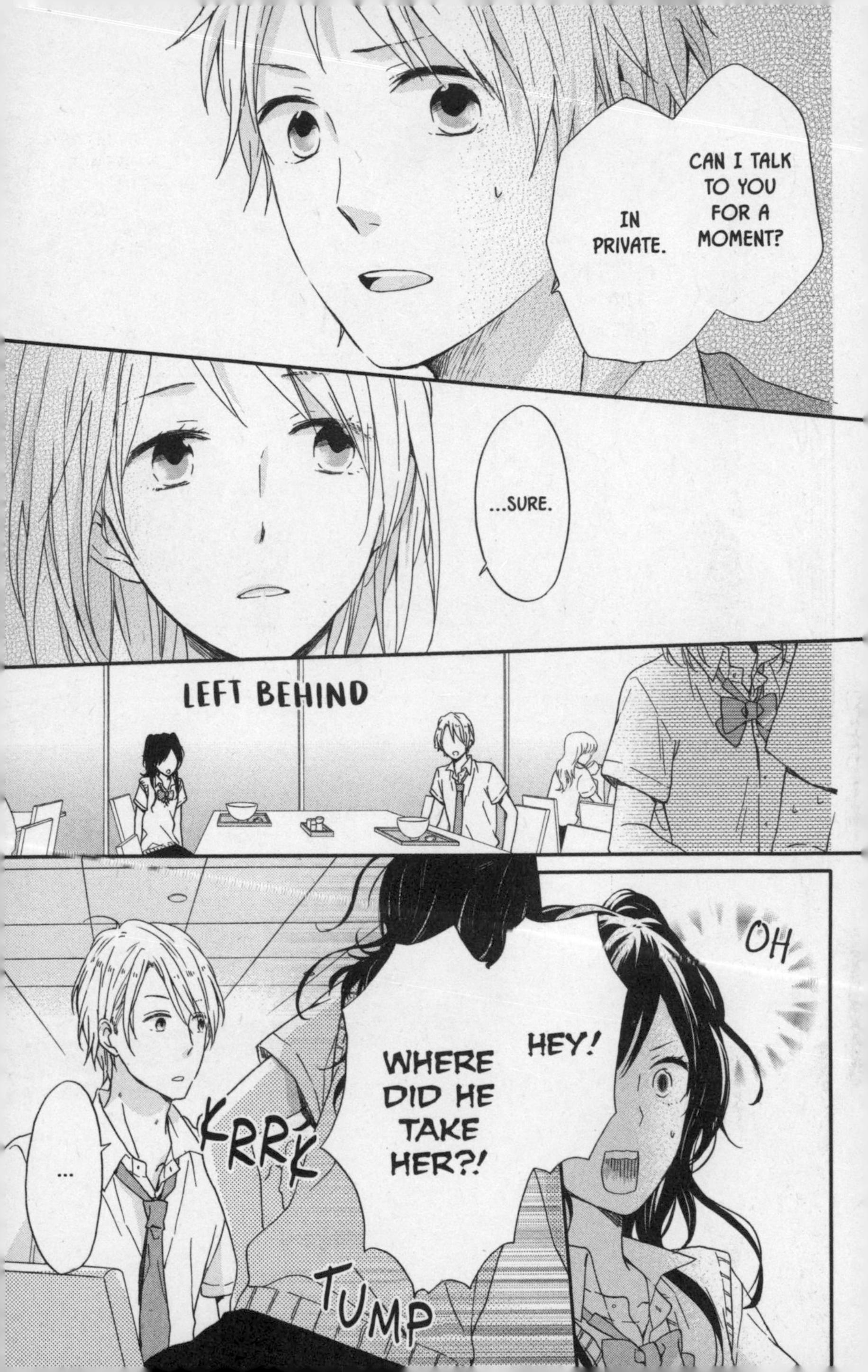
CAN I TALK TO YOU FOR A MOMENT?
IN PRIVATE.
...SURE.
LEFT BEHIND
OH
HEY!
WHERE DID HE TAKE HER?!
KRRK
TUMP
...

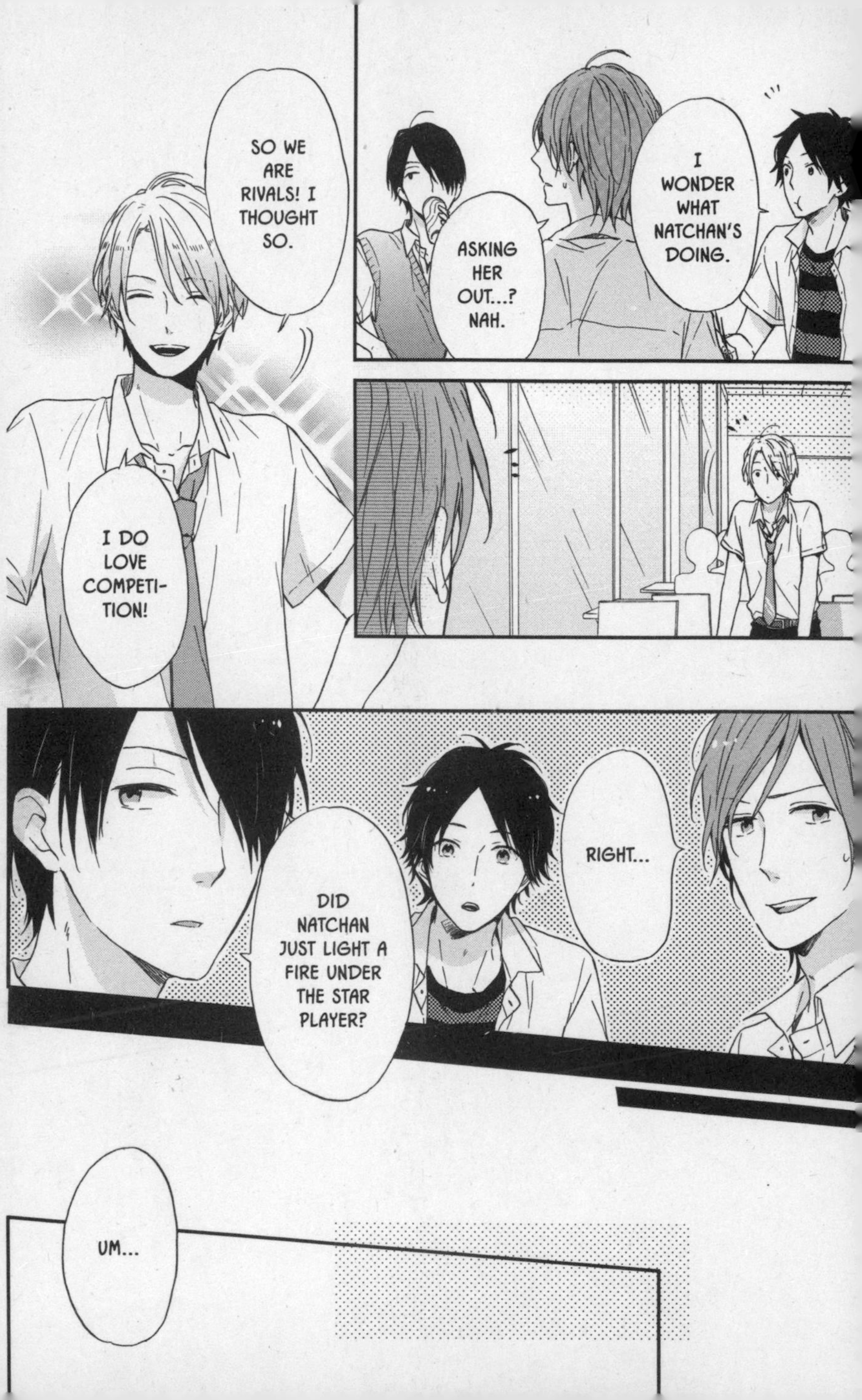
I WONDER WHAT NATCHAN'S DOING.
ASKING HER OUT...? NAH.
SO WE ARE RIVALS! I THOUGHT SO.
I DO LOVE COMPETITION!
RIGHT...
DID NATCHAN JUST LIGHT A FIRE UNDER THE STAR PLAYER?
UM...

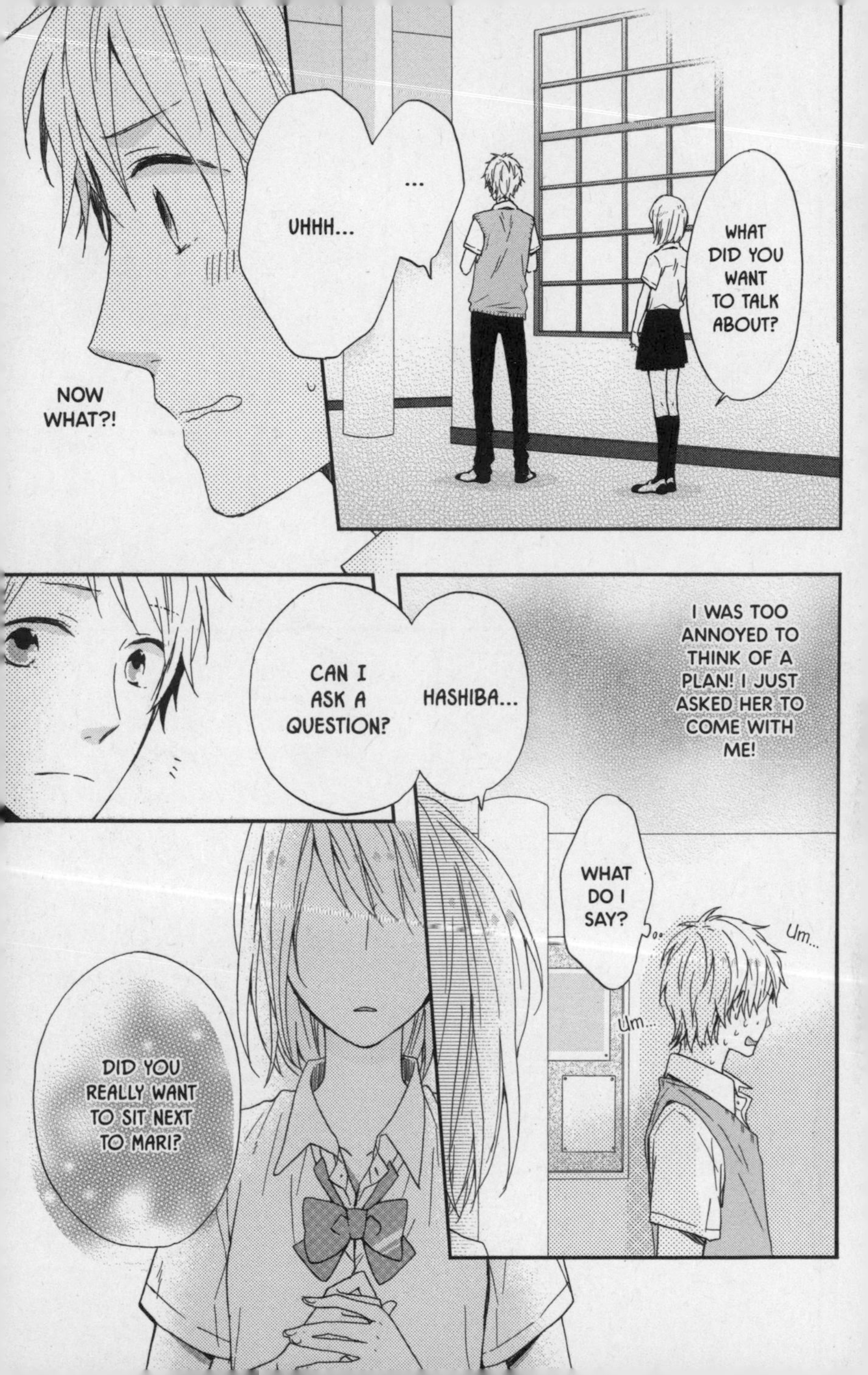
WHAT DID YOU WANT TO TALK ABOUT?
...
UHHH...
NOW WHAT?!
I WAS TOO ANNOYED TO THINK OF A PLAN! I JUST ASKED HER TO COME WITH ME!
WHAT DO I SAY?
Um...
Um...
HASHIBA...
CAN I ASK A QUESTION?
DID YOU REALLY WANT TO SIT NEXT TO MARI?

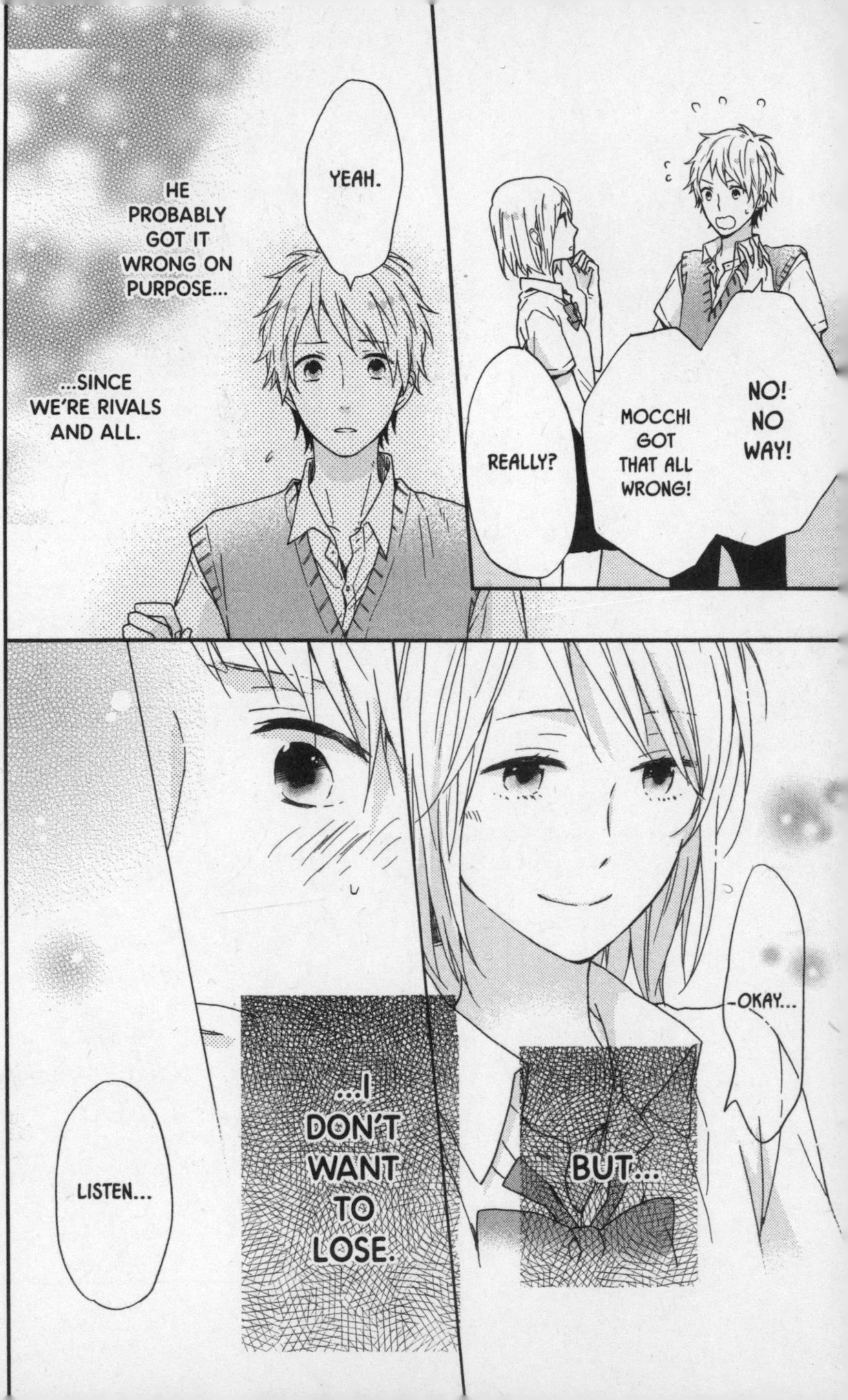
NO! NO WAY!
MOCCHI GOT THAT ALL WRONG!
REALLY?
YEAH.
HE PROBABLY GOT IT WRONG ON PURPOSE...
...SINCE WE'RE RIVALS AND ALL.
-OKAY...
BUT...
...I DON'T WANT TO LOSE.
LISTEN...

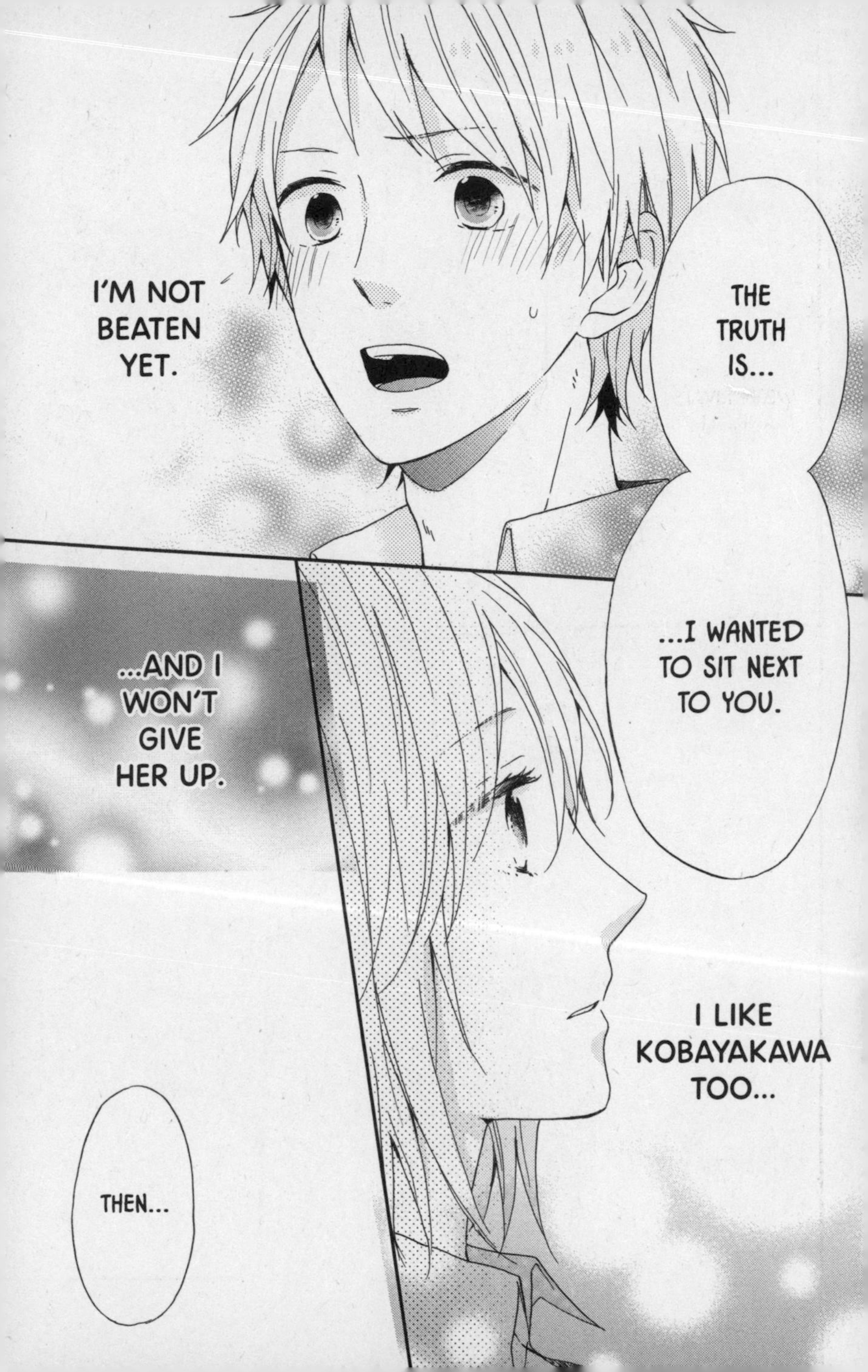
THE TRUTH IS...
...I WANTED TO SIT NEXT TO YOU.
I'M NOT BEATEN YET.
...AND I WON'T GIVE HER UP.
I LIKE KOBAYAKAWA TOO...
THEN...

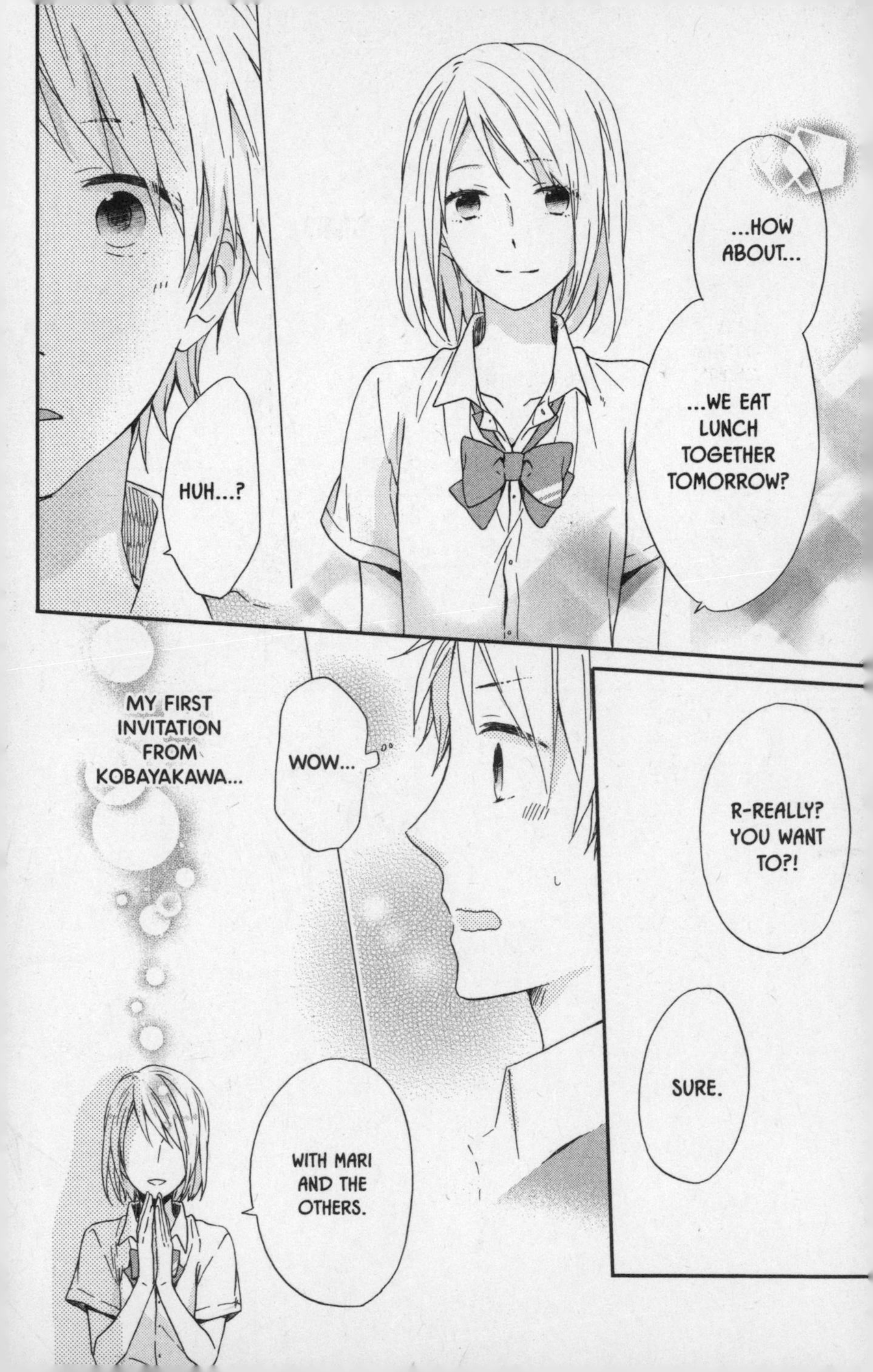
...HOW ABOUT...
...WE EAT LUNCH TOGETHER TOMORROW?
HUH...?
R-REALLY? YOU WANT TO?!
SURE.
WOW...
MY FIRST INVITATION FROM KOBAYAKAWA...
WITH MARI AND THE OTHERS.

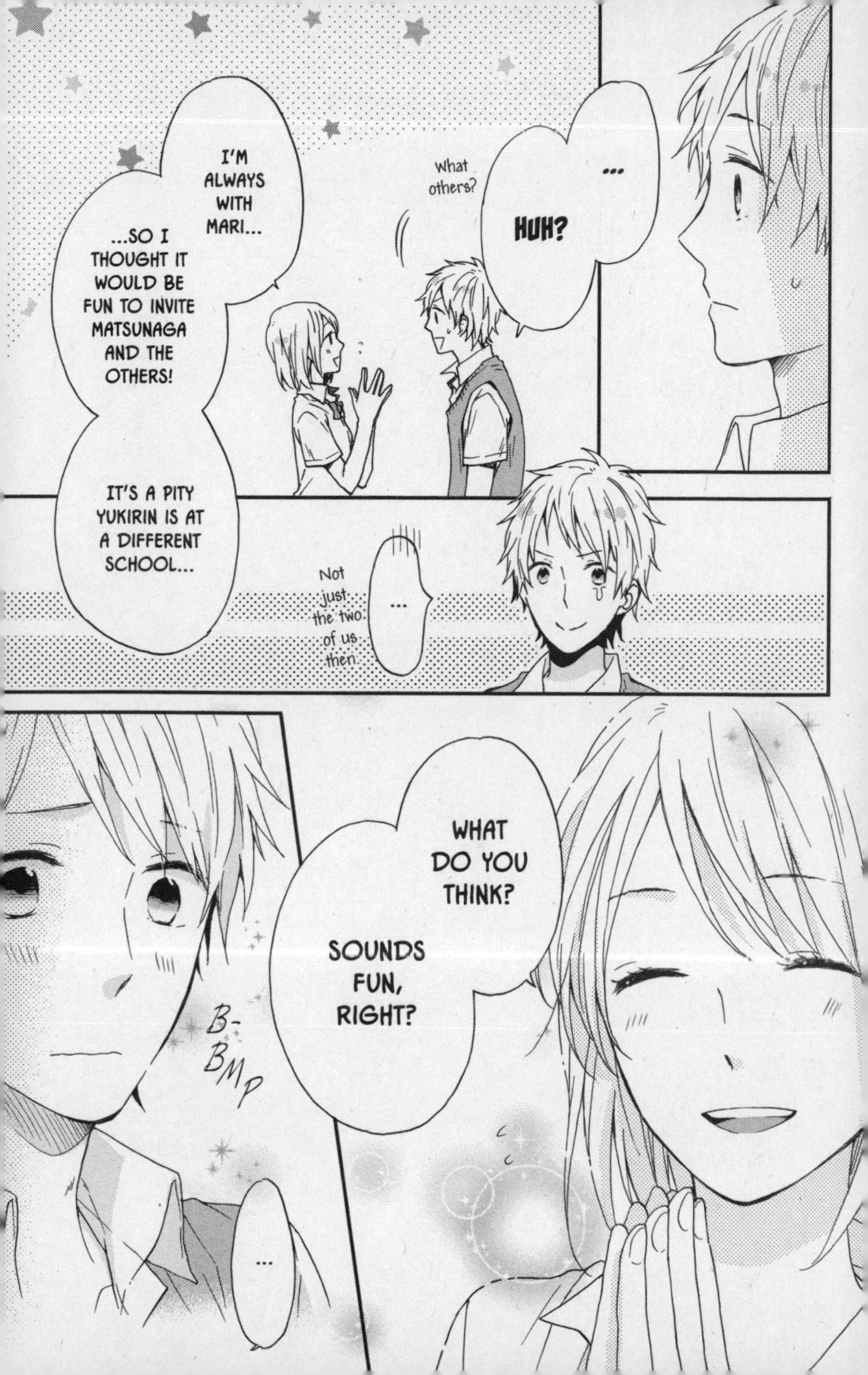
...
HUH?
What others?
I'M ALWAYS WITH MARI...
...SO I THOUGHT IT WOULD BE FUN TO INVITE MATSUNAGA AND THE OTHERS!
IT'S A PITY YUKIRIN IS AT A DIFFERENT SCHOOL...
...
Not just the two of us then.
WHAT DO YOU THINK?
SOUNDS FUN, RIGHT?
B-BMP
...

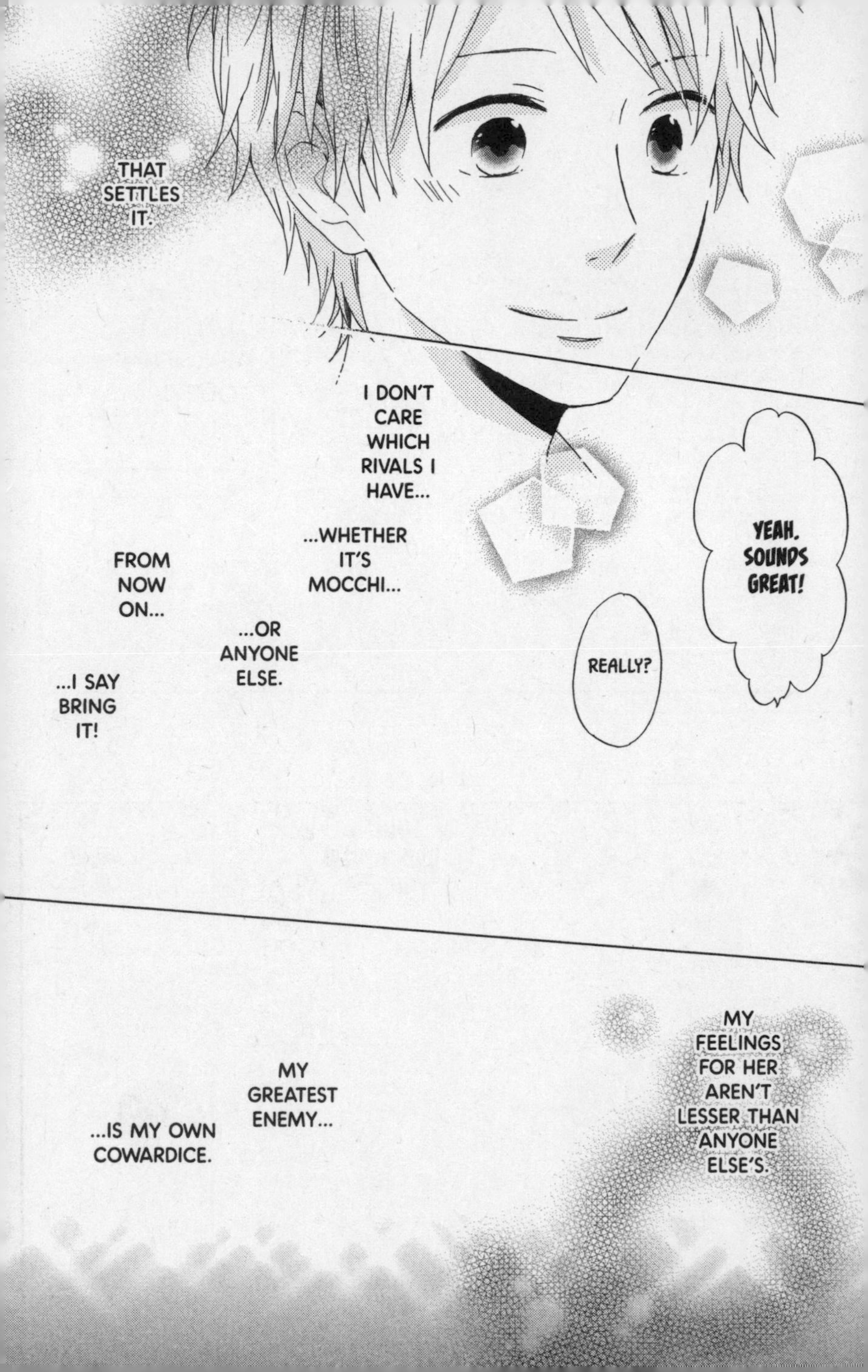
THAT SETTLES IT.
YEAH. SOUNDS GREAT!
REALLY?
I DON'T CARE WHICH RIVALS I HAVE...
...WHETHER IT'S MOCCHI...
...OR ANYONE ELSE.
FROM NOW ON...
...I SAY BRING IT!
MY FEELINGS FOR HER AREN'T LESSER THAN ANYONE ELSE'S.
MY GREATEST ENEMY...
...IS MY OWN COWARDICE.

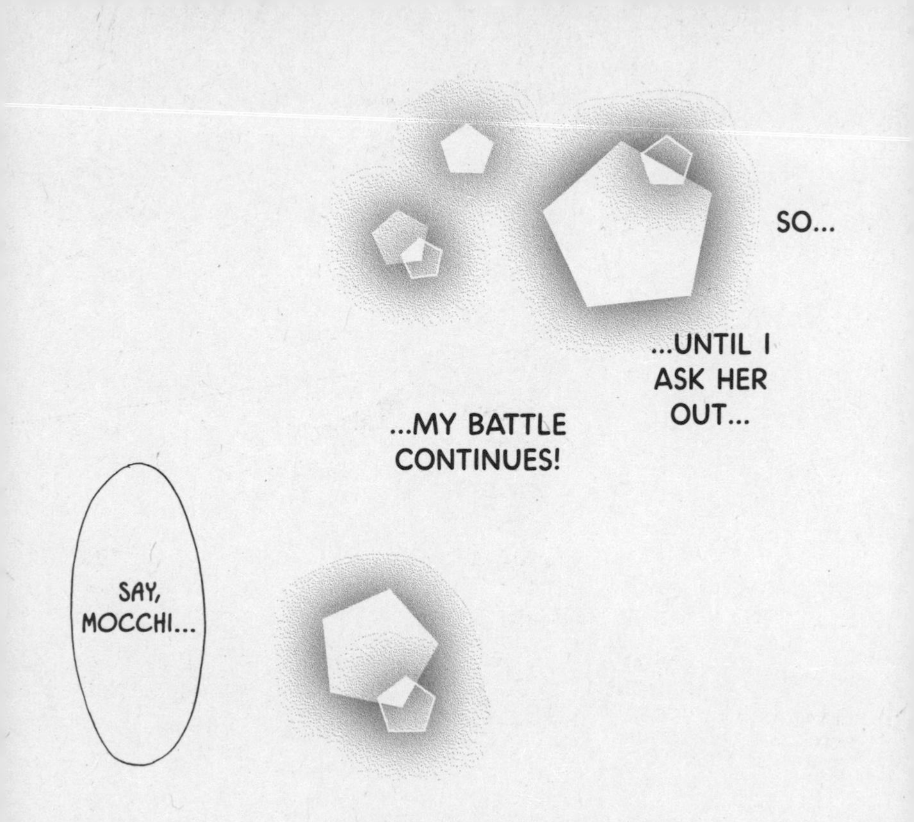
SO...
...UNTIL I ASK HER OUT...
...MY BATTLE CONTINUES!
SAY, MOCCHI...

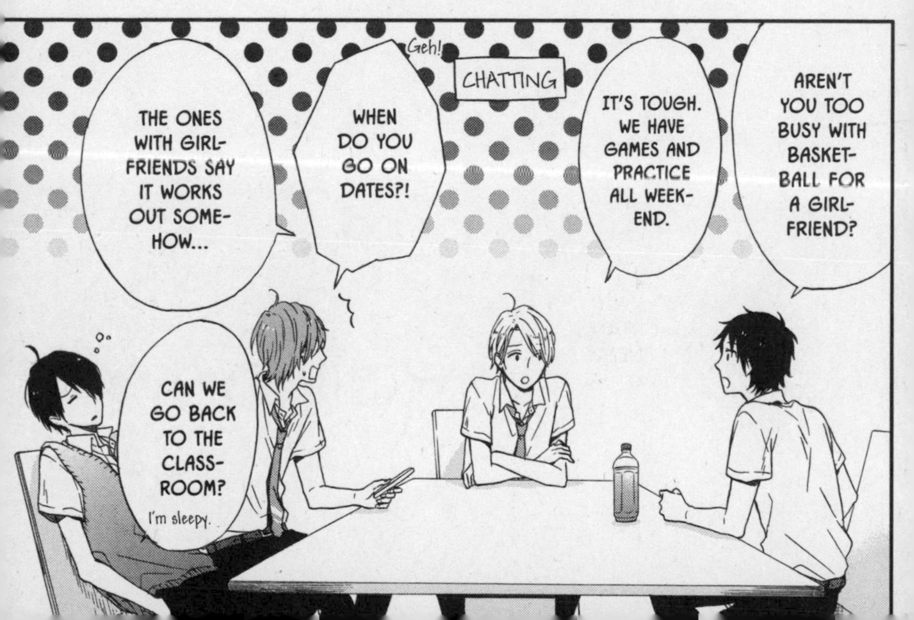
AREN'T YOU TOO BUSY WITH BASKET-BALL FOR A GIRL-FRIEND?
IT'S TOUGH. WE HAVE GAMES AND PRACTICE ALL WEEK-END.
CHATTING
Geh!
WHEN DO YOU GO ON DATES?!
THE ONES WITH GIRL-FRIENDS SAY IT WORKS OUT SOME-HOW...
CAN WE GO BACK TO THE CLASS-ROOM?
I'm sleepy.

Rainbow
Days

■ ■ ■ ■ ■ ■ ■ ■

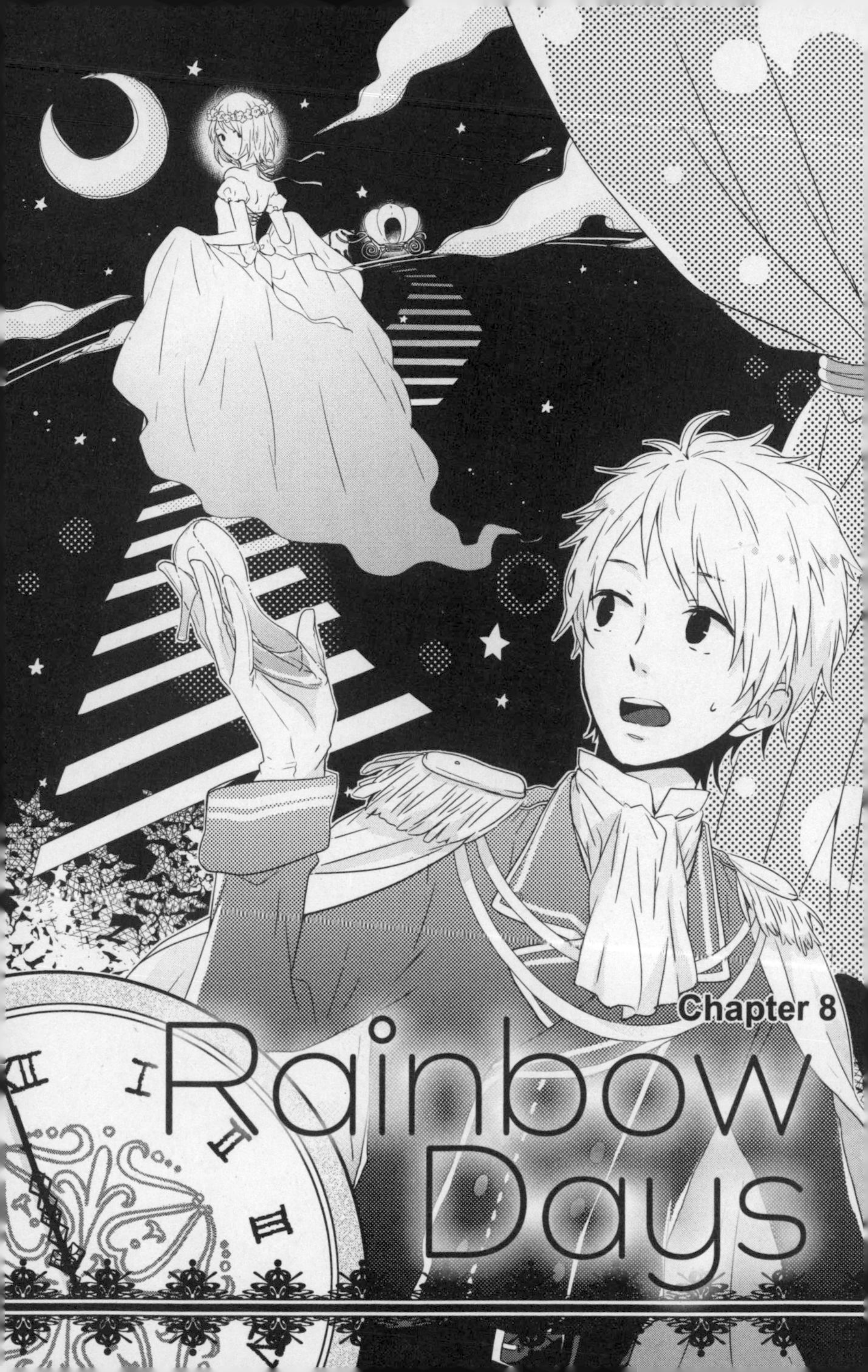
Chapter 8
Rainbow Days

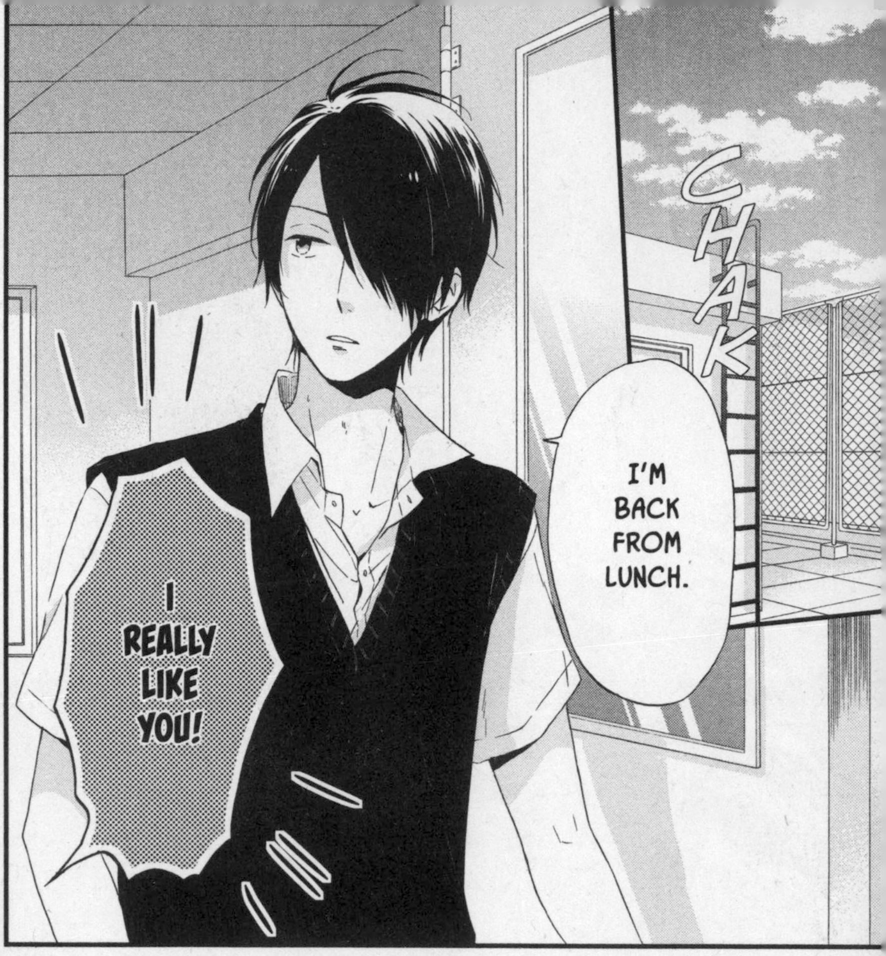
CHAK
I'M BACK FROM LUNCH.
I REALLY LIKE YOU!

I dream a lot when I sleep.
I remember my dreams pretty well.

From nursery school to the first couple years of elementary school, I had a recurring dream. Bakatono was in it...

I had that dream so many times I lost count. It went exactly the same way every time.

What was that about, I wonder...?

*Bakatono ("Stupid Lord") is a character played by comedian Ken Shimura.

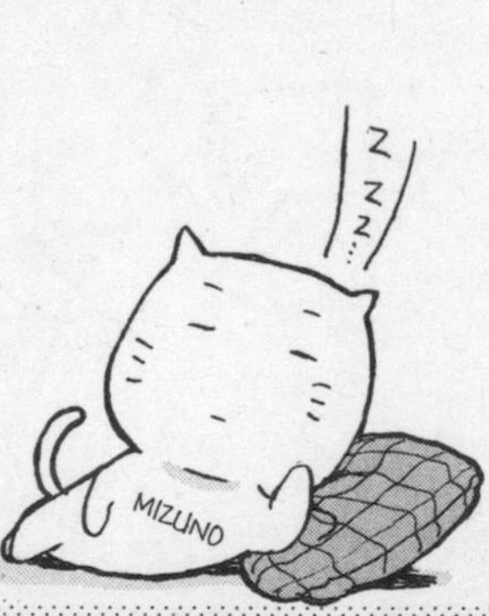
Z Z Z...
MIZUNO

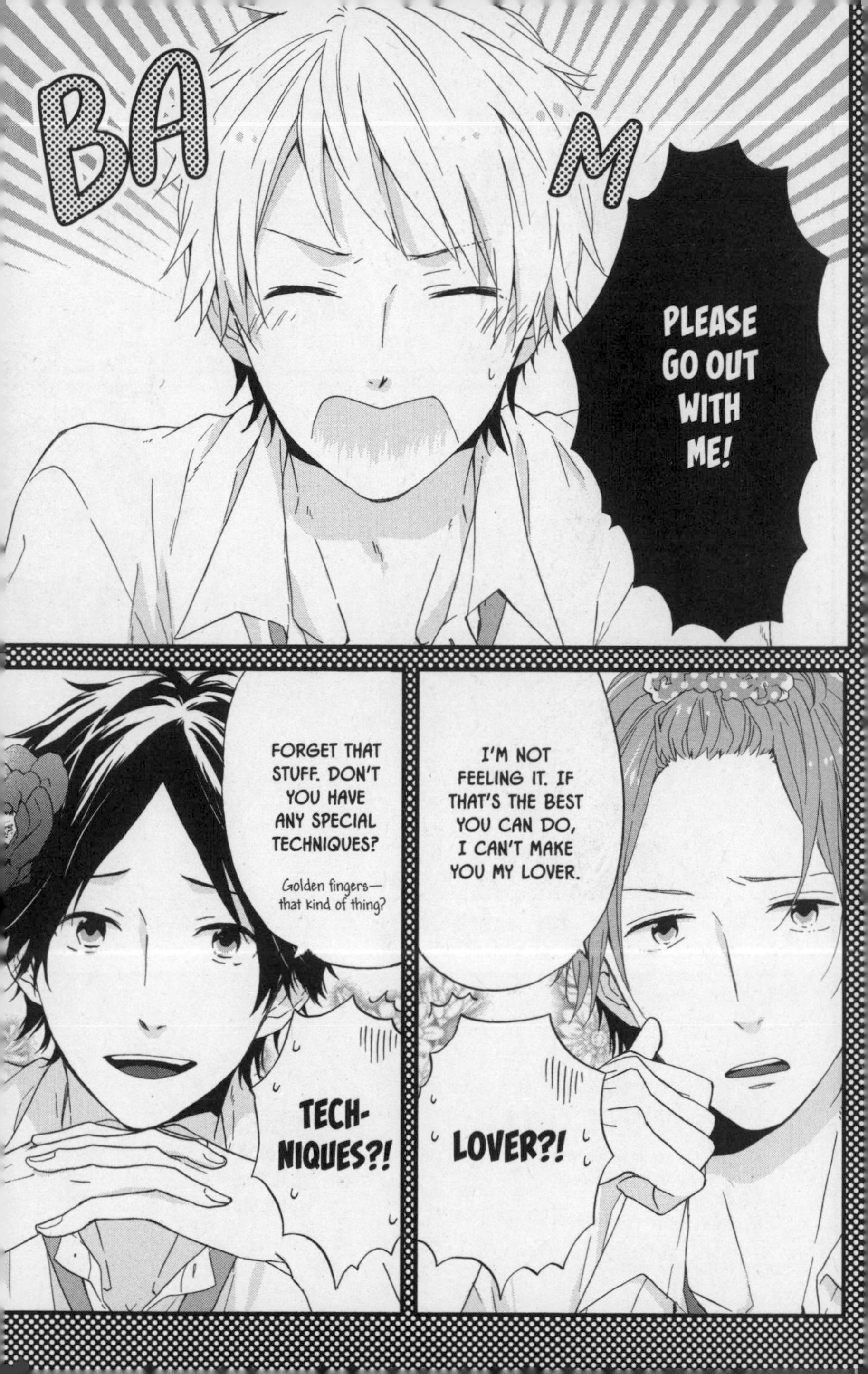
BAM
PLEASE GO OUT WITH ME!
I'M NOT FEELING IT. IF THAT'S THE BEST YOU CAN DO, I CAN'T MAKE YOU MY LOVER.
LOVER?!
FORGET THAT STUFF. DON'T YOU HAVE ANY SPECIAL TECHNIQUES?
Golden fingers— that kind of thing?
TECH-NIQUES?!

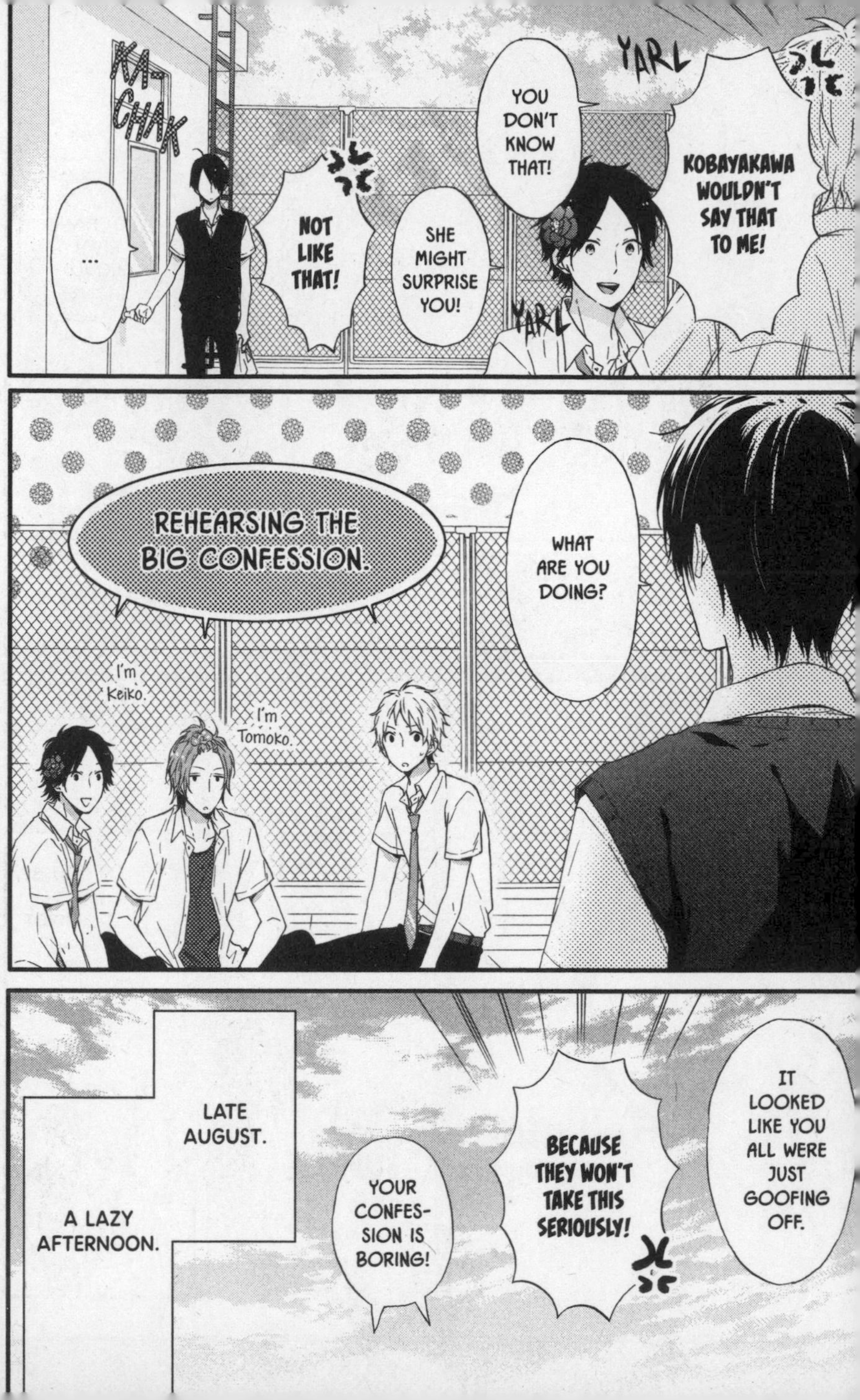
YARL
KOBAYAKAWA WOULDN'T SAY THAT TO ME!
YOU DON'T KNOW THAT!
YARL
SHE MIGHT SURPRISE YOU!
NOT LIKE THAT!
KA-CHAK
...
WHAT ARE YOU DOING?
REHEARSING THE BIG CONFESSION.
I'm Tomoko.
I'm Keiko.
IT LOOKED LIKE YOU ALL WERE JUST GOOFING OFF.
BECAUSE THEY WON'T TAKE THIS SERIOUSLY!
YOUR CONFES-SION IS BORING!
LATE AUGUST.
A LAZY AFTERNOON.

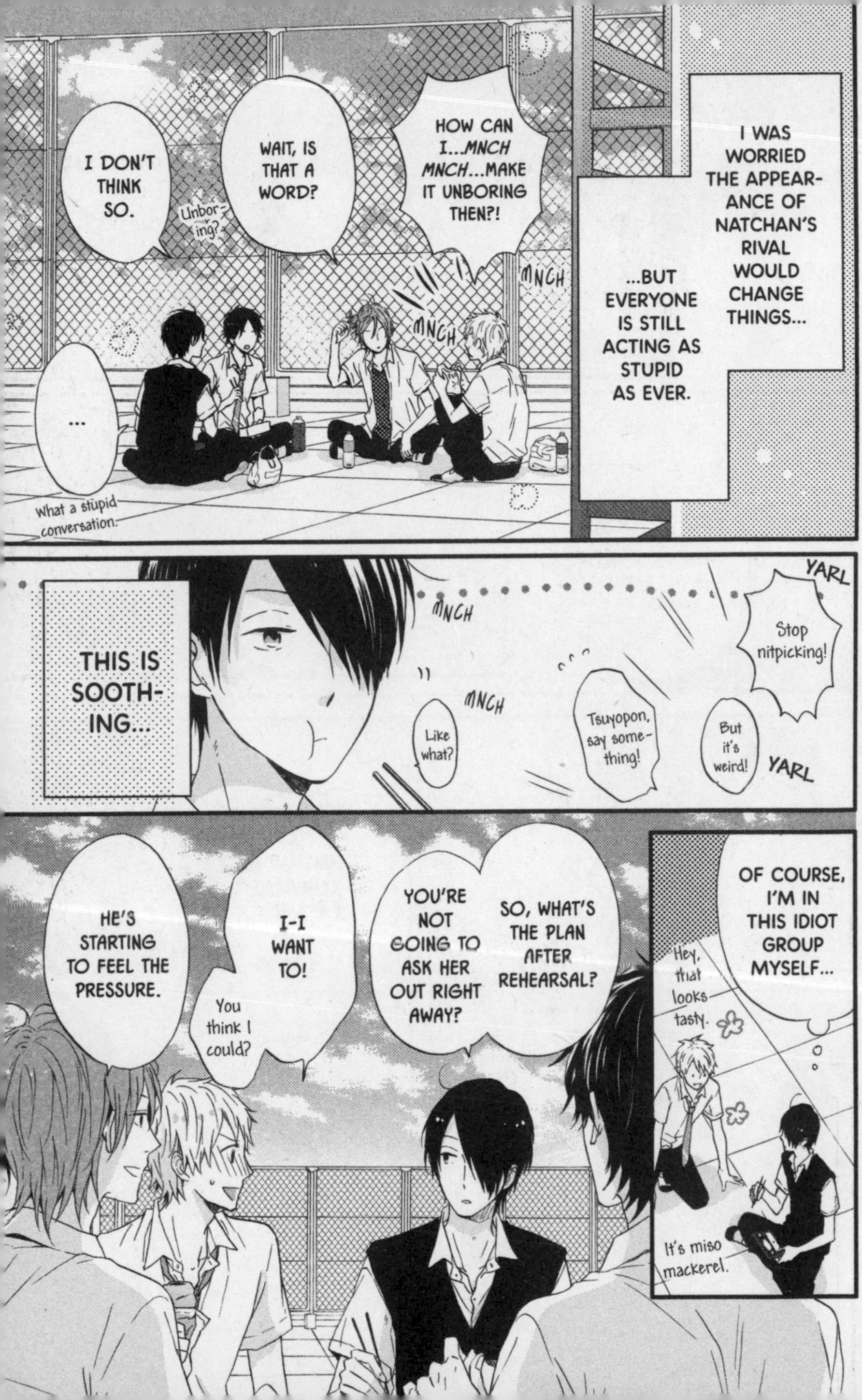
I WAS WORRIED THE APPEARANCE OF NATCHAN'S RIVAL WOULD CHANGE THINGS...
...BUT EVERYONE IS STILL ACTING AS STUPID AS EVER.
MNCH
MNCH
HOW CAN I...MNCH MNCH...MAKE IT UNBORING THEN?!
WAIT, IS THAT A WORD?
Unbor-ing?
I DON'T THINK SO.
...
What a stupid conversation.
YARL
Stop nitpicking!
But it's weird!
YARL
Tsuyopon, say something!
Like what?
MNCH
MNCH
THIS IS SOOTHING...
OF COURSE, I'M IN THIS IDIOT GROUP MYSELF...
Hey, that looks tasty.
It's miso mackerel.
SO, WHAT'S THE PLAN AFTER REHEARSAL?
YOU'RE NOT GOING TO ASK HER OUT RIGHT AWAY?
I-I WANT TO!
You think I could?
HE'S STARTING TO FEEL THE PRESSURE.

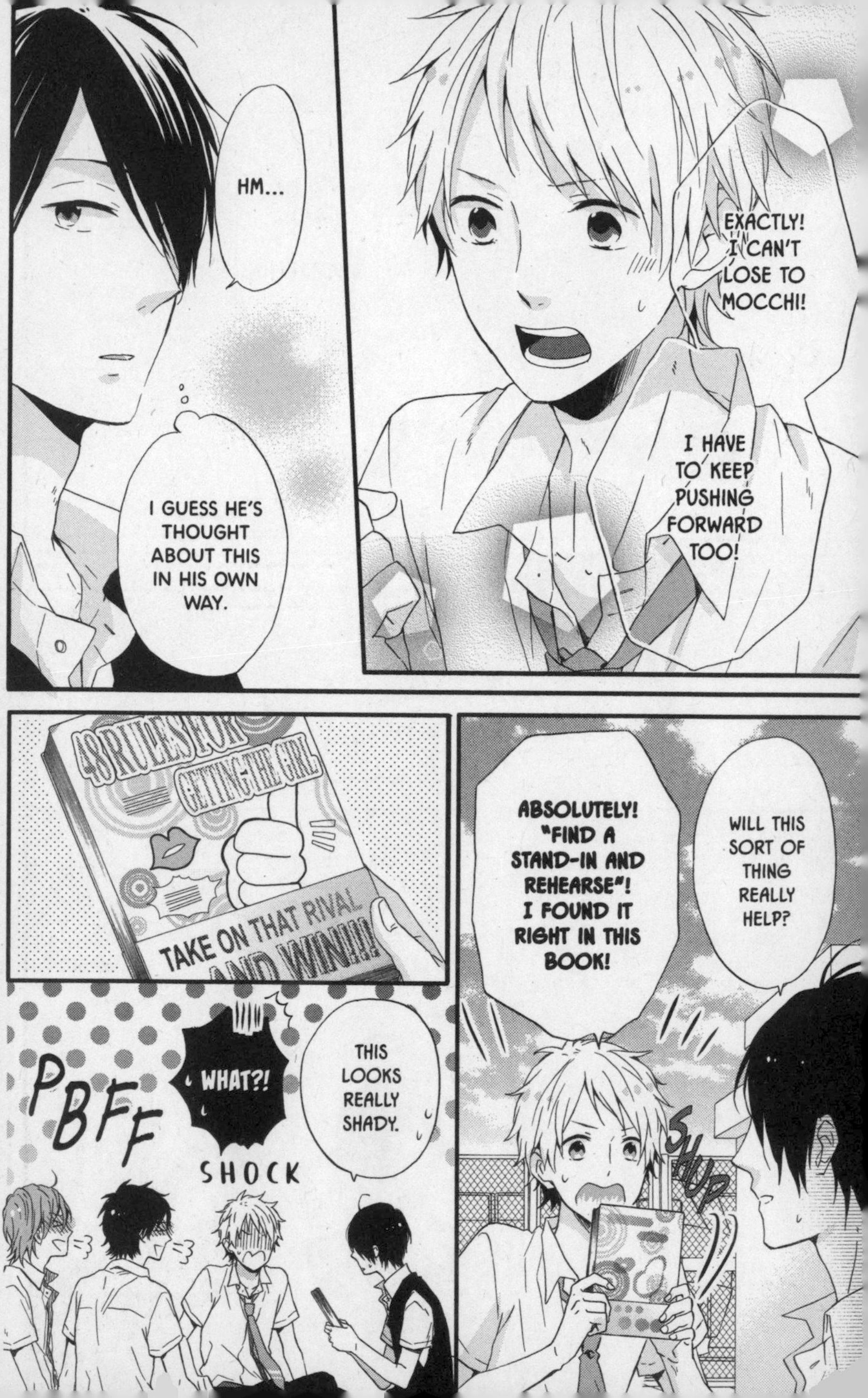
EXACTLY! I CAN'T LOSE TO MOCCHI!
I HAVE TO KEEP PUSHING FORWARD TOO!
HM...
I GUESS HE'S THOUGHT ABOUT THIS IN HIS OWN WAY.
WILL THIS SORT OF THING REALLY HELP?
ABSOLUTELY! "FIND A STAND-IN AND REHEARSE"! I FOUND IT RIGHT IN THIS BOOK!
SHUP
48 RULES FOR GETTING THE GIRL
TAKE ON THAT RIVAL AND WIN!!!
THIS LOOKS REALLY SHADY.
WHAT?!
PBFF
SHOCK

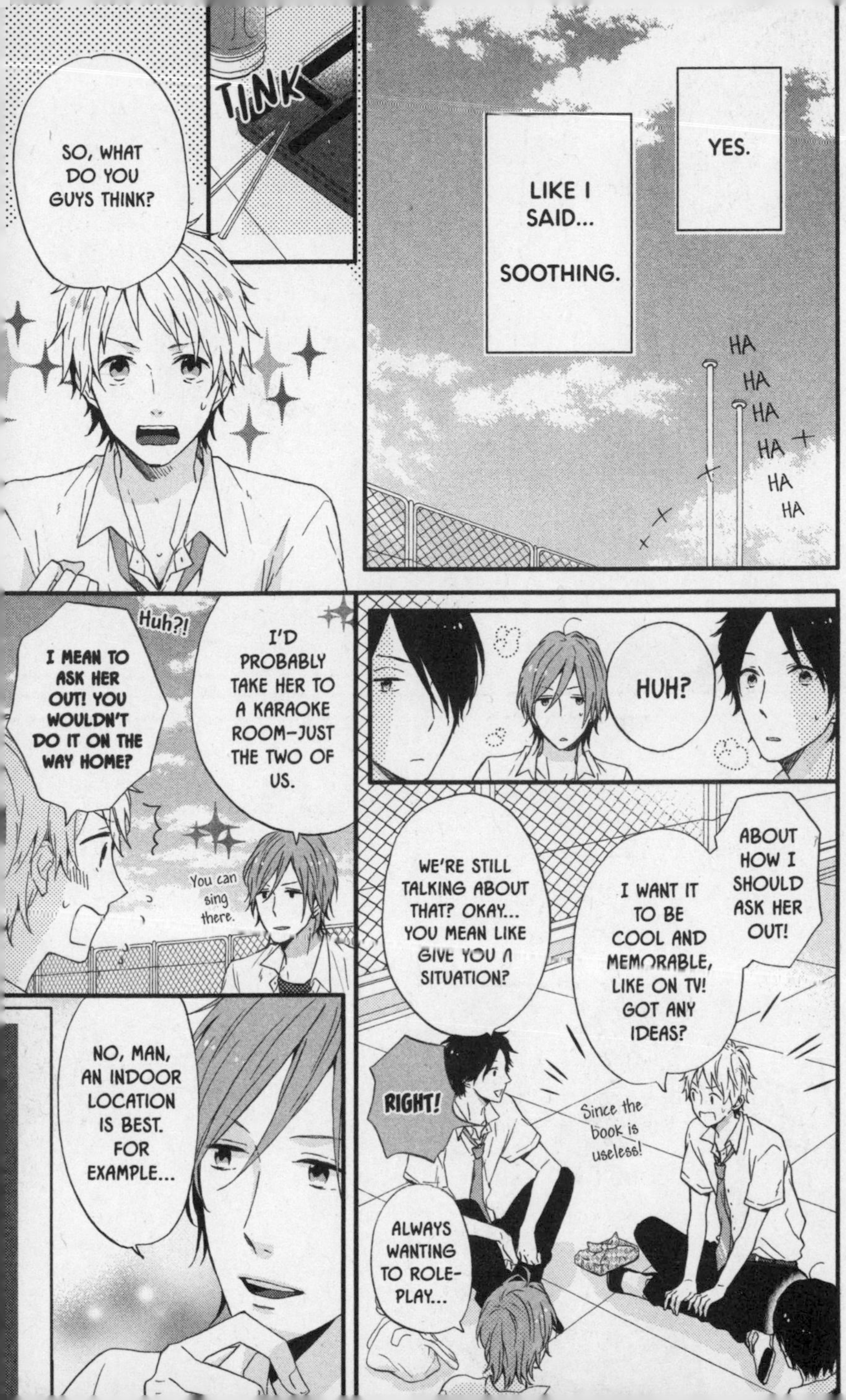
YES.
LIKE I SAID... SOOTHING.
HA HA HA HA HA HA
TINK
SO, WHAT DO YOU GUYS THINK?
HUH?
ABOUT HOW I SHOULD ASK HER OUT!
I WANT IT TO BE COOL AND MEMORABLE, LIKE ON TV! GOT ANY IDEAS?
WE'RE STILL TALKING ABOUT THAT? OKAY... YOU MEAN LIKE GIVE YOU A SITUATION?
Since the book is useless!
RIGHT!
ALWAYS WANTING TO ROLE-PLAY...
I'D PROBABLY TAKE HER TO A KARAOKE ROOM—JUST THE TWO OF US.
You can sing there.
Huh?!
I MEAN TO ASK HER OUT! YOU WOULDN'T DO IT ON THE WAY HOME?
NO, MAN, AN INDOOR LOCATION IS BEST. FOR EXAMPLE...

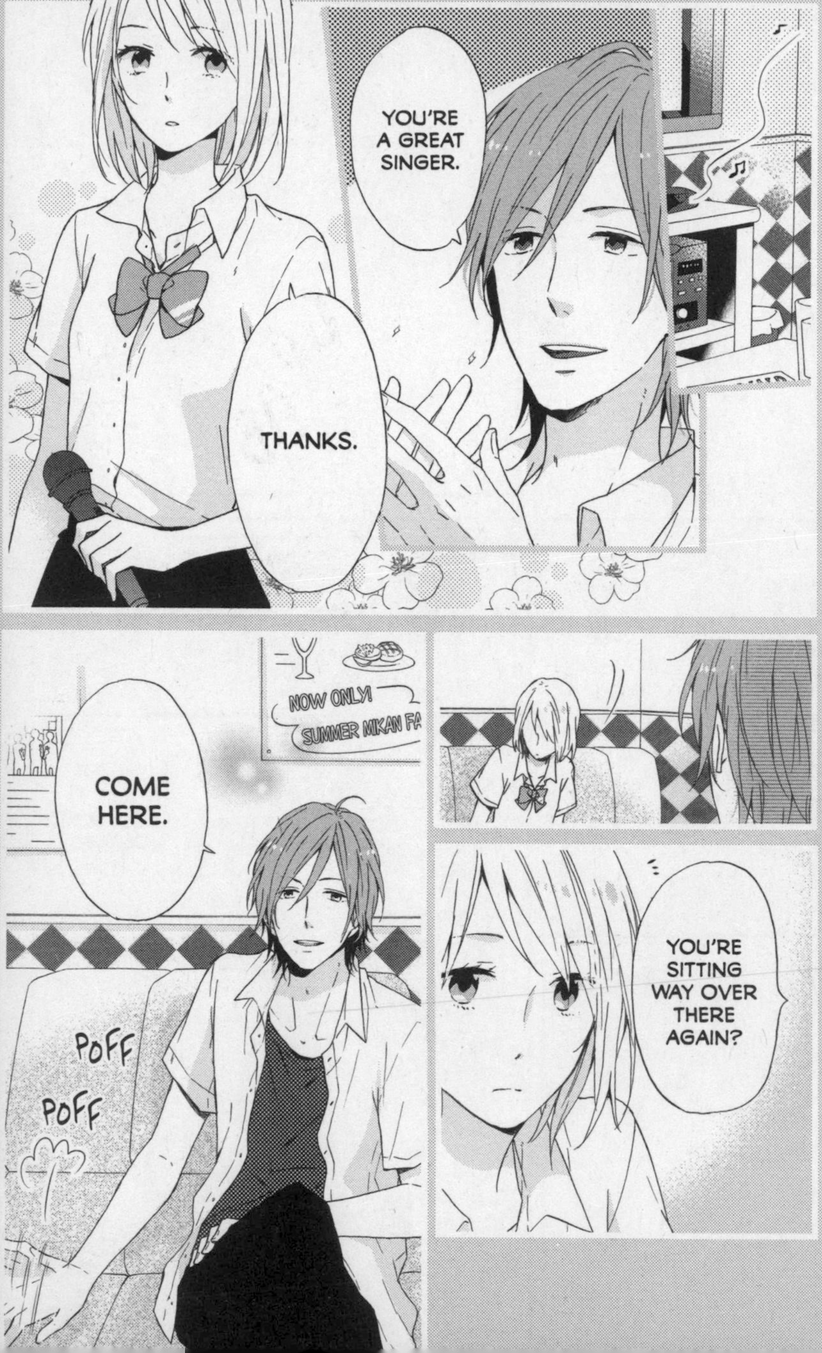
YOU'RE A GREAT SINGER.
THANKS.
YOU'RE SITTING WAY OVER THERE AGAIN?
COME HERE.
NOW ONLY!
SUMMER MIKAN FA
POFF
POFF

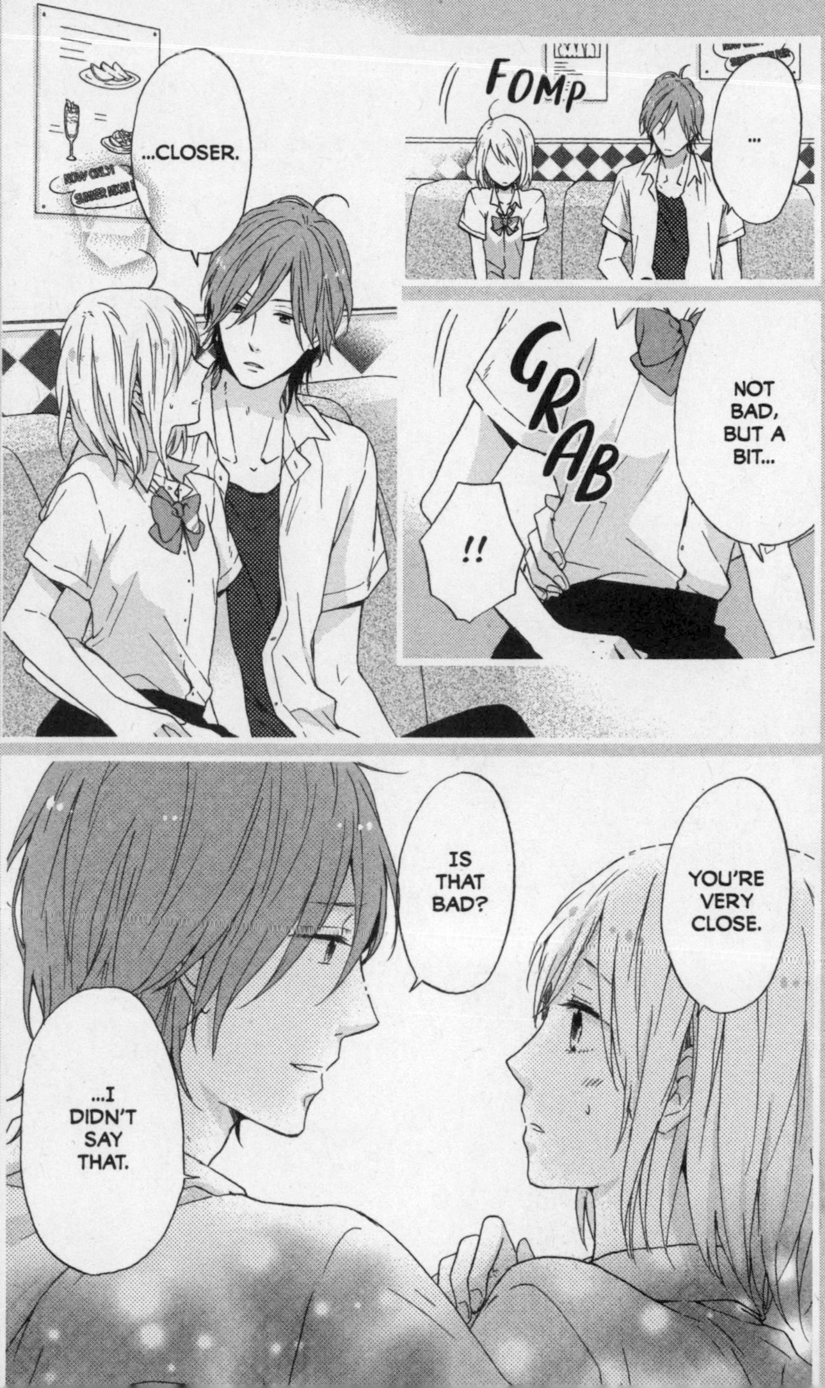
FOMP
...
NOT BAD, BUT A BIT...
GRAB
!!
...CLOSER.
YOU'RE VERY CLOSE.
IS THAT BAD?
...I DIDN'T SAY THAT.

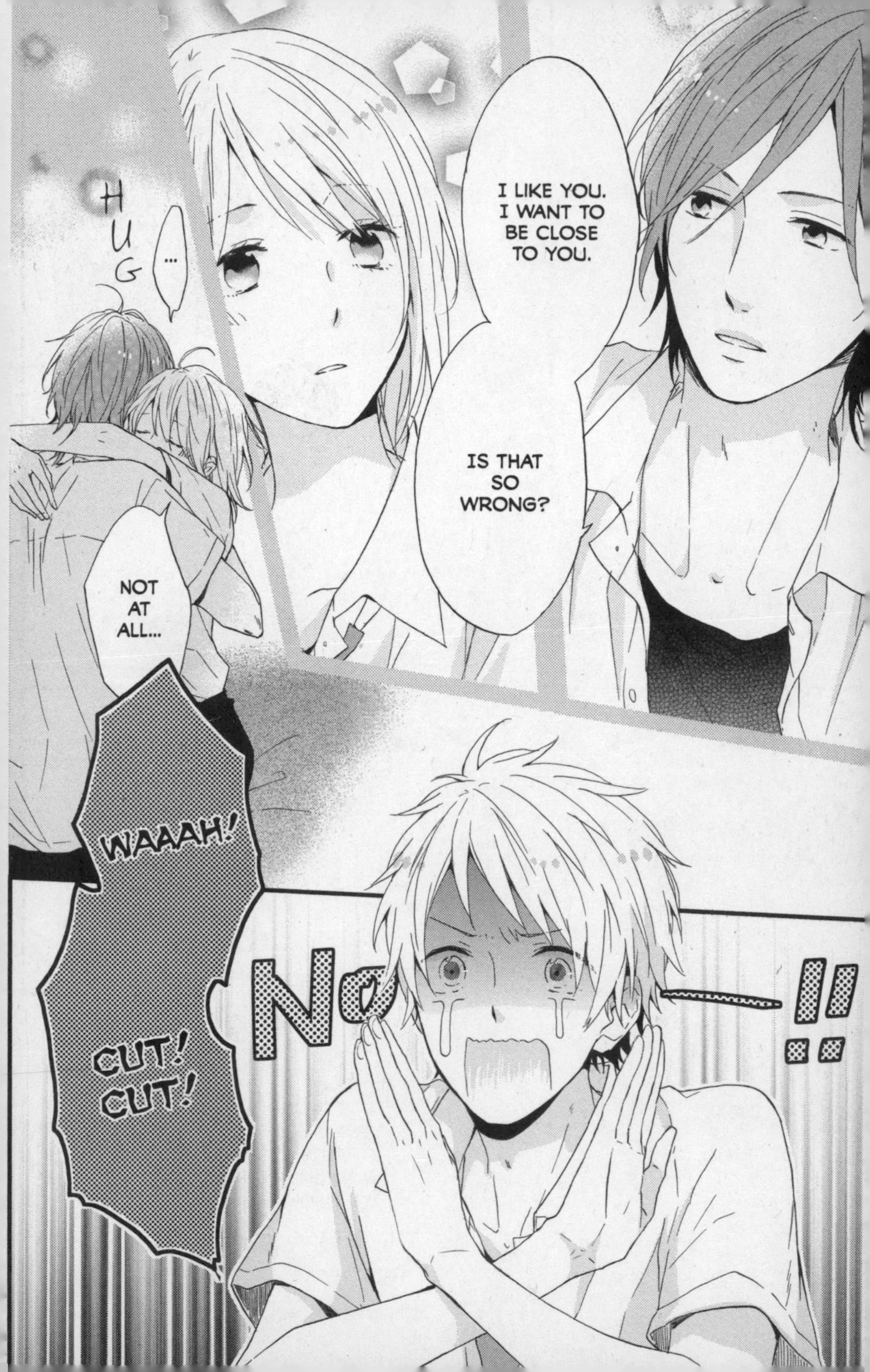
I LIKE YOU. I WANT TO BE CLOSE TO YOU.
IS THAT SO WRONG?
...
HUG
NOT AT ALL...
WAAAH!
CUT! CUT!
NO—!!

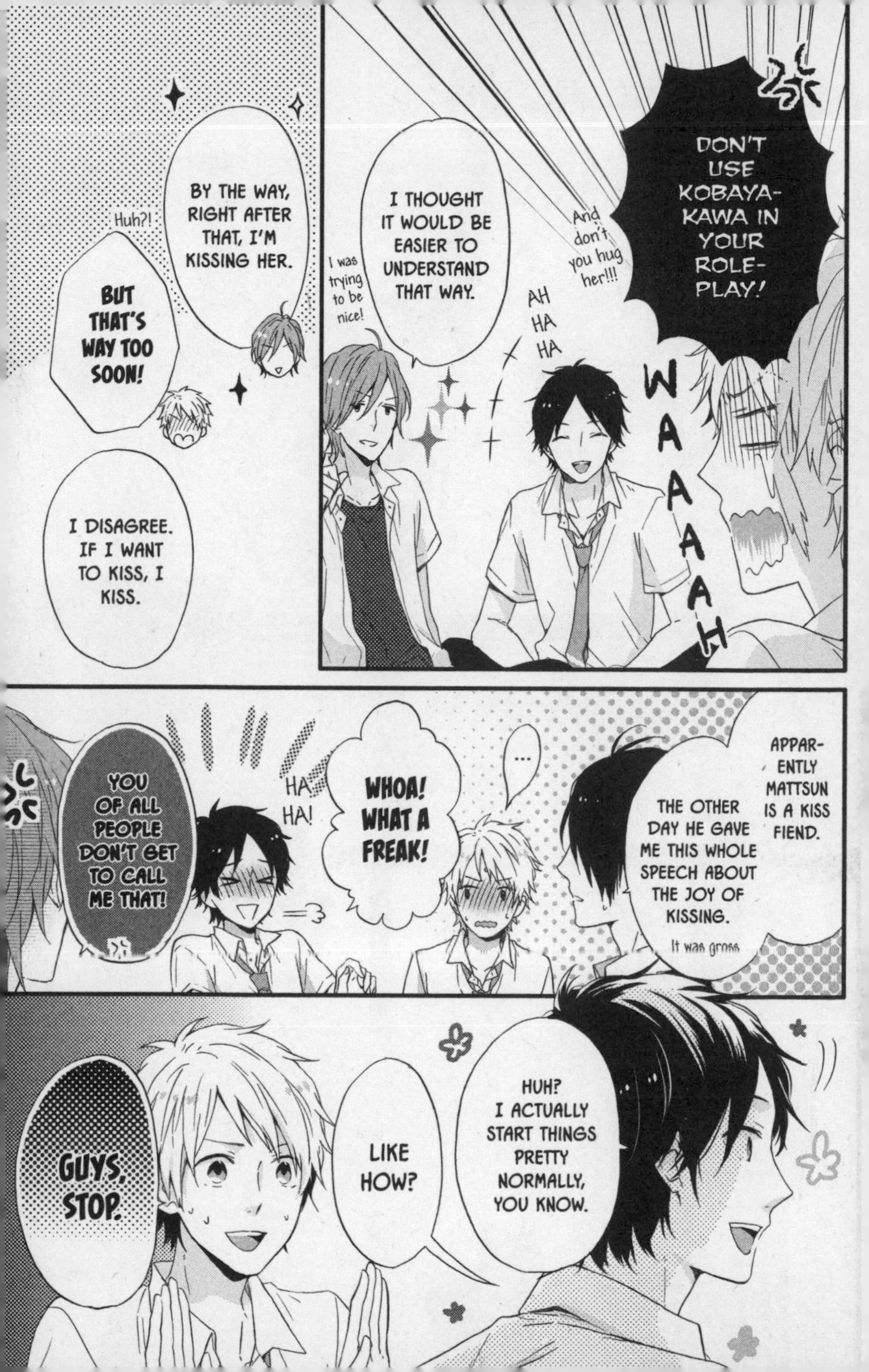
DON'T USE KOBAYA-KAWA IN YOUR ROLE-PLAY!
And don't you hug her!!!
WAAAAAH
AH HA HA
I THOUGHT IT WOULD BE EASIER TO UNDERSTAND THAT WAY.
I was trying to be nice!
BY THE WAY, RIGHT AFTER THAT, I'M KISSING HER.
Huh?!
BUT THAT'S WAY TOO SOON!
I DISAGREE. IF I WANT TO KISS, I KISS.
APPAR-ENTLY MATTSUN IS A KISS FIEND.
THE OTHER DAY HE GAVE ME THIS WHOLE SPEECH ABOUT THE JOY OF KISSING.
It was gross
...
WHOA! WHAT A FREAK!
HA HA!
YOU OF ALL PEOPLE DON'T GET TO CALL ME THAT!
HUH? I ACTUALLY START THINGS PRETTY NORMALLY, YOU KNOW.
LIKE HOW?
GUYS, STOP.

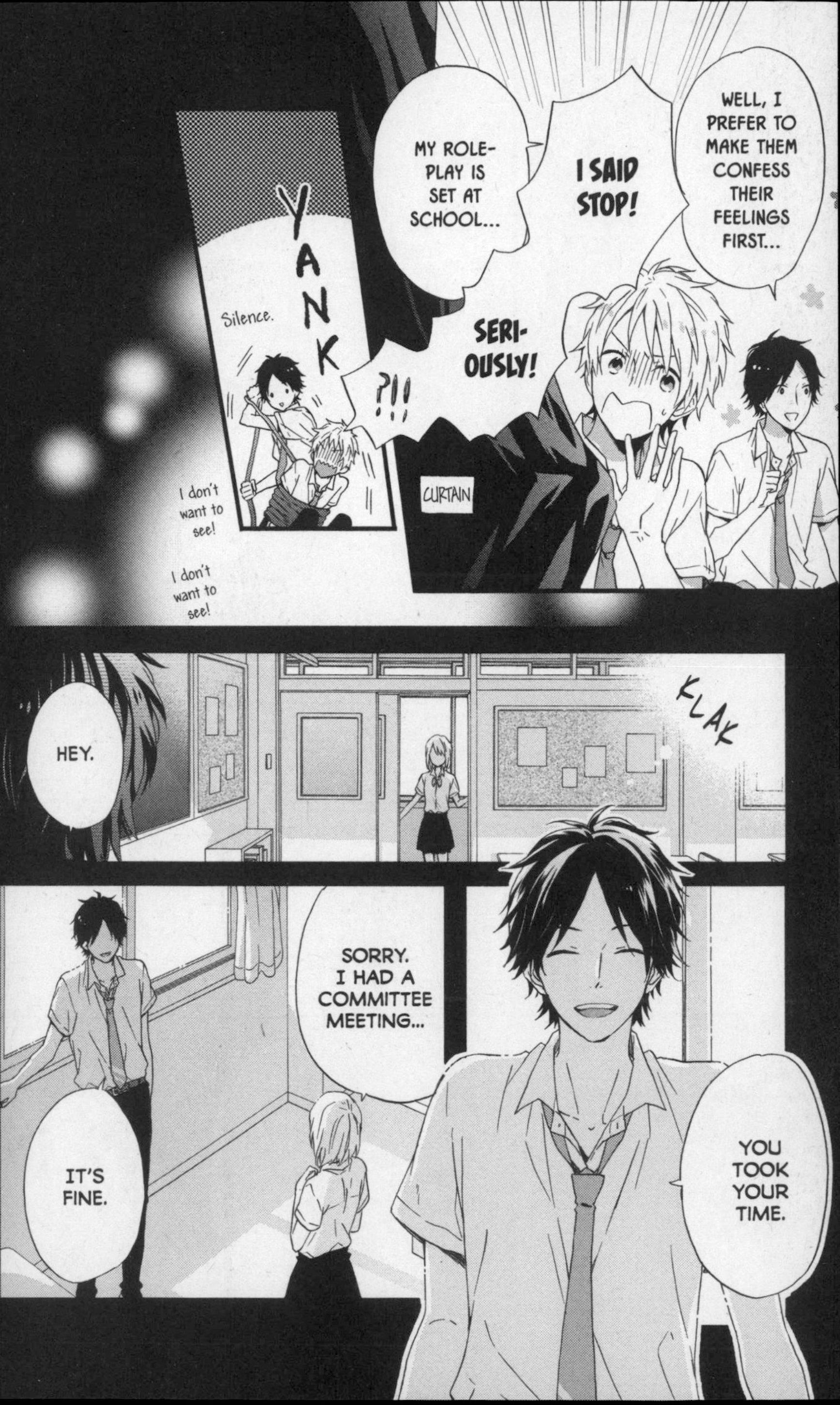
WELL, I PREFER TO MAKE THEM CONFESS THEIR FEELINGS FIRST...
I SAID STOP!
MY ROLE-PLAY IS SET AT SCHOOL...
SERI-OUSLY!
?!!
CURTAIN
YANK
Silence.
I don't want to see!
I don't want to see!
KLAK
HEY.
YOU TOOK YOUR TIME.
SORRY. I HAD A COMMITTEE MEETING...
IT'S FINE.

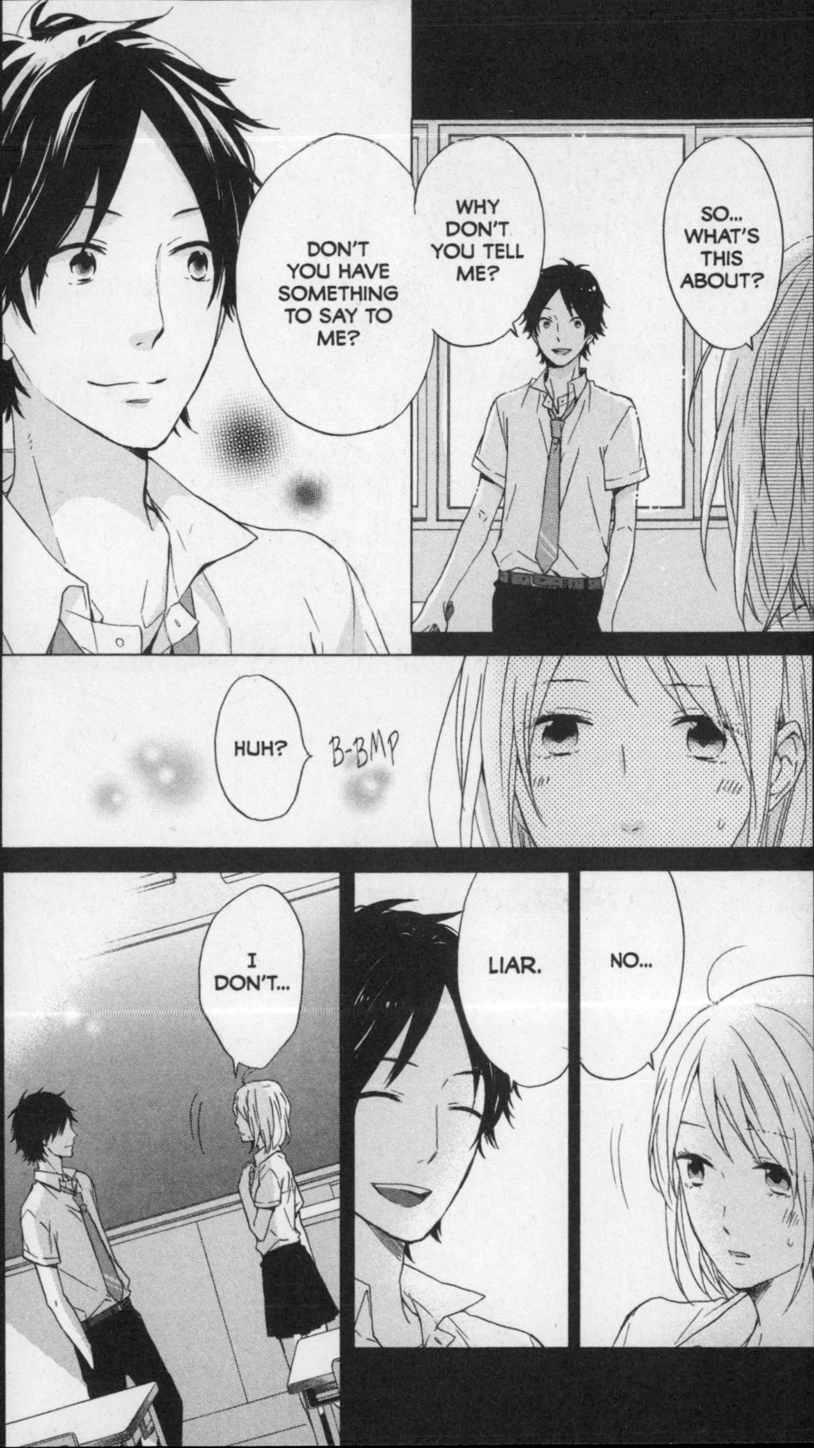
SO... WHAT'S THIS ABOUT?
WHY DON'T YOU TELL ME?
DON'T YOU HAVE SOMETHING TO SAY TO ME?
HUH?
B-BMP
NO...
LIAR.
I DON'T...

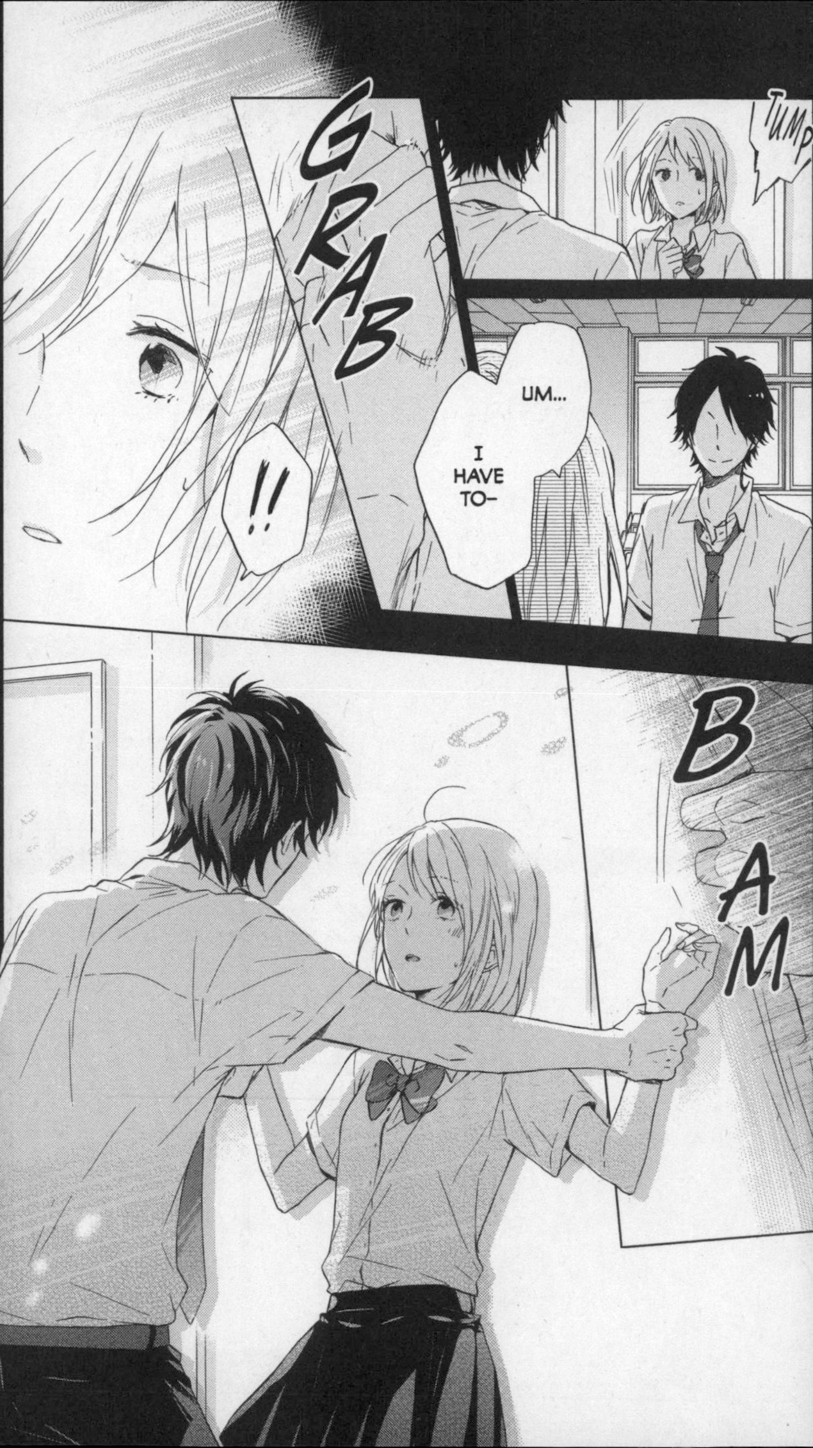
TUMP
UM...
I HAVE TO–
GRAB
!!
BAM

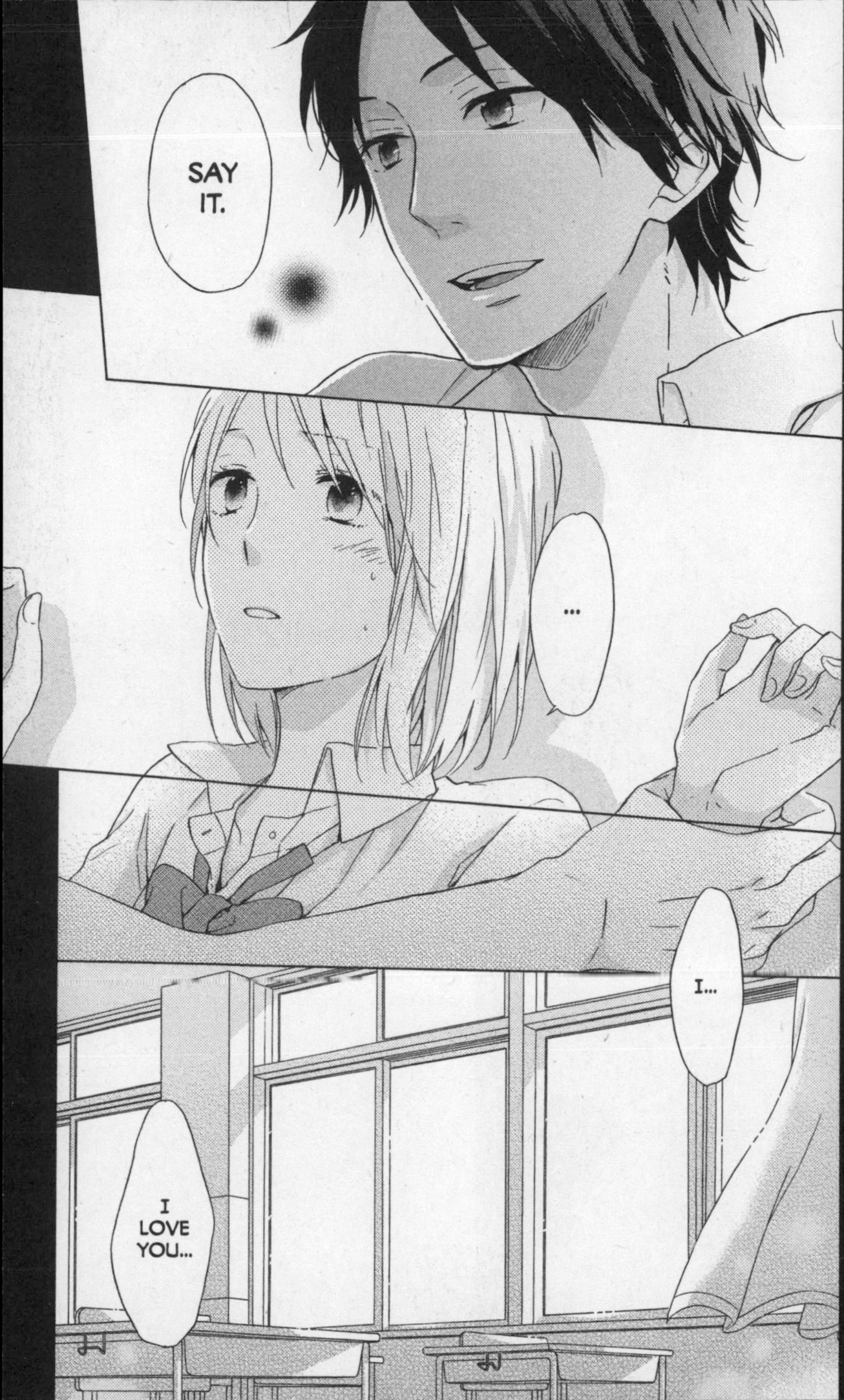
SAY IT.
...
I...
I LOVE YOU...

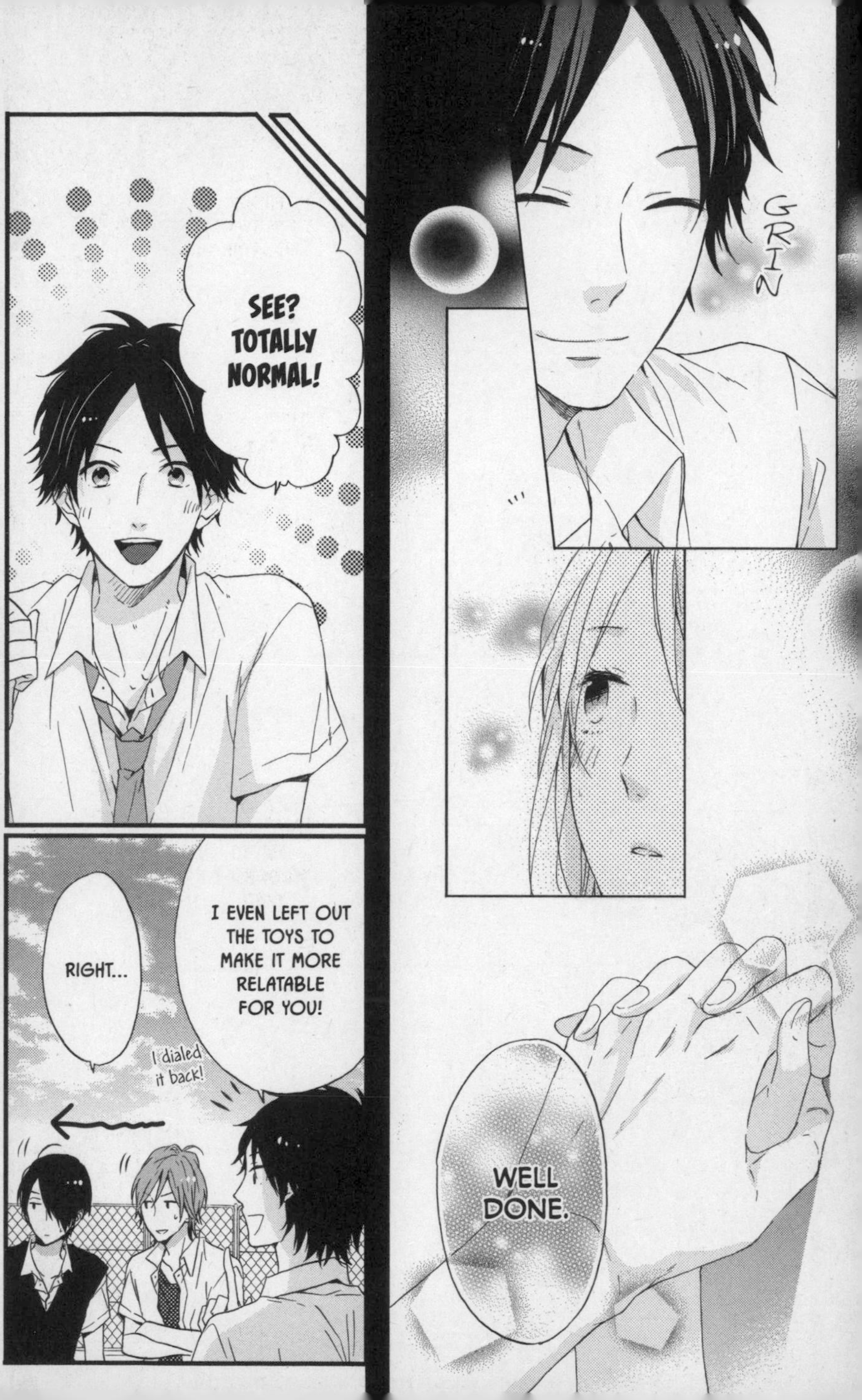
GRIN
WELL DONE.
SEE? TOTALLY NORMAL!
I EVEN LEFT OUT THE TOYS TO MAKE IT MORE RELATABLE FOR YOU!
RIGHT...
I dialed it back!

MY ASSISTANTS & I

When one of my assistants who likes Kobayakawa saw this page, she said...

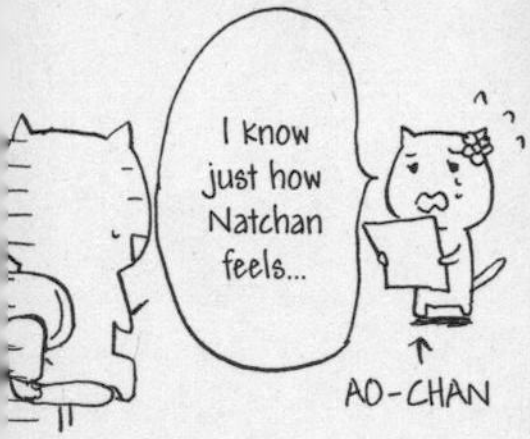
I know just how Natchan feels...
AO-CHAN

...which left a deep impression. Sorry about that.

Also, when I was drawing Chapter 9, it was around Valentine's Day, and one of my assistants made me a cheesecake. It was sooo good!

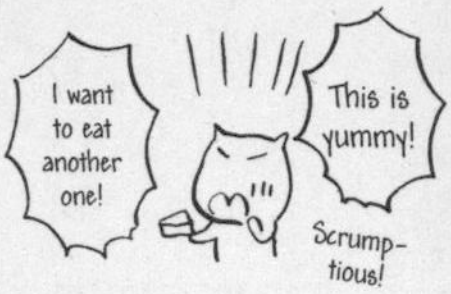
This is yummy!
I want to eat another one!
Scrumptious!

Incidentally, that assistant's name is also Matsunaga! (They've been on the team since the tennis chapter.)

Making sweets...
My hat goes off to Matsunaga-san's girl power...

Hey! I just realized that Mattsun also makes sweets!!! They're the same!!!

I should learn from the two of them and try some baking...

Wait, I can't. I don't have an oven.

Maybe I'll buy one...

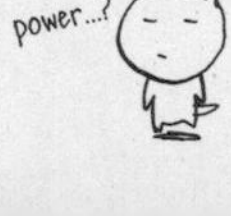
Girl power...?

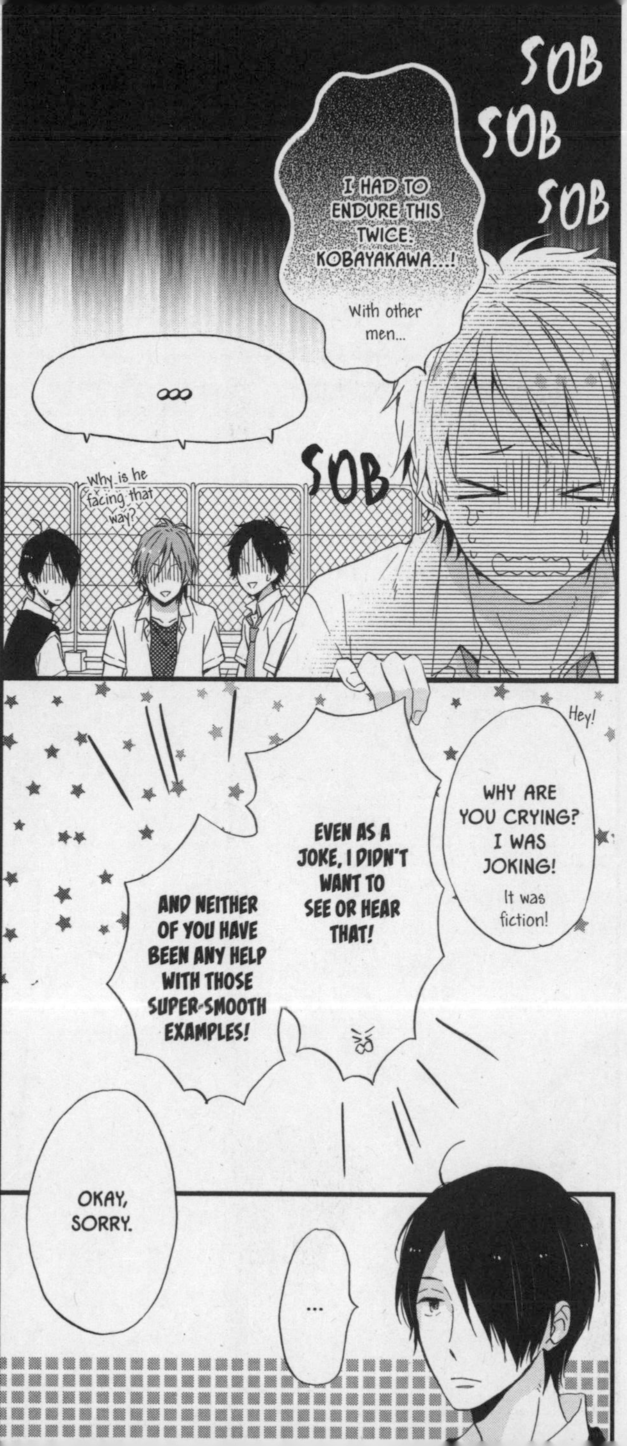
SOB SOB SOB
I HAD TO ENDURE THIS TWICE. KOBAYAKAWA...!
With other men...
...
SOB
Why is he facing that way?
Hey!
WHY ARE YOU CRYING? I WAS JOKING!
It was fiction!
EVEN AS A JOKE, I DIDN'T WANT TO SEE OR HEAR THAT!
AND NEITHER OF YOU HAVE BEEN ANY HELP WITH THOSE SUPER-SMOOTH EXAMPLES!
...
OKAY, SORRY.

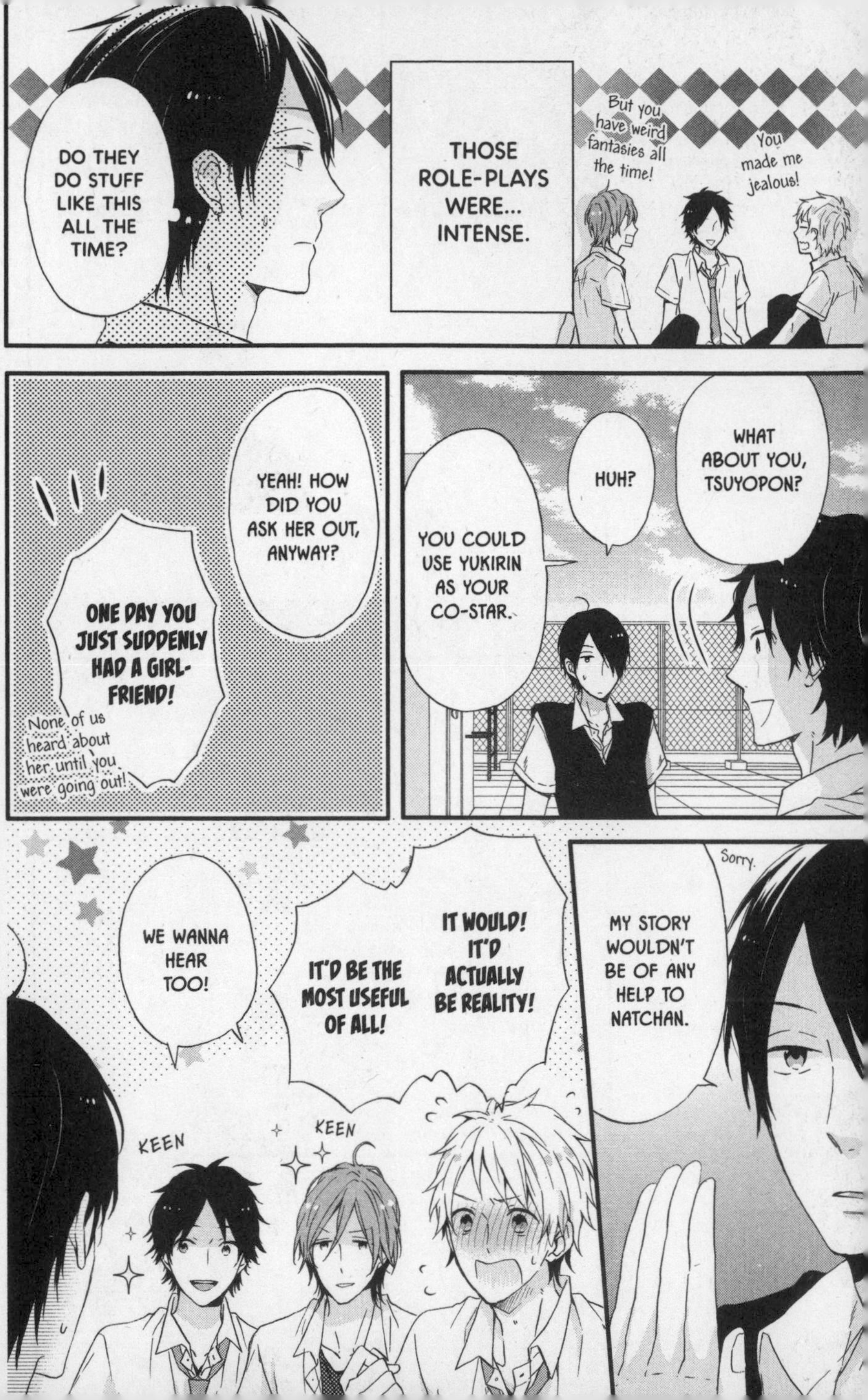
You made me jealous!
But you have weird fantasies all the time!
THOSE ROLE-PLAYS WERE... INTENSE.
DO THEY DO STUFF LIKE THIS ALL THE TIME?
WHAT ABOUT YOU, TSUYOPON?
HUH?
YOU COULD USE YUKIRIN AS YOUR CO-STAR.
YEAH! HOW DID YOU ASK HER OUT, ANYWAY?
ONE DAY YOU JUST SUDDENLY HAD A GIRL-FRIEND!
None of us heard about her until you were going out!
Sorry.
MY STORY WOULDN'T BE OF ANY HELP TO NATCHAN.
IT WOULD! IT'D ACTUALLY BE REALITY!
IT'D BE THE MOST USEFUL OF ALL!
WE WANNA HEAR TOO!
KEEN
KEEN

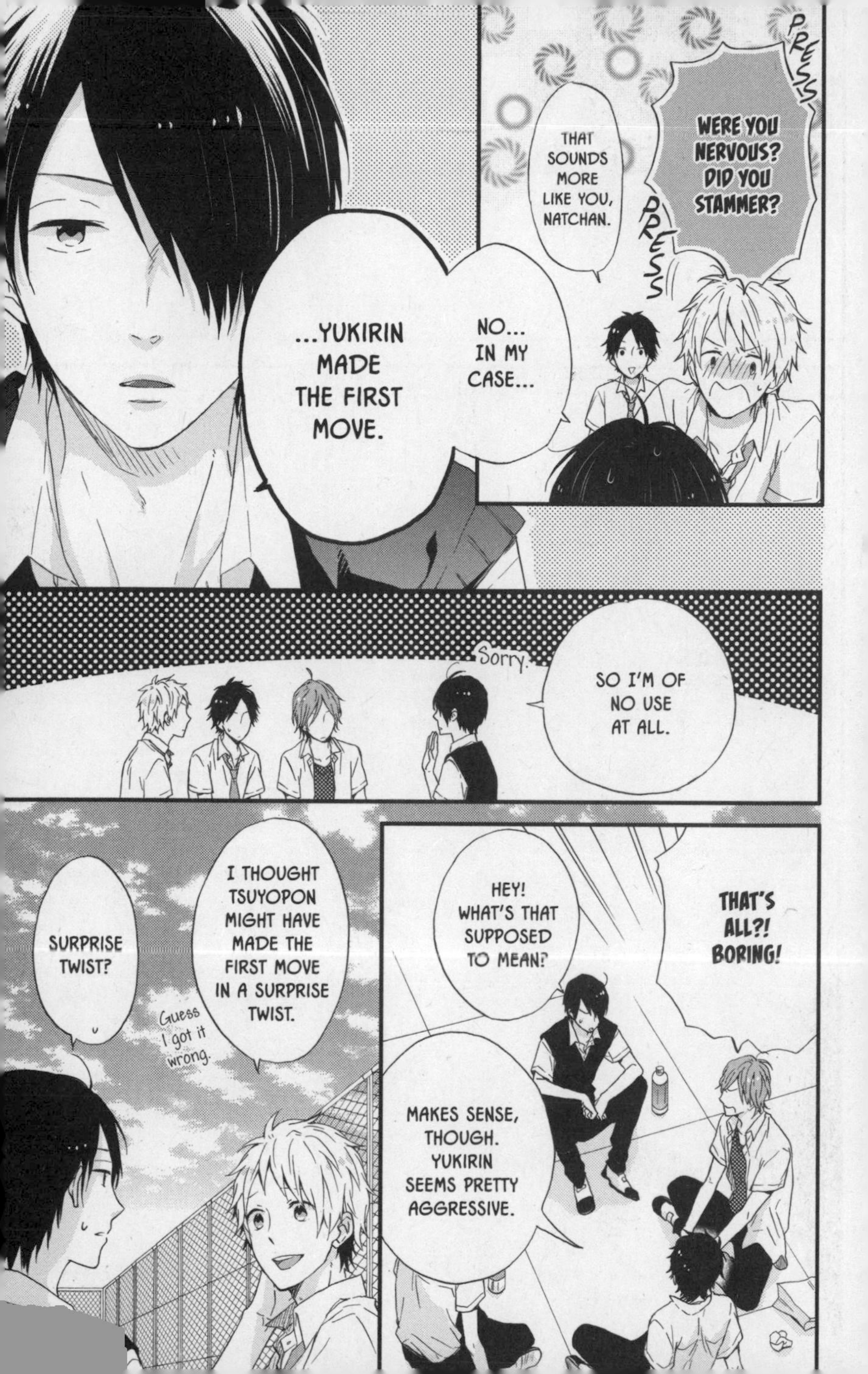
PRESS
WERE YOU NERVOUS? DID YOU STAMMER?
PRESS
THAT SOUNDS MORE LIKE YOU, NATCHAN.
NO... IN MY CASE...
...YUKIRIN MADE THE FIRST MOVE.
SO I'M OF NO USE AT ALL.
Sorry.
THAT'S ALL?! BORING!
HEY! WHAT'S THAT SUPPOSED TO MEAN?
MAKES SENSE, THOUGH. YUKIRIN SEEMS PRETTY AGGRESSIVE.
I THOUGHT TSUYOPON MIGHT HAVE MADE THE FIRST MOVE IN A SURPRISE TWIST.
Guess I got it wrong.
SURPRISE TWIST?

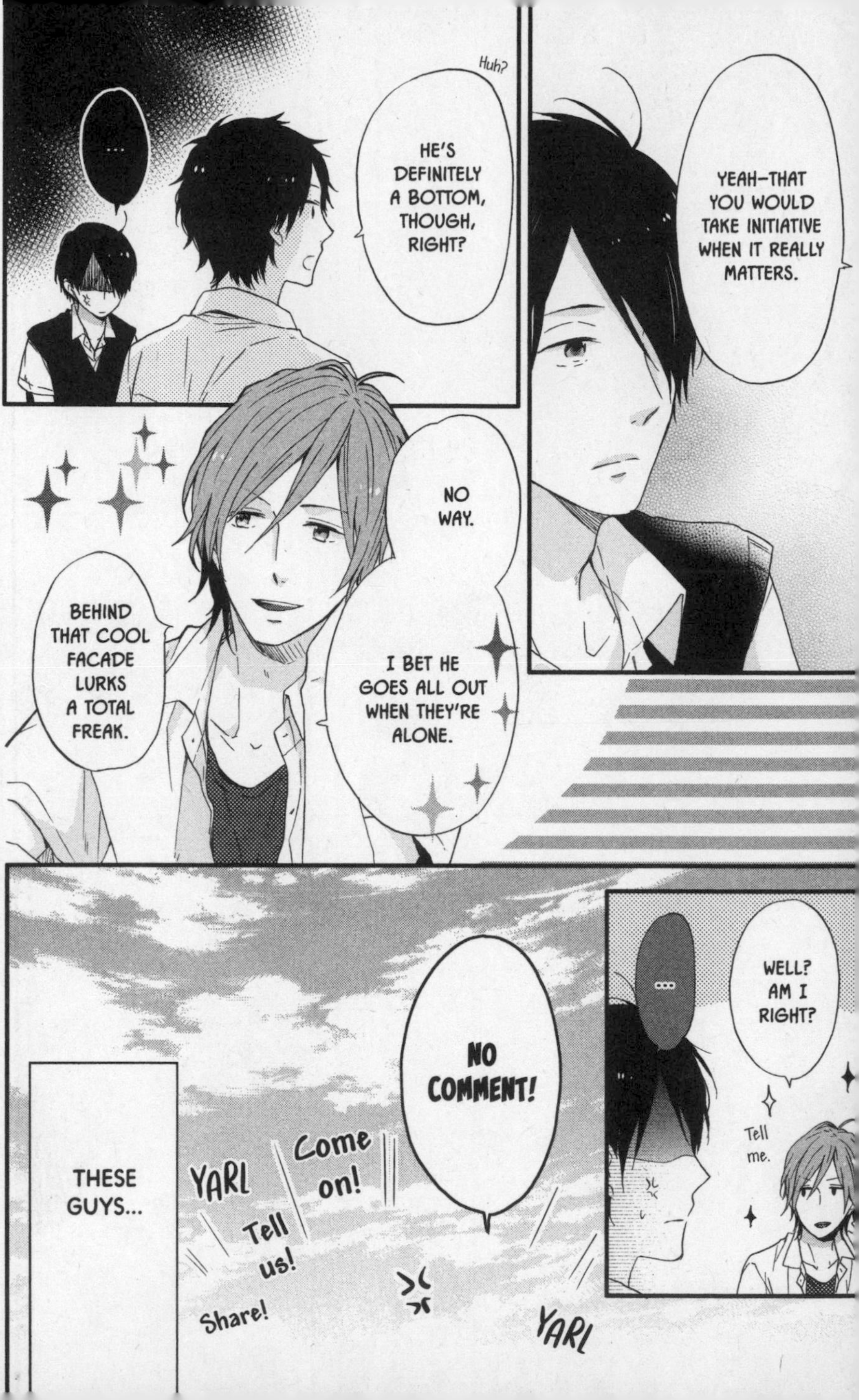
YEAH—THAT YOU WOULD TAKE INITIATIVE WHEN IT REALLY MATTERS.
Huh?
HE'S DEFINITELY A BOTTOM, THOUGH, RIGHT?
...
NO WAY.
I BET HE GOES ALL OUT WHEN THEY'RE ALONE.
BEHIND THAT COOL FACADE LURKS A TOTAL FREAK.
...
WELL? AM I RIGHT?
Tell me.
NO COMMENT!
Come on!
YARL
Tell us!
Share!
YARL
THESE GUYS...

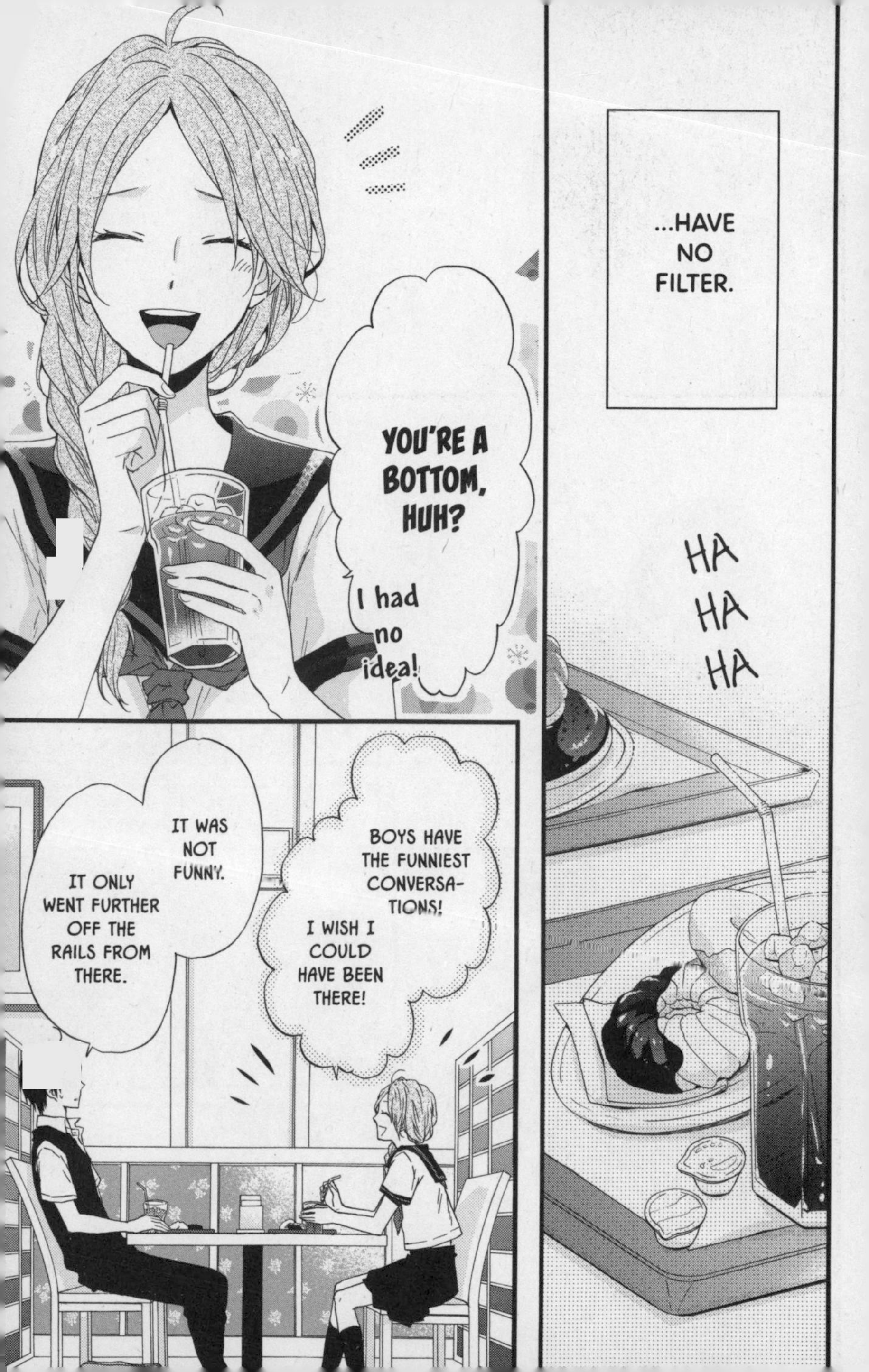
...HAVE NO FILTER.
HA HA HA
YOU'RE A BOTTOM, HUH?
I had no idea!
BOYS HAVE THE FUNNIEST CONVERSA-TIONS!
I WISH I COULD HAVE BEEN THERE!
IT WAS NOT FUNNY.
IT ONLY WENT FURTHER OFF THE RAILS FROM THERE.

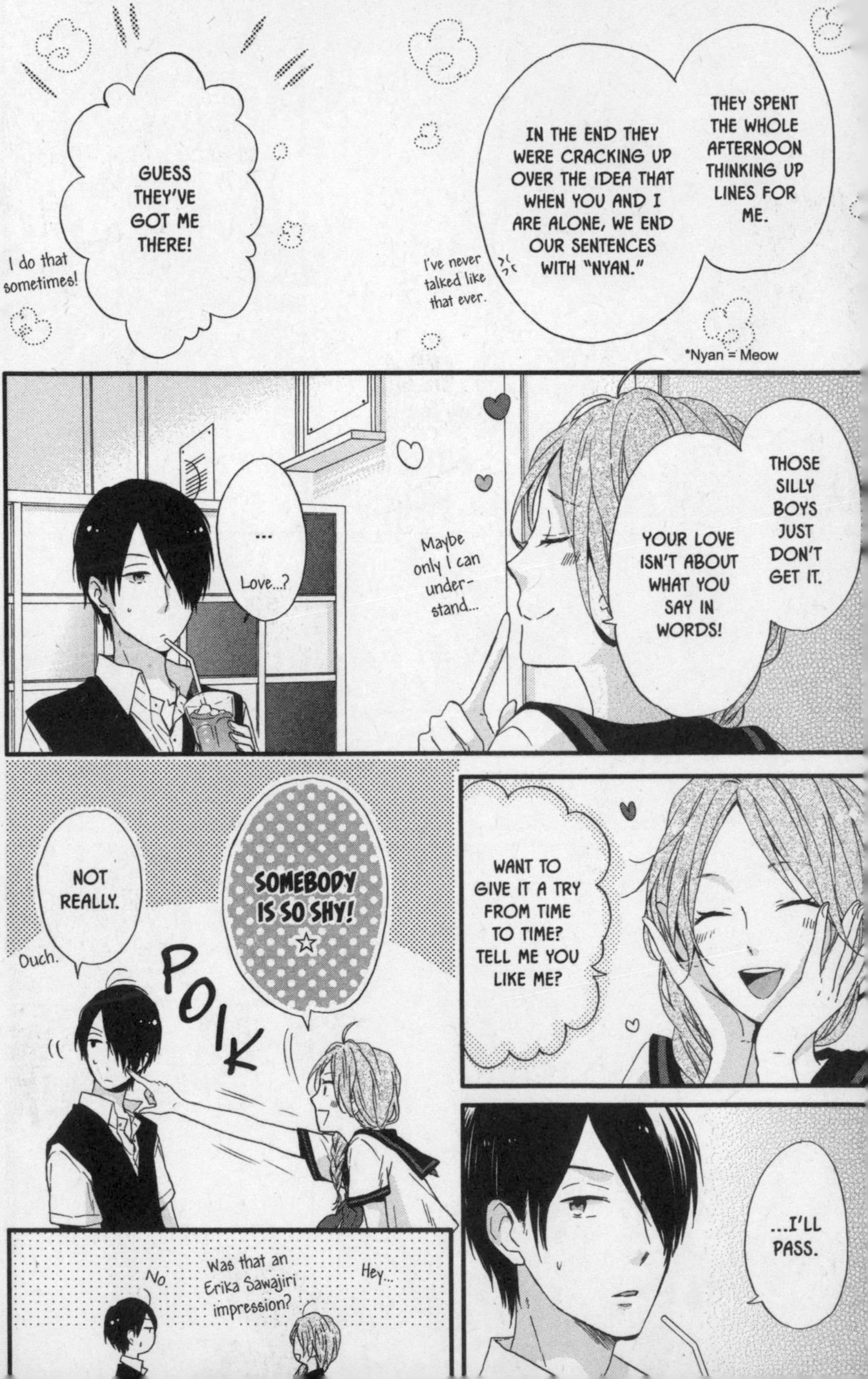
THEY SPENT THE WHOLE AFTERNOON THINKING UP LINES FOR ME.
IN THE END THEY WERE CRACKING UP OVER THE IDEA THAT WHEN YOU AND I ARE ALONE, WE END OUR SENTENCES WITH "NYAN."
I've never talked like that ever.
GUESS THEY'VE GOT ME THERE!
I do that sometimes!
*Nyan = Meow
THOSE SILLY BOYS JUST DON'T GET IT.
YOUR LOVE ISN'T ABOUT WHAT YOU SAY IN WORDS!
Maybe only I can under-stand...
... Love...?
WANT TO GIVE IT A TRY FROM TIME TO TIME? TELL ME YOU LIKE ME?
...I'LL PASS.
SOMEBODY IS SO SHY! ☆
POIK
NOT REALLY.
Ouch.
Hey...
Was that an Erika Sawajiri impression?
No.

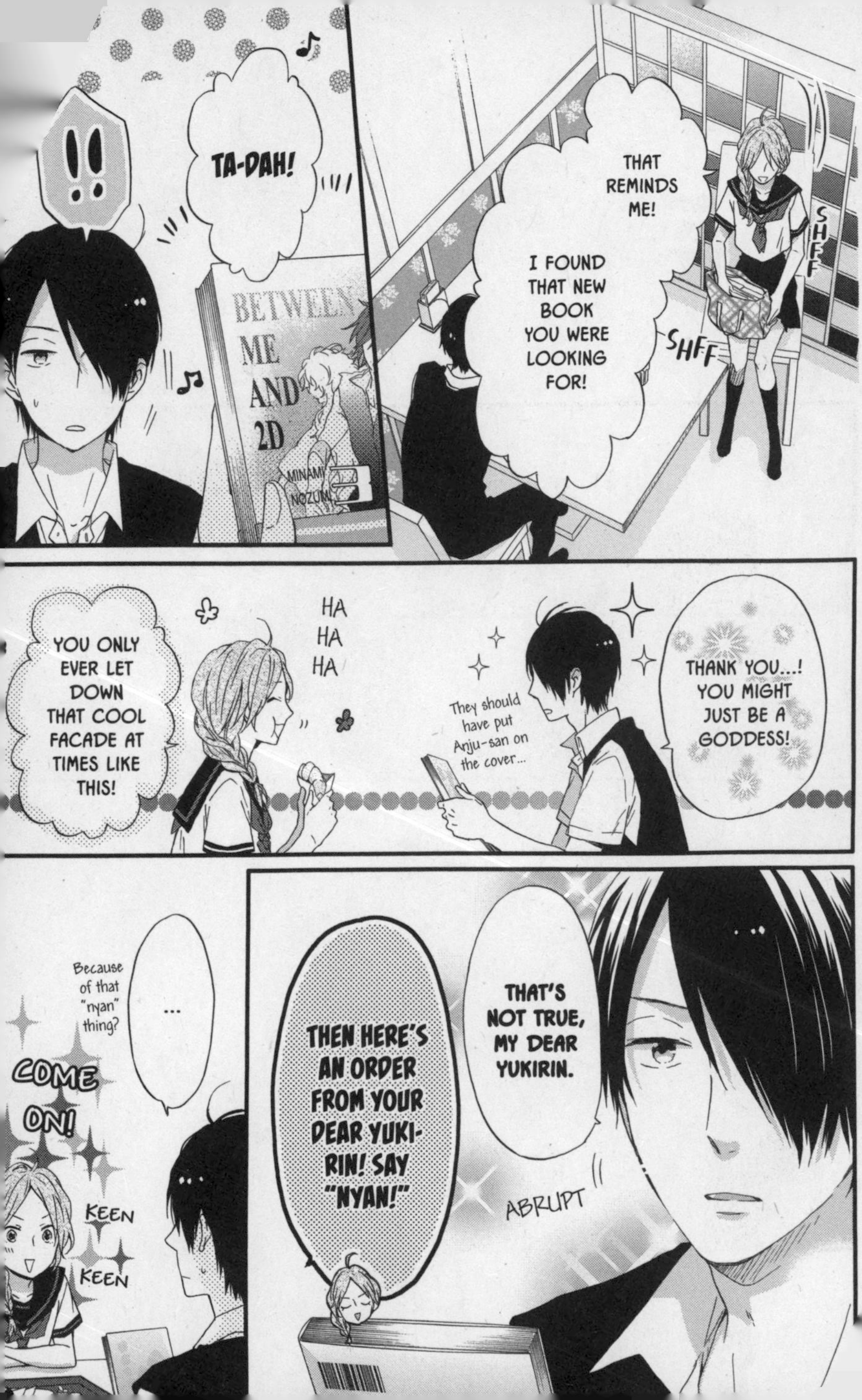
THAT REMINDS ME!
I FOUND THAT NEW BOOK YOU WERE LOOKING FOR!
SHFF
SHFF
!!
TA-DAH!
BETWEEN ME AND 2D
MINAMI NOZUMI
THANK YOU...! YOU MIGHT JUST BE A GODDESS!
They should have put Anju-san on the cover...
HA HA HA
YOU ONLY EVER LET DOWN THAT COOL FACADE AT TIMES LIKE THIS!
THAT'S NOT TRUE, MY DEAR YUKIRIN.
ABRUPT
THEN HERE'S AN ORDER FROM YOUR DEAR YUKI-RIN! SAY "NYAN!"
...
Because of that "nyan" thing?
COME ON!
KEEN
KEEN

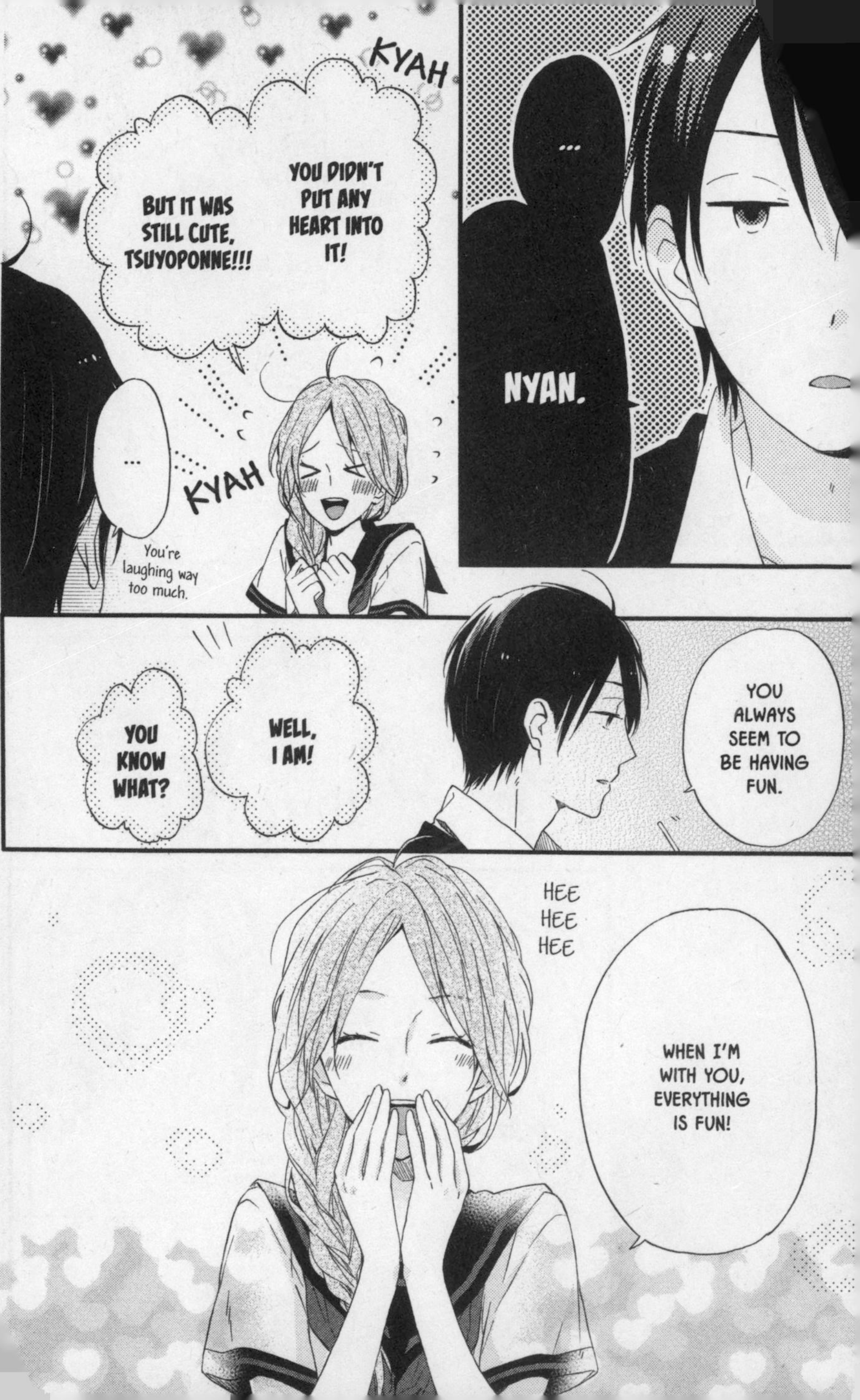
...
NYAN.
KYAH
YOU DIDN'T PUT ANY HEART INTO IT!
BUT IT WAS STILL CUTE, TSUYOPONNE!!!
...
KYAH
You're laughing way too much.
YOU ALWAYS SEEM TO BE HAVING FUN.
WELL, I AM!
YOU KNOW WHAT?
WHEN I'M WITH YOU, EVERYTHING IS FUN!
HEE HEE HEE

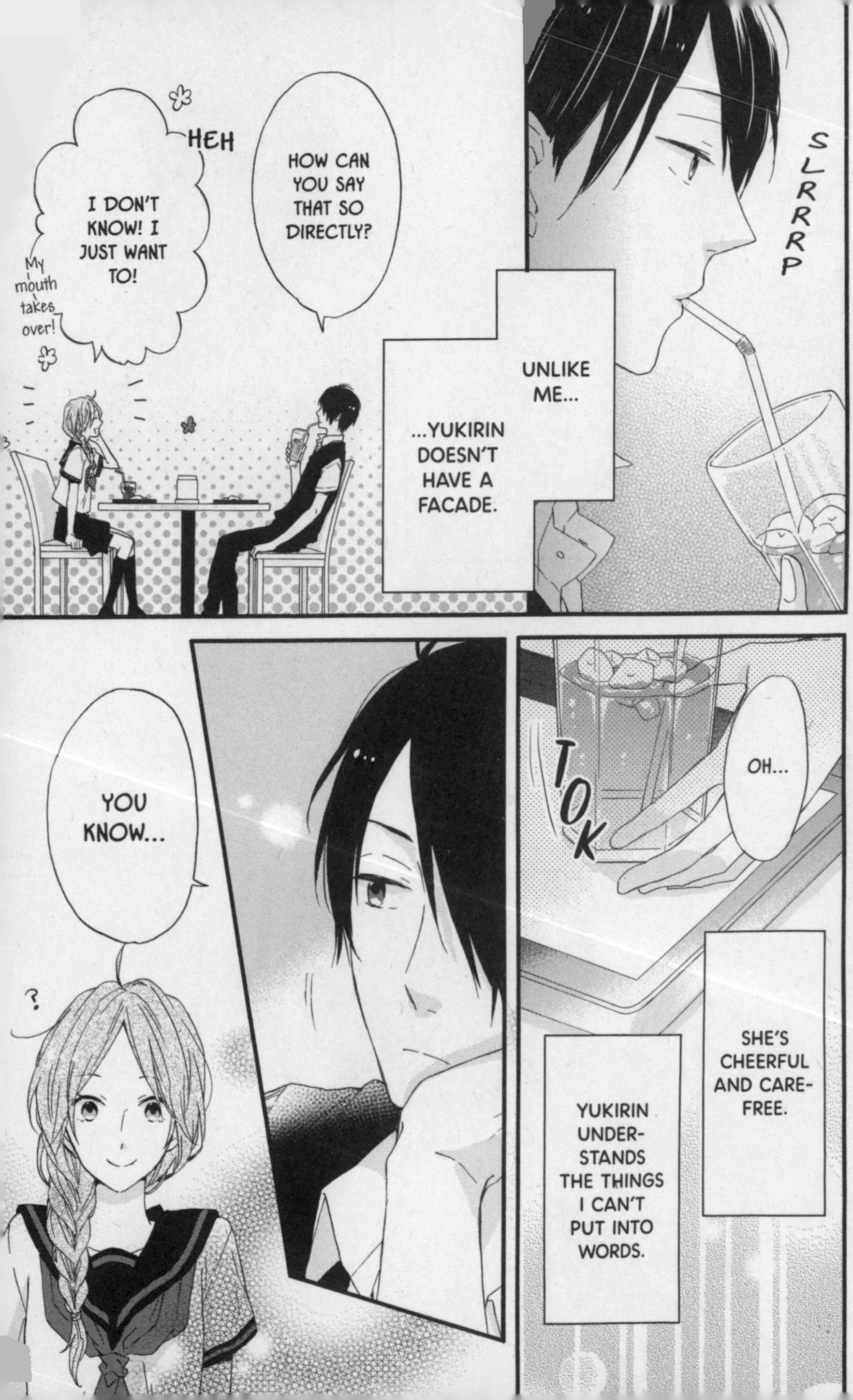
SLRRRP
UNLIKE ME...
...YUKIRIN DOESN'T HAVE A FACADE.
HOW CAN YOU SAY THAT SO DIRECTLY?
HEH
I DON'T KNOW! I JUST WANT TO!
My mouth takes over!
TOK
OH...
SHE'S CHEERFUL AND CARE-FREE.
YUKIRIN UNDERSTANDS THE THINGS I CAN'T PUT INTO WORDS.
YOU KNOW...
?

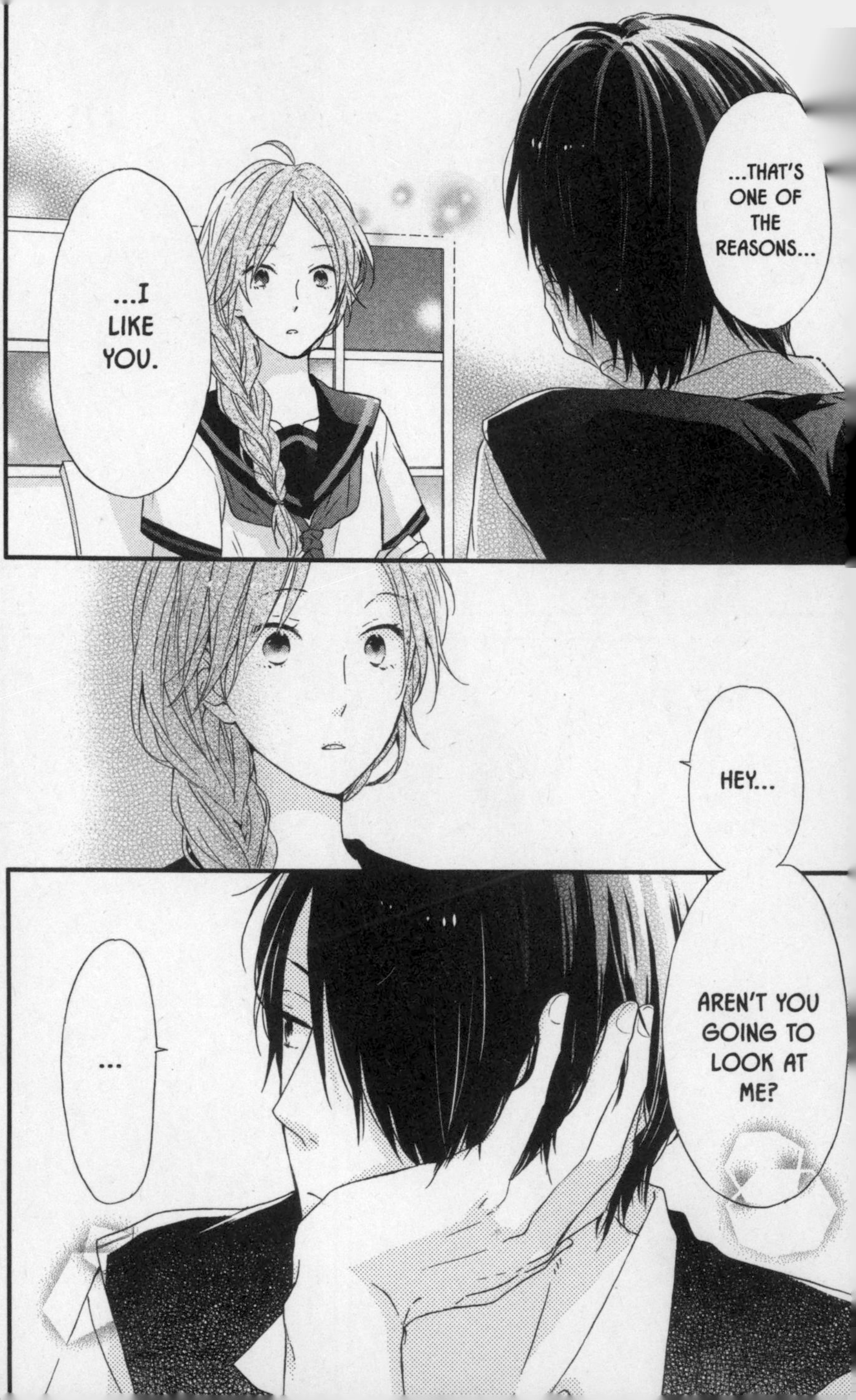
...THAT'S ONE OF THE REASONS...
...I LIKE YOU.
HEY...
AREN'T YOU GOING TO LOOK AT ME?
...

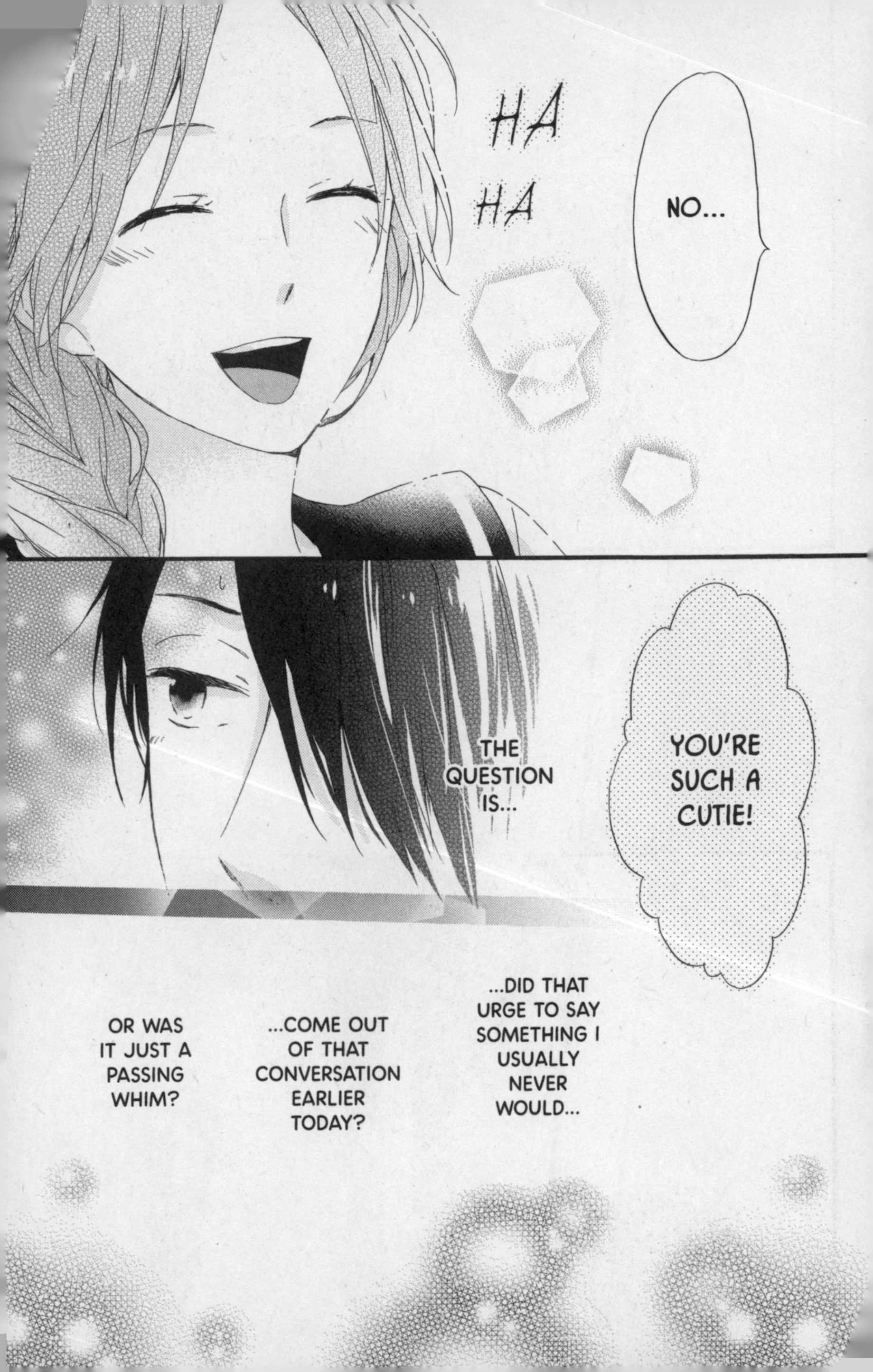
NO...
HA HA
YOU'RE SUCH A CUTIE!
THE QUESTION IS...
...DID THAT URGE TO SAY SOMETHING I USUALLY NEVER WOULD...
...COME OUT OF THAT CONVERSATION EARLIER TODAY?
OR WAS IT JUST A PASSING WHIM?

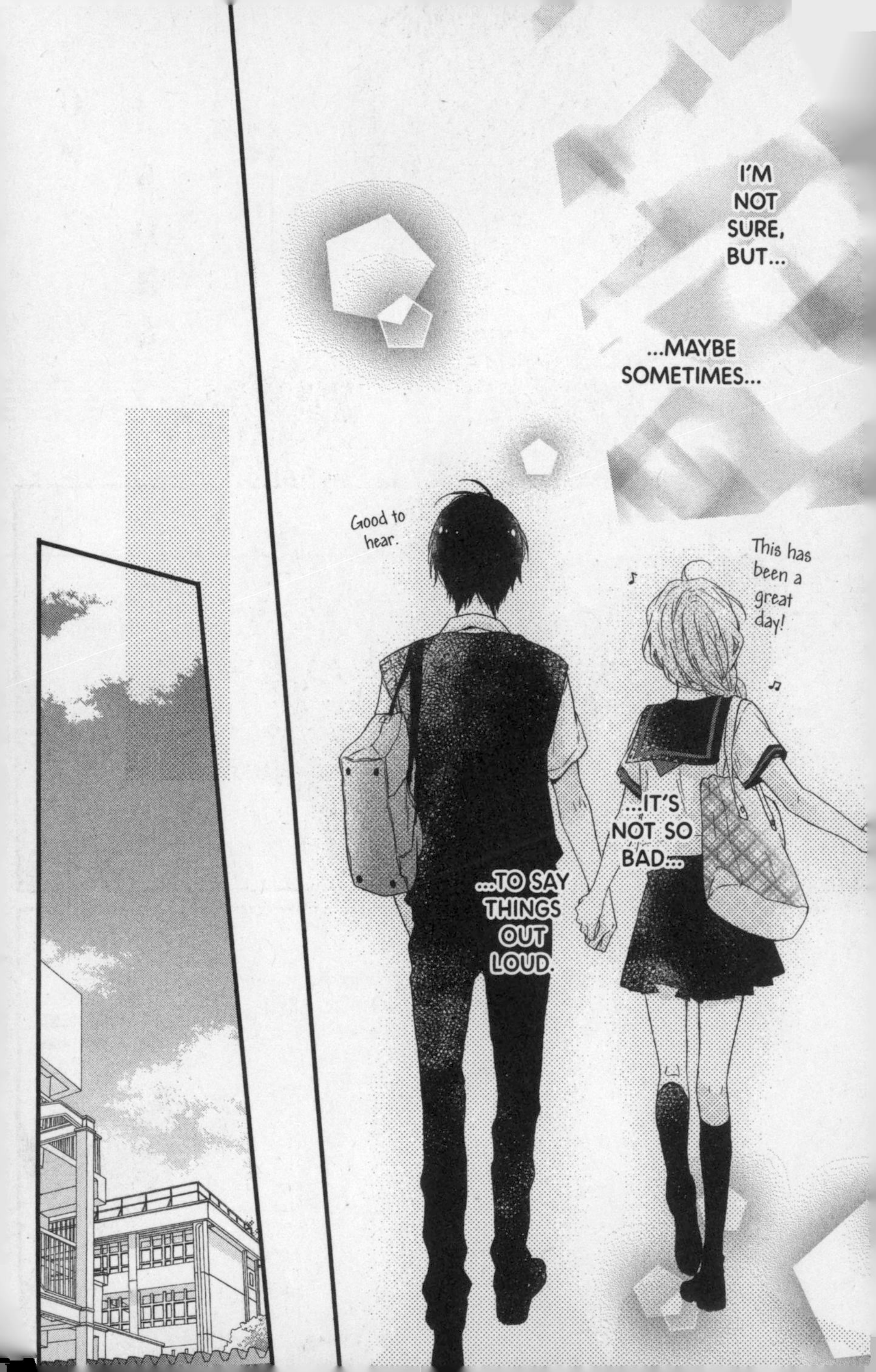
I'M NOT SURE, BUT...
...MAYBE SOMETIMES...
This has been a great day!
...IT'S NOT SO BAD...
...TO SAY THINGS OUT LOUD.
Good to hear.

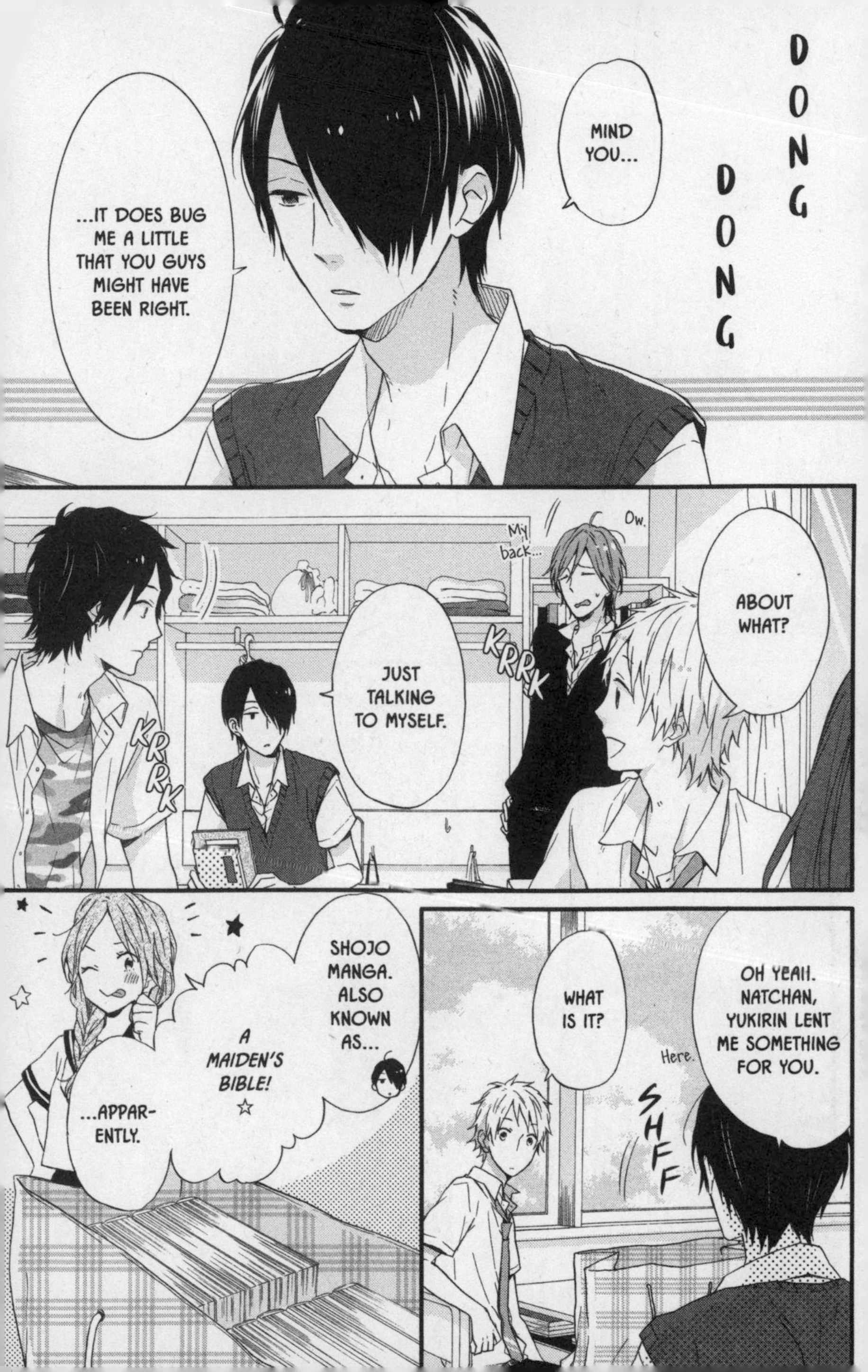
DONG
DONG
MIND YOU...
...IT DOES BUG ME A LITTLE THAT YOU GUYS MIGHT HAVE BEEN RIGHT.
ABOUT WHAT?
Ow.
My back...
KRRK
JUST TALKING TO MYSELF.
KRRK
OH YEAH. NATCHAN, YUKIRIN LENT ME SOMETHING FOR YOU.
Here.
SHFF
WHAT IS IT?
SHOJO MANGA. ALSO KNOWN AS...
A MAIDEN'S BIBLE!
...APPARENTLY.

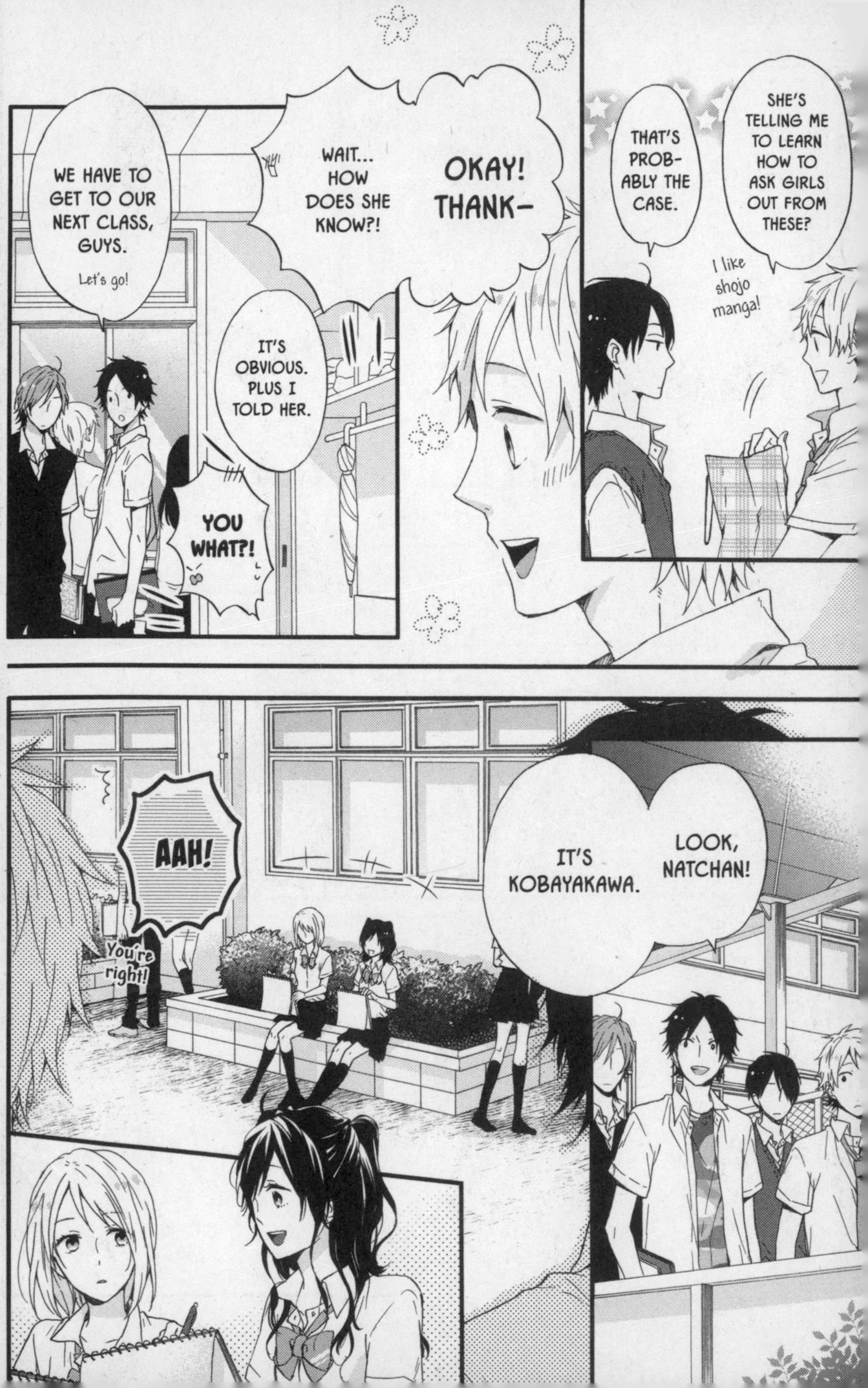
SHE'S TELLING ME TO LEARN HOW TO ASK GIRLS OUT FROM THESE?
I like shojo manga!
THAT'S PROB-ABLY THE CASE.
OKAY! THANK–
WAIT... HOW DOES SHE KNOW?!
IT'S OBVIOUS. PLUS I TOLD HER.
YOU WHAT?!
WE HAVE TO GET TO OUR NEXT CLASS, GUYS.
Let's go!
LOOK, NATCHAN!
IT'S KOBAYAKAWA.
AAH!
You're right!

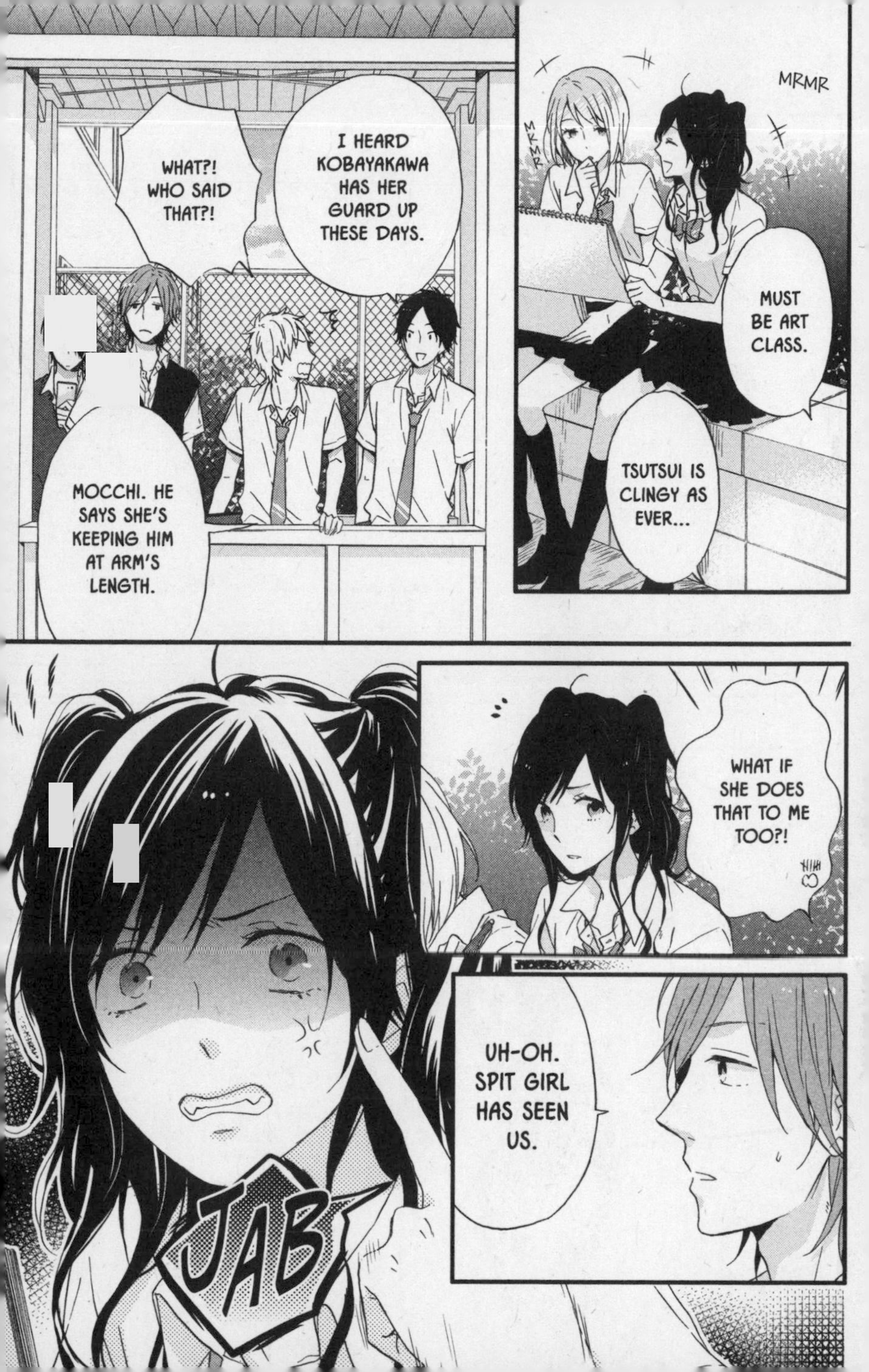
MRMR
MKMR
MUST BE ART CLASS.
TSUTSUI IS CLINGY AS EVER...
I HEARD KOBAYAKAWA HAS HER GUARD UP THESE DAYS.
WHAT?! WHO SAID THAT?!
MOCCHI. HE SAYS SHE'S KEEPING HIM AT ARM'S LENGTH.
WHAT IF SHE DOES THAT TO ME TOO?!
UH-OH. SPIT GIRL HAS SEEN US.
JAB

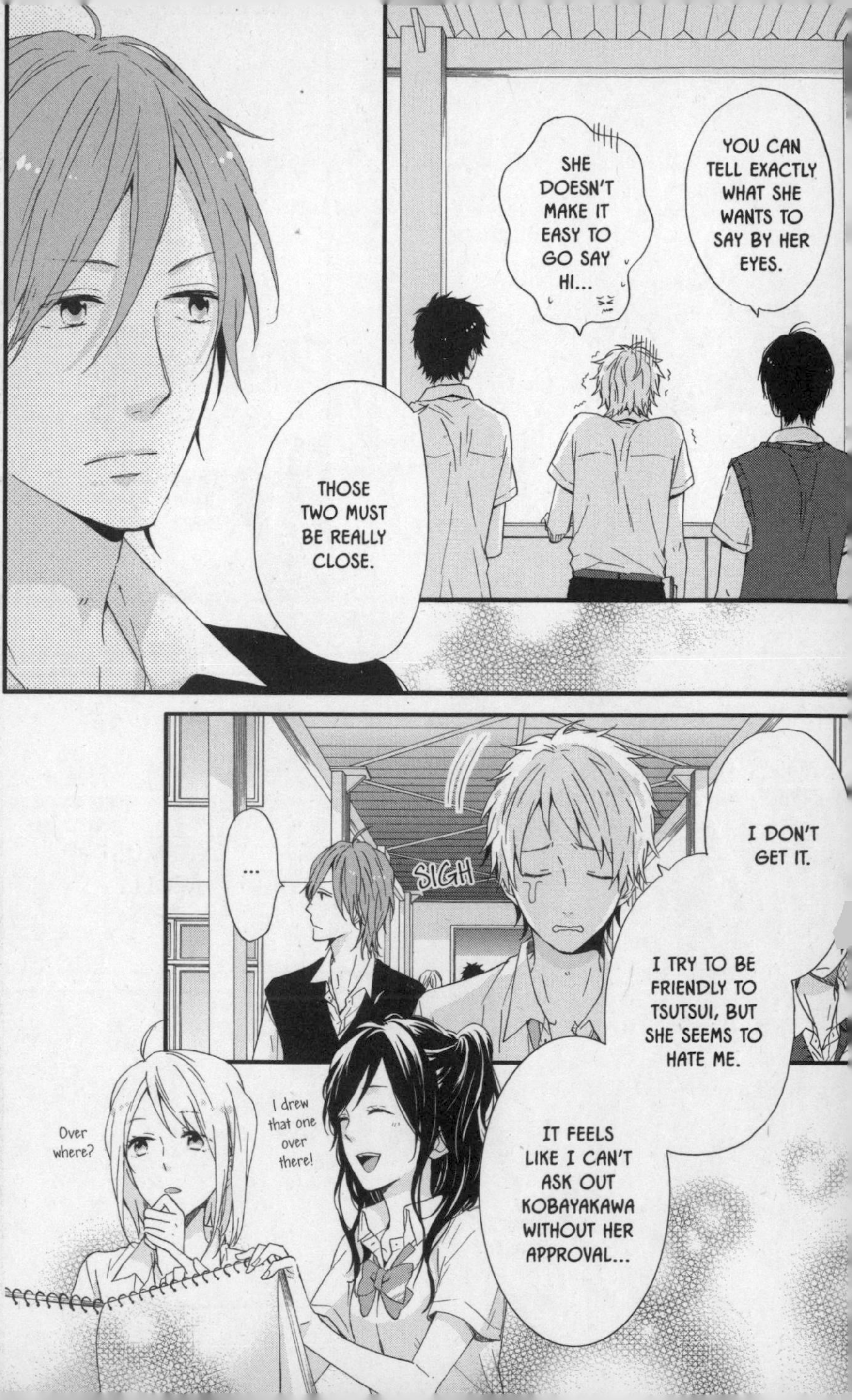
YOU CAN TELL EXACTLY WHAT SHE WANTS TO SAY BY HER EYES.
SHE DOESN'T MAKE IT EASY TO GO SAY HI...
THOSE TWO MUST BE REALLY CLOSE.
I DON'T GET IT.
I TRY TO BE FRIENDLY TO TSUTSUI, BUT SHE SEEMS TO HATE ME.
IT FEELS LIKE I CAN'T ASK OUT KOBAYAKAWA WITHOUT HER APPROVAL...
SIGH
...
I drew that one over there!
Over where?

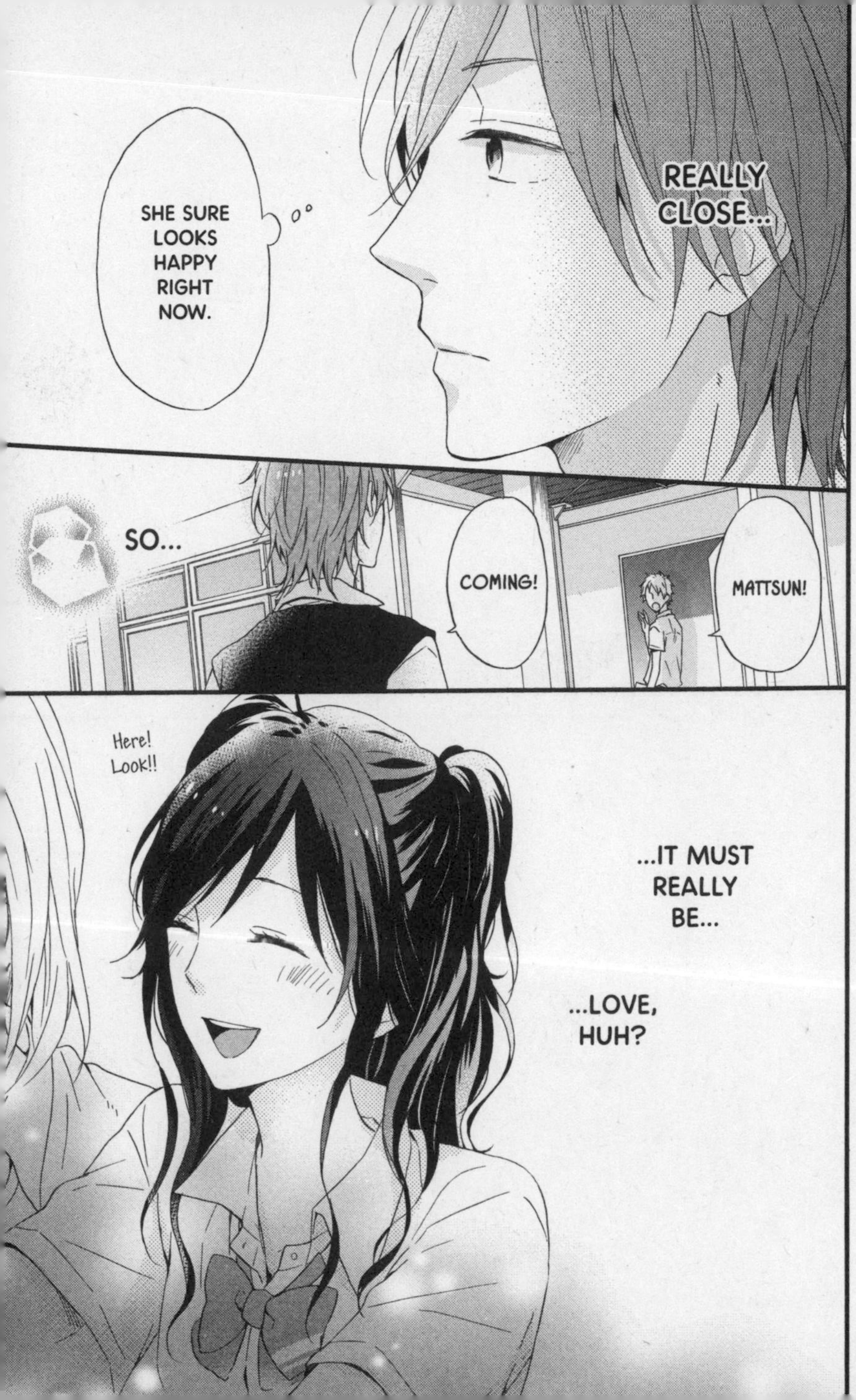
REALLY CLOSE...
SHE SURE LOOKS HAPPY RIGHT NOW.
MATTSUN!
COMING!
SO...
...IT MUST REALLY BE...
...LOVE, HUH?
Here! Look!!

Rainbow
Days

■　■　■　■　■　■　■

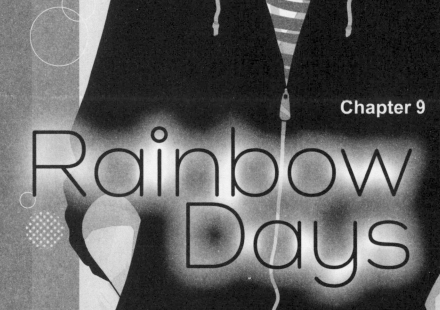

Chapter 9

Rainbow
Days

Rainbow
Days

■ ■ ■ ■ ■ ■ ■

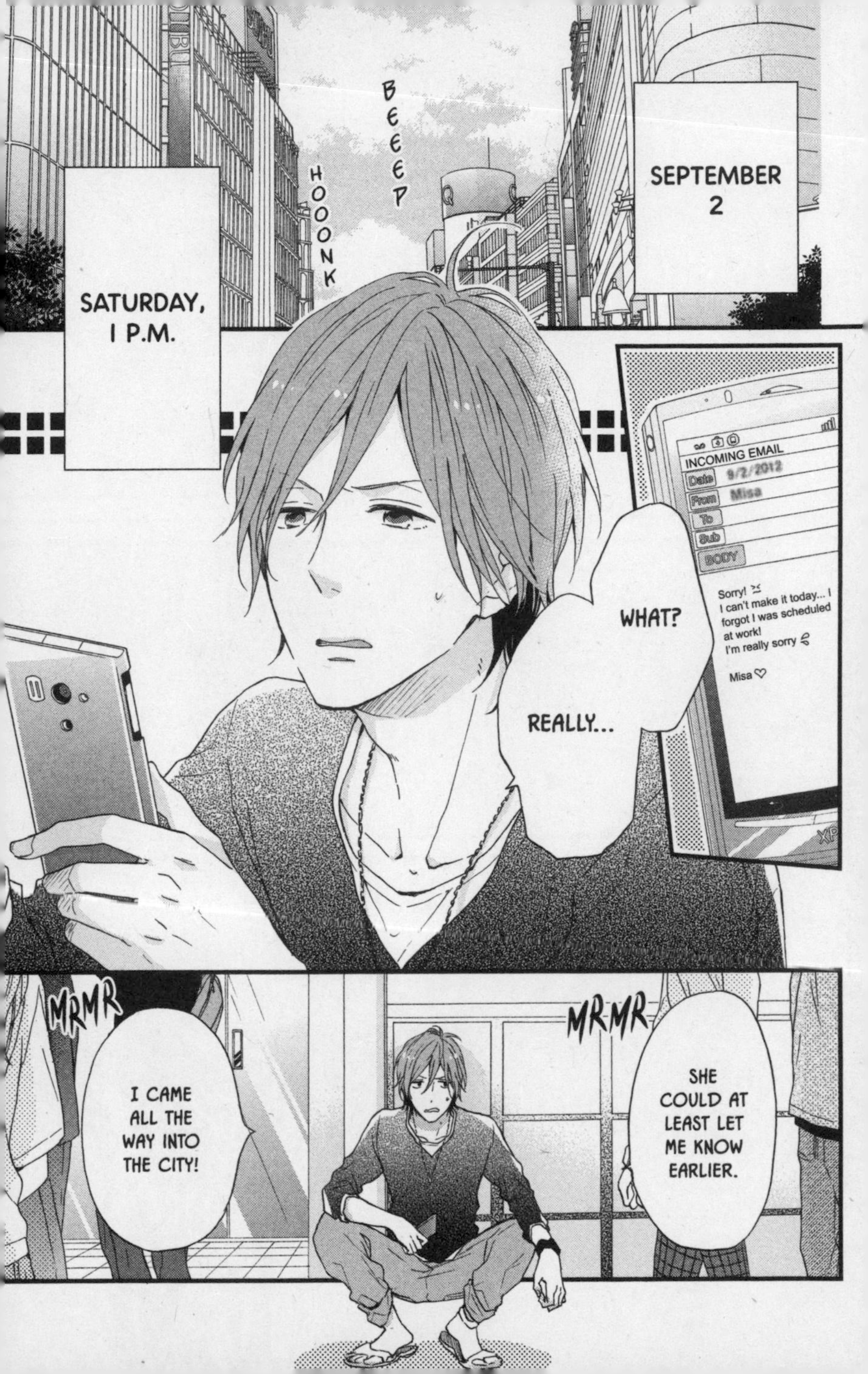
SEPTEMBER 2
BEEEEP
HOOOONK
SATURDAY, 1 P.M.
INCOMING EMAIL
Date 9/2/2012
From Misa
To
Sub
BODY
Sorry! I can't make it today... I forgot I was scheduled at work! I'm really sorry
Misa
WHAT?
REALLY...
MRMR
SHE COULD AT LEAST LET ME KNOW EARLIER.
MRMR
I CAME ALL THE WAY INTO THE CITY!

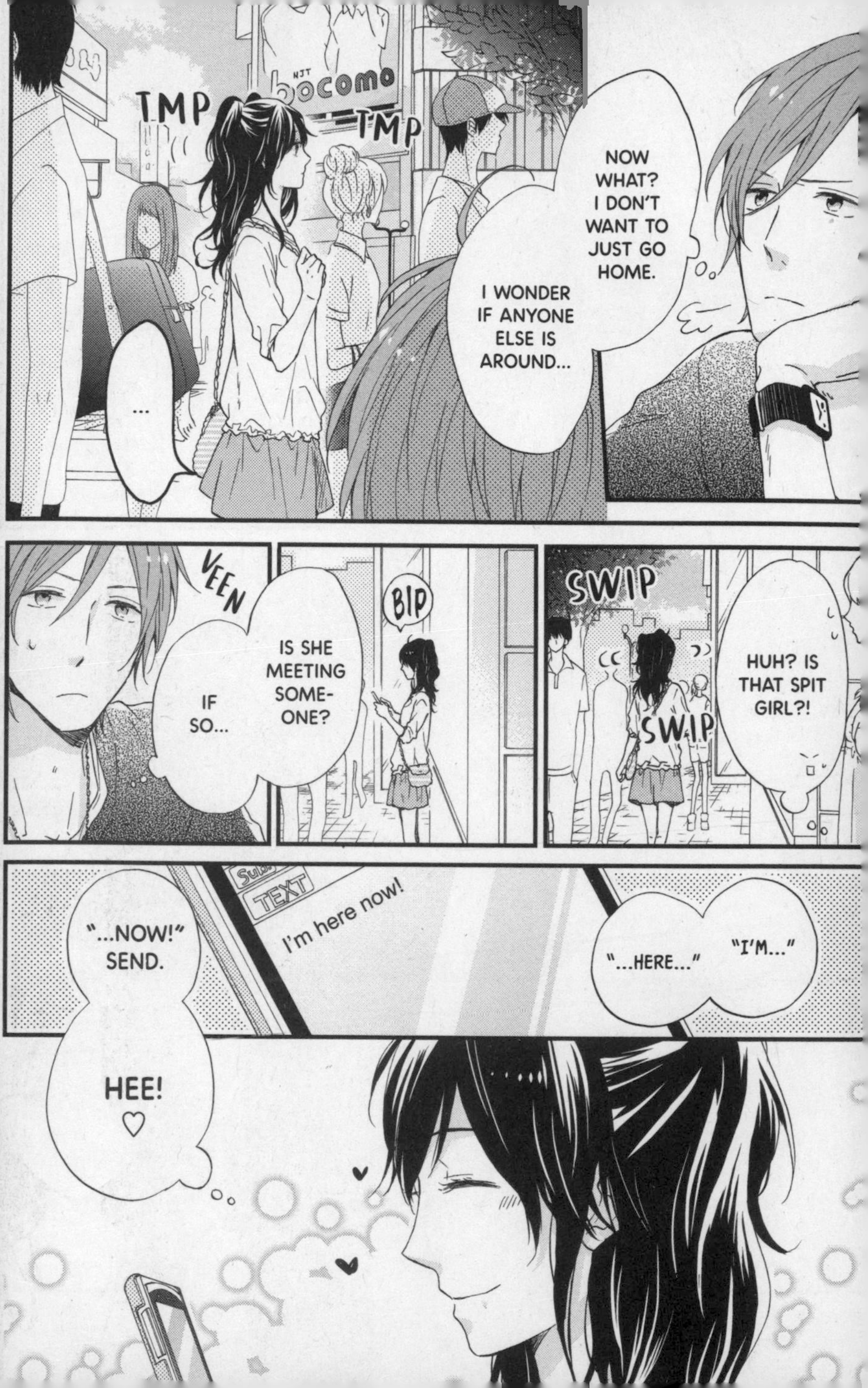
NOW WHAT? I DON'T WANT TO JUST GO HOME.
I WONDER IF ANYONE ELSE IS AROUND...
TMP
NJT bocomo
TMP
...
HUH? IS THAT SPIT GIRL?!
SWIP
SWIP
BIP
VEEN
IS SHE MEETING SOME-ONE?
IF SO...
"I'M..."
"...HERE..."
TEXT
I'm here now!
"...NOW!" SEND.
HEE! ♡

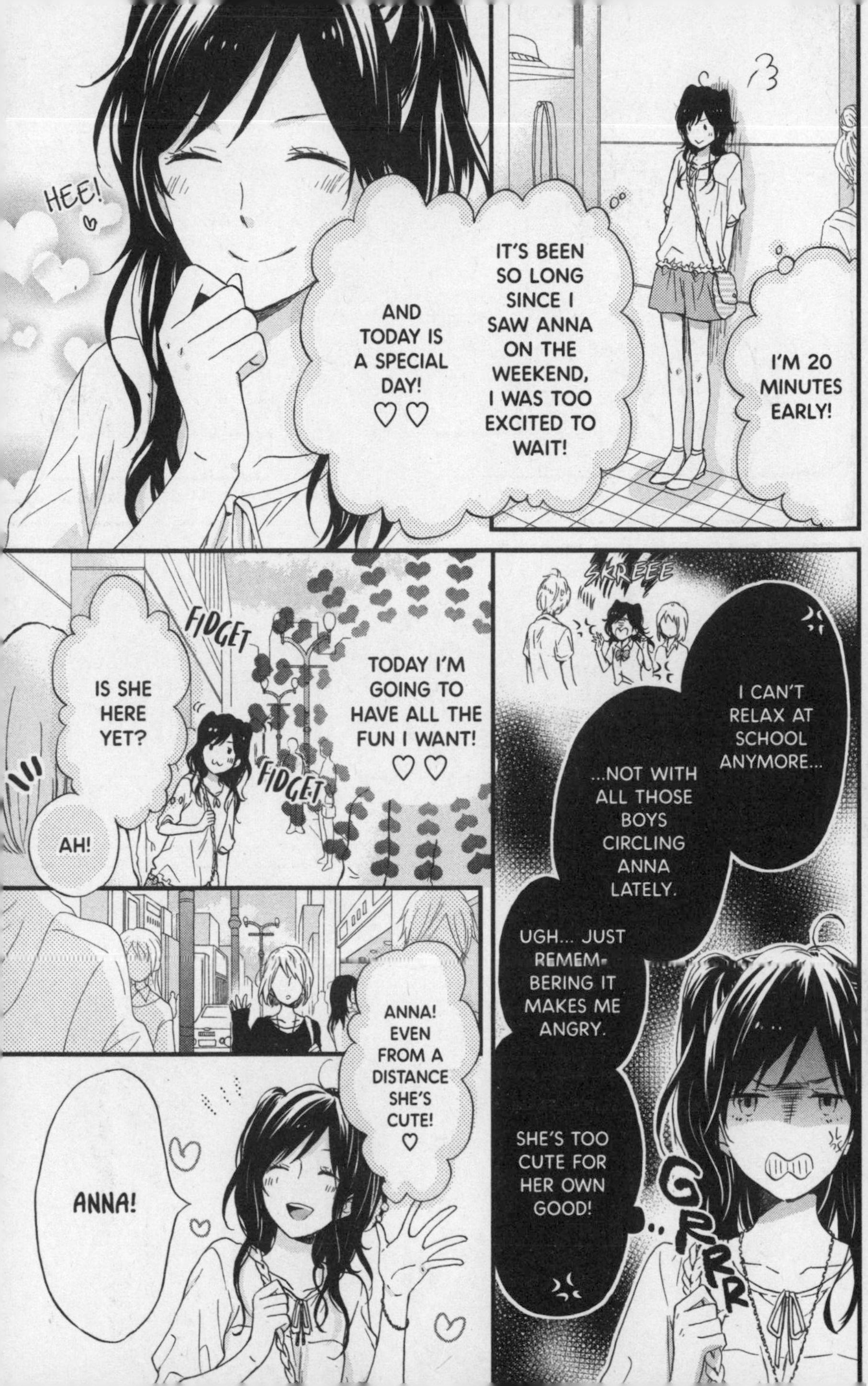
I'M 20 MINUTES EARLY!
IT'S BEEN SO LONG SINCE I SAW ANNA ON THE WEEKEND, I WAS TOO EXCITED TO WAIT!
AND TODAY IS A SPECIAL DAY! ♡ ♡
HEE! ♡
SKREEE
I CAN'T RELAX AT SCHOOL ANYMORE...
...NOT WITH ALL THOSE BOYS CIRCLING ANNA LATELY.
UGH... JUST REMEM-BERING IT MAKES ME ANGRY.
SHE'S TOO CUTE FOR HER OWN GOOD!
GRRR
TODAY I'M GOING TO HAVE ALL THE FUN I WANT! ♡ ♡
FIDGET
FIDGET
IS SHE HERE YET?
AH!
ANNA! EVEN FROM A DISTANCE SHE'S CUTE! ♡
ANNA!

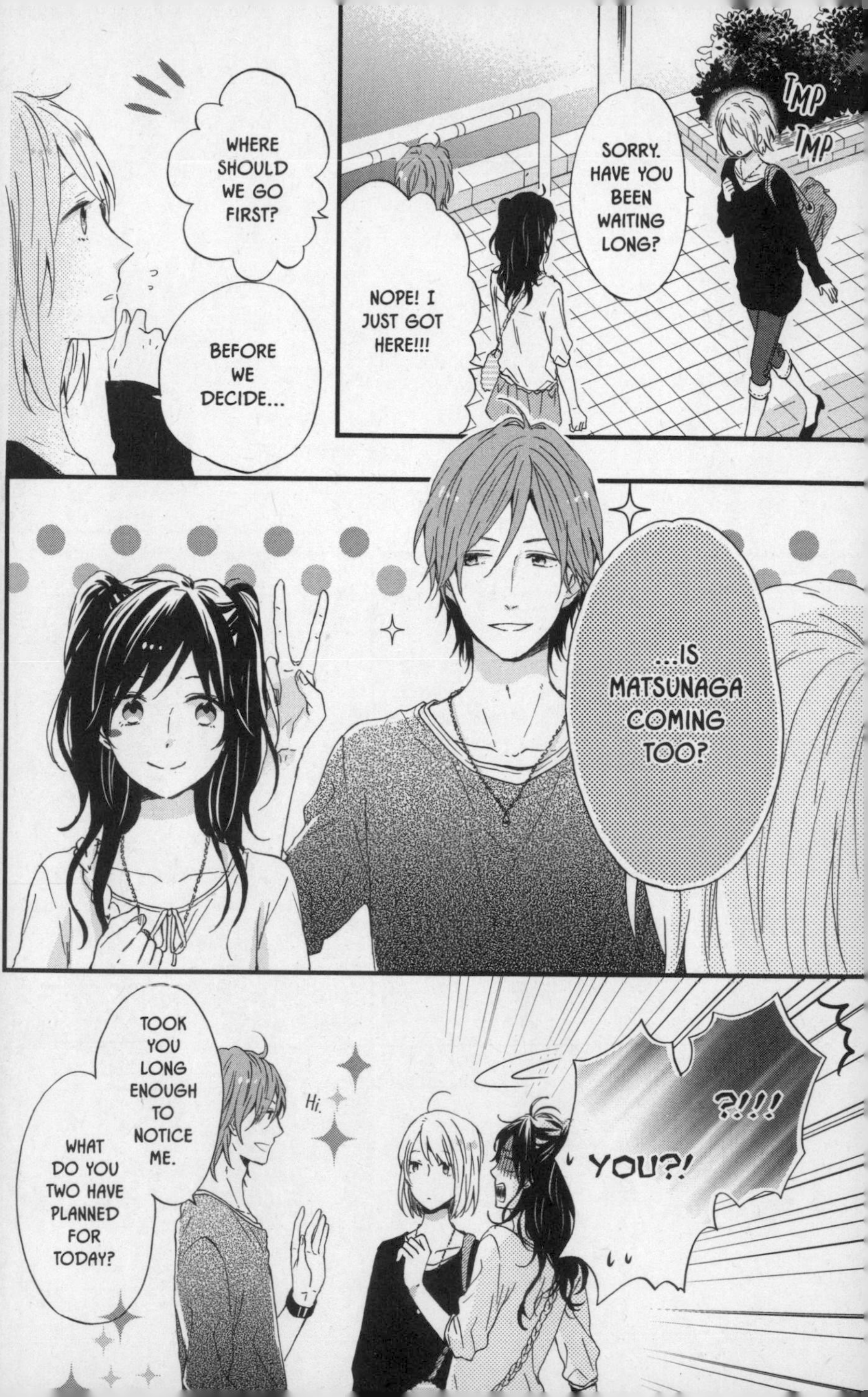
TMP TMP
SORRY. HAVE YOU BEEN WAITING LONG?
NOPE! I JUST GOT HERE!!!
WHERE SHOULD WE GO FIRST?
BEFORE WE DECIDE...
...IS MATSUNAGA COMING TOO?
?!!!
YOU?!
Hi.
TOOK YOU LONG ENOUGH TO NOTICE ME.
WHAT DO YOU TWO HAVE PLANNED FOR TODAY?

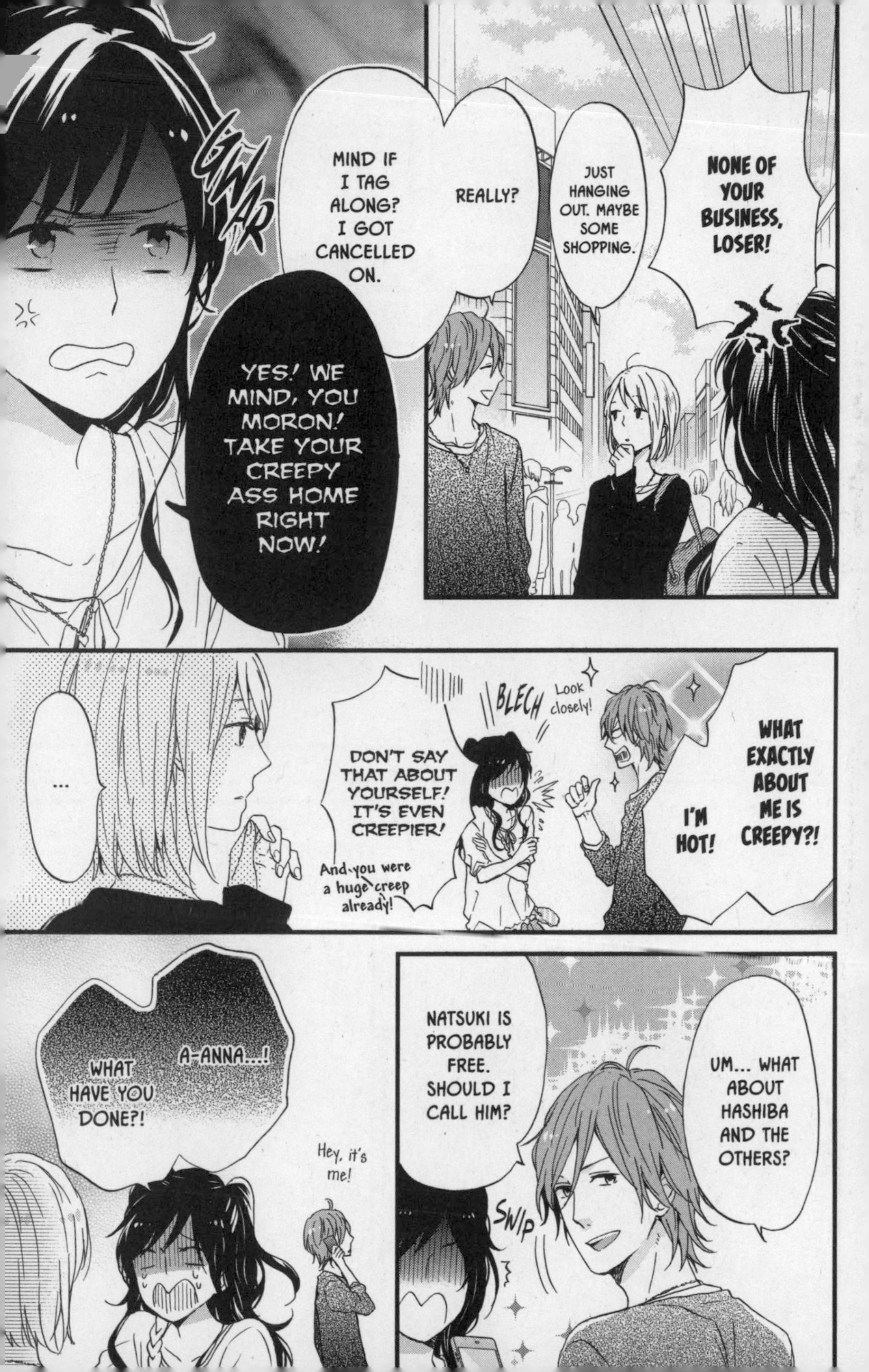

NONE OF YOUR BUSINESS, LOSER!
JUST HANGING OUT. MAYBE SOME SHOPPING.
REALLY?
MIND IF I TAG ALONG? I GOT CANCELLED ON.
GWAR
YES! WE MIND, YOU MORON! TAKE YOUR CREEPY ASS HOME RIGHT NOW!
WHAT EXACTLY ABOUT ME IS CREEPY?!
I'M HOT!
Look closely!
BLECH
DON'T SAY THAT ABOUT YOURSELF! IT'S EVEN CREEPIER!
And you were a huge creep already!
...
UM... WHAT ABOUT HASHIBA AND THE OTHERS?
NATSUKI IS PROBABLY FREE. SHOULD I CALL HIM?
SWIP
Hey, it's me!
A-ANNA...!
WHAT HAVE YOU DONE?!

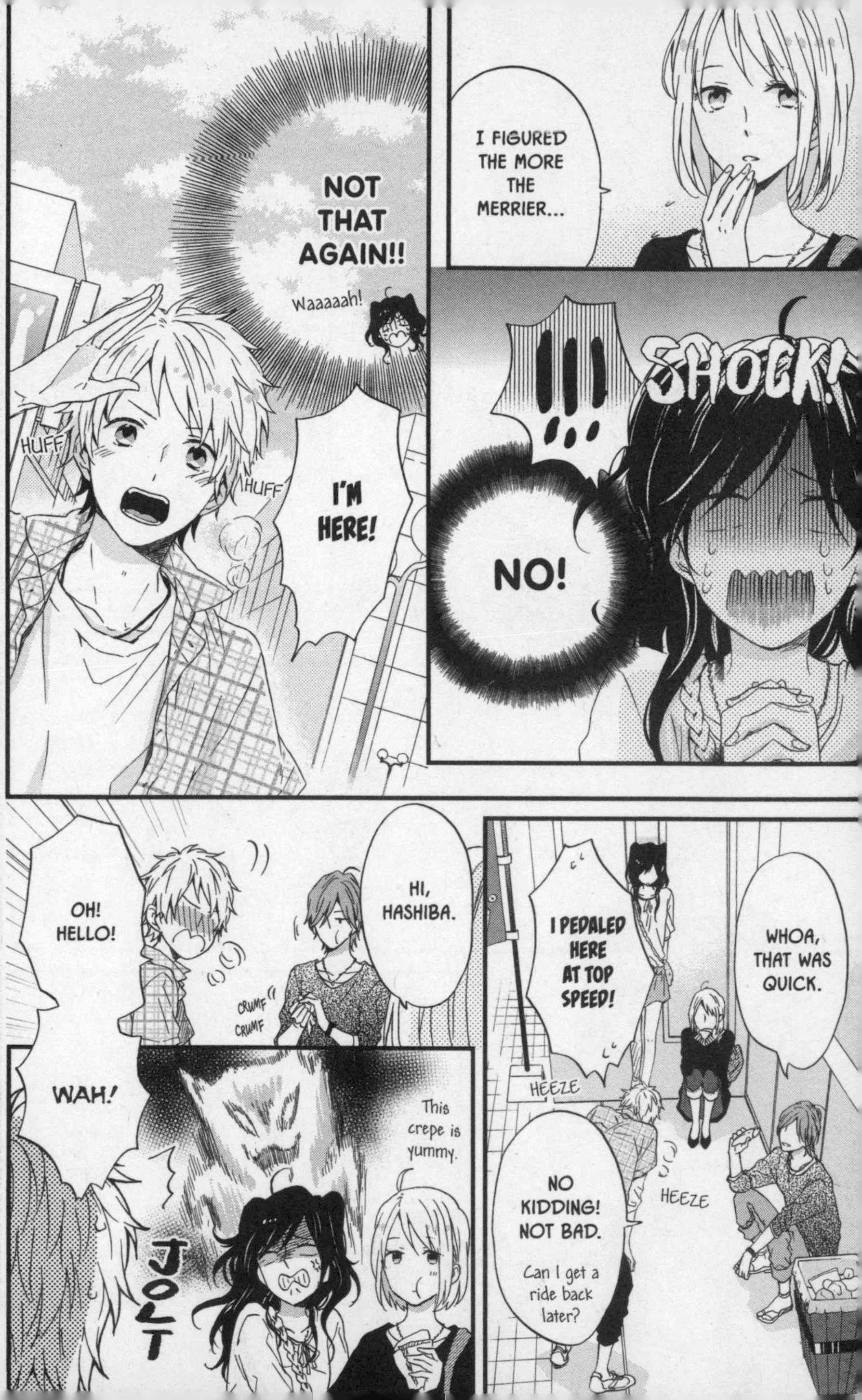
I FIGURED THE MORE THE MERRIER...
!!!
SHOCK!
NO!
NOT THAT AGAIN!!
Waaaaah!
HUFF
HUFF
I'M HERE!
WHOA, THAT WAS QUICK.
I PEDALED HERE AT TOP SPEED!
HEEZE
HEEZE
NO KIDDING! NOT BAD.
Can I get a ride back later?
HI, HASHIBA.
OH! HELLO!
CRUMF CRUMF
This crepe is yummy.
WAH!
JOLT

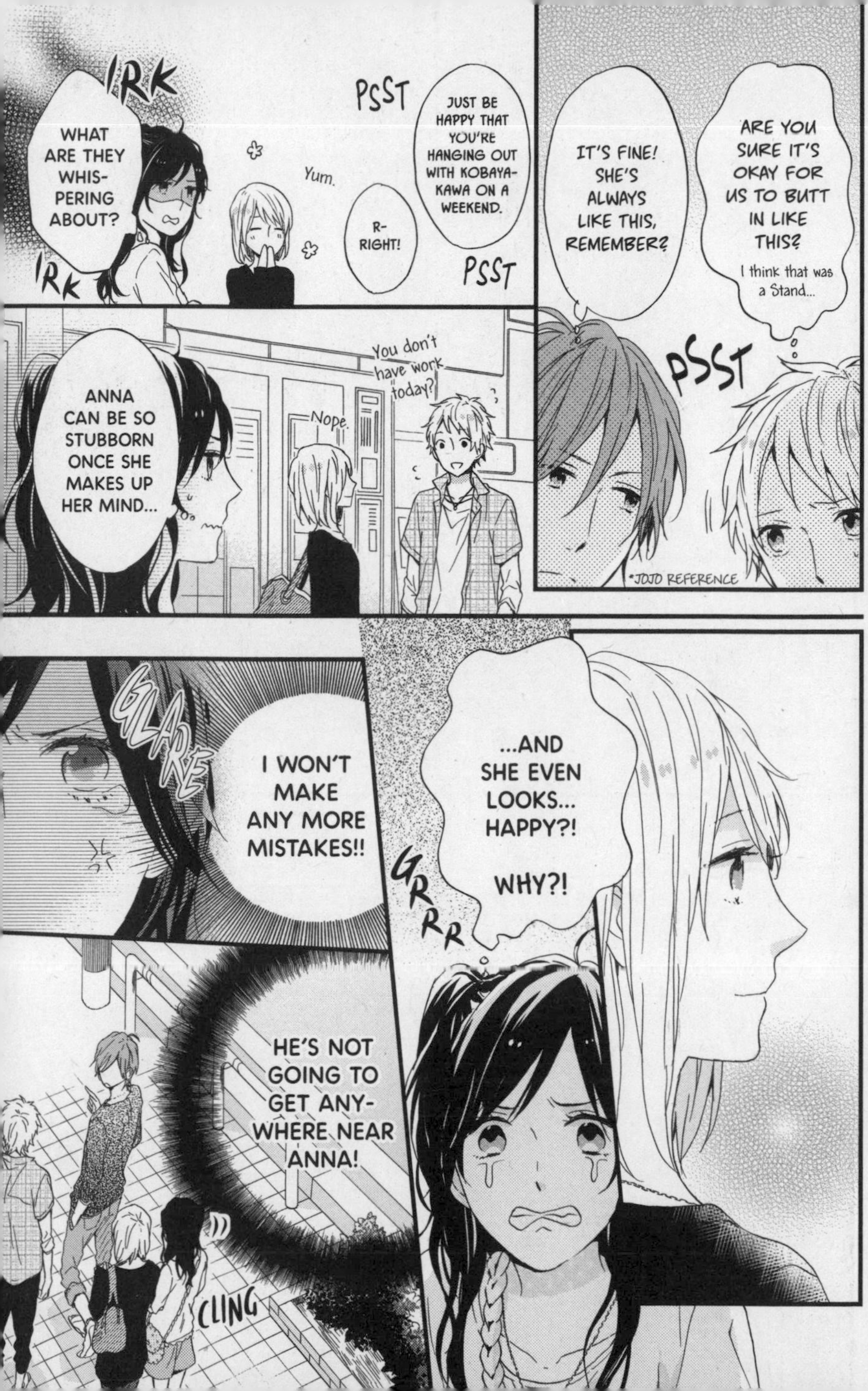
ARE YOU SURE IT'S OKAY FOR US TO BUTT IN LIKE THIS?
I think that was a Stand...
IT'S FINE! SHE'S ALWAYS LIKE THIS, REMEMBER?
PSST
*JOJO REFERENCE
PSST
JUST BE HAPPY THAT YOU'RE HANGING OUT WITH KOBAYA-KAWA ON A WEEKEND.
R-RIGHT!
PSST
Yum.
IRK
WHAT ARE THEY WHIS-PERING ABOUT?
IRK
You don't have work today?
Nope.
ANNA CAN BE SO STUBBORN ONCE SHE MAKES UP HER MIND...
...AND SHE EVEN LOOKS... HAPPY?!
WHY?!
GRRR
GLARE
I WON'T MAKE ANY MORE MISTAKES!!
HE'S NOT GOING TO GET ANY-WHERE NEAR ANNA!
CLING

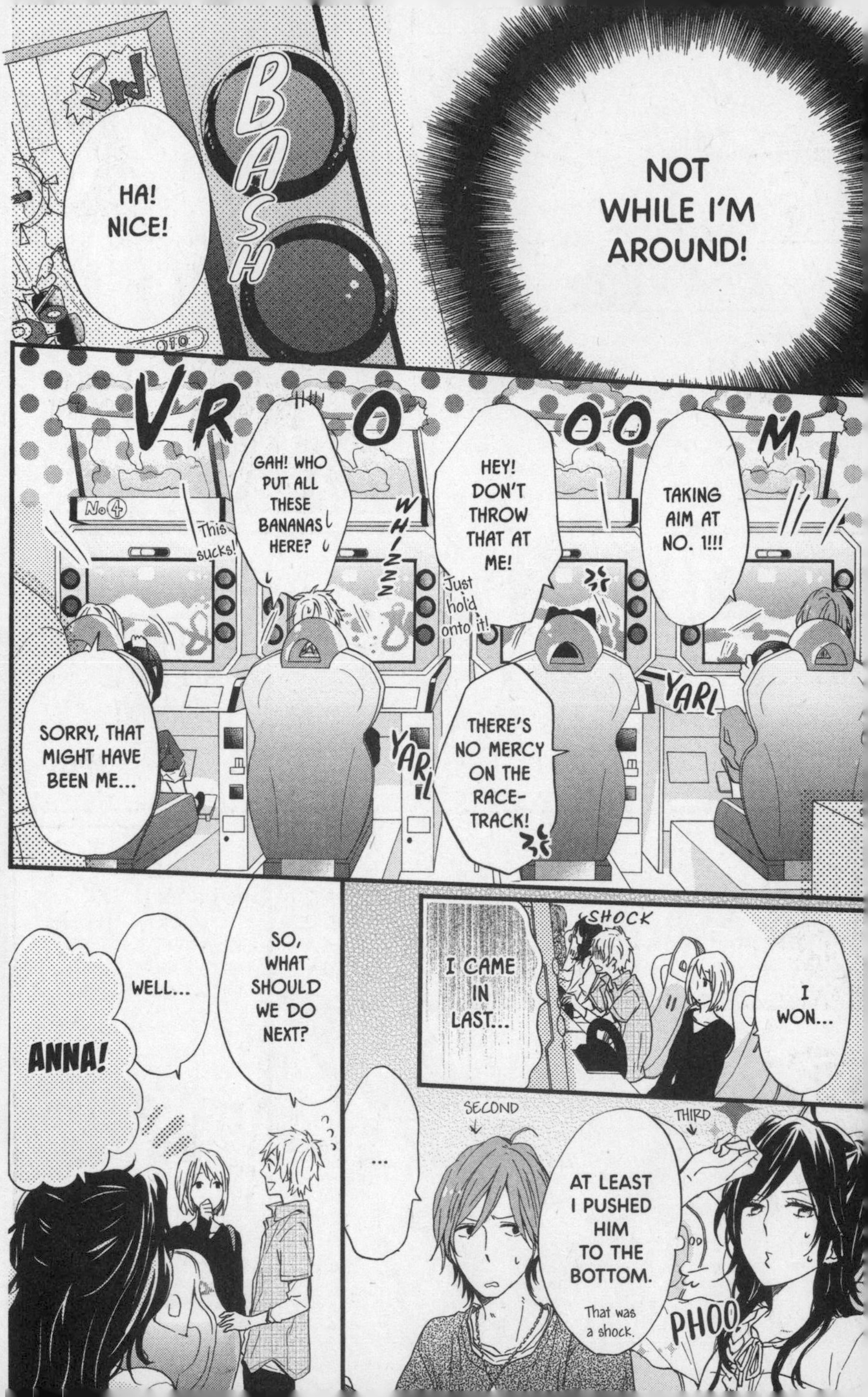
NOT WHILE I'M AROUND!
BASH
HA! NICE!
3rd
VROOOOM
TAKING AIM AT NO. 1!!!
HEY! DON'T THROW THAT AT ME!
Just hold onto it!
YARL
WHIZZZ
GAH! WHO PUT ALL THESE BANANAS HERE?
This sucks!
No 4
THERE'S NO MERCY ON THE RACE-TRACK!
YARL
SORRY, THAT MIGHT HAVE BEEN ME...
I WON...
SHOCK
I CAME IN LAST...
THIRD
PHOO
AT LEAST I PUSHED HIM TO THE BOTTOM.
That was a shock.
SECOND
...
SO, WHAT SHOULD WE DO NEXT?
WELL...
ANNA!

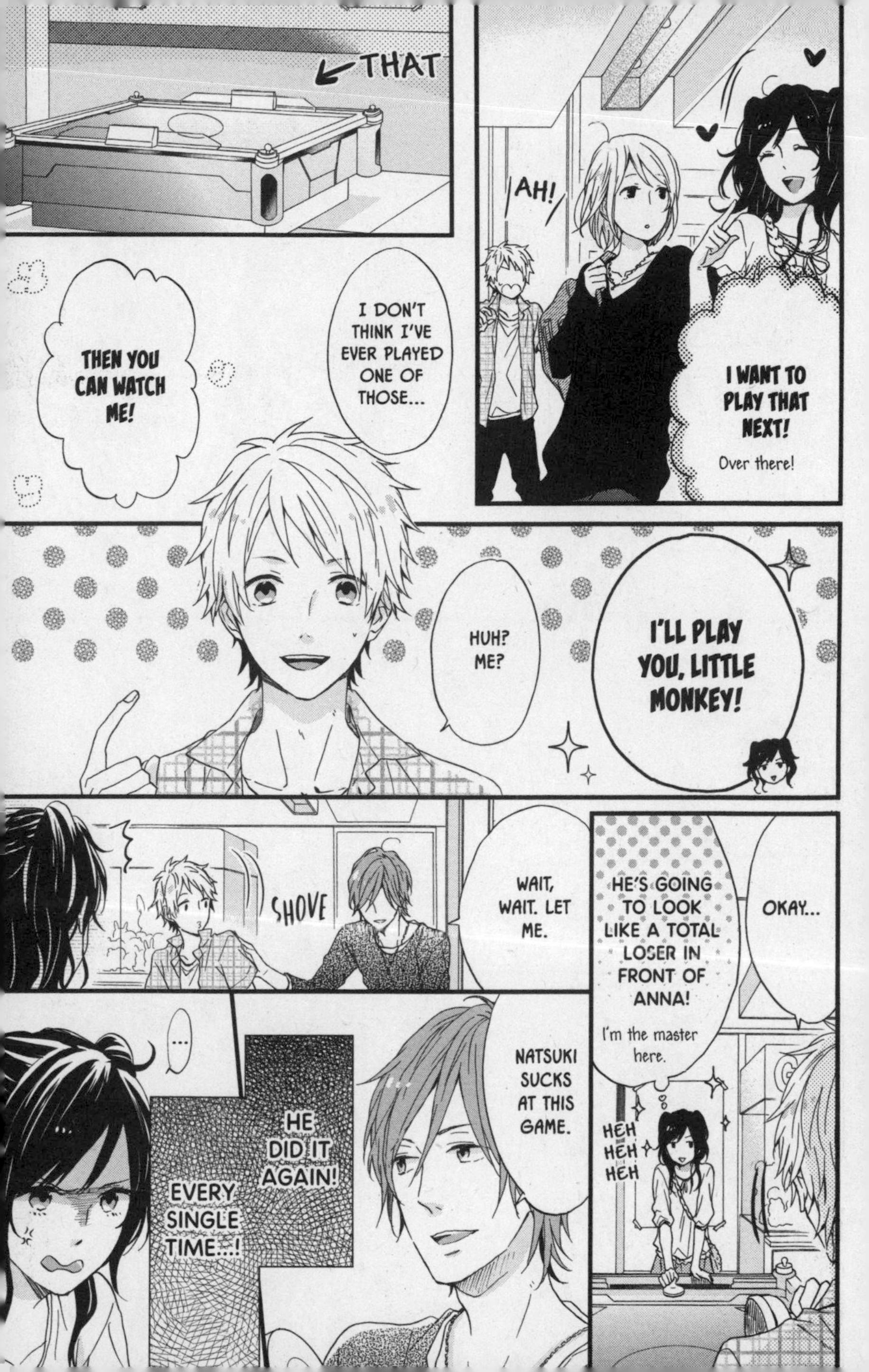
AH!
I WANT TO PLAY THAT NEXT!
Over there!
THAT
I DON'T THINK I'VE EVER PLAYED ONE OF THOSE...
THEN YOU CAN WATCH ME!
I'LL PLAY YOU, LITTLE MONKEY!
HUH? ME?
OKAY...
HE'S GOING TO LOOK LIKE A TOTAL LOSER IN FRONT OF ANNA!
I'm the master here.
HEH HEH HEH
WAIT, WAIT. LET ME.
SHOVE
NATSUKI SUCKS AT THIS GAME.
...
HE DID IT AGAIN!
EVERY SINGLE TIME...!

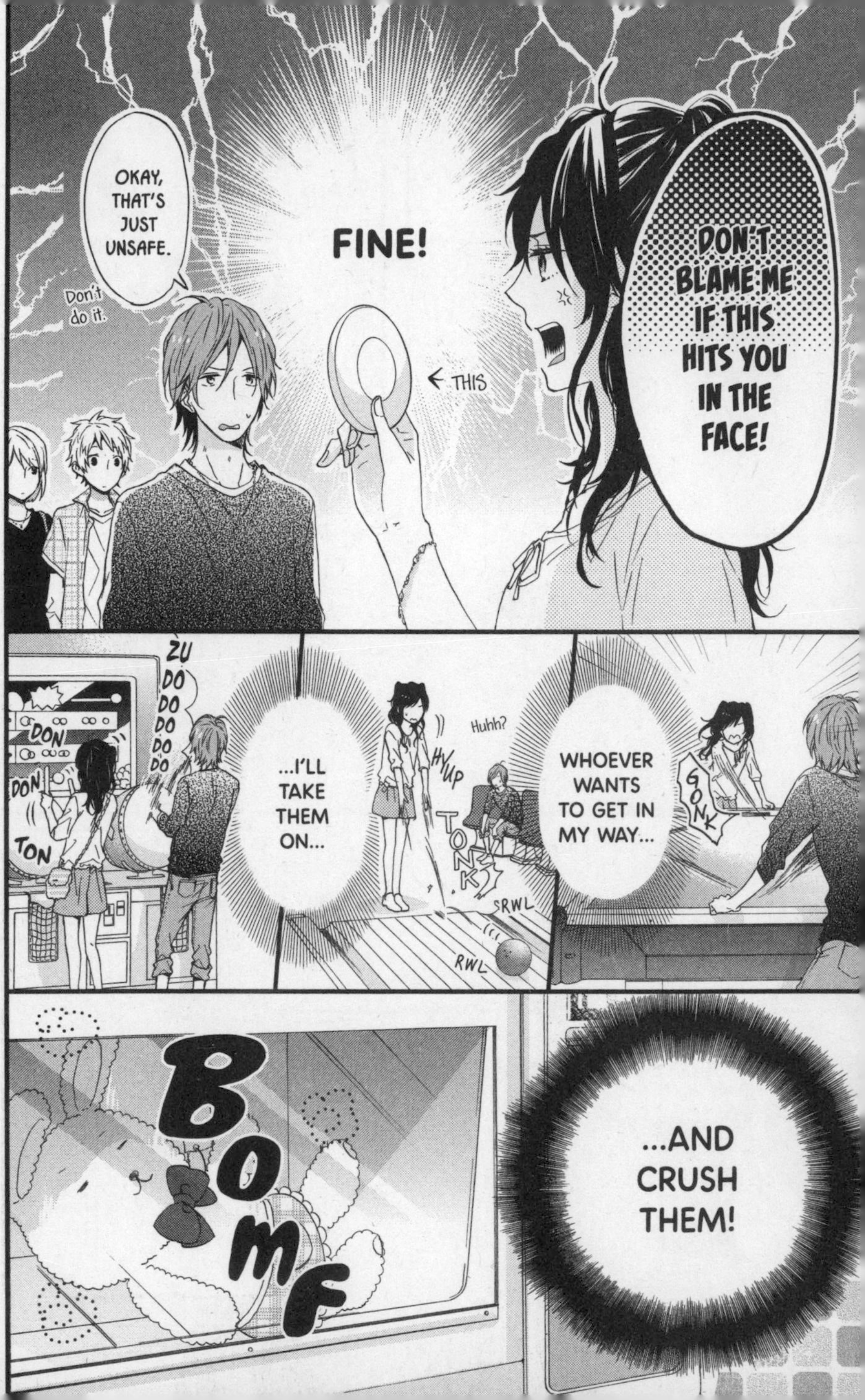
DON'T BLAME ME IF THIS HITS YOU IN THE FACE!
← THIS
FINE!
OKAY, THAT'S JUST UNSAFE.
Don't do it.
GONK
WHOEVER WANTS TO GET IN MY WAY...
Huhh?
HYUP
TONK
SRWL
RWL
...I'LL TAKE THEM ON...
ZU DO DO DO DO DO DO
DON
DON
TON
...AND CRUSH THEM!
BOMF

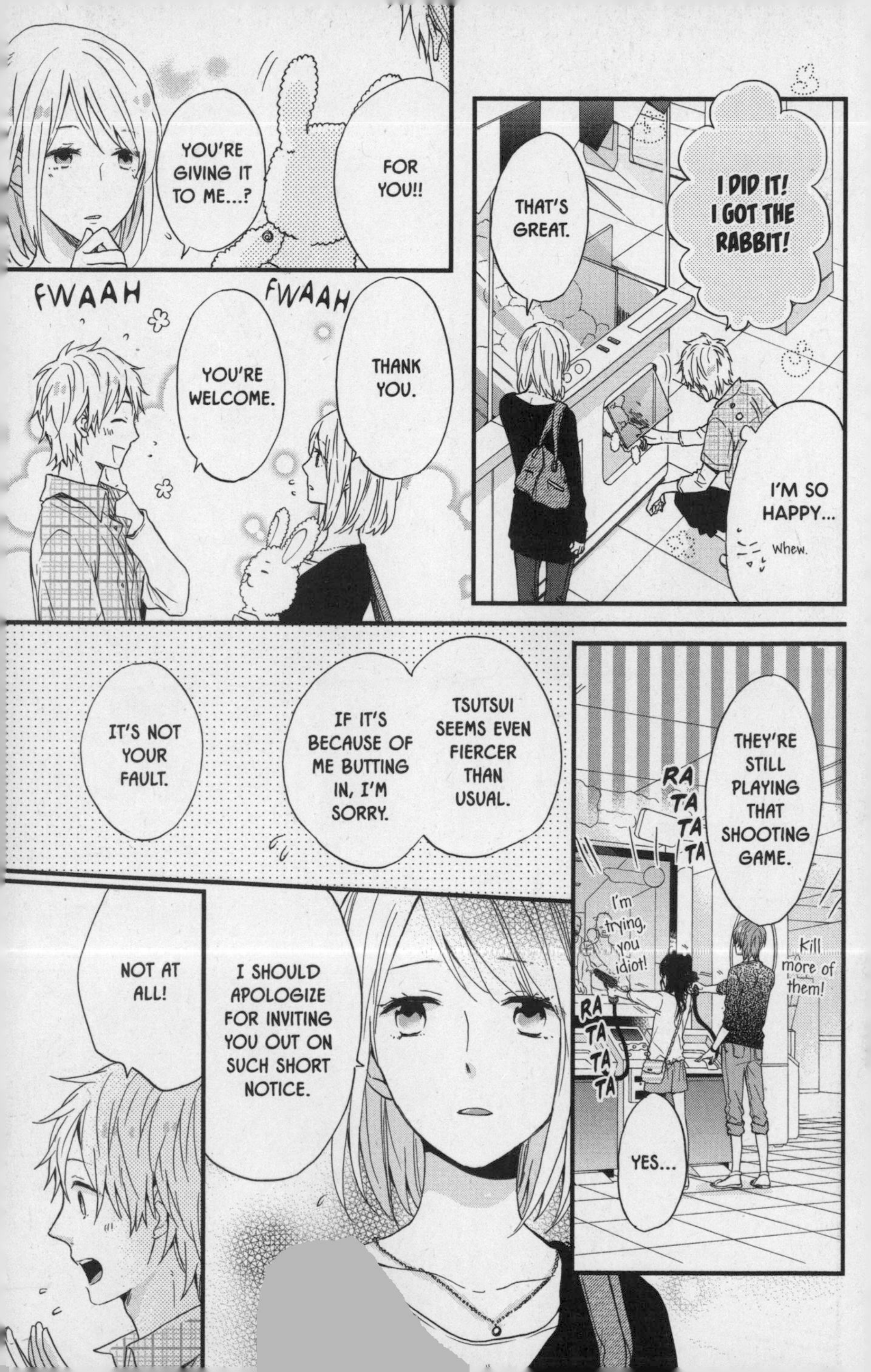
I DID IT! I GOT THE RABBIT!
THAT'S GREAT.
I'M SO HAPPY...
Whew.
FOR YOU!!
YOU'RE GIVING IT TO ME...?
FWAAH
FWAAH
THANK YOU.
YOU'RE WELCOME.
THEY'RE STILL PLAYING THAT SHOOTING GAME.
RA TA TA TA
Kill more of them!
I'm trying, you idiot!
RA TA TA TA
YES...
TSUTSUI SEEMS EVEN FIERCER THAN USUAL.
IF IT'S BECAUSE OF ME BUTTING IN, I'M SORRY.
IT'S NOT YOUR FAULT.
I SHOULD APOLOGIZE FOR INVITING YOU OUT ON SUCH SHORT NOTICE.
NOT AT ALL!

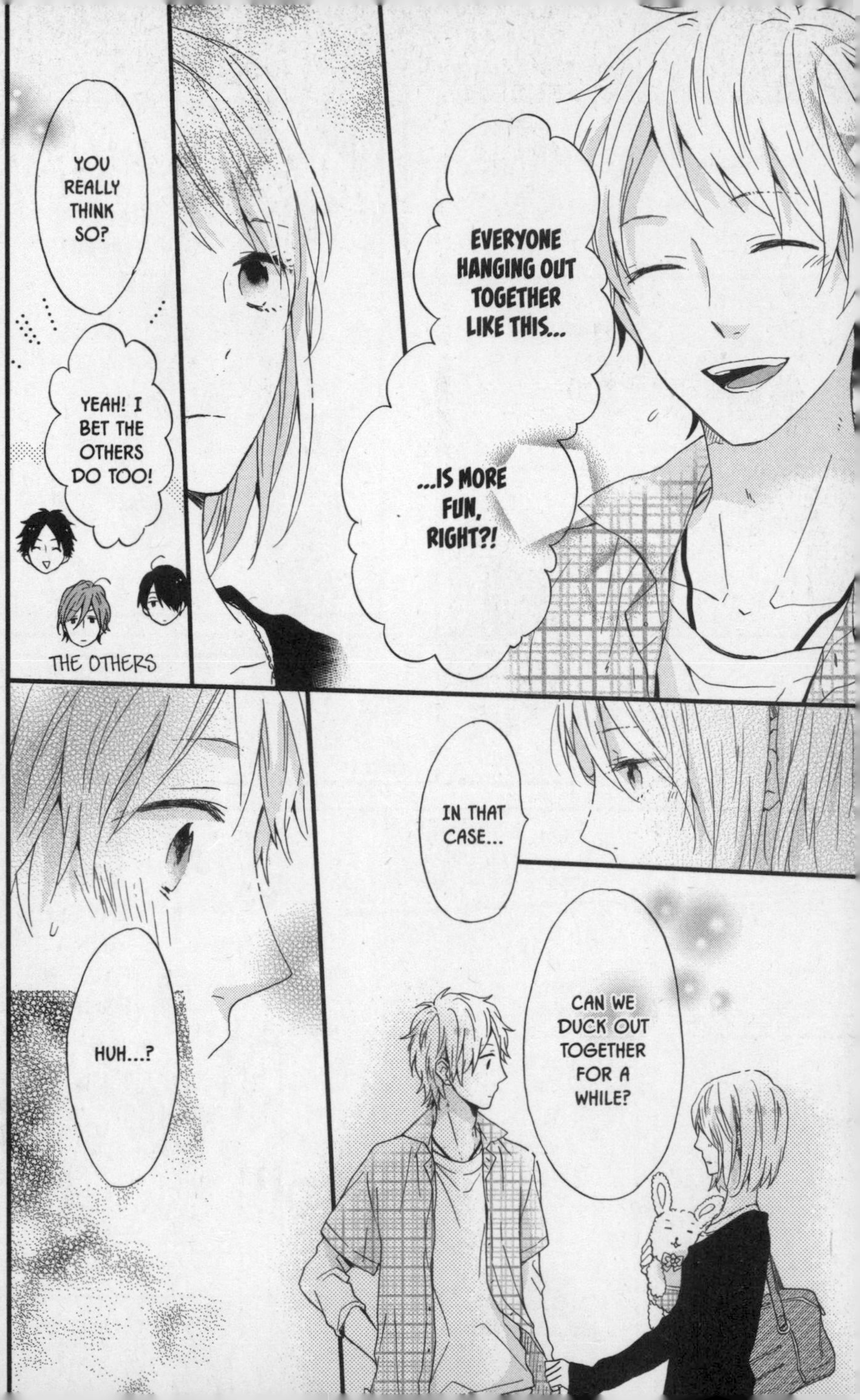
EVERYONE HANGING OUT TOGETHER LIKE THIS...
...IS MORE FUN, RIGHT?!
YOU REALLY THINK SO?
YEAH! I BET THE OTHERS DO TOO!
THE OTHERS
IN THAT CASE...
CAN WE DUCK OUT TOGETHER FOR A WHILE?
HUH...?

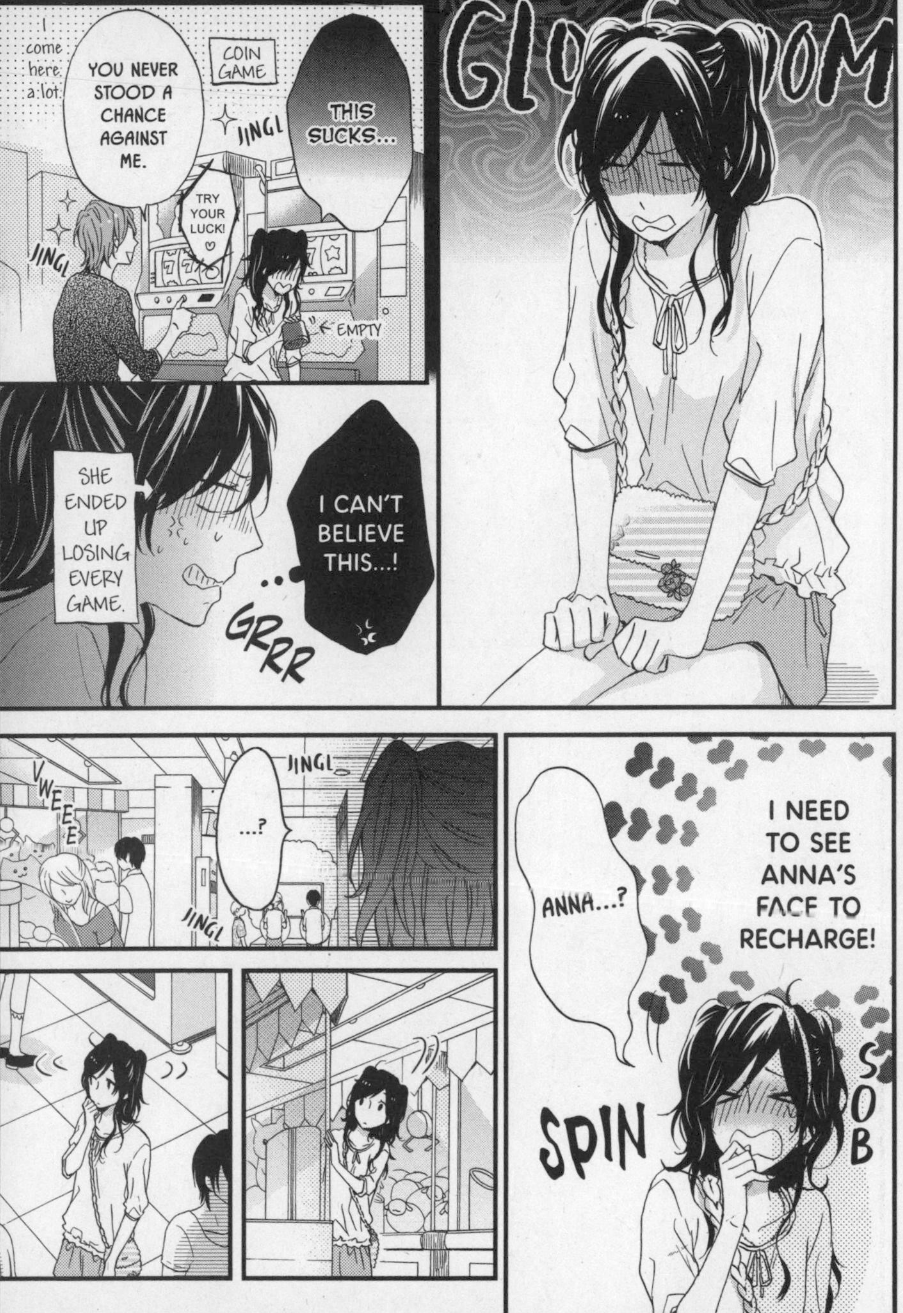
GLOOOM
I come here a lot.
YOU NEVER STOOD A CHANCE AGAINST ME.
COIN GAME
JINGL
THIS SUCKS...
TRY YOUR LUCK! ♡
JINGL
EMPTY
SHE ENDED UP LOSING EVERY GAME.
I CAN'T BELIEVE THIS...!
...
GRRR
ANNA...?
I NEED TO SEE ANNA'S FACE TO RECHARGE!
SOB
SPIN
JINGL
...?
VWEEE
JINGL

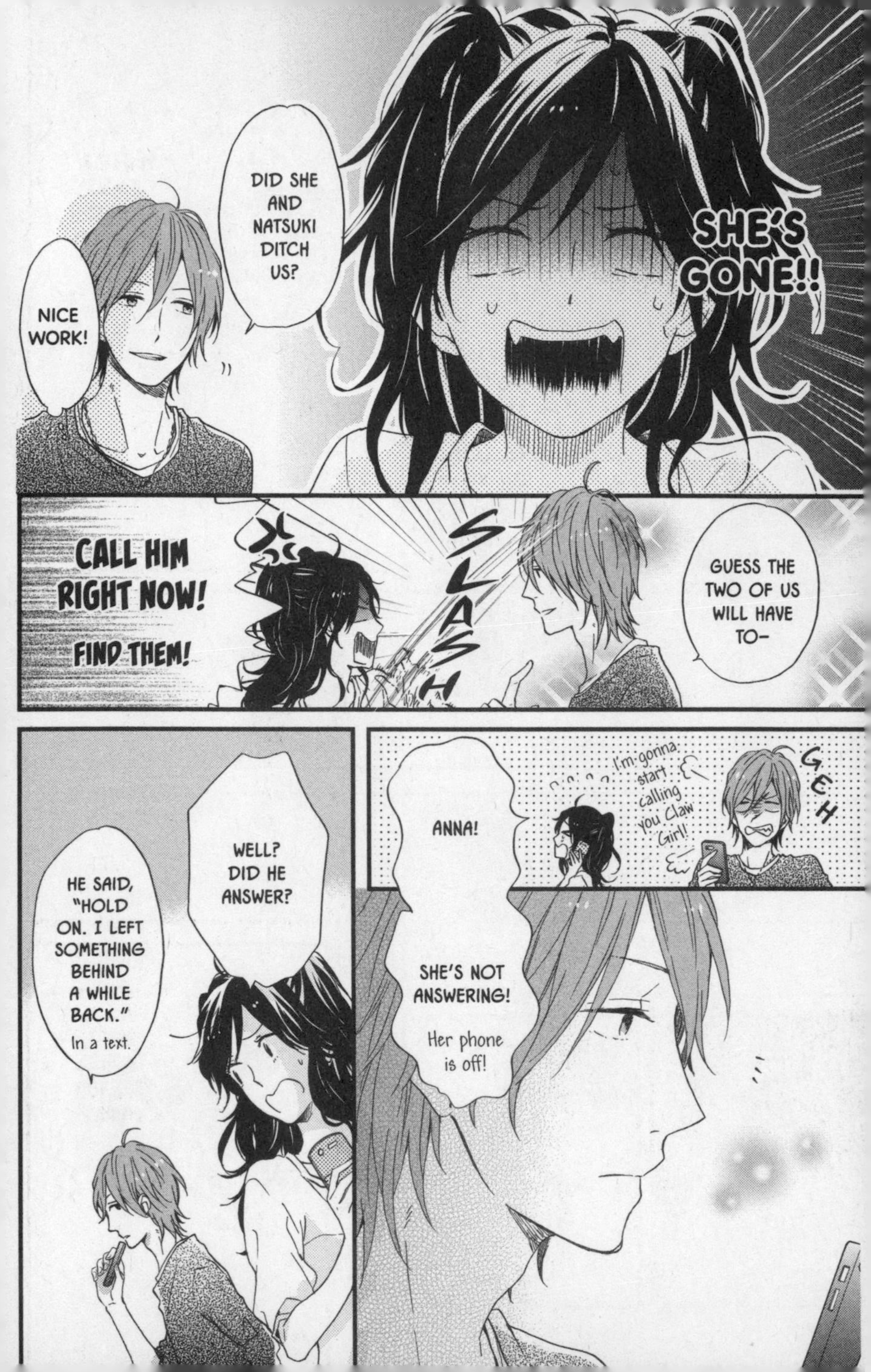
SHE'S GONE!!
DID SHE AND NATSUKI DITCH US?
NICE WORK!
GUESS THE TWO OF US WILL HAVE TO—
SLASH
CALL HIM RIGHT NOW!
FIND THEM!
GEH
I'm gonna start calling you Claw Girl!
ANNA!
SHE'S NOT ANSWERING!
Her phone is off!
WELL? DID HE ANSWER?
HE SAID, "HOLD ON. I LEFT SOMETHING BEHIND A WHILE BACK."
In a text.

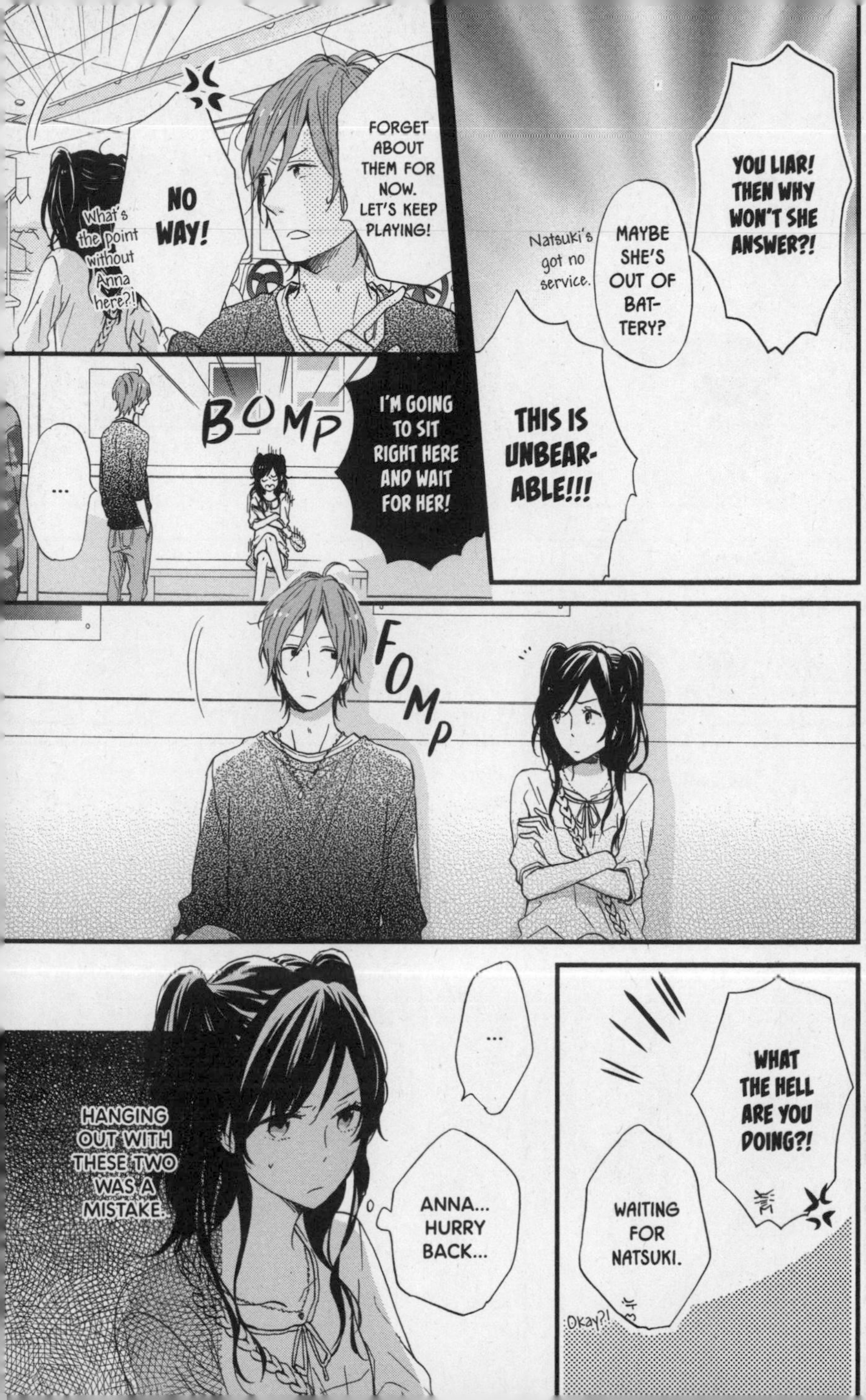
YOU LIAR! THEN WHY WON'T SHE ANSWER?!
MAYBE SHE'S OUT OF BAT-TERY?
Natsuki's got no service.
THIS IS UNBEARABLE!!!
FORGET ABOUT THEM FOR NOW. LET'S KEEP PLAYING!
NO WAY!
What's the point without Anna here?!
I'M GOING TO SIT RIGHT HERE AND WAIT FOR HER!
BOMP
...
FOMP
WHAT THE HELL ARE YOU DOING?!
WAITING FOR NATSUKI.
Okay?!
...
ANNA... HURRY BACK...
HANGING OUT WITH THESE TWO WAS A MISTAKE.

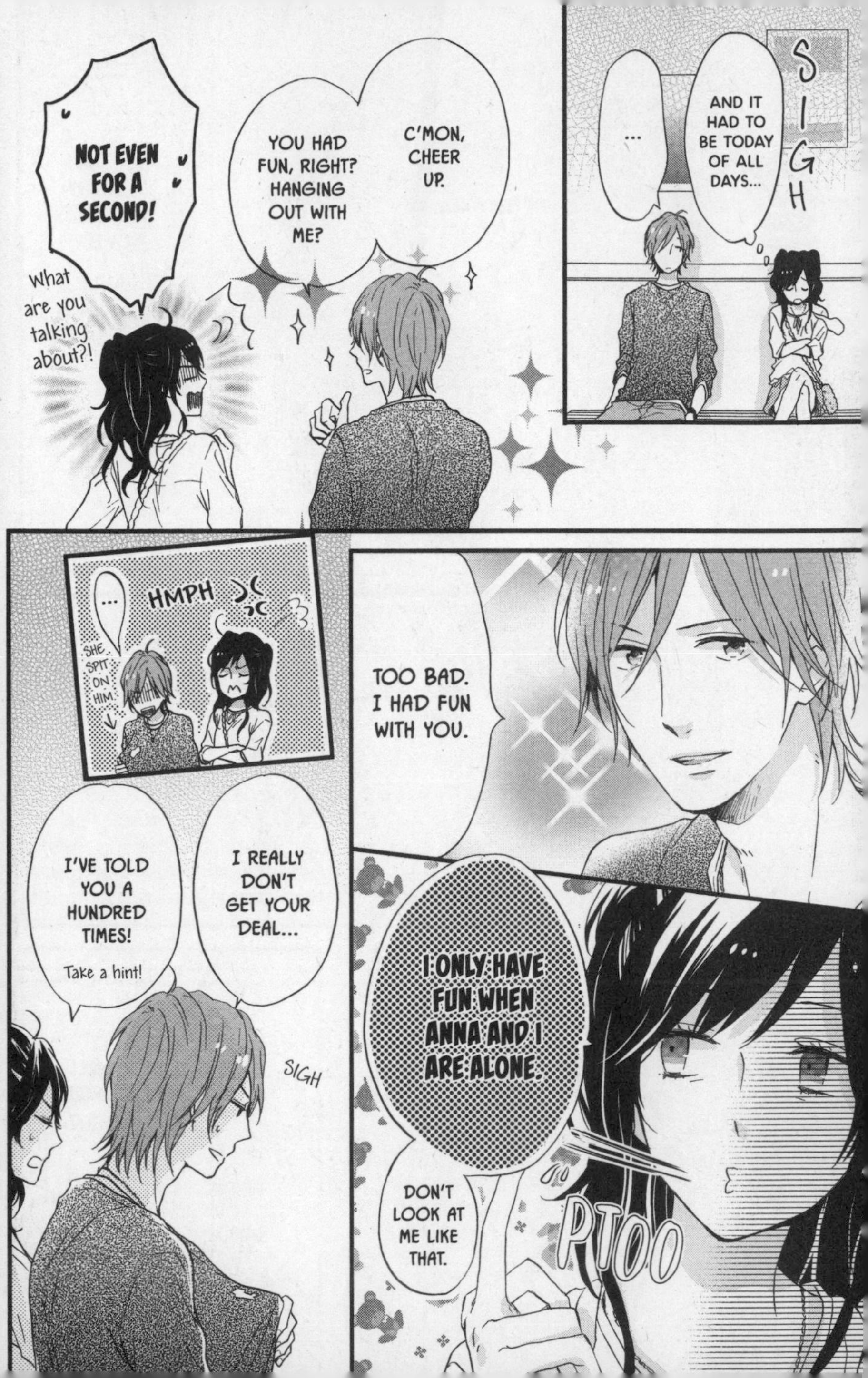
AND IT HAD TO BE TODAY OF ALL DAYS...
SIGH
...
C'MON, CHEER UP.
YOU HAD FUN, RIGHT? HANGING OUT WITH ME?
NOT EVEN FOR A SECOND!
What are you talking about?!
TOO BAD. I HAD FUN WITH YOU.
I ONLY HAVE FUN WHEN ANNA AND I ARE ALONE.
PTOO
DON'T LOOK AT ME LIKE THAT.
...
HMPH
SHE SPIT ON HIM.
I REALLY DON'T GET YOUR DEAL...
I'VE TOLD YOU A HUNDRED TIMES!
Take a hint!
SIGH

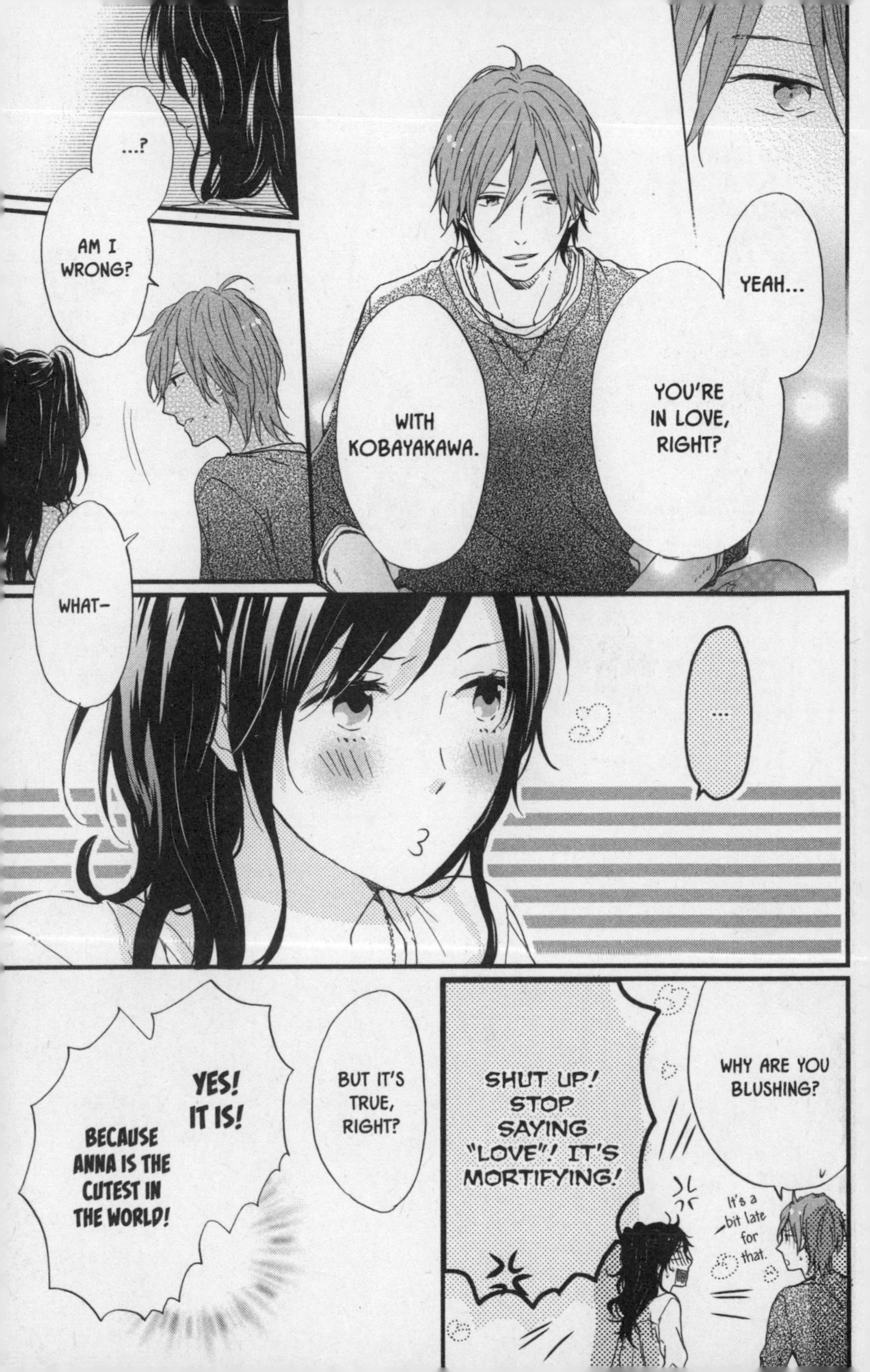
YEAH...
YOU'RE IN LOVE, RIGHT?
WITH KOBAYAKAWA.
...?
AM I WRONG?
WHAT-
...
WHY ARE YOU BLUSHING?
SHUT UP! STOP SAYING "LOVE"! IT'S MORTIFYING!
It's a bit late for that.
BUT IT'S TRUE, RIGHT?
YES! IT IS!
BECAUSE ANNA IS THE CUTEST IN THE WORLD!

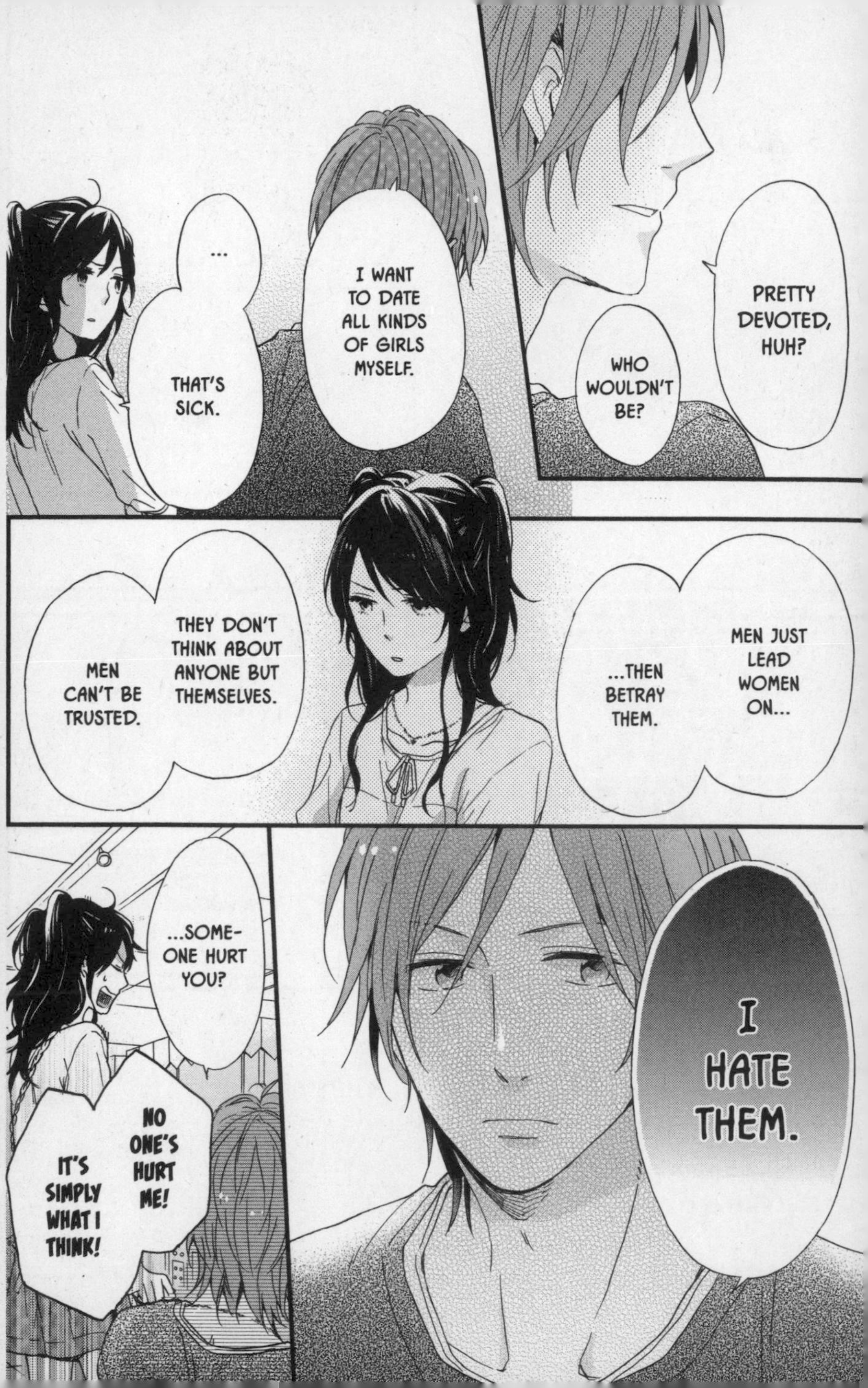
PRETTY DEVOTED, HUH?
WHO WOULDN'T BE?
I WANT TO DATE ALL KINDS OF GIRLS MYSELF.
...
THAT'S SICK.
MEN JUST LEAD WOMEN ON...
...THEN BETRAY THEM.
THEY DON'T THINK ABOUT ANYONE BUT THEMSELVES.
MEN CAN'T BE TRUSTED.
I HATE THEM.
...SOME-ONE HURT YOU?
NO ONE'S HURT ME!
IT'S SIMPLY WHAT I THINK!

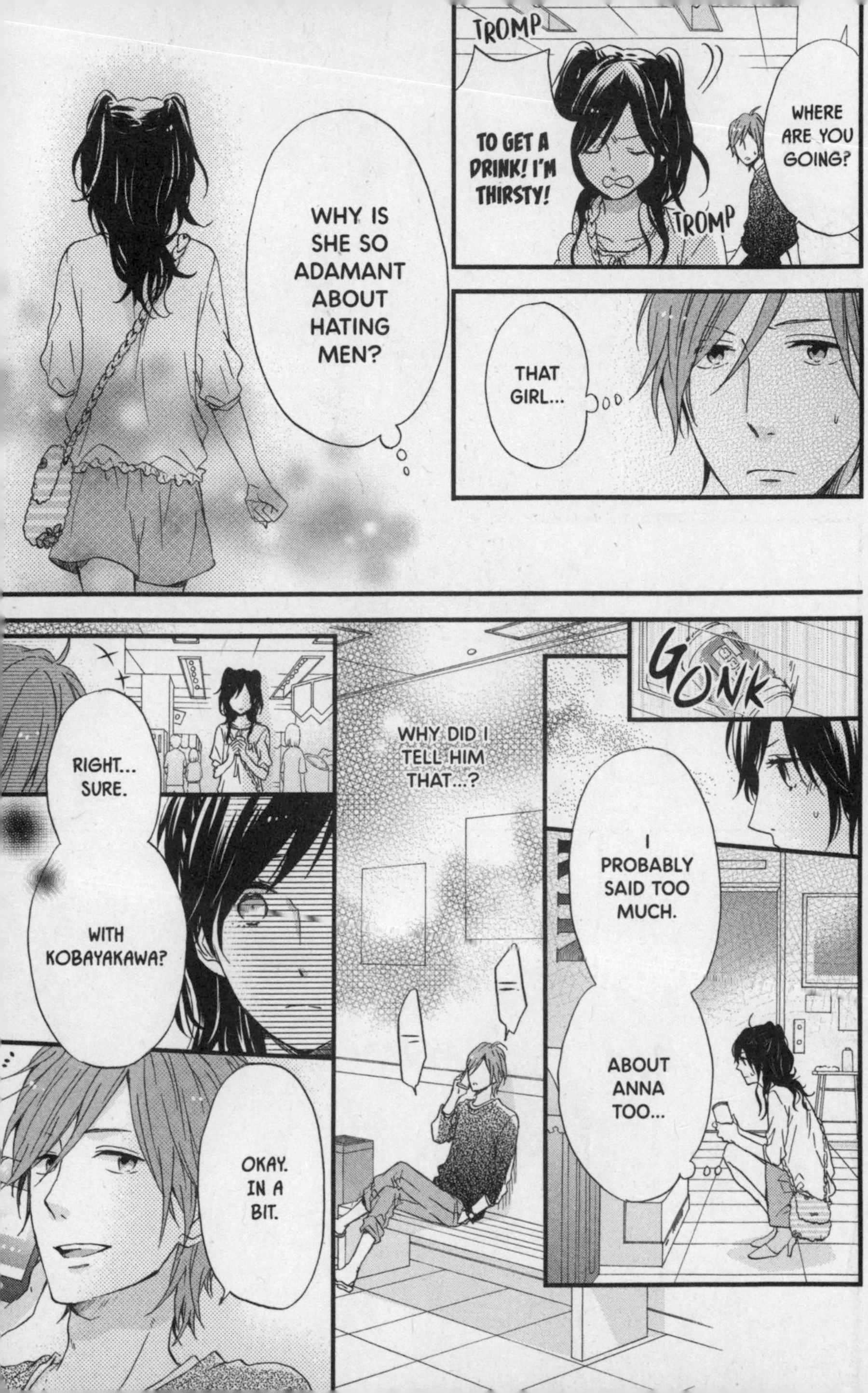
WHERE ARE YOU GOING?
TROMP
TO GET A DRINK! I'M THIRSTY!
TROMP
THAT GIRL...
WHY IS SHE SO ADAMANT ABOUT HATING MEN?
GONK
I PROBABLY SAID TOO MUCH.
ABOUT ANNA TOO...
WHY DID I TELL HIM THAT...?
—
—
RIGHT... SURE.
WITH KOBAYAKAWA?
...
OKAY. IN A BIT.

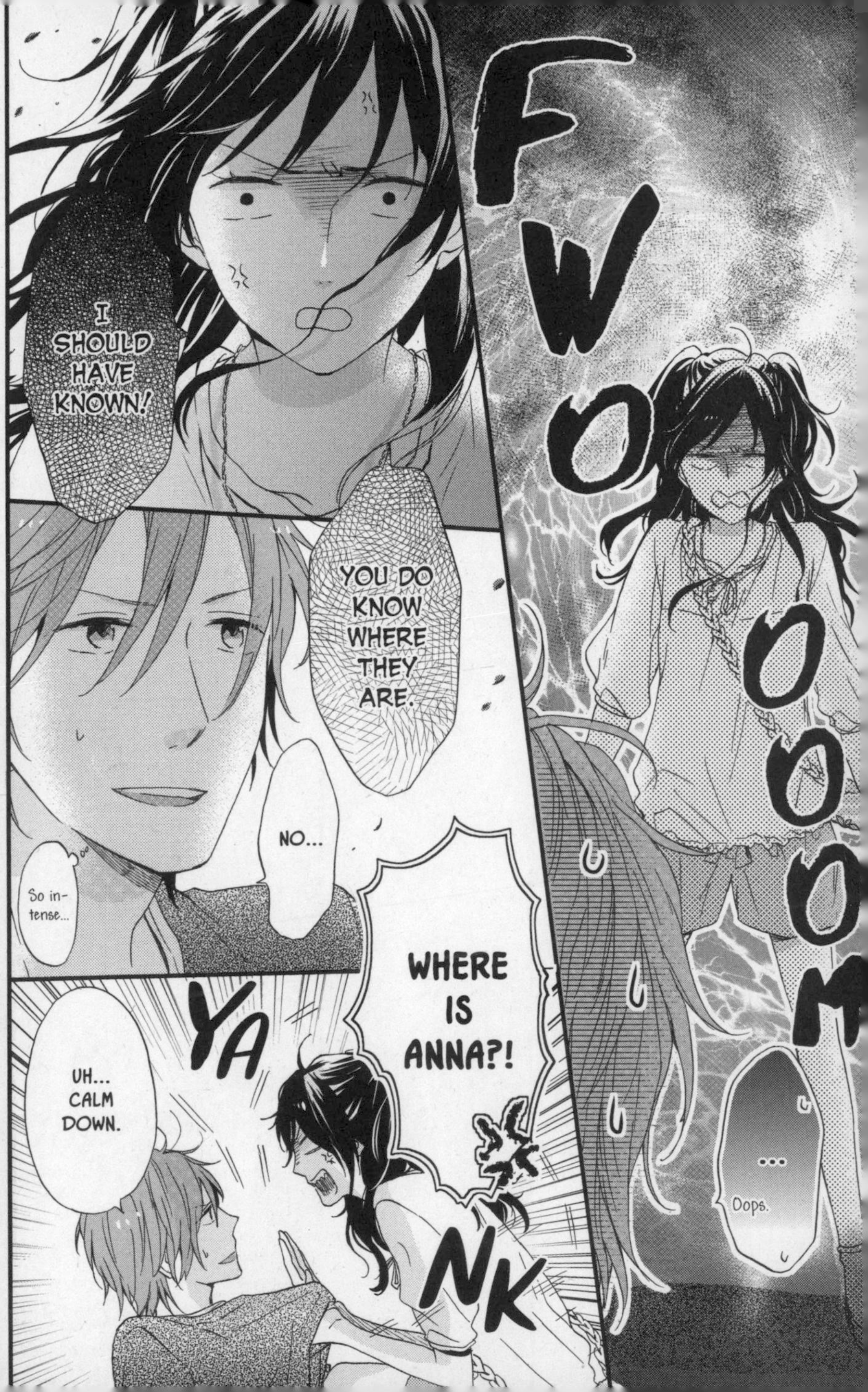
FWOOOOOM
...
Oops.
I SHOULD HAVE KNOWN!
YOU DO KNOW WHERE THEY ARE.
NO...
So intense...
WHERE IS ANNA?!
YANK
UH... CALM DOWN.

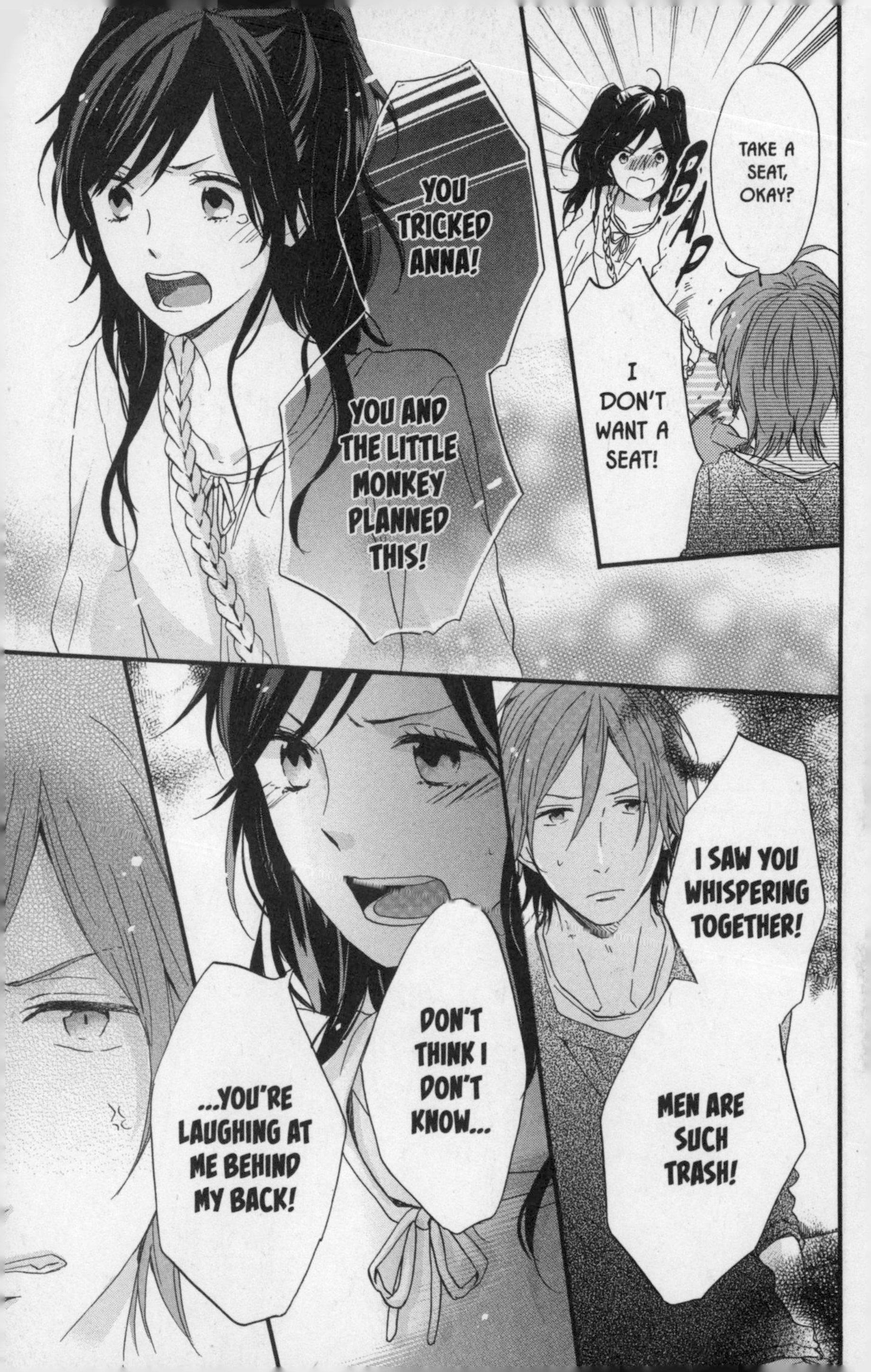
TAKE A SEAT, OKAY?
BAP
I DON'T WANT A SEAT!
YOU TRICKED ANNA!
YOU AND THE LITTLE MONKEY PLANNED THIS!
I SAW YOU WHISPERING TOGETHER!
MEN ARE SUCH TRASH!
DON'T THINK I DON'T KNOW...
...YOU'RE LAUGHING AT ME BEHIND MY BACK!

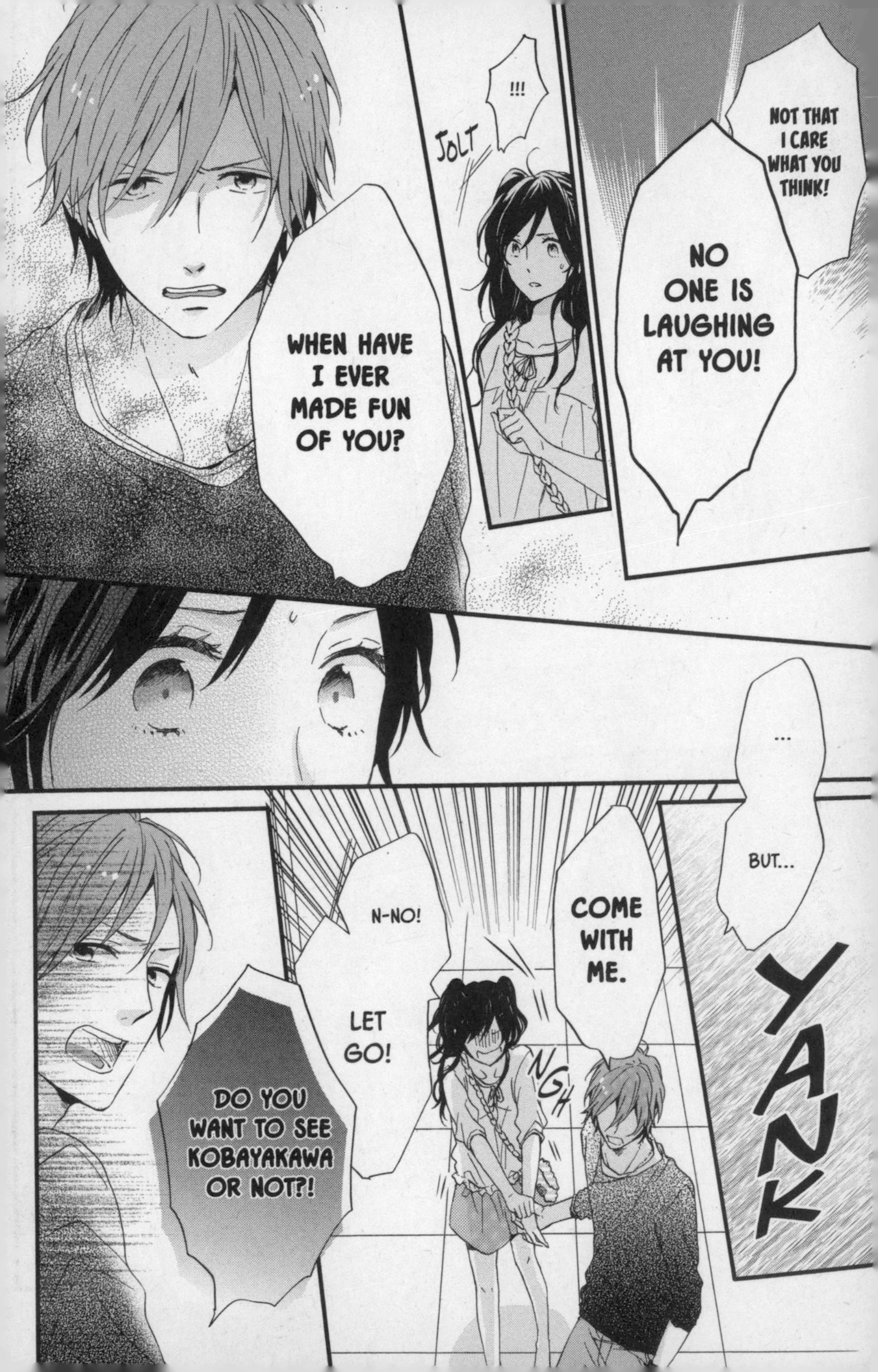
NOT THAT I CARE WHAT YOU THINK!
NO ONE IS LAUGHING AT YOU!
JOLT
!!!
WHEN HAVE I EVER MADE FUN OF YOU?
...
BUT...
YANK
COME WITH ME.
N-NO!
LET GO!
NGH
DO YOU WANT TO SEE KOBAYAKAWA OR NOT?!

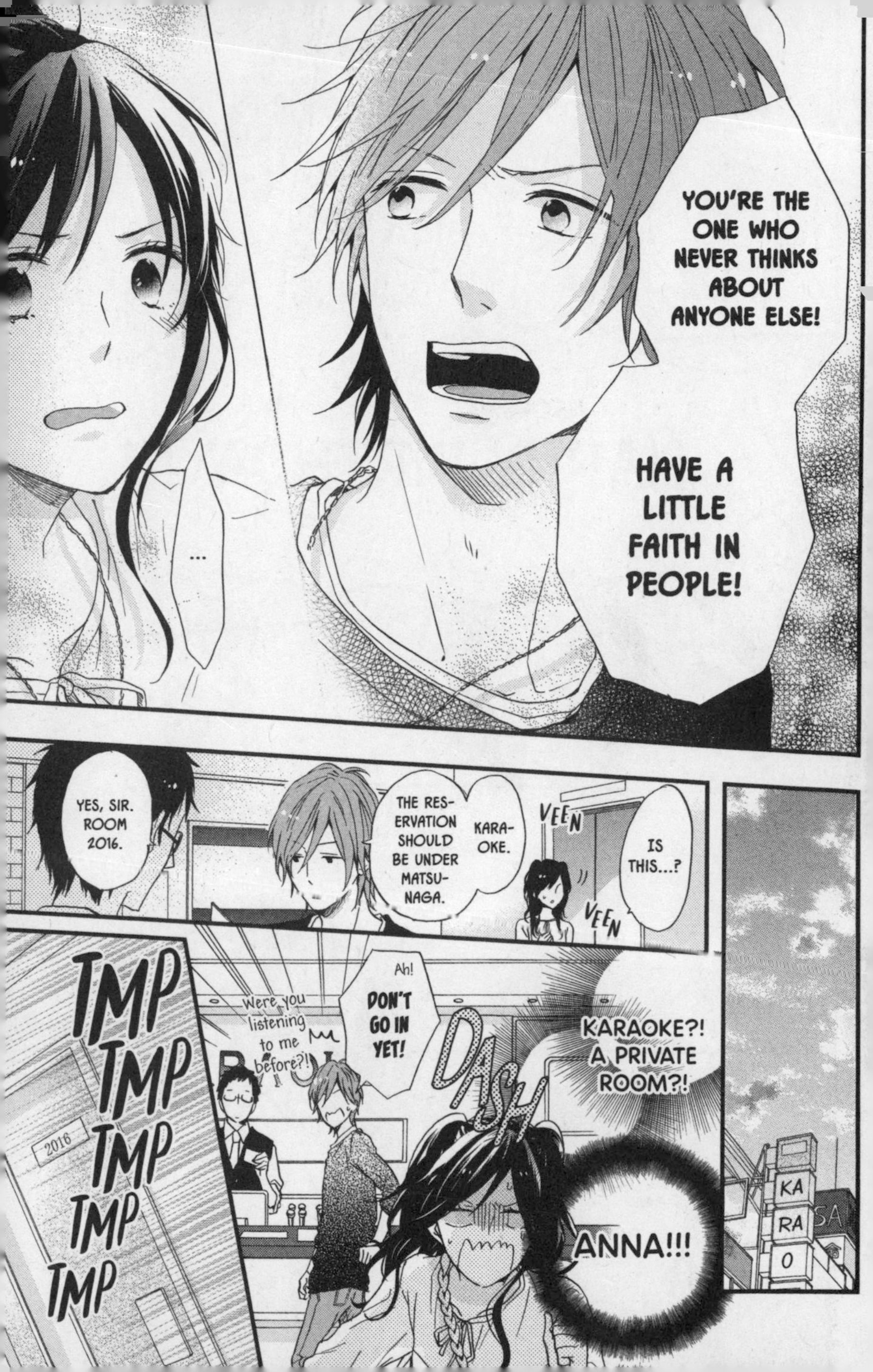
YOU'RE THE ONE WHO NEVER THINKS ABOUT ANYONE ELSE!
HAVE A LITTLE FAITH IN PEOPLE!
...
KA RA O
IS THIS...?
VEEN
VEEN
KARA-OKE.
THE RES-ERVATION SHOULD BE UNDER MATSU-NAGA.
YES, SIR. ROOM 2016.
KARAOKE?! A PRIVATE ROOM?!
ANNA!!!
DASH
Ah!
DON'T GO IN YET!
Were you listening to me before?!
2016
TMP TMP TMP TMP TMP

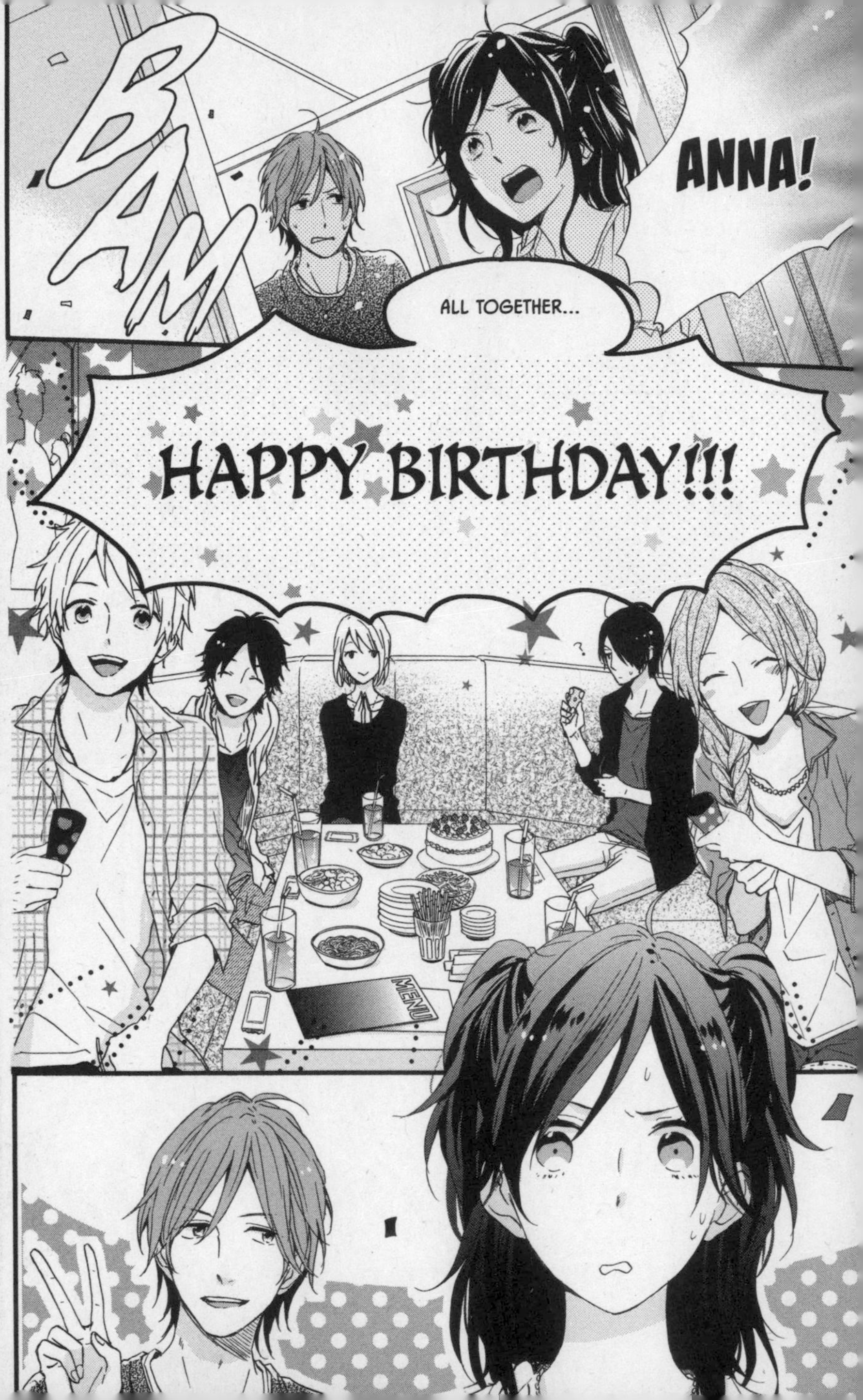
ANNA!
ALL TOGETHER...
BAM
HAPPY BIRTHDAY!!!
MENU

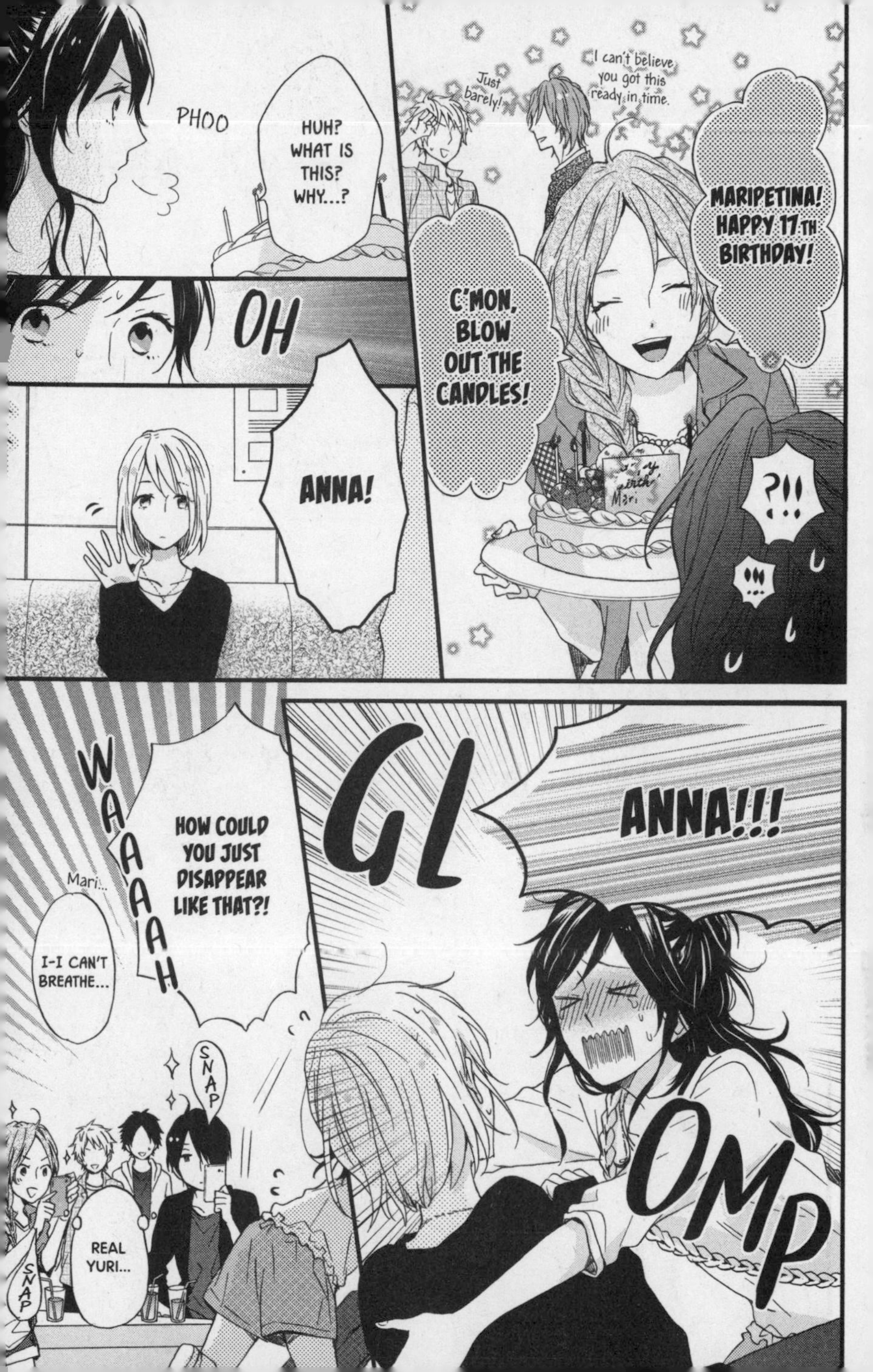
I can't believe you got this ready in time.
Just barely!
MARIPETINA! HAPPY 17TH BIRTHDAY!
C'MON, BLOW OUT THE CANDLES!
?!!
HUH? WHAT IS THIS? WHY...?
PHOO
OH
ANNA!
ANNA!!!
GLOMP
WAAAAAH
HOW COULD YOU JUST DISAPPEAR LIKE THAT?!
Mari...
I-I CAN'T BREATHE...
SNAP
REAL YURI...
SNAP

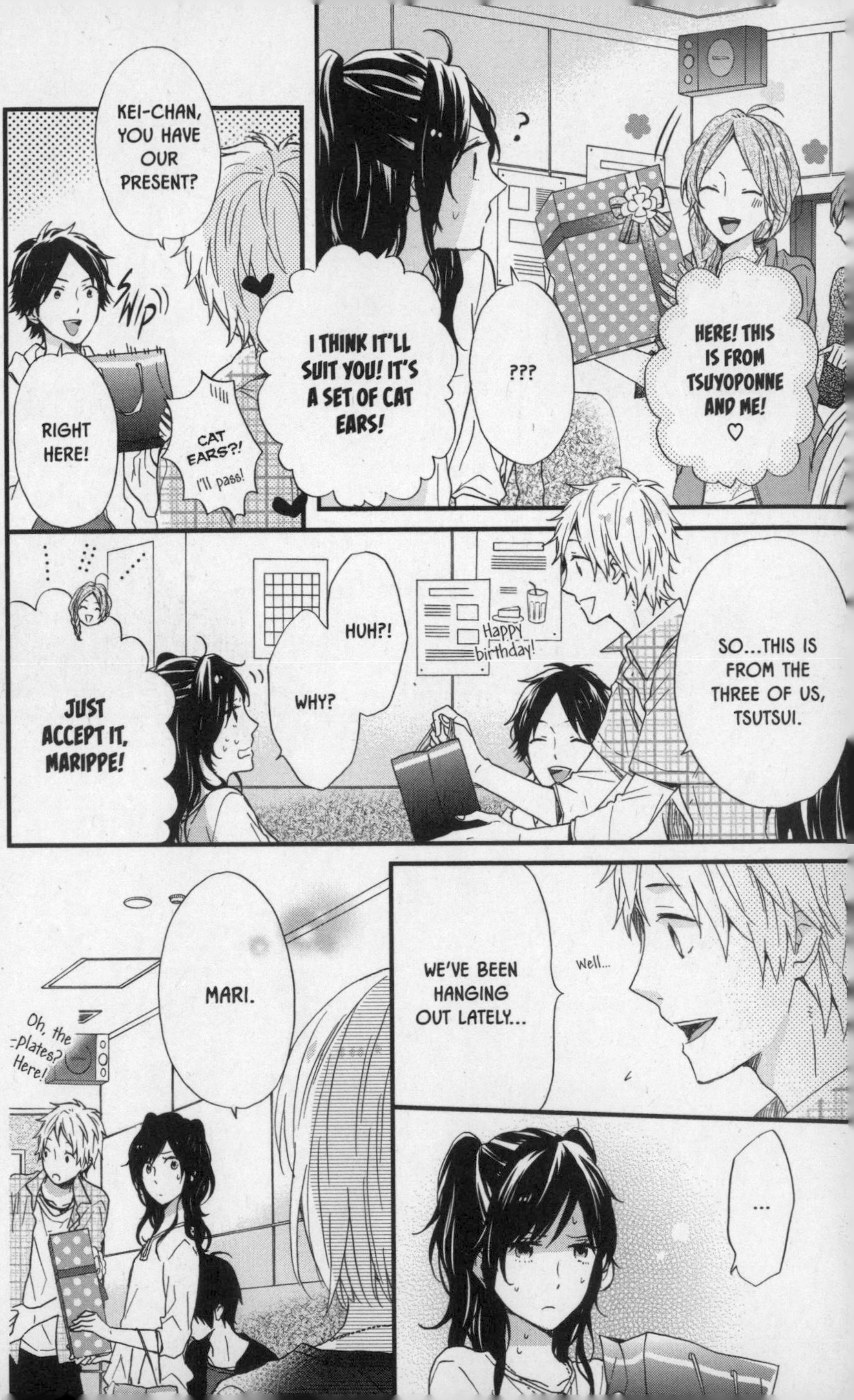

HERE! THIS IS FROM TSUYOPONNE AND ME! ♡
???
I THINK IT'LL SUIT YOU! IT'S A SET OF CAT EARS!
KEI-CHAN, YOU HAVE OUR PRESENT?
SWIP
RIGHT HERE!
CAT EARS?!
I'll pass!
SO...THIS IS FROM THE THREE OF US, TSUTSUI.
Happy birthday!
HUH?!
WHY?
JUST ACCEPT IT, MARIPPE!
Well...
WE'VE BEEN HANGING OUT LATELY...
...
MARI.
Oh, the plates? Here!

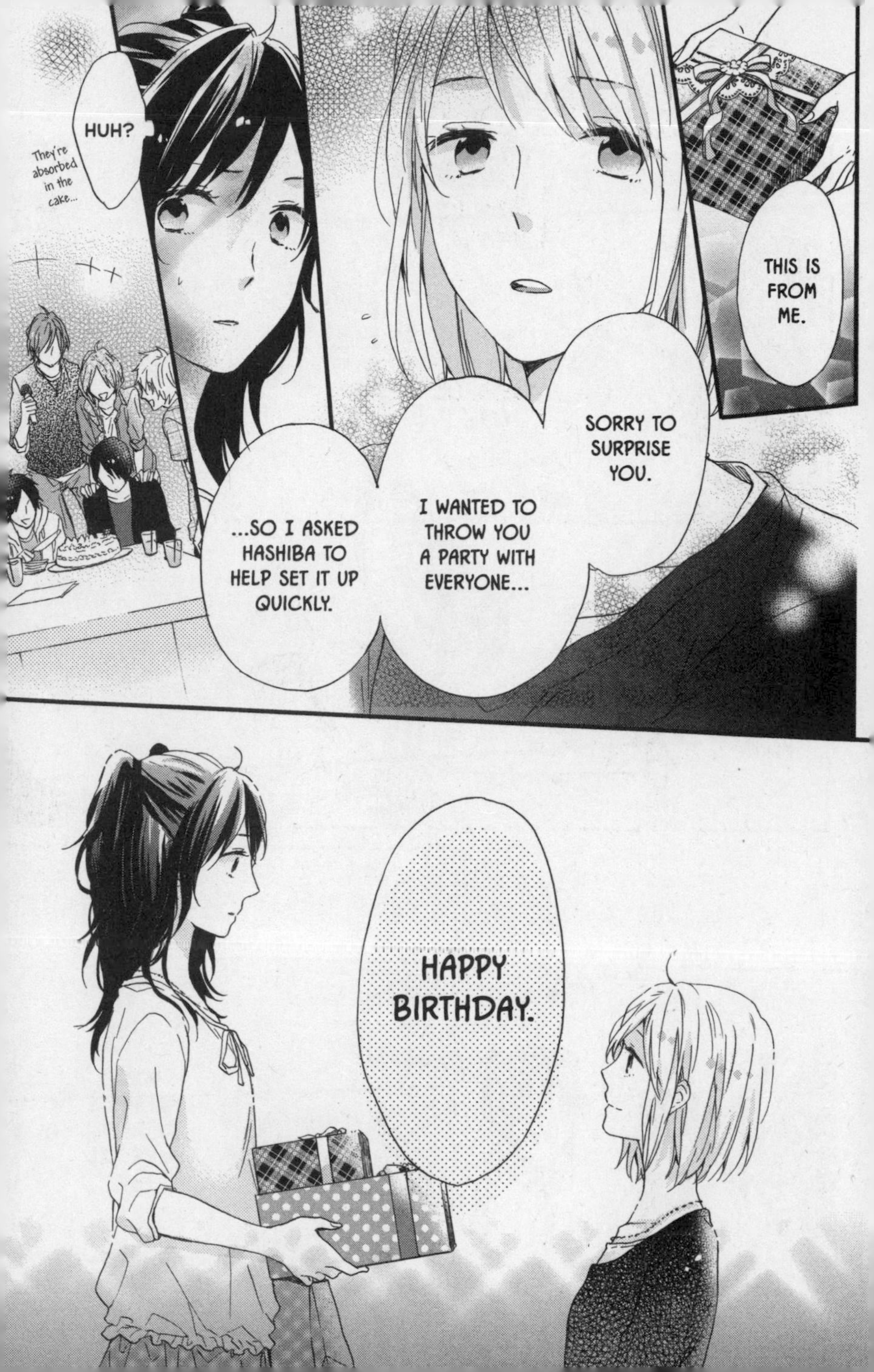
THIS IS FROM ME.
SORRY TO SURPRISE YOU.
I WANTED TO THROW YOU A PARTY WITH EVERYONE...
...SO I ASKED HASHIBA TO HELP SET IT UP QUICKLY.
HUH?
They're absorbed in the cake...
HAPPY BIRTHDAY.

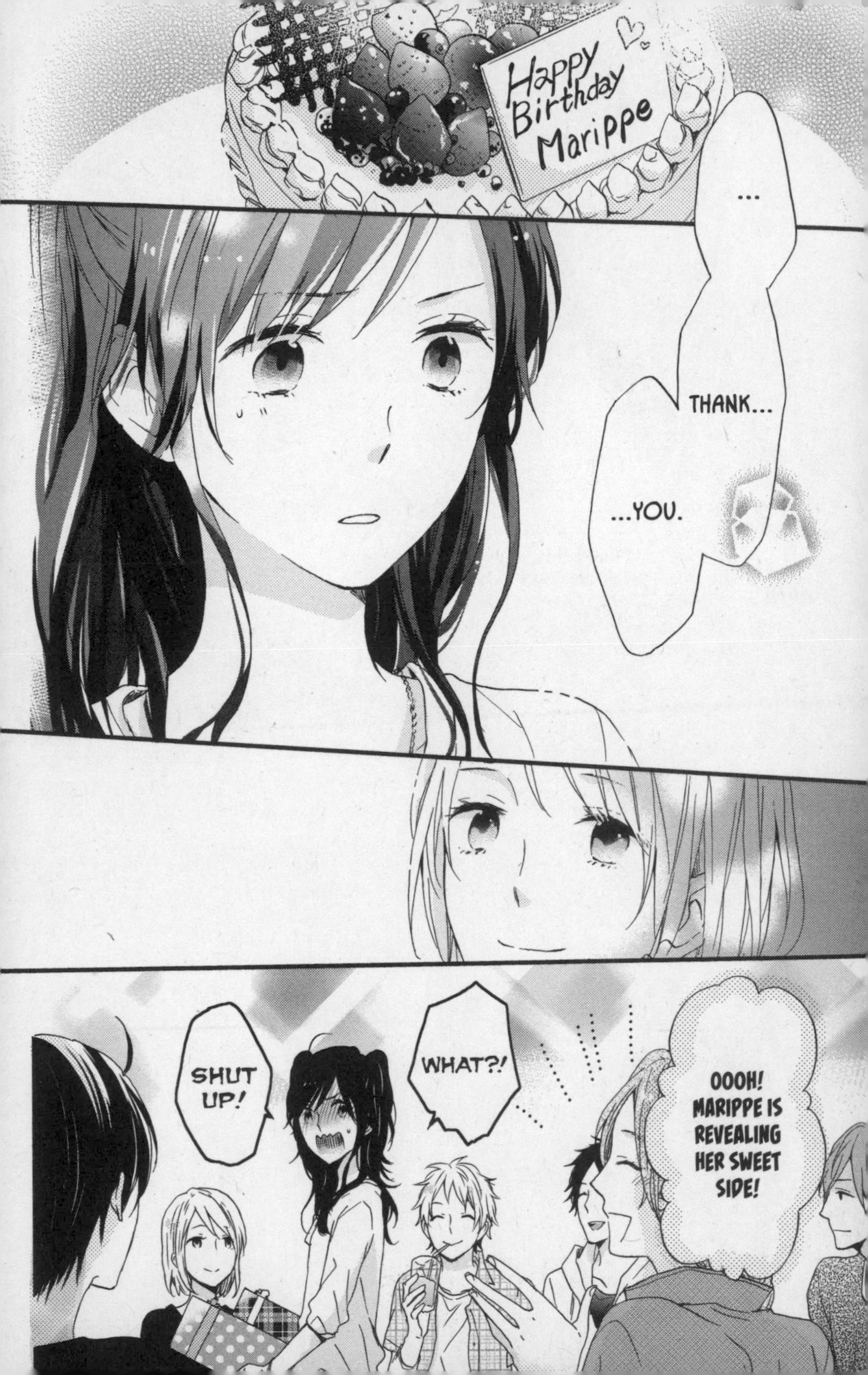
Happy Birthday Marippe
...
THANK...
...YOU.
OOOH! MARIPPE IS REVEALING HER SWEET SIDE!
WHAT?!
SHUT UP!

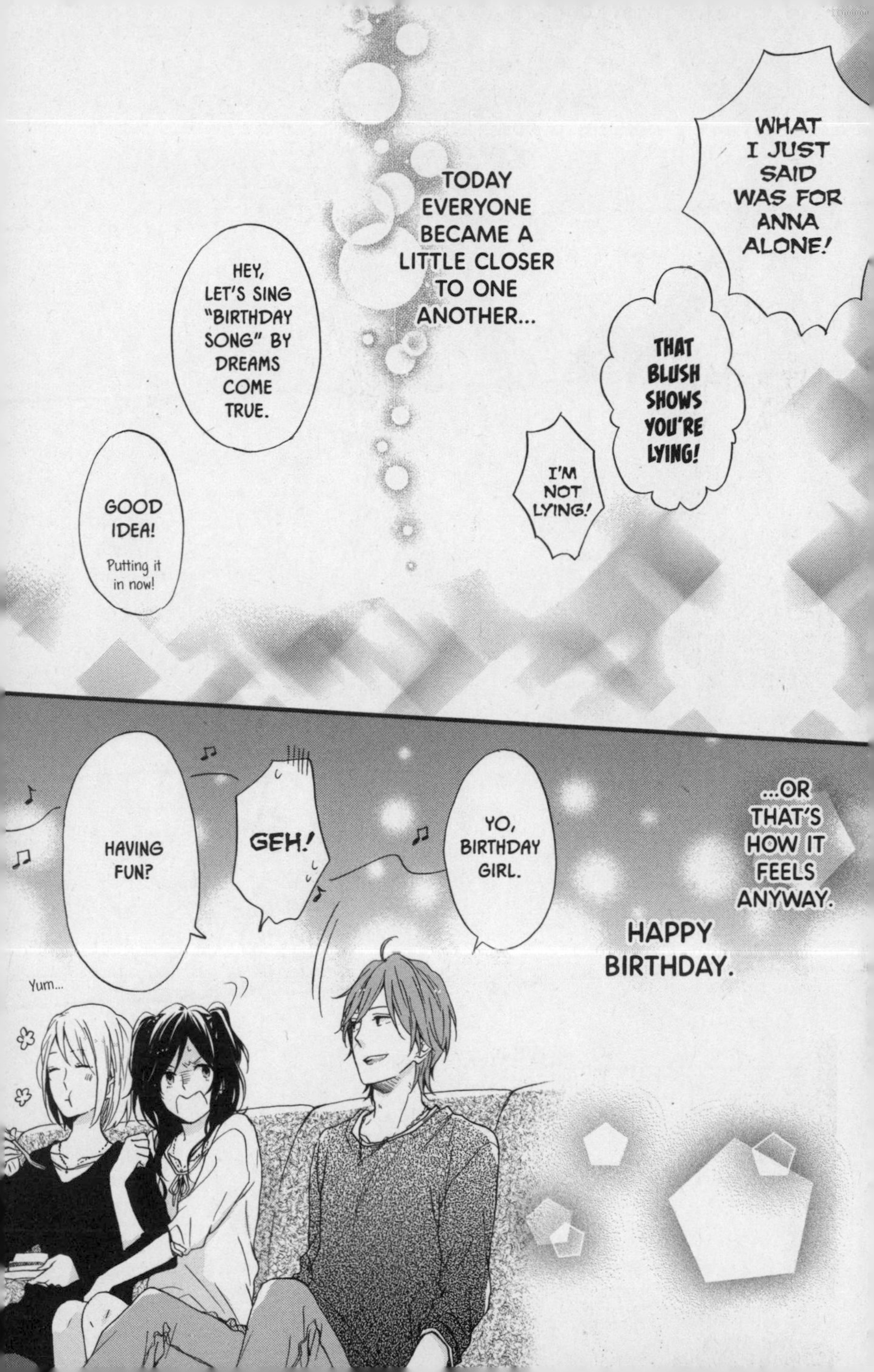
WHAT I JUST SAID WAS FOR ANNA ALONE!
THAT BLUSH SHOWS YOU'RE LYING!
I'M NOT LYING!
TODAY EVERYONE BECAME A LITTLE CLOSER TO ONE ANOTHER...
HEY, LET'S SING "BIRTHDAY SONG" BY DREAMS COME TRUE.
GOOD IDEA!
Putting it in now!
...OR THAT'S HOW IT FEELS ANYWAY.
HAPPY BIRTHDAY.
YO, BIRTHDAY GIRL.
GEH!
HAVING FUN?
Yum...

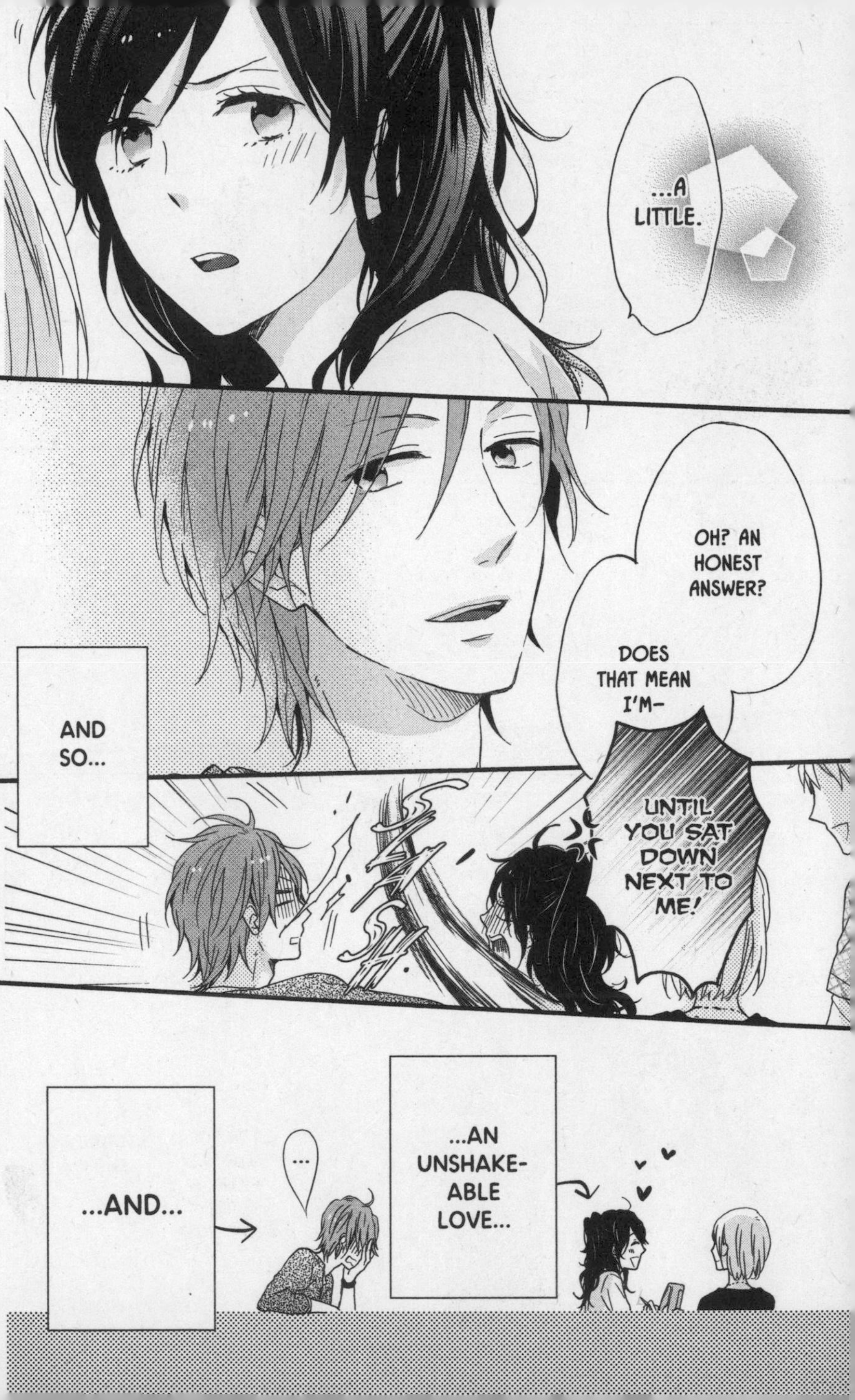
...A LITTLE.
OH? AN HONEST ANSWER?
DOES THAT MEAN I'M—
UNTIL YOU SAT DOWN NEXT TO ME!
AND SO...
...AN UNSHAKE-ABLE LOVE...
...
...AND...

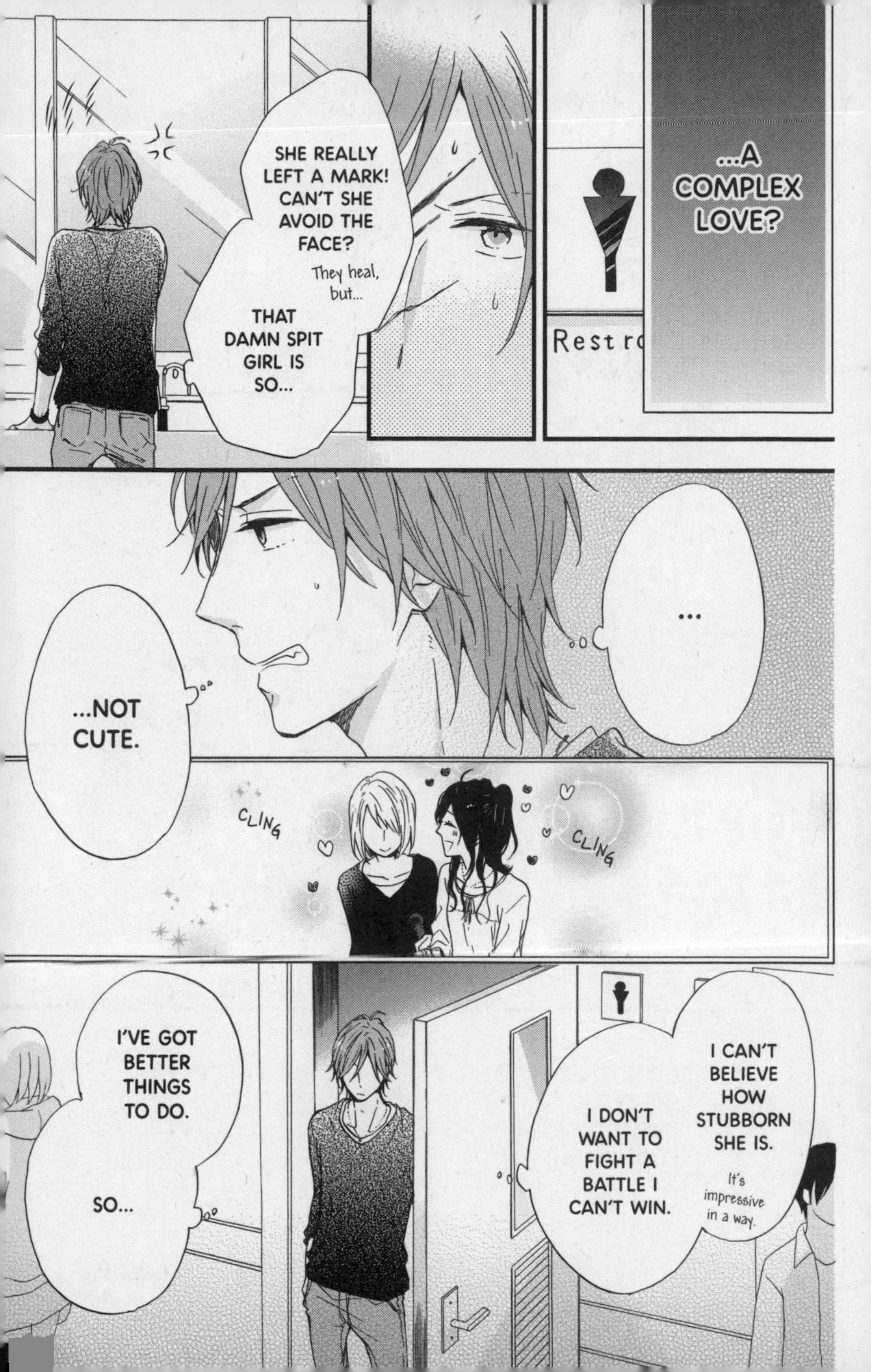
...A COMPLEX LOVE?
Restr
SHE REALLY LEFT A MARK! CAN'T SHE AVOID THE FACE?
They heal, but...
THAT DAMN SPIT GIRL IS SO...
...
...NOT CUTE.
CLING
CLING
I CAN'T BELIEVE HOW STUBBORN SHE IS.
It's impressive in a way.
I DON'T WANT TO FIGHT A BATTLE I CAN'T WIN.
I'VE GOT BETTER THINGS TO DO.
SO...

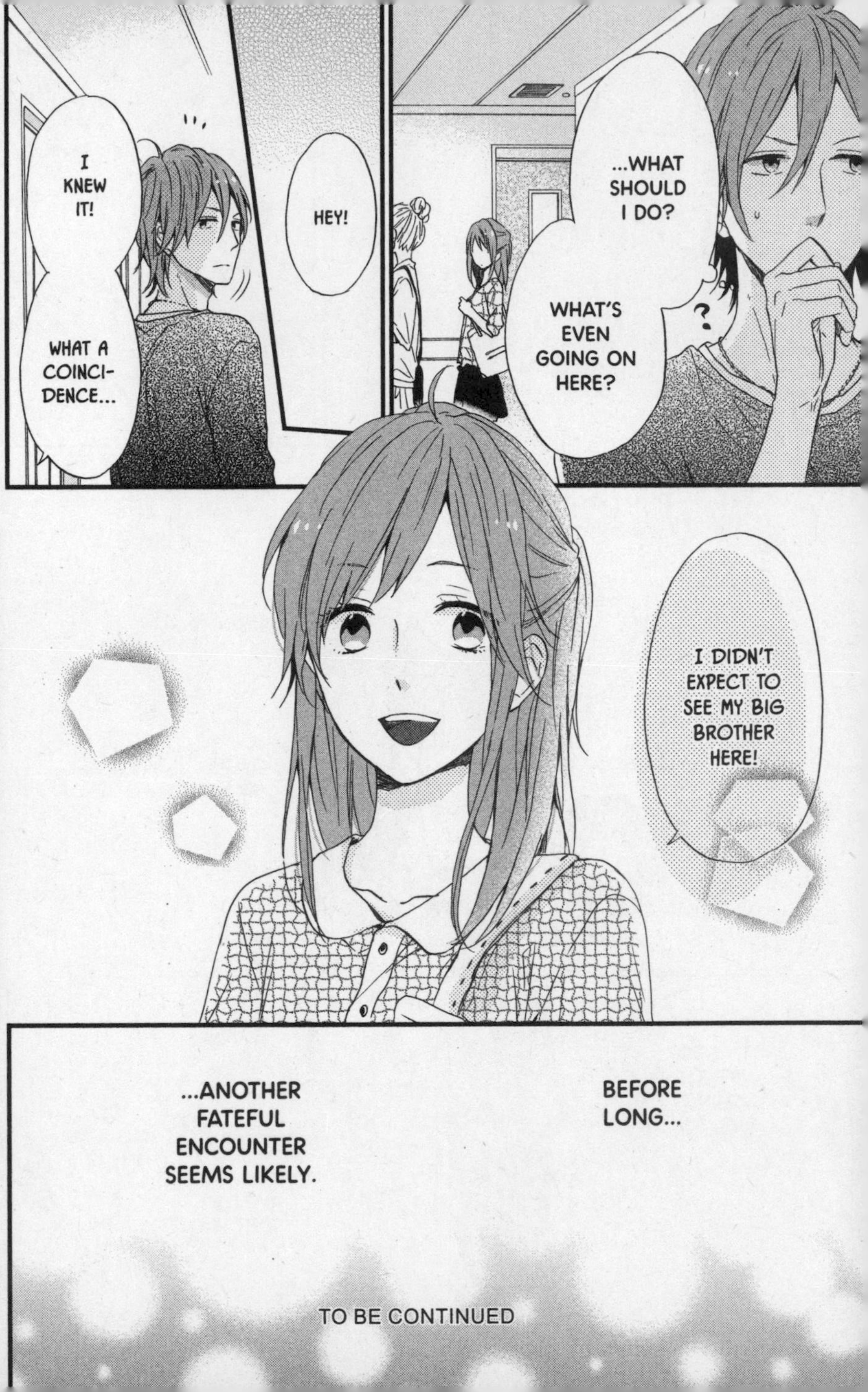
...WHAT SHOULD I DO?
WHAT'S EVEN GOING ON HERE?
?
HEY!
I KNEW IT!
WHAT A COINCIDENCE...
I DIDN'T EXPECT TO SEE MY BIG BROTHER HERE!
BEFORE LONG...
...ANOTHER FATEFUL ENCOUNTER SEEMS LIKELY.
TO BE CONTINUED

WEARING HER PRESENTS

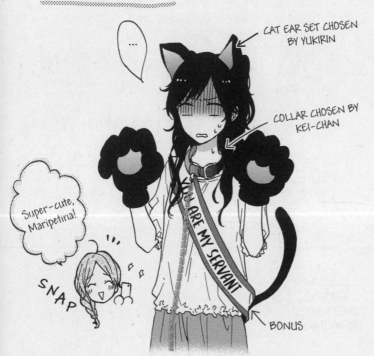

CAT EAR SET CHOSEN BY YUKIRIN
...
COLLAR CHOSEN BY KEI-CHAN
ARE MY SERVANT
BONUS
Super-cute, Maripetina!
SNAP

③

I think this is the first time I've ever rambled so much in these scribblings, but here's part 3.

This series has the usual hubbub and confusion, but I hope you will stick with our four merry pals for a while yet! I'll do my best to make sure you enjoy it!

Finally, the VOMIC!! *Rainbow Days* has become a VOMIC! I think it should start streaming when the books go on sale in Japan. I was able to sit in on the recording, and it blew me away! I thought, "So this is what it means to breathe life into characters...!" The boys and girls were both cool and cute! ♥

Okay, then! Hope to see you in volume 4!

Minami Mizuno

Sorry my handwriting is so bad!

*Vomic = Videos combining the original comic art with voiceover performances

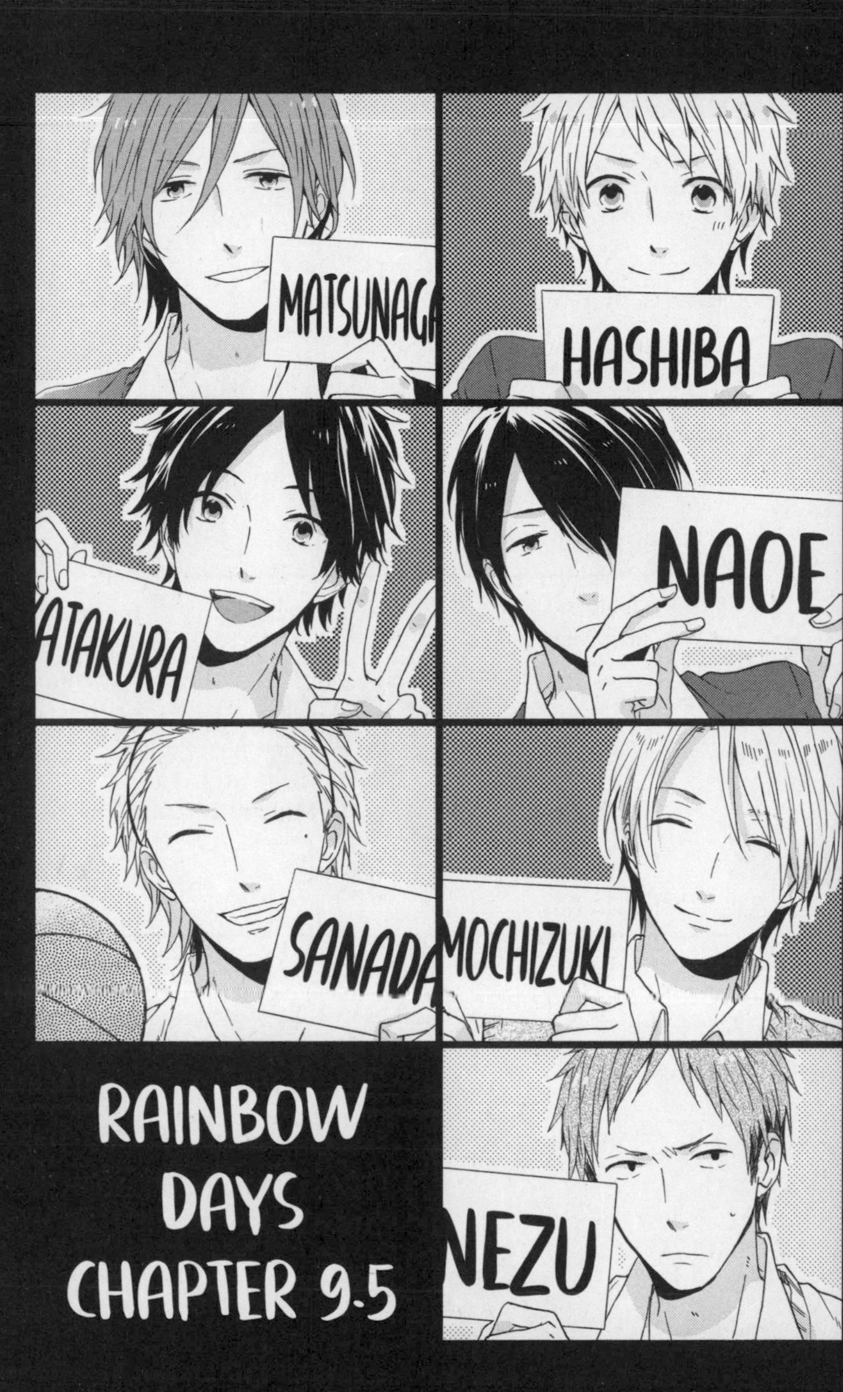
HASHIBA
MATSUNAGA
NAOE
ATAKURA
MOCHIZUKI
SANADA
NEZU
RAINBOW DAYS CHAPTER 9.5

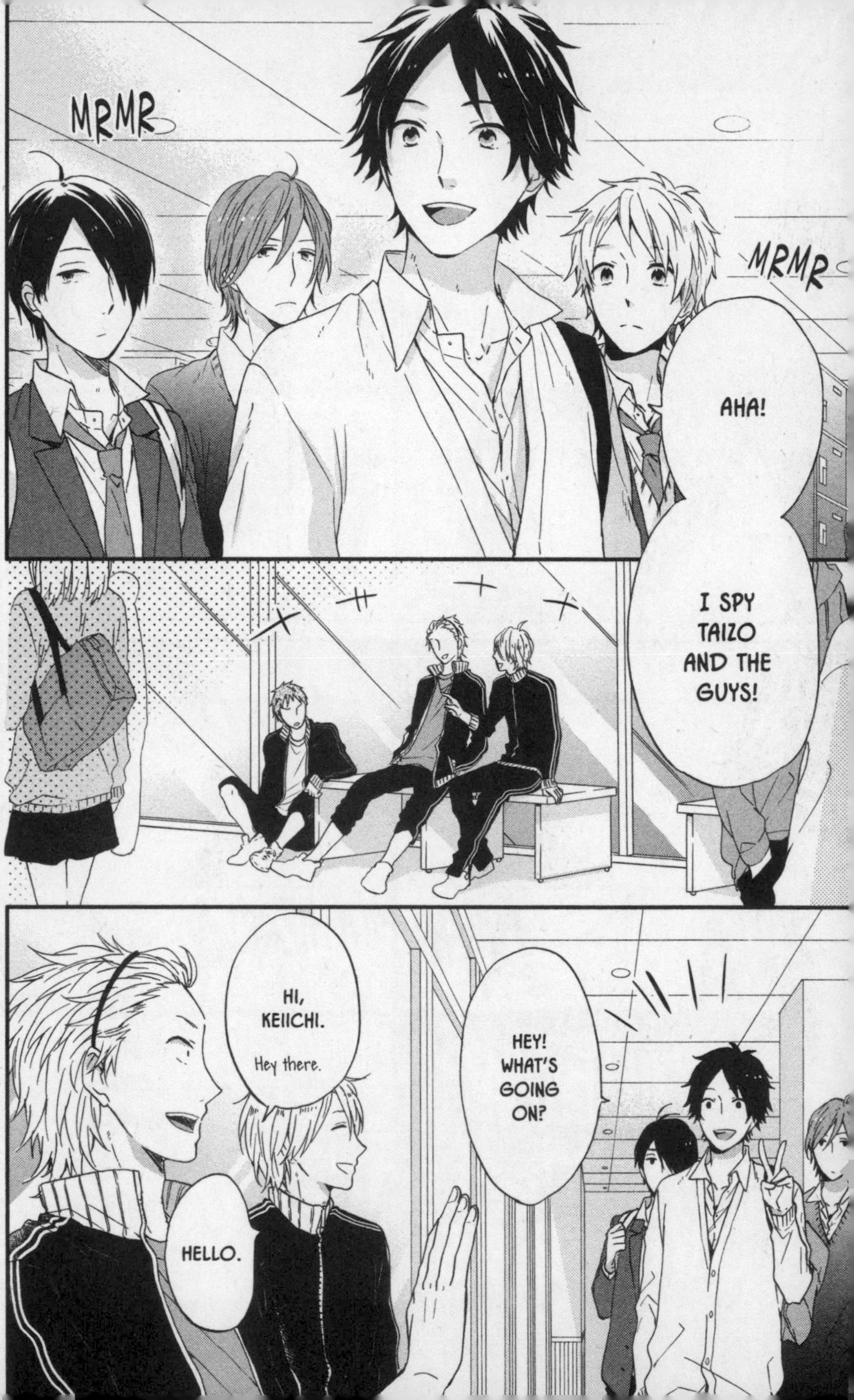
MRMR
MRMR
AHA!
I SPY TAIZO AND THE GUYS!
HEY! WHAT'S GOING ON?
HI, KEIICHI.
Hey there.
HELLO.

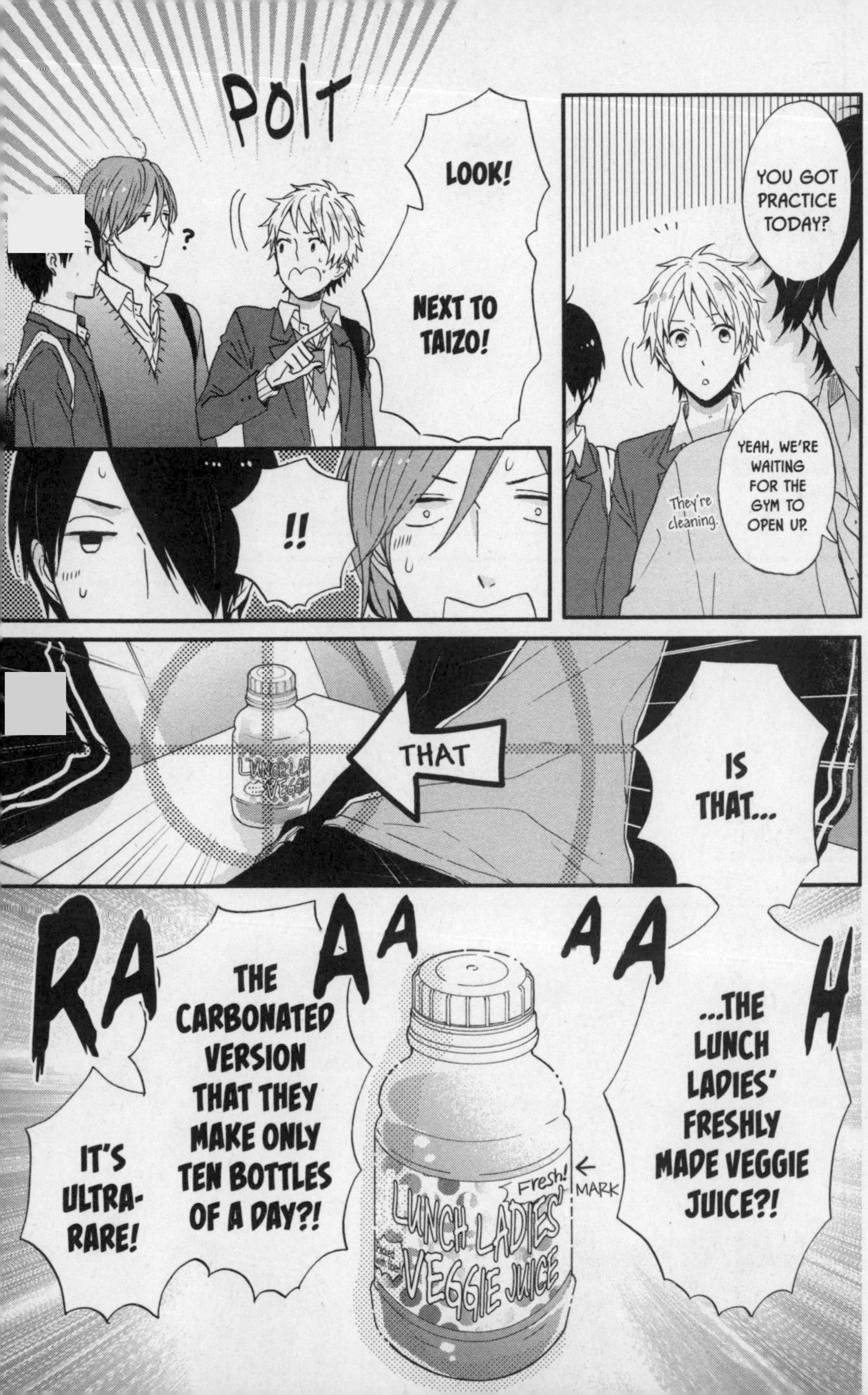

YOU GOT PRACTICE TODAY?
YEAH, WE'RE WAITING FOR THE GYM TO OPEN UP.
They're cleaning.
POIT
LOOK!
NEXT TO TAIZO!
?
!!
IS THAT...
THAT
RAAAAAH
...THE LUNCH LADIES' FRESHLY MADE VEGGIE JUICE?!
THE CARBONATED VERSION THAT THEY MAKE ONLY TEN BOTTLES OF A DAY?!
IT'S ULTRA-RARE!
Fresh!
← MARK
LUNCH LADIES' VEGGIE JUICE

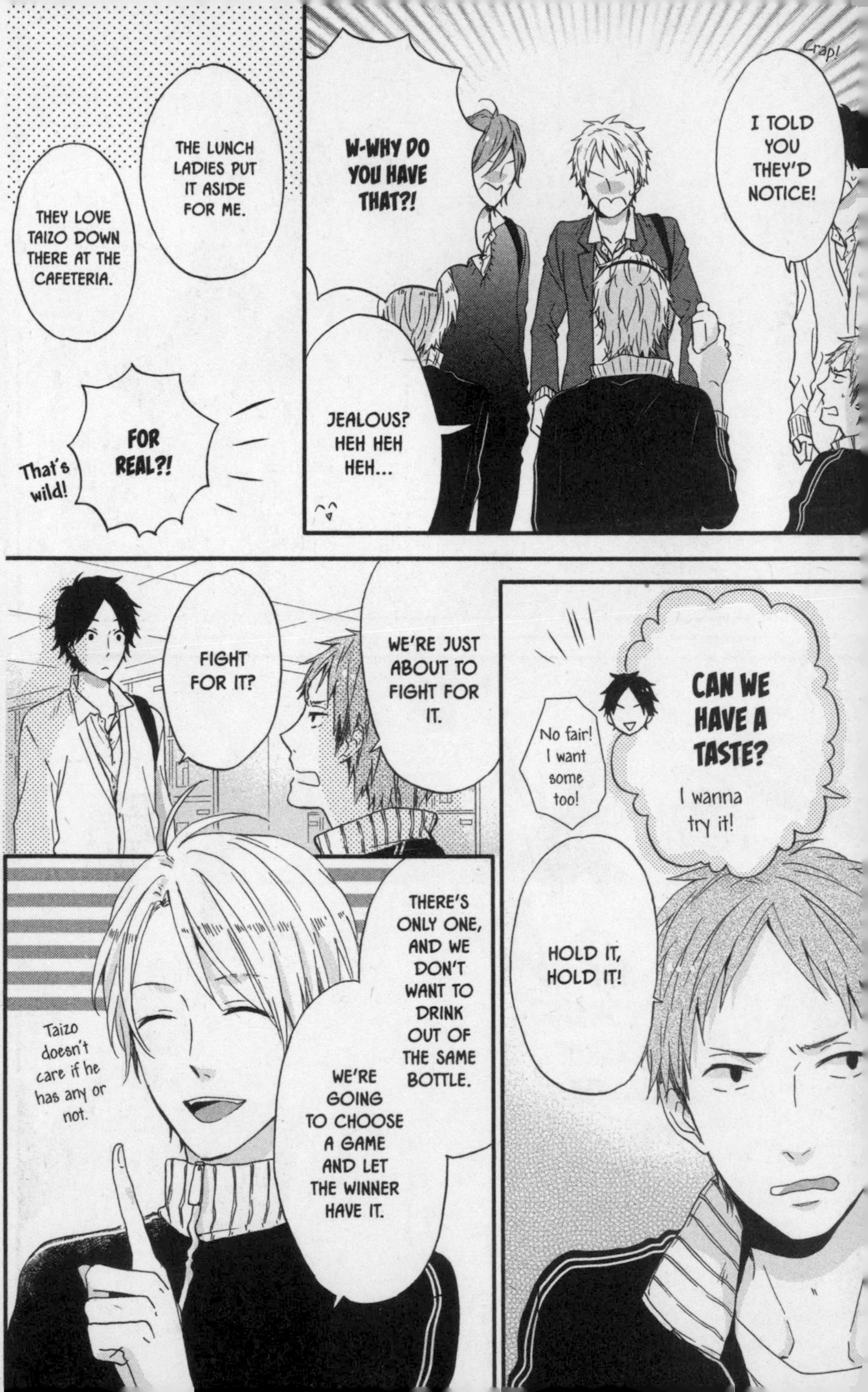
Crap!
I TOLD YOU THEY'D NOTICE!
W-WHY DO YOU HAVE THAT?!
JEALOUS? HEH HEH HEH...
THE LUNCH LADIES PUT IT ASIDE FOR ME.
THEY LOVE TAIZO DOWN THERE AT THE CAFETERIA.
FOR REAL?!
That's wild!
CAN WE HAVE A TASTE?
I wanna try it!
No fair! I want some too!
HOLD IT, HOLD IT!
WE'RE JUST ABOUT TO FIGHT FOR IT.
FIGHT FOR IT?
THERE'S ONLY ONE, AND WE DON'T WANT TO DRINK OUT OF THE SAME BOTTLE.
WE'RE GOING TO CHOOSE A GAME AND LET THE WINNER HAVE IT.
Taizo doesn't care if he has any or not.

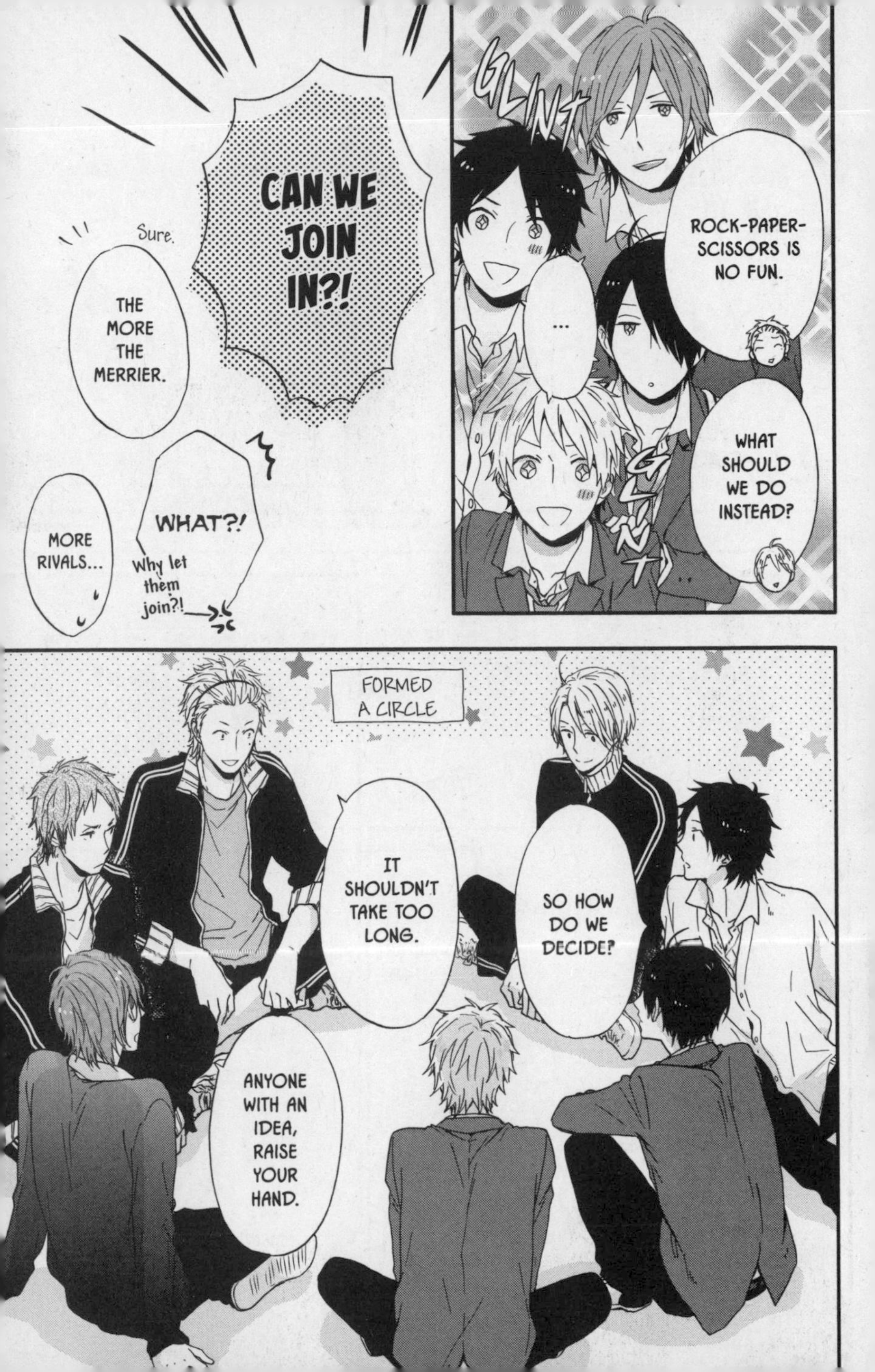
GLINT
ROCK-PAPER-SCISSORS IS NO FUN.
...
WHAT SHOULD WE DO INSTEAD?
GLINT
CAN WE JOIN IN?!
Sure.
THE MORE THE MERRIER.
WHAT?!
Why let them join?!
MORE RIVALS...
FORMED A CIRCLE
SO HOW DO WE DECIDE?
IT SHOULDN'T TAKE TOO LONG.
ANYONE WITH AN IDEA, RAISE YOUR HAND.

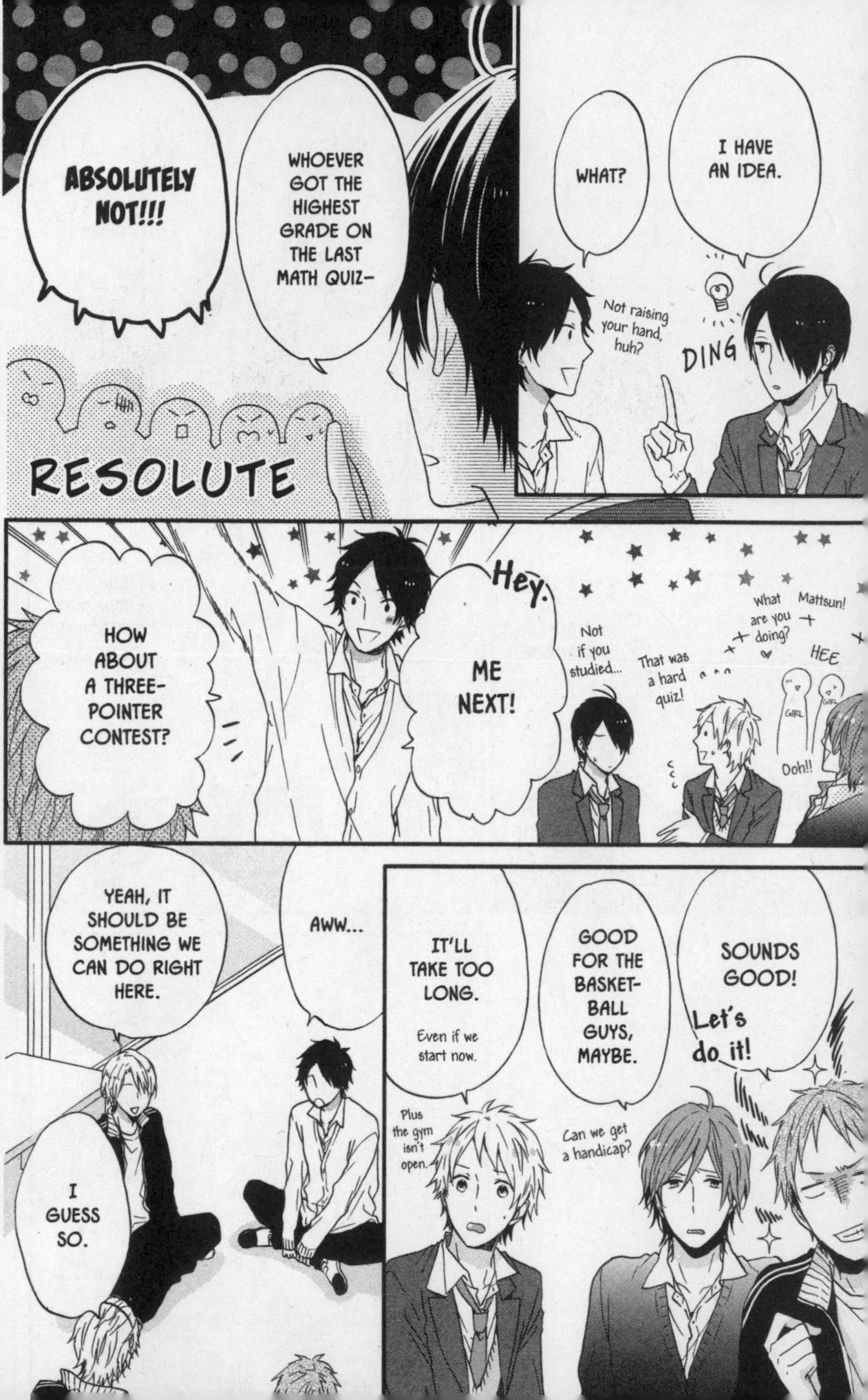
I HAVE AN IDEA.
WHAT?
Not raising your hand, huh?
DING
WHOEVER GOT THE HIGHEST GRADE ON THE LAST MATH QUIZ—
ABSOLUTELY NOT!!!
RESOLUTE
Mattsun!
What are you doing?
HEE
GIRL
GIRL
Ooh!!
That was a hard quiz!
Not if you studied...
Hey.
ME NEXT!
HOW ABOUT A THREE-POINTER CONTEST?
SOUNDS GOOD!
Let's do it!
GOOD FOR THE BASKETBALL GUYS, MAYBE.
Can we get a handicap?
IT'LL TAKE TOO LONG.
Even if we start now.
Plus the gym isn't open.
AWW...
YEAH, IT SHOULD BE SOMETHING WE CAN DO RIGHT HERE.
I GUESS SO.

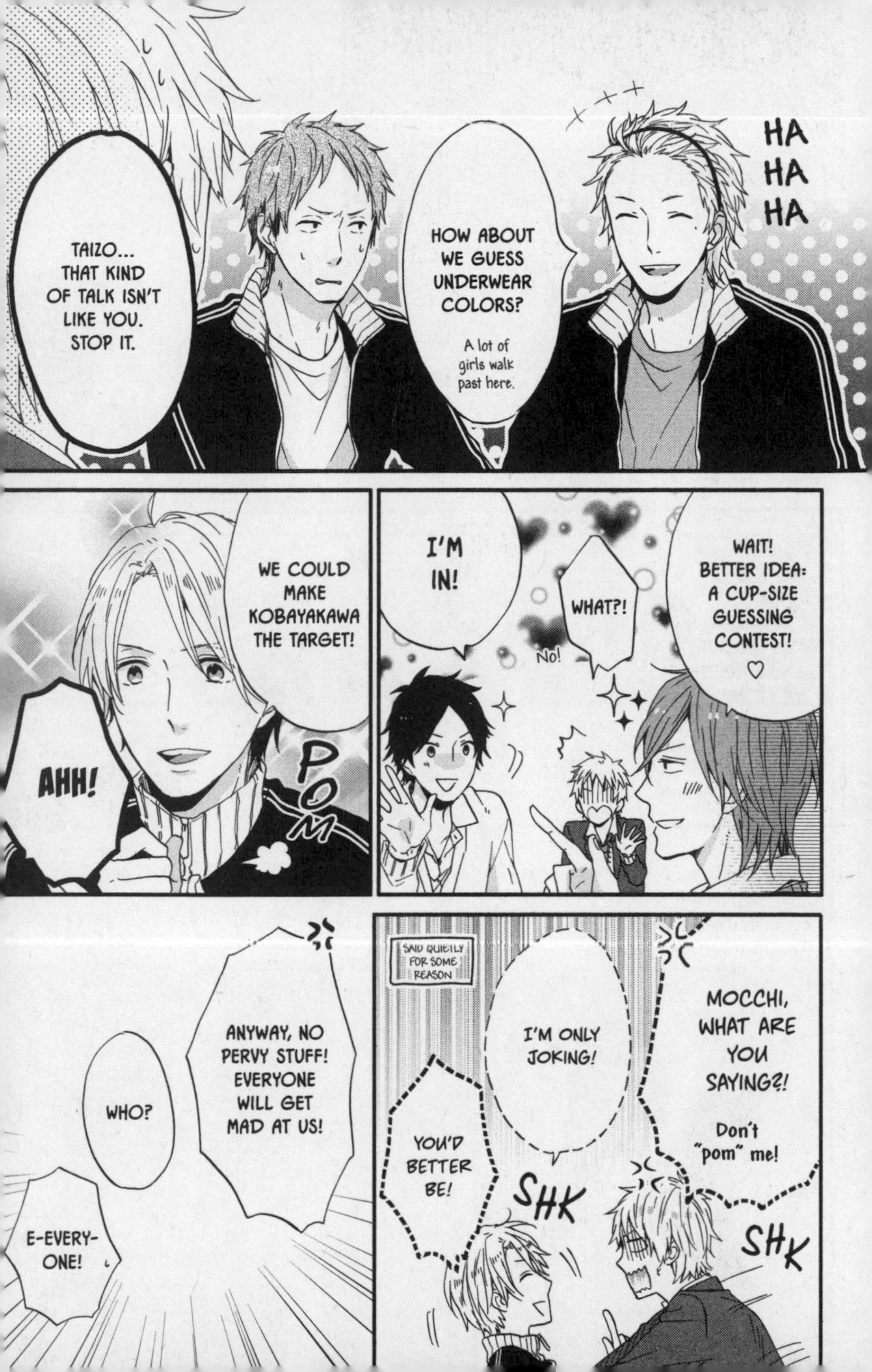
HA HA HA
HOW ABOUT WE GUESS UNDERWEAR COLORS?
A lot of girls walk past here.
TAIZO... THAT KIND OF TALK ISN'T LIKE YOU. STOP IT.
WAIT! BETTER IDEA: A CUP-SIZE GUESSING CONTEST! ♡
WHAT?!
No!
I'M IN!
WE COULD MAKE KOBAYAKAWA THE TARGET!
POM
AHH!
MOCCHI, WHAT ARE YOU SAYING?!
Don't "pom" me!
SHK
I'M ONLY JOKING!
SAID QUIETLY FOR SOME REASON
SHK
YOU'D BETTER BE!
ANYWAY, NO PERVY STUFF! EVERYONE WILL GET MAD AT US!
WHO?
E-EVERY-ONE!

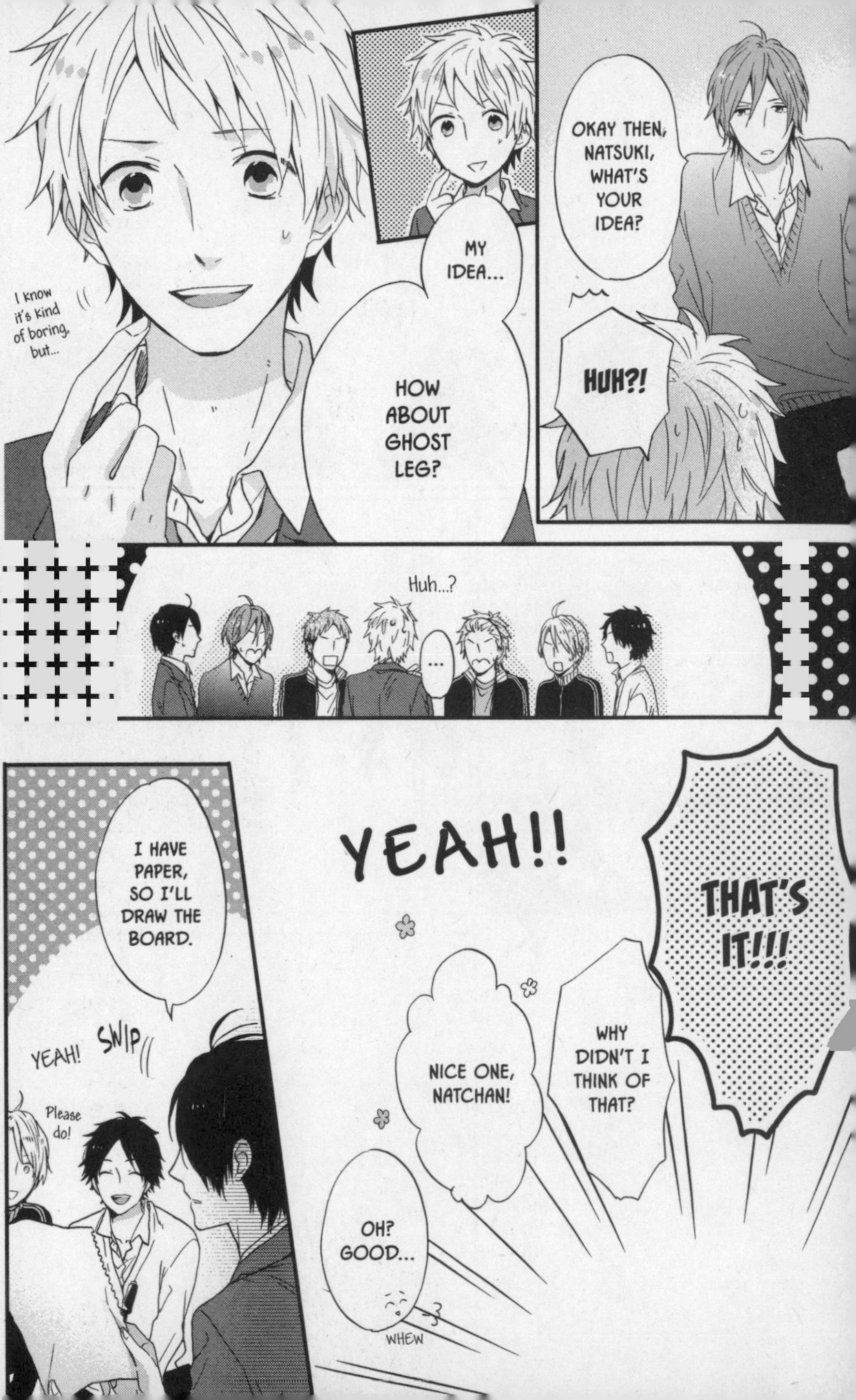
OKAY THEN, NATSUKI, WHAT'S YOUR IDEA?
HUH?!
MY IDEA...
HOW ABOUT GHOST LEG?
I know it's kind of boring, but...
Huh...?
...
THAT'S IT!!!
YEAH!!
WHY DIDN'T I THINK OF THAT?
NICE ONE, NATCHAN!
OH? GOOD...
WHEW
I HAVE PAPER, SO I'LL DRAW THE BOARD.
SWIP
YEAH!
Please do!

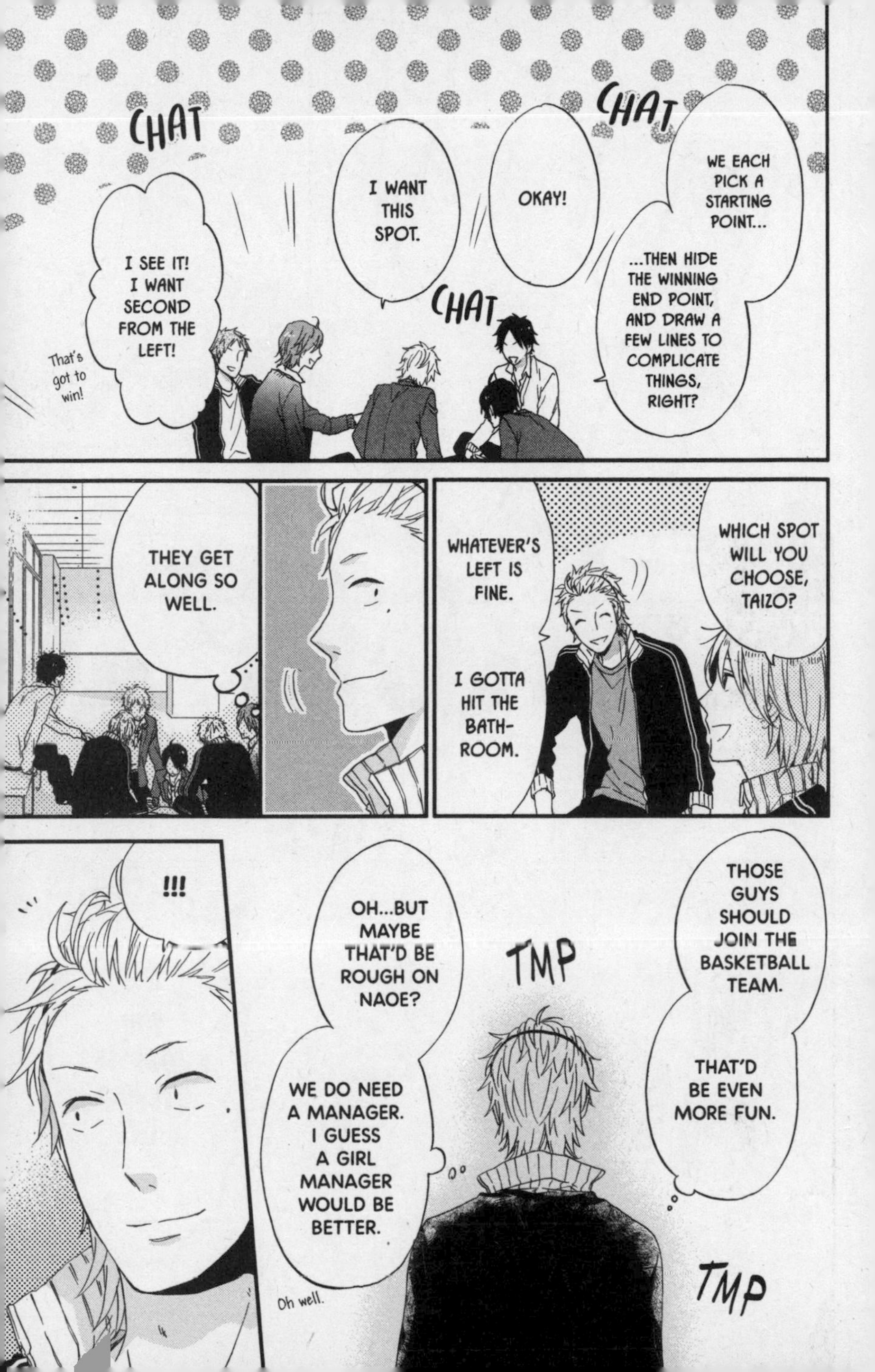
WE EACH PICK A STARTING POINT...
...THEN HIDE THE WINNING END POINT, AND DRAW A FEW LINES TO COMPLICATE THINGS, RIGHT?
CHAT
OKAY!
CHAT
I WANT THIS SPOT.
CHAT
I SEE IT! I WANT SECOND FROM THE LEFT!
That's got to win!
WHICH SPOT WILL YOU CHOOSE, TAIZO?
WHATEVER'S LEFT IS FINE.
I GOTTA HIT THE BATH-ROOM.
THEY GET ALONG SO WELL.
THOSE GUYS SHOULD JOIN THE BASKETBALL TEAM.
THAT'D BE EVEN MORE FUN.
TMP
OH...BUT MAYBE THAT'D BE ROUGH ON NAOE?
WE DO NEED A MANAGER. I GUESS A GIRL MANAGER WOULD BE BETTER.
TMP
Oh well.
!!!

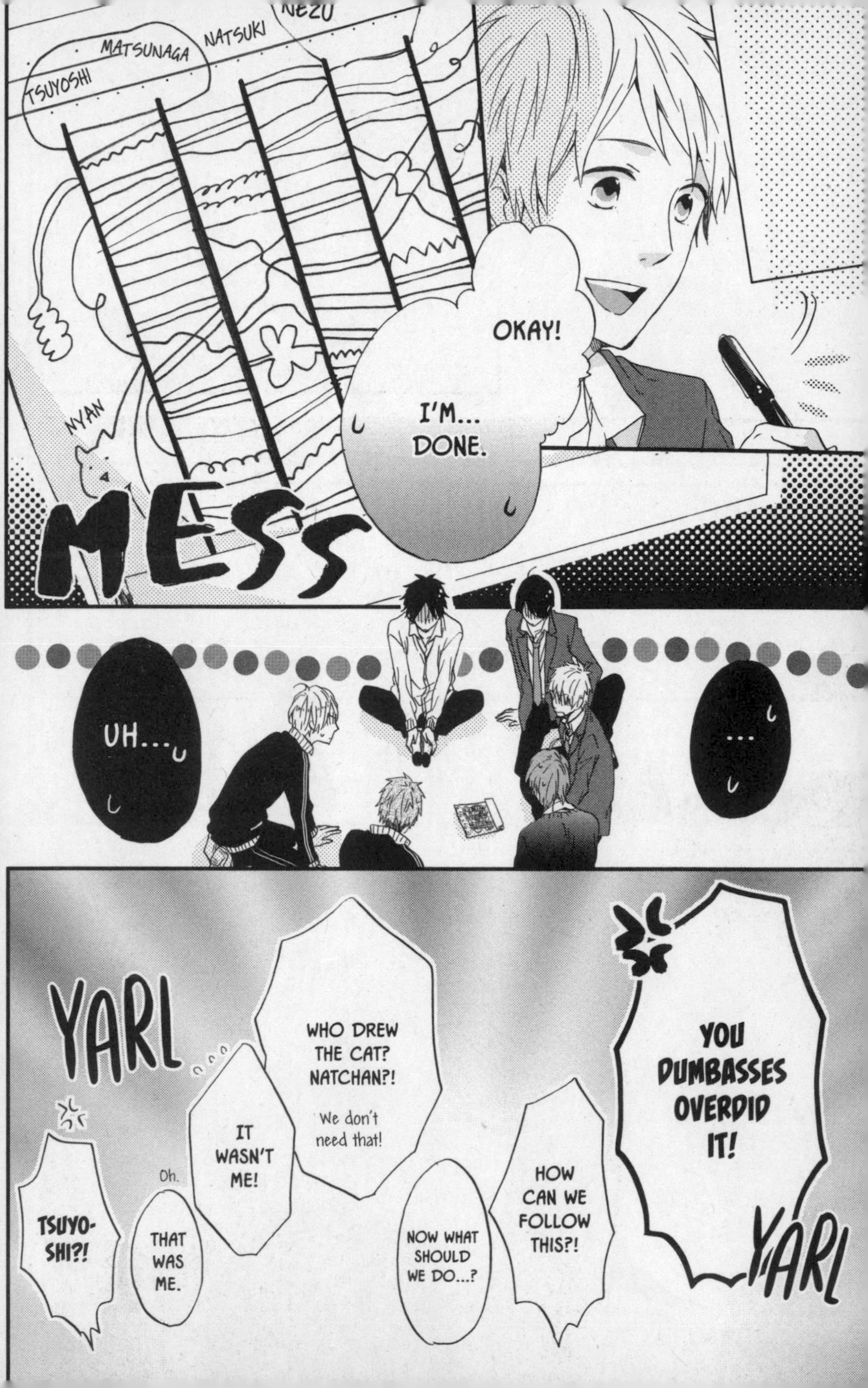
NEZU
NATSUKI
MATSUNAGA
TSUYOSHI
OKAY!
I'M... DONE.
NYAN
MESS
...
UH...
YOU DUMBASSES OVERDID IT!
YARL
HOW CAN WE FOLLOW THIS?!
NOW WHAT SHOULD WE DO...?
WHO DREW THE CAT? NATCHAN?!
We don't need that!
IT WASN'T ME!
Oh.
THAT WAS ME.
YARL
TSUYO-SHI?!

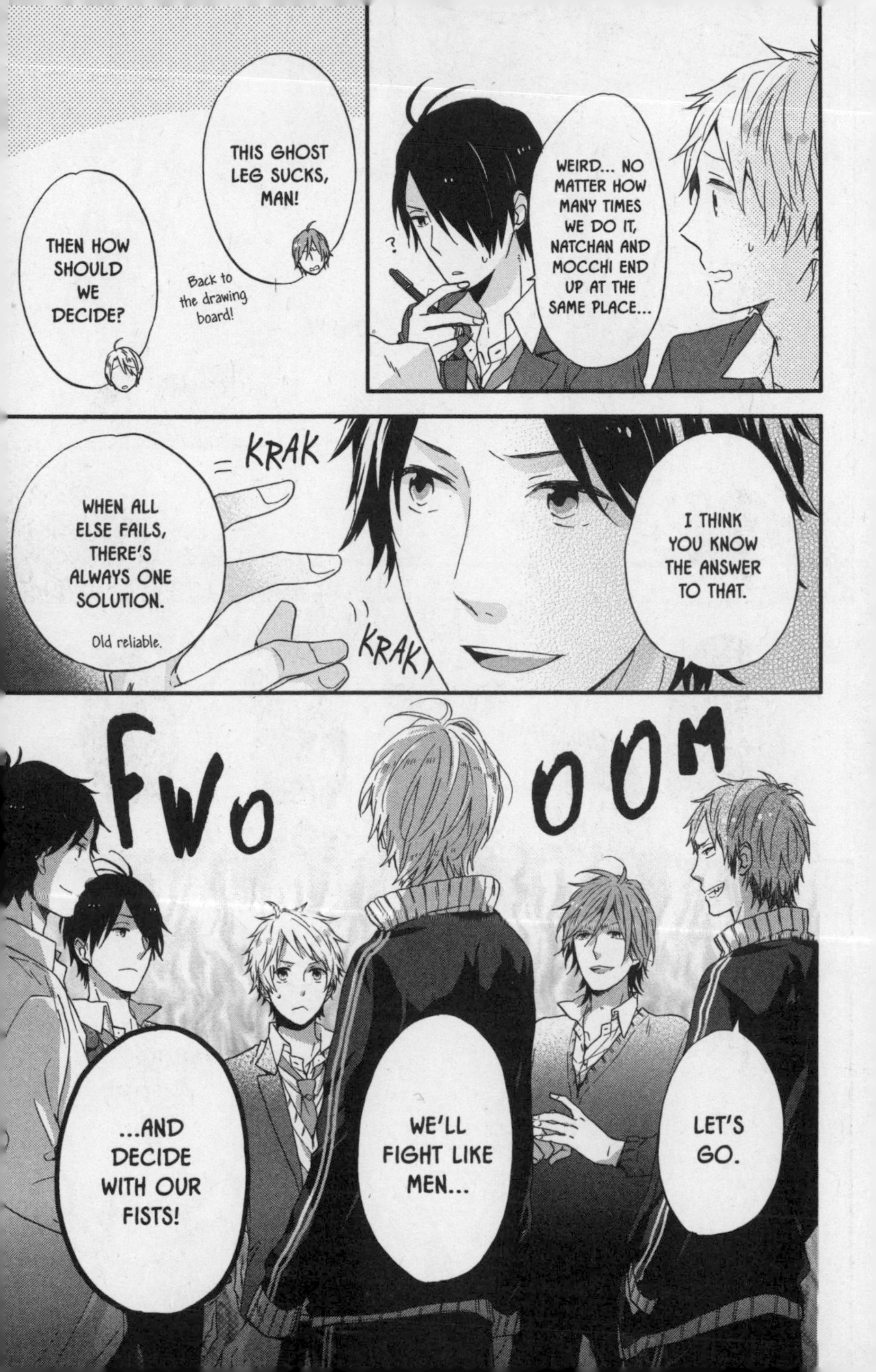
WEIRD... NO MATTER HOW MANY TIMES WE DO IT, NATCHAN AND MOCCHI END UP AT THE SAME PLACE...
?
THIS GHOST LEG SUCKS, MAN!
Back to the drawing board!
THEN HOW SHOULD WE DECIDE?
I THINK YOU KNOW THE ANSWER TO THAT.
KRAK
KRAK
WHEN ALL ELSE FAILS, THERE'S ALWAYS ONE SOLUTION.
Old reliable.
FWOOOM
LET'S GO.
WE'LL FIGHT LIKE MEN...
...AND DECIDE WITH OUR FISTS!

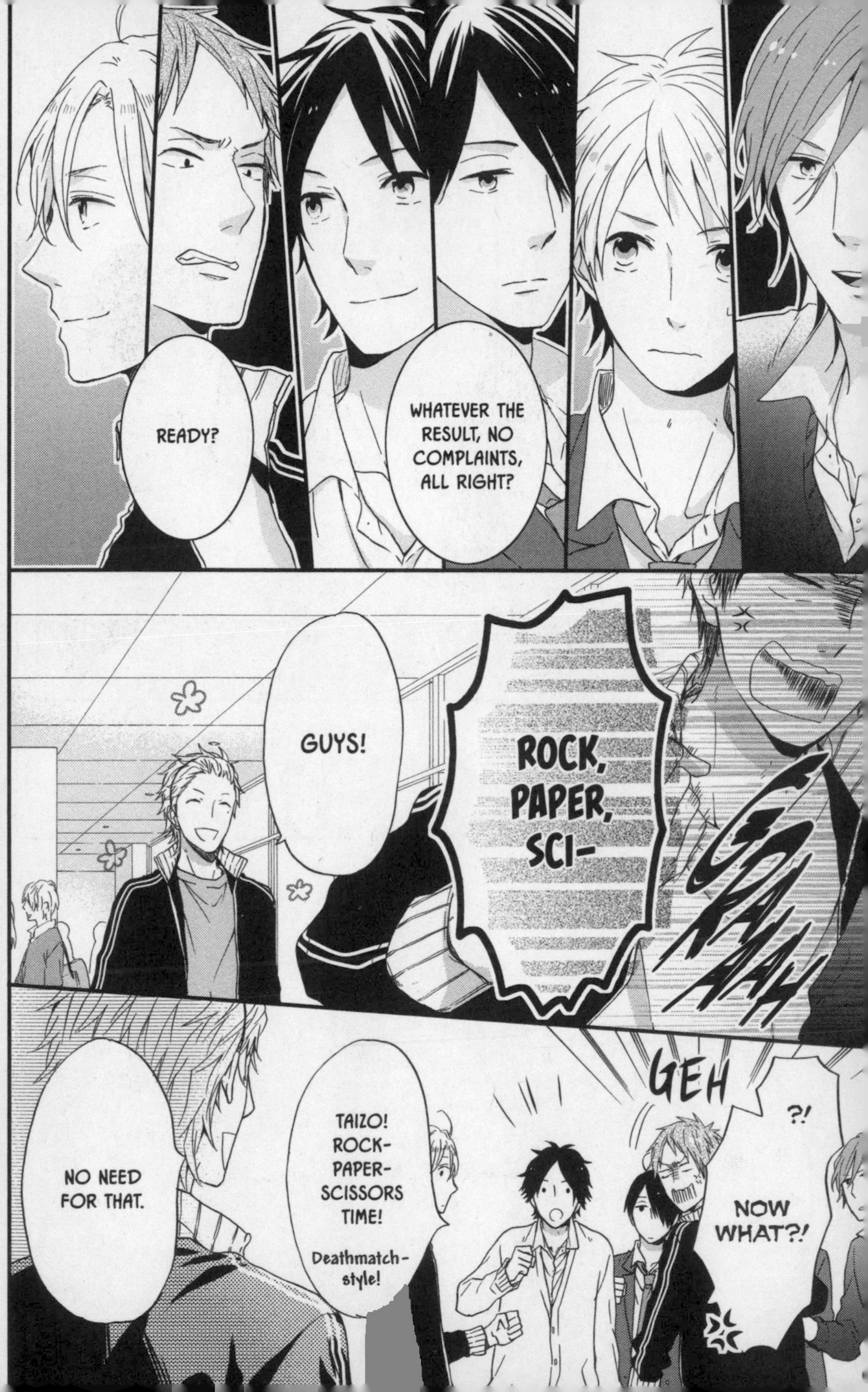
WHATEVER THE RESULT, NO COMPLAINTS, ALL RIGHT?
READY?
ROCK, PAPER, SCI-
GAHAAH
GUYS!
NOW WHAT?!
?!
GEH
TAIZO! ROCK-PAPER-SCISSORS TIME!
Deathmatch-style!
NO NEED FOR THAT.

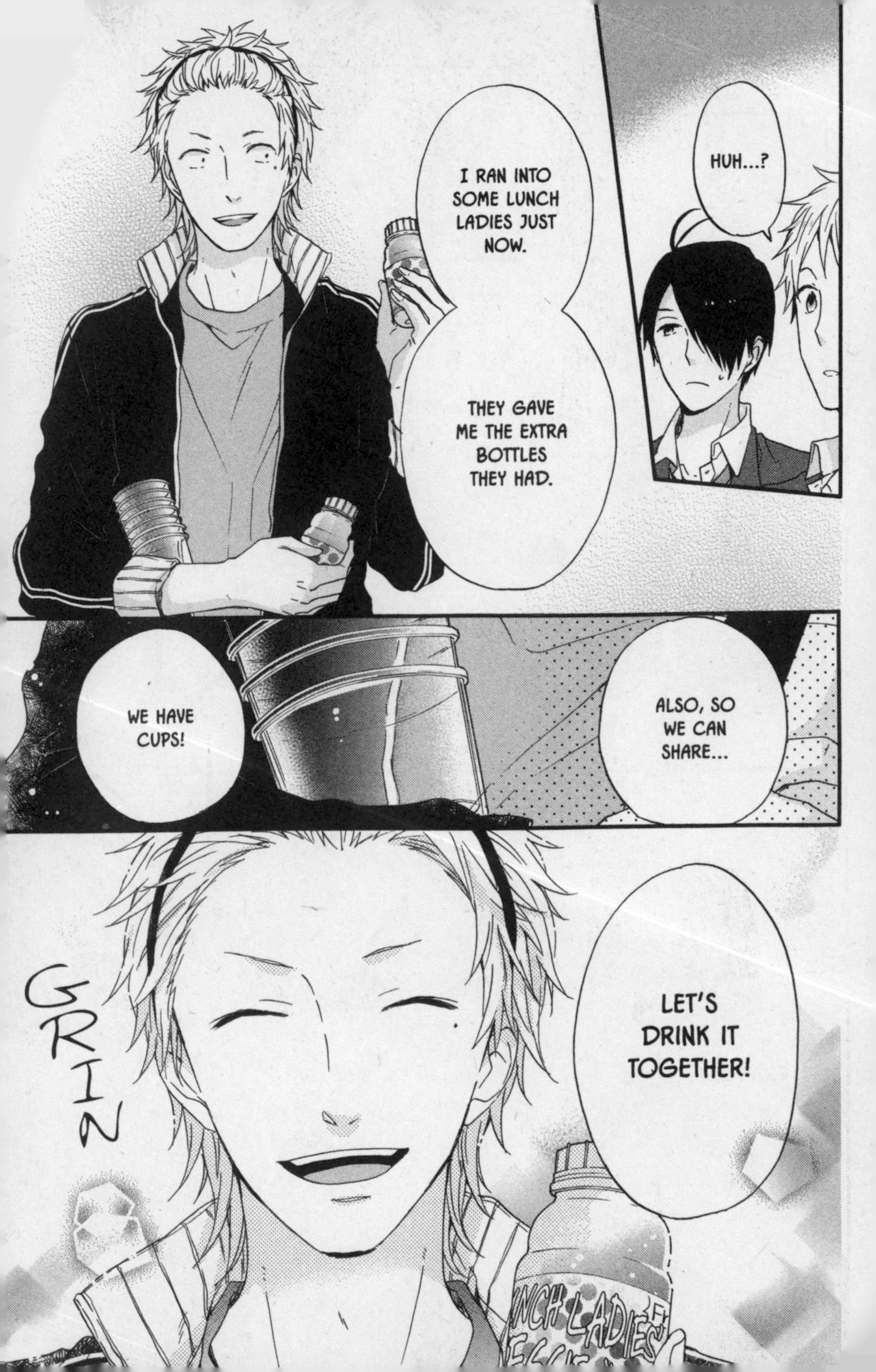
HUH...?
I RAN INTO SOME LUNCH LADIES JUST NOW.
THEY GAVE ME THE EXTRA BOTTLES THEY HAD.
ALSO, SO WE CAN SHARE...
WE HAVE CUPS!
LET'S DRINK IT TOGETHER!
GRIN

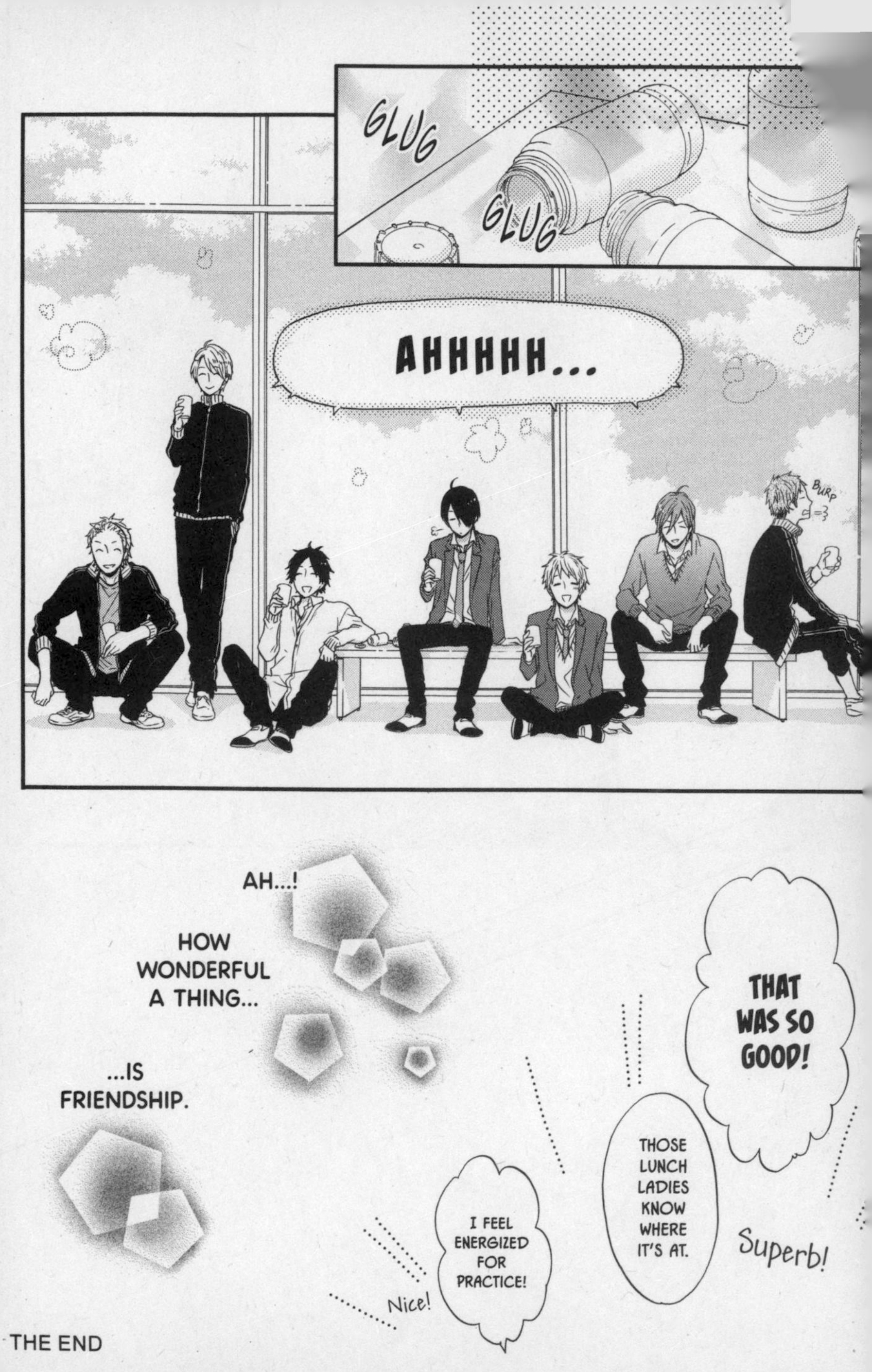
GLUG
GLUG
AHHHHH...
BURP
THAT WAS SO GOOD!
Superb!
THOSE LUNCH LADIES KNOW WHERE IT'S AT.
I FEEL ENERGIZED FOR PRACTICE!
Nice!
AH...!
HOW WONDERFUL A THING...
...IS FRIENDSHIP.
THE END

SPECIAL THANKS

Cozmi
Ao Suzuki
Kei Tanaka
Rui Hase
Erina Matsunaga
Mochio Mochi

Kgr
Nao

Editor   Yabu
Designer Kawatani

My family

And you!!!

Minami Mizuno

Blog:
 http://mizunoiro.jugem.jp

Twitter:
 http://twitter.com/mizuno007

I love soup curry. There was a period of time in which I was going to my favorite restaurant for it four times a week. My topping of choice? Natto, of course.

Minami Mizuno

Minami Mizuno was born on July 30 in Sapporo, Japan.
She debuted with *Tama ni wa Konna Watashi to Anata*
(We Get like This Sometimes, You and I) in 2006.
Rainbow Days was nominated for the 40th Kodansha Manga Award
in 2016, and her subsequent work, *We Don't Know Love Yet*,
was nominated for the 66th Shogakukan Manga Award in 2020.

Rainbow Days

Volume 3
Shojo Beat Edition

Story and Art by
Minami Mizuno

TRANSLATION + ADAPTATION **Max Greenway**
TOUCH-UP ART + LETTERING **Inori Fukuda Trant**
DESIGN **Shawn Carrico**
EDITOR **Nancy Thistlethwaite**

NIJIIRO DAYS © 2011 by Minami Mizuno
All rights reserved.
First published in Japan in 2011 by SHUEISHA Inc., Tokyo.
English translation rights arranged by SHUEISHA Inc.

The stories, characters, and incidents mentioned
in this publication are entirely fictional.

Printed in Canada

Published by VIZ Media, LLC
P.O. Box 77010
San Francisco, CA 94107

10 9 8 7 6 5 4 3 2 1
First printing, April 2023

PARENTAL ADVISORY
RAINBOW DAYS is rated T+ for Older Teen
and is recommended for ages 16 and up. This
volume may contain suggestive situations.

viz.com   shojobeat.com

Stop!

You may be reading the wrong way.

In keeping with the original Japanese comic format, this book reads from right to left—so action, sound effects, and word balloons are completely reversed to preserve the orientation of the original artwork. Check out the diagram shown here to get the hang of things, and then turn to the other side of the book to get started!

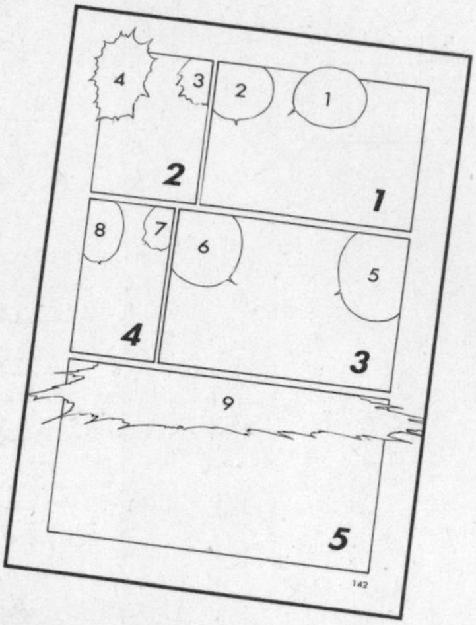
1
2
3
4
1
2
5
6
7
8
3
4
9
5
142

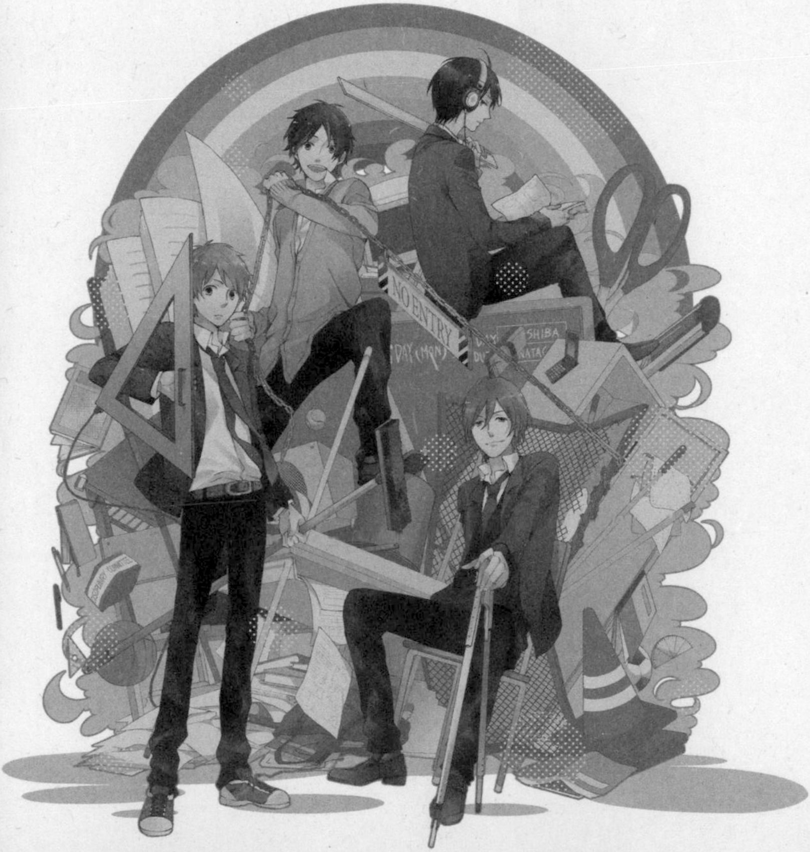
NO ENTRY